The LOST

SECOND BOOK

of ARISTOTLE'S

POETICS

The LOST SECOND BOOK *of* ARISTOTLE'S POETICS

WALTER WATSON

The UNIVERSITY *of* CHICAGO PRESS

CHICAGO *and* LONDON

The University of Chicago Press, Chicago 60637

The University of Chicago Press, Ltd., London

© 2012 by The University of Chicago

All rights reserved. Published 2012.

Paperback edition 2015.

Printed in the United States of America

24 23 22 21 20 19 18 17 16 15   2 3 4 5 6

ISBN-13: 978-0-226-87508-8 (cloth)

ISBN-13: 978-0-226-27411-9 (paper)

ISBN-13: 978-0-226-87510-1 (e-book)

10.7208/chicago/9780226875101.001.0001

Library of Congress Cataloging-in-Publication Data

Watson, Walter, 1925–

  The lost second book of Aristotle's Poetics / Walter Watson.

    p. cm.

  Includes bibliographical references and index.

  ISBN-13: 978-0-226-87508-8 (hardcover : alkaline paper)

  ISBN-10: 0-226-87508-3 (hardcover : alkaline paper)

  1. Aristotle. Poetics. 2. Poetry—History and criticism. I. Title.

  PN1040.A753W38 2012

  808.2—dc23

                    2011034675

♾ This paper meets the requirements of ANSI/NISO

Z39.48-1992 (Permanence of Paper).

IN MEMORY OF

Richard McKeon,

WITH ENDURING GRATITUDE

FOR HIS HAVING TAUGHT ME

SO MUCH THAT I COULD NEVER

HAVE LEARNED BUT FOR THE

GREAT GOOD FORTUNE OF

FINDING SUCH A MENTOR.

CONTENTS

ACKNOWLEDGMENTS

Without Richard Janko's book *Aristotle on Comedy*, the present book would not have been written. Seeing his text of the so-called Tractatus Coisliniaus, with what appeared to be four-cause analyses of both catharsis and the laughable, I thought, "We know the lion by his paw," as Johann Bernoulli is said to have remarked of Newton's anonymous solution to the brachistochrone problem Bernoulli had proposed. I have since consulted Janko's book a thousand times, but I am grateful to him for more than his book. He encouraged my work at an early stage and read a later draft of the entire manuscript. His many corrections have saved me from embarrassing errors, and his many suggestions have greatly improved the book.

Many of my Stony Brook colleagues have also read the manuscript of the book, or portions of it, at various stages of completion, and have provided valuable comments. They include Bruce Bashford, Homer Goldberg, and the late Richard Levin of the Department of English; and Robert Crease and David Dilworth of the Department of Philosophy. Richard Levin in particular I consulted many times on questions relating to Shakespeare and to poetic theory, and his understanding of the *Poetics* enabled him to express unqualified agreement with the key point of the book, the interpretation of the distinction between imitative and nonimitative poetry, long before the full argument was worked out. Robert Watson of the UCLA Department of English, Richard Brooks of the Vermont Law School, and the late Richard Wynne contributed helpful comments at an early stage.

I am indebted to Eugene Gendlin not only for specific suggestions, but for many enlightening and enjoyable e-mail exchanges on problems of Aristotelian interpretation and for the magnificent example of his *Line by Line Commentary on Aristotle's "De Anima."* I am grateful to my Stony Brook friend and colleague Bill Godfrey for teaching me Latin and for being a never-failing source of jokes and of information on all recondite subjects. The late Kenneth Telford was my friend from graduate school days, and we were colleagues for a while at the New School during the 1960s. I am grateful to him for the discussions that we had on his translation and interpretation of the *Poetics* as well as on countless other matters. The encouragement and steadfast support of my work by Douglas Mitchell of the University of

Chicago Press has been invaluable to me. Finally, I am grateful to my wife, Norma, formerly a professional editor, for securing for me uninterrupted mornings in which to work and for her unfailing willingness to interrupt her many civic and musical activities to provide editorial and scholarly assistance.

INTRODUCTION

1. HISTORY OF THE PROBLEM

The surviving manuscripts of Aristotle's *Poetics* consist of a single book. In this book, Aristotle says that he will speak of comedy, but this he does not do in the surviving book. This book concludes with the problem of whether tragedy or epic is more achieving of their common end, but this problem is left unresolved. In the *Politics*, when Aristotle uses the word "catharsis," he says that he will say more clearly what the word means when he comes to speak of it in the *Poetics*, but this he does not do in the surviving book. These things give us reason to think that there was a second book in which the expectations they raise were met.

There is also evidence that a second book actually existed. In the *Rhetoric*, Aristotle says that he has distinguished the forms of the laughable in the *Poetics*, and has said what homonyms and synonyms are, neither of which is done in the surviving book. A lexicographer of the second or third century CE known as the Anti-Atticist lists as used in Aristotle's *Poetics* the word *kuntotaton* (an alteration of *kuntaton*, "most doglike" or "most shameless"), and this word is not in the surviving book. Simplicius in the sixth century quotes Porphyry in the third as quoting a definition of synonymy from the *Poetics* that is not in the surviving book (Janko 1984, 172). A two-book *Poetics* is listed among Aristotle's works by Diogenes Laertius in the third century, by Ptolemy *al garíb* (the unknown) in the fourth century, and by Hesychius of Miletus in the middle of the sixth century (ibid., 65). After this, we have no references to a second book as existing.

The *Poetics* was the final work in the series of manuscripts that, as published by Andronicus of Rhodes in the first century BCE, constitute what has come to be known as the Aristotelian corpus. The second book of the *Poetics* would have been the last scroll in the corpus or the last pages of a manuscript volume and in either case would have been particularly vulnerable to loss. It is reasonable to conclude that there was in fact a second book, and that it probably became lost sometime after the middle of the sixth century.

In 1839, three manuscript pages that appeared to be an abstract or epitome of the missing book came to light. They were discovered by J. A. Cramer in the De Coislin collection in the Bibliothèque Nationale in Paris. They have been called the "Tractatus Coislinianus" from the collection in which they

were found. The earliest known location of the manuscript is the monas-
tery of the Great Lavra on Mt. Athos, c. 1218 (ibid., 5). It is thought to be an
early-tenth-century copy of a sixth-century original (ibid., 5, 8, 18).

Cramer thought the manuscript was written by a commentator on Aristotle's *Poetics* who seemed to have had a fuller text than that which has
reached us, especially in the analysis of humor (Janko 1984, 1–2). The text
certainly contains material that is not in our *Poetics*, but its form is that of
an abstract or summary, not a commentary. The first full examination of
the Tractatus was by Jacob Bernays (1853). After presenting the text of the
Tractatus, he begins his examination:

> A series of statements, for the most part without any stylistic con-
> nection, are held together only by this unity, that they all concern the
> doctrine of comedy, and say only so much of tragedy and the other
> kinds of poetry as seems indispensable for contrast, and stand in some
> relation to Aristotle's *Poetics*, to which clues glance forth throughout. In
> what relation, if all the statements alike approach it, can only be learned
> through an examination of the particulars.
>
> There is in the beginning of the first paragraph little that is encourag-
> ing. In the whole schematic division of the poetic species there is noth-
> ing that is in any way Aristotelian except the subdivision of "imitative
> poetry," determined in the third chapter of the *Poetics*, into "narrated"
> (epic) and "acted" (dramatic). But in this itself lies an offense against
> Aristotle. For him poetry is so essentially imitative, that in the precise
> terminology of a division to speak of "imitative poetry" he can as little
> permit as to speak of fiery fire. The schematizer must indeed permit it
> to himself, because he places next to imitative poetry as a coordinate
> genus a "nonimitative" (*amimētos*) poetry. With this, however, he
> strikes Aristotelian doctrine so hard in its face that he now makes us
> cease to care, and it scarcely still especially stands out, since his "theo-
> retical poetry" can be no other than the physiological-didactic, a field
> that nobody cultivated with greater renown than honest Empedocles,
> of whom Aristotle (1.1447b29) explicitly says, that one must call him
> only a natural philosopher, not a poet, because he does not imitate.
> (Bernays 1853, 140–41; my trans.)

Bernays argues that three phrases at the beginning of the Tractatus—
imitative poetry, nonimitative poetry, and theoretical poetry—are inconsistent with Book I. The three inconsistencies pop up like three red flags as
if to warn him that an illegal operation has been performed. The principle

of Aristotelian interpretation that Bernays has violated is stated in the first book of the *Poetics*: "Whenever a word seems to signify an incongruity one ought to examine the number of ways it might be significant in what has been expressed" (*Poet.* 25.1461a31–3, trans. Telford[1]). Bernays has thus overlooked the possibility that Aristotle at the beginning of Book II introduces a new meaning for "imitation."

Science for Aristotle requires that the words in which it is stated have definite meanings. The words of ordinary language include multiple meanings in a sort of confused whole. Aristotle in his technical treatises deals with this problem by giving restricted technical meanings to the words of ordinary language. "Imitation" is a word of ordinary language that is introduced at the beginning of Book I in its ordinary sense, but later, in the definition of tragedy, is used to designate the genus of tragedy, which requires a technical meaning, although none is stated. Like all discussion of the end of imitation, on which differences in its meaning presumably depend, this is deferred to Book II. We would expect it to appear at the beginning of Book II because a shift to the discussion of a new kind of cause of the subject of a treatise, as here the shift to the end of imitation, is ordinarily marked by beginning a new book. If Aristotle has begun Book II by introducing a restricted technical meaning for "imitative," this would blow away Bernays's entire argument, for the distinction between the ordinary and technical meanings of "imitative" would give rise to the possibility of poetry that, like all poetry, is imitative in the ordinary sense, but may be either imitative or nonimitative in the technical sense, and also to the possibility of a theoretical poetry that, unlike the natural philosophy of Empedocles, is imitative in the ordinary sense but not in the technical sense.

All this will be discussed more fully later, but what is important to note here is that the hard blow in the face to Aristotelian doctrine does not come from the Tractatus but from Bernays's method of interpreting it. He supposes that Aristotle's meanings are independent of context, but this contradicts a fundamental feature of Aristotle's philosophy, in which parts and whole are interdependent, and the same term may have different meanings in different contexts.

Bernays has objections to other parts of the Tractatus as well. "In the opening words of the following paragraph [section 4 of the Tractatus] one believes at first look that he has found a priceless treasure, one in our *Poetics* so sorely missed, a definition of comedy, probably from an Aristotelian source! Unfortunately, it appears already on a second look only a gem of coal (*Kohlenschatz*), as the Greeks say, completely black. [The same Greek word, *anthrax*, means both coal and a red gem such as a carbuncle, ruby, or garnet, presumably from their resemblance to a glowing coal.] What should be the definition of comedy is nothing other than a sorry, unhistorical travesty of the Aristotelian definition of tragedy" (1880, 145). Nevertheless, Bernays also argues that some parts of the Tractatus, particularly the analysis of humor, do derive from Aristotle. He attempts to reconcile this with the supposed inauthenticity of other parts by the hypothesis that the author lacked a complete text of the second book and was trying to reconstruct the missing parts. This hypothesis refutes itself, however, for it is not credible that anyone attempting to reconstruct missing parts of Book II would begin with what appears to explicitly contradict Book I. Only Aristotle himself would do that!

There are many difficulties with Bernays's analysis, but the view that some parts of the Tractatus are Aristotelian and some are not prevailed for the next fifty years. It is expressed by G. Kaibel when he says that Bernays tried to prove Cramer's suggestion, "with the result, however, that he showed that no small amount of extraneous and silly material is jumbled together with what is truly Aristotelian" (1899, 50; trans. and quoted by Janko 1984, 2). This view is compatible with the admiration for the treatment of comedy expressed by two British classicists. W. G. Rutherford writes, "Even the scrimp and grudging abstract, now the sole relic of the section in the *Poetics* concerned with comedy, will convince anybody who keeps it in his head as he listens to Greek comic *prosōpa* [persons of the drama] that a Greek had indeed read for Greeks the most secret heart of 'the mother of comedy,' and, probe in hand, had made clear wherefore it beat, and what it was made of—unconventionality, spite, malice, impudence, devilment, ribaldry, whimsicality, extravagance, insincerity, nonsensicalness, inconsequence, equivoque, drivel, pun, parody, incongruity in all sorts and sizes" (1905, 435; quoted in Cooper 1922, 6). W. J. M. Starkie writes, "The value of this fragment was not fully recognized till Bernays demonstrated that it represented a summary, mutilated and misunderstood in parts, of Aristotle's analysis of the laughter in comedy. The 'tractate' has not yet been fully recognized by the student of Aristophanes. Holzinger, Müller, and v. Leeuwen never refer to it; Rutherford alone has shown a due appreciation of its value. In the following pages some attempt is made to classify, according to the divisions of Aristotle, the various methods of exciting laughter employed by the writers of old comedy, especially Aristophanes" (1909, xxxviii, references omitted).

In the same year that Starkie's work was published, the distinguished classical scholar Ingram Bywater published an edition of the *Poetics* in which he extends Bernays's negative judgment of parts of the Tractatus to the entire work. He argues that the mechanical fashion in which the text of *Poetics* I is repeated indicates that the author did not have access to any part of *Poetics* II. He cites three instances in which there is such a repetition. The first is the definition of comedy, "which has no doubt a certain Aristotelian look; any one can see, however, by simple inspection that it is nothing more than an adaptation, or rather, as Bernays calls it, a travesty, of the well known definition of Tragedy in the existing *Poetics*" (1909, xxi–ii). It is, he says, a "sorry fabrication." The second instance is attributing to comedy the same six parts of poetry that Aristotle finds in tragedy—plot, character, thought, diction, melody, and spectacle—but calling them the matter of comedy rather than forms, as they are called in Book I. The third is attributing to comedy the same quantitative parts as those of tragedy—prologue, choral part, episode, exode. Bywater notes that these parts are also attributed to comedy by John Tzetzes (twelfth century), who cites as his source Euclides, described by Bywater as "a grammarian of doubtful date but apparently of the classical period." From this Bywater concludes that Book II was lost or inaccessible even before Euclides. "It would seem, therefore, that even at the time of this Euclides Bk. II of the Poetics was lost or inaccessible. It is difficult to believe that in the course of a comparatively short treatise, Aristotle repeated himself in the purely mechanical fashion of these later compilations on Comedy" (1909, xxii).

Bywater is right to think that mechanical repetitions of doctrine in Aristotle's technical treatises would be prima facie evidence of inauthenticity, for Aristotle in his final set of technical treatises almost never repeats his doctrines. The scheme of disciplines and causes that structures his inquiries (to be discussed in the first two chapters of this book) insures that he is always addressing new problems. Repetitions of doctrine occur only if it happens that the same statement is called for in two different contexts and the reason why it is required in the second context prevents Aristotle from simply referring back to what was said earlier. I know of only one case in which such circumstances actually occur, the repetition of the account of causes in the *Physics* in the lexicon of metaphysical terms in the *Metaphysics*.

Another kind of repetition, however, is characteristically Aristotelian and found in all three of Bywater's examples. This is the repetition of generic or common features when their form in a new species is discussed. Thus the genus of tragedy and comedy is imitation, and poetic imitation is differentiated by its causes: its object, means, manner, and end. The definition of tragedy specifies these to tragedy, and the definition of comedy specifies them to comedy. Repetition of the form of the definition is therefore required. The differentiae themselves are repeated if they happen to be the same in the two species, as tragedy and comedy have the same means and manner of imitation. This repetition is not mechanical, for it requires a new judgment as to what the differentiae of comedy are.

The six parts of tragedy also derive from what poetry is as imitation, and are therefore found also in comedy. The discussion of what these parts should be in comedy therefore also requires a repetition of the parts, but the account of what they should be involves no repetition. The objection that the parts are called forms in Book I and matter in Book II repeats Bernays's error of supposing that Aristotle's meanings are independent of context. There is no reason why the six parts should not be forms in one context and matter in another.

Since both tragedy and comedy have the same means and manner of imitation, there is a third element common to both, the quantitative parts, and the account of what they are is again not a mechanical repetition, for they are differently defined to suit the difference between tragic and comic plots. There is thus nothing in any of these repetitions that is in any way mechanical or non-Aristotelian.

Not only do Bywater's three instances fail to support his claim that the Tractatus repeats Book I in a purely mechanical fashion, they actually support the authenticity of the Tractatus, for these three instances correspond to the three respects in which tragedy and comedy have generic or common features that require repetition in the account of comedy. This authenticity is further supported by the appearance of its account of the quantitative parts also in Tzetzes, from which Bywater concludes that Book II seems to have been lost before the end of the classical period. We cited earlier the evidence that Book II was known for centuries after the classical period, and therefore the appearance of the same account in both Tzetzes and the epitome is not evidence that both lacked the second book, but that both possessed it.

Bywater has accepted the negative judgments of Bernays and fabricated in his own mind the view that the Tractatus is wholly spurious, unaware that what he is taking as evidence for this actually supports the contrary view. Everything that is said against the Tractatus presupposes its inauthenticity, and viewed as arguments they simply beg the question. Bywater is simply giving expression to his own strongly held opinion in forceful language. This is more effective rhetorically with most people than arguments, however, particularly when the author is held in high repute. Bywater thus initiated a second phase in the history of the Tractatus in which none of it could be taken as authentic.

The predicament in which this put anyone who, like Rutherford and Starkie, valued the account of comedy is well illustrated by Lane Cooper, who shared Rutherford's view that the Tractatus *is* the best analysis of comedy that we have. The Tractatus, he writes, "schematic though it is, is by all odds the most important technical treatise on comedy that has come down to us from the ancients. And modern times give us nothing of comparable worth in its field" (1922, viii). He wished to make it available to all students of literature, but, faced with the prevailing scholarly skepticism, he did not attempt to defend any part of it as authentic, and argued only that "when all possible objections have been urged against the fragment, there remain certain elements in it that, we may contend, preserve if not an original Aristotelianism, at all events an early Peripatetic tradition" (ibid., 3). He did the best he could to exhibit whatever authenticity the Tractatus possesses by melding it with the existing *Poetics* to form a coherent whole. "I contend that . . . the *Poetics* can be metamorphosed into a treatise on comedy; whereupon the authentic elements of the *Tractatus Coislinianus* (if such there be) become an addendum, very significant in any case, subordinated to the main Aristotelian theory of comedy, and improperly estimated unless viewed in a perspective of the whole" (ibid., 17).

This did not alter the prevailing view. Janko's summary of attitudes toward the Tractatus after Cooper shows the extent to which the prevailing skepticism led to its general neglect. "Subsequently, writers on ancient literary criticism, such as D'Alton, Atkins, Duckworth, Plebe, Grube, Fuhrmann and Russell still continue to follow Bernays; Cantarella rejects both the Tractatus and the idea of a second book; scholars of the *Poetics* are either non-committal, like Else, as negative as Bywater, like Kassel, or entirely silent, like D. W. Lucas or Gallavotti. So too writers on comedy, such as Feibleman, Swabey, or Gurewich" (1984, 3; references omitted).

Richard Janko's *Aristotle on Comedy* (1984) dramatically challenged the prevailing view by arguing that the whole of the work derives from Aristotle, along with two other works that have parts in common with it, an anonymous Prolegomenon to Comedy dating from late antiquity and parts of which survive in several manuscripts, and parts of Tzetzes's *Iambi de Comoedia*, the work to which Bywater was referring. The first two of these, Janko argues, derive from a hypothetical archetypal epitome of the lost *Poetics* II. He collates the three texts to produce as complete a text as possible of this epitome. The text is accompanied by a translation, an investigation of its origin and authorship, an extensive commentary in which he gives a full discussion of each of its parts, and a hypothetical reconstruction of *Poetics* II. His extremely thorough scholarly arguments show how much positive evidence there is for the derivation of the whole Tractatus from *Poetics* II and how insubstantial are most of the arguments of Bernays and others against it. He made the results of his work available to nonclassicists in his 1987 translation of the *Poetics* and surviving fragments of Aristotle's other writings on poetry, which contains a slightly revised translation of the Tractatus, an improved hypothetical reconstruction of *Poetics* II, and extensive interpretive notes that summarize and update his earlier work.

Since the publication of Janko's book, a few leading scholars have accepted Janko's thesis of the derivation of the Tractatus from the lost Book II (Janko 2001), but even among these there remain skeptical doubts as to its reliability. Jonathan Barnes writes, "We could accept Janko's main contention and still maintain that TC omitted vital points of Aristotle's arguments, added non-Aristotelian items, and garbled the Aristotelian material that it preserves" (Barnes 1985, 104). Malcolm Heath summarizes the reception of Janko's book by calling it "a book widely admired and disbelieved." Speaking for himself, he says, "I am willing to believe that the *Tractatus* descends from an epitome of *Poetics* II but fear that it has suffered more distortion — and is less useful — in detail than Janko contends," and cites Barnes in support of this judgment (Heath 1989, 344n1).

To Barnes's argument it must be said that any document may contain omissions of vital points, additions of extraneous items, or garbling. Objections to authenticity on these grounds have no validity except in relation to specific points and supported by specific reasons. Barnes does indeed present a number of specific objections that are plausible and deserve answers, particularly his criticism of Janko's answer to Bernays's objection to nonimitative poetry. These arguments justify further investigation, but not a general claim of unreliability. Barnes thus joins Bernays and Bywater in their role of influential Aristotelian scholars who, with good intentions but a limited understanding of Aristotle (a condition which affects us all), have delayed for well over a century and a half the recognition of what the Tractatus for the most part truly is, a straightforward and reliable summary in Aristotle's own words of the lost second book of the *Poetics*, or at least this is what I shall argue.

The present situation is well illustrated by Stephen Halliwell in *Greek Laughter* (2008). He dissents from Janko's thesis on the Aristotelian credentials of the Tractatus (393n11) and regards it as an unreliable guide to the second book of the *Poetics* (392), but gives no reasons. His book says much about the relation of laughter to virtue in Aristotle, nothing about what is laughable.

Before proceeding further, we need a better way of referring to the work we are discussing than as the Tractatus Coislinianus, or Tractatus, or Tractate, or TC, for none of these names has anything to do with what the work is about, and they are either awkward or overly general or an ambiguous abbreviation. Janko refers to the archetype of the Tractatus as an epitome, but Barnes mildly objects, "TC is hardly long or discursive enough to count as an epitome, at least as ancient epitomators typically produced them" (Barnes 1985, 104). But even though this document is more abbreviated than a typical epitome, Janko's edited text is the closest thing to an epitome of the lost second book that we possess or are likely to possess. Against calling it an epitome it might also be urged that in prevailing modern usage, an epitome is a paradigmatic or exemplary case rather than an abstract, and this can cause initial confusion. But it also makes the name more distinctive than it would have been when epitomes were plentiful and Francis Bacon condemned their use in history: "As for the corruptions and moths of history, which are epitomes, the use of them deserves to be banished, as all men of sound judgment have confessed, as those that have fretted and corroded the sound bodies of many excellent histories, and wrought them into base and unprofitable dregs" (Bacon 1605, 82). I shall therefore refer to Janko's edited version of the Tractatus as the epitome of *Poetics* II, or simply as the epitome.

2. AIMS OF THE PRESENT BOOK

Investigations of the epitome fall naturally into three phases. First is a philological phase, focusing on the text of the epitome, its editing, its provenance, its authenticity, and its relation to other texts of various kinds. Next comes a philosophical phase, focusing on the meaning of the new text. Last comes a poetic phase, focusing on how the meaning of the new text bears on questions of literary creation and appreciation.

The long philological phase has now culminated in Janko's improved text backed by widely admired philology. The philosophical investigation of the meaning of the text could now begin, were it not for residual doubts as to its authenticity and reliability. No one can be expected to be much interested in the interpretation of a text that is thought to be inauthentic or unreliable. I therefore propose to begin the present book by supplementing Janko's philological arguments on behalf of the epitome with a philosophic argument that aims to make its authenticity and general reliability evident to everyone. It is my hope that philology and philosophy can together do what philology alone has not been able to do, save a whole treasure chest of priceless gems from an eternity in scholarly limbo.

The philosophical argument for the epitome's authenticity resembles a method used in ancient Greece to guarantee contractual claims. A vertebra or other hard, durable object was broken in half, and each of the contracting parties kept one of the halves to guarantee his claims under the contract. So here, the *Poetics* has been broken in half, and the claim of the epitome to represent the missing half can be established by the way it fits together with Book I to form a complete whole. Each of the halves of the broken bone was called a *sumbolon*, from which the English word "symbol" is derived. In order to have a name for the proposed argument, I shall call it the symbolon argument.

The symbolon argument would not be diffcult to construct if we knew the design of the *Poetics* as a whole, but one consequence of the loss of Book II is that there is no general agreement on the design of the whole. The usual supposition that Book I is about tragedy and Book II about comedy is evidently not adequate, for Book I treats the genesis of comedy and Book II is generally supposed to have treated the end of tragedy. Sir David Ross, for example, says that the reference in the *Politics* to a fuller account of catharsis in the *Poetics* "is doubtless to the missing second book" (Ross 1949, 283). Aristotle's technical treatises are, as we shall see, organized by the causes of their subject, and the best evidence for the causal structure of the whole would be the causal structure of Book I, but there is no generally accepted account of the causal structure of Book I. This, too, is collateral damage from the loss of Book II. Further evidence that we have not understood the design of the *Poetics* as a whole can be derived from the opening words of the *Poetics*: "About *both* poetics itself *and* its species (*Peri poētikēs autēs te kai tōn eidōn autēs*) . . . we propose to speak" (italics are mine, I need hardly say, for the ancient Greeks did not have a lower case, let alone italics and other fonts). The appearance of the distinction between the generic and specific treatment of poetry in the very first words of the *Poetics* strongly suggests that it plays a primary role in organizing the whole *Poetics*. Such a distinction is not peculiar to Aristotle, but is familiar to us as the difference between books on the theory of literature and books on particular literary species such as tragedy or comedy. If Aristotle's poetics is to fulfill its program, or have anything like completeness with respect to its subject, it must speak about both. Yet we have no theory at all as to how this distinction applies to the *Poetics*.

All this shows that the epitome has a quite unexpected importance, for it can not only tell us what was in the lost Book II, but it can also lead us to a new understanding of Book I and of the *Poetics* as a whole. It shows also that we cannot simply rely on what others have said about *Poetics* I, but must construct our argument from the ground up.

If the epitome is authentic and reliable, it is a priceless treasure that will make important contributions to our understanding of Aristotle's *Poetics* and to poetics in general. Although previous authors, including Rutherford, Starkie, Cooper, and Janko have done much in interpreting the epitome, it should, if authentic, contain riches that are yet to be discovered. Finding them is not the work of any one individual, but requires the combined effort of many scholars working over time and from different points of view. What Aristotle says about the judgment of music and poetry applies also to the judgment of his poetic theory. "The many are better judges than a single man of music and poetry, for some understand one part and some another, and among them they understand the whole" (*Pol.* iii.11.1281b7–10, trans. Jowett). I can hope to find undiscovered riches in the epitome, but not to exhaust them.

In this book, then, I propose to present the symbolon argument for the epitome's authenticity and to follow this by interpreting the epitome in the light of the whole body of Aristotle's works with a view to contributing what I can to the understanding of Aristotle's *Poetics* and to poetics in general.

3. METHOD TO BE FOLLOWED

The history of the interpretation of the epitome suggests that we must be careful to interpret it in accordance with Aristotle's own philosophy, and the same is true of interpreting Book I in order to discover the design of the *Poetics* as a whole. I have for convenience adapted two Greek words to designate two possible modes of interpretation. Every interpretation involves two philosophies, the philosophy of the interpreter and the philosophy embodied in the text that is being interpreted. If the two are the same, the interpretation may be called *endothenic,* that is, from within, or *ab intra;* if they are different, the interpretation can be called *exothenic,* that is, from without, or *ab extra* (Watson 1990, 364). The distinction is descriptive, not valuative — valuable interpretations can be made in either mode. But both the interpretation of *Poetics* I for its relation to a supposed second book and the interpretation of a highly abbreviated epitome are particularly suited to endothenic interpretation, for they depend upon discerning the internal connectedness within Aristotle's philosophy. This connectedness is most evident in endothenic interpretation, for any exothenic component in the interpreter's philosophy tends to obscure or transform the connectedness in accordance with its own requirements.

Our problem, then, is to interpret *Poetics* I and the epitome in accordance with Aristotle's own philosophy. One thing that can be done is to consider how Aristotle himself treats a problem like one that we face or how he says such a problem should be treated. We have already cited his statement of how to treat apparent inconsistencies, a method neglected by both Bernays and Bywater. We do not always have such explicit guidance, however, and we need also the guidance provided by the general features of Aristotle's philosophy. His view of philosophies, as we shall see in the first chapter of this book, is that they are self-determined by their own principles, which in Greek are called *archai*. These *archai*, as we shall see in the second chapter, are of four different kinds. Thus a philosophy is determined in a general way by a set of four *archai*, for which David Dilworth has coined the convenient phrase "archic profile" (Dilworth 1989, 17). I have worked out the theory of the self-determination of philosophies by their *archai* in my *Architectonics of Meaning: Foundations of the New Pluralism* (1985). That book was an attempt to understand philosophy as a whole composed of different philosophies (philosophic pluralism); the present book is an application of this theory to a particular philosophy (Aristotle's) and to a particular part of that philosophy (what was in *Poetics* II), but the present book stands on its own and does not presuppose an understanding of the earlier book. What is needed for the present purpose is simply the archic profile of Aristotle himself, which then functions as a hypothesis to be tested by its ability to solve the problems that concern us here.

Aristotle's archic profile comprises: (1) *disciplinary perspectives,* which are perspectives constituted by the human mind and within which we know things; (2) *essential realities* as what is to be known within these perspectives, that is, the experienced realities of general kinds of things; (3) the *resolutive method* as the method by which these realities are known, that is, the method in which these realities are constituted by reciprocally determining wholes and parts or form and matter; and (4) *reflexive principles* as the principles in accordance with which these wholes function, that is, principles that make this functioning self-determined. It is of course not possible to understand these *archai* solely from such an initial statement, but their meaning will become clearer as we proceed and find them exemplified in the material that we treat. The whole book is an exposition of the meaning of these *archai* as well as a test of the validity of assigning them to Aristotle.

We have already encountered Aristotle's method of interdependent parts and wholes in arguing that first impressions of the epitome are misleading because they do not take the context of its statements into account. The interdependence of parts and wholes appeared again in the difficulty of discovering that context in the absence of Book II. The method can be illustrated further by showing how it structures the whole of the present book. It implies that we can begin either from the parts or from the whole in order to understand their unity. The natural beginning is from whichever we know best. The *Poetics* is a whole which is a part of the larger whole of Aristotle's arts and sciences. We know all the other arts and sciences better than we know the *Poetics* because we have the whole of these other arts and sciences but only half of the *Poetics*. But whatever is true of all the arts and sciences simply because they are arts or sciences will also be true of the *Poetics*, which is an art that is also a science in a qualified sense. We therefore begin in chapter 1 by considering Aristotle's idea of scientific rationality and what it means to be a science. A science for Aristotle is knowledge of the causes of its subject matter, or subject genus, and therefore in chapter 2 we consider Aristotle's general idea of causation. This completes the examination of the arts and sciences as a whole. The remainder of the inquiry is an inquiry into the *Poetics*. Of the *Poetics* we know only its first half, which is *Poetics* I. Chapters 3 and 4 of the present book are concerned with what we know of *Poetics* I that relates it to *Poetics* II. This gives rise to expectations of Book II, to which are added expectations derived from explicit or implicit references to Book II in the works of Aristotle and other authors. These expectations are the concern of chapter 5. Chapter 6 is the epitome, and chapter 7 compares the epitome with our expectations. This completes the symbolon argument, and the remainder of the book is the interpretation of the epitome itself. What we know best about the second book we know from the epitome, and what we know best about the epitome is the statements of which it is composed, and it is accordingly interpreted part by part. The principal parts of the interpretation correspond to the three principal parts of the epitome, which concern respectively the kinds of poetry, the end of tragedy, and comedy.

4. PROSPECTIVE READERS

I shall continue along the path begun by Lane Cooper and Janko and address not only classical scholars and experts on Aristotle and the *Poetics*, but those I like to call educated readers, who may not know Greek or be expert in either Aristotle or his *Poetics* but have a general interest in important achievements of the arts and sciences. Such readers are likely to have some initial acquaintance with the *Poetics*, for *Poetics* I, in spite of being only one-half of a poetics, has still become by far our most important and influential work on literary theory. Many of its doctrines are widely familiar, for example, that poetry for Aristotle is imitation, that a plot should imitate a single action and have a beginning, middle, and end united by probability or necessity, that the tragic hero should suffer misfortune not from vice or depravity but from a mistake (*hamartia*), and that tragedy should achieve through pity and fear a catharsis of such emotions. What was in the missing half of the *Poetics* is, I think, of interest to the educated reader.

The missing book of the *Poetics* has in fact already attracted the interest of many who are not classical scholars. The best-selling novel by Umberto Eco, *The Name of the Rose* (Eco 1983), imagines an effort to suppress the second book, which contained Aristotle's analysis of comedy, because it was seen as inimical to the Christian religion, Jesus being supposed never to have laughed. Eco actually includes in his novel a summary of the contents of the second book taken directly from the epitome (ibid., 468). With respect to the hypothesis of the novel, permit me to say this much here. A central thesis of the present book is that the epitome clarifies in a way that has never been done before Aristotle's conception of the autonomy of art, and this conception has two consequences. The first is that *The Name of the Rose* can be an excellent novel regardless of whether its account of *Poetics* II is accurate. Nevertheless, Eco's attempt to give an accurate account of *Poetics* II by including the epitome's summary in the novel may contribute to the reader's belief in the probability of the events of the novel. The second consequence of the autonomy of poetry is that *Poetics* II explains how to produce laughter but has nothing to say about the proper place of laughter in human life, which is fully treated in Aristotle's *Ethics*. Nevertheless, the existence of a book by Aristotle on comedy, regardless of what it contains, may seem to give more seriousness to laughter than it deserves.

Since the present book is intended not only for experts in Aristotle, whatever knowledge of his doctrines that is needed to understand the arguments of the book must be presented in the book itself, not presupposed or referred to by citations. Most of this knowledge can best be presented in relation to the particular interpretation for which it is needed. But there is also a general knowledge of Aristotle's philosophy that is presupposed at the outset and is better presented before the interpretation. This is in fact the subject of the first two chapters, on science and causes, which I have called the groundwork of the book. The first chapter in particular has been conceived as a general introduction to Aristotle in the modern world for readers who may know little or nothing of his works.

The book as a whole consists of three principle parts: the groundwork, concerned with Aristotle's works as a whole; the symbolon argument, concerned with the authenticity and reliability of the epitome; and the interpretation of the epitome itself. This division is useful in accommodating the book to the differing interests of prospective readers. Some readers will be experts on Aristotle, and— although the two groundwork chapters contain new views on most of Aristotle's arts and sciences, a new conception of the unity of the whole of his works, and a new approach to the problem of causation, which make them of interest in themselves—those experts on Aristotle who are interested primarily in the epitome and its authenticity and meaning may wish to skip the two groundwork chapters and go directly to the symbolon argument, which begins in chapter 3. Some readers, now or in the future, will already be convinced of the epitome's authenticity, and, although the symbolon argument contains new interpretations of the causal structure of Poetics I and the sequence of its arguments, which are of interest in themselves, these readers may wish to skip most of the symbolon argument and go directly to the epitome in chapter 6, either with or without reading the two groundwork chapters.

In addition to the need for background knowledge, there is another difficulty for the educated reader that must be addressed. This is a difficulty in understanding anything that Aristotle says. It is identified by Aristotle as the unfamiliarity of the way in what he says is expressed. "The effect which lectures produce on a hearer depends on his habits; for we demand the language we are accustomed to, and that which is different from this seems not in keeping but somewhat unintelligible and alien because of its unfamiliarity. For it is the familiar that is intelligible. . . . Hence one must already have been educated to know how to take each sort of argument, for it would be out of place to seek at the same time science and a mode of the science; and it is not easy to get even one of the two" (Metaph. ii.3.994b33–995a14, after Ross). We are today unfamiliar with the way in which Aristotle expresses himself, which seems not in keeping but somewhat unintelligible and alien. He begins his Poetics, for example, by saying that poetry is imitation, which is not how we think of poetry. The remedy lies in being educated to know how to take what Aristotle says. With time and experience what is alien in the way Aristotle expresses himself can come to seem accidental to what is expressed, and what he says can be understood as expressing in simple, direct language what is true of our common experience.

I cannot, however, presuppose that the educated reader has already been educated in how Aristotle expresses himself, or that he will have the required time and experience needed to remove that unfamiliarity, any more than I can presuppose knowledge of what Aristotle has said. Here a second principle of endothenic interpretation comes to our aid. Aristotle's realities are essential realities, the experienced realities of general kinds of things. An essential reality is a "such," which is what it is independently of the time and place of its occurrence, as contrasted with an existential reality, which is a "this," and is what it is only in a particular time and place. Aristotle's poetics, for example, is concerned with what poetry is regardless of the time or place of its occurrence, and his meanings can be illustrated by the poetry of any time or place. More generally, illustrations of any of Aristotle's meanings can be sought within our own experience, and I shall try throughout the book to find such illustrations in the hope that they will provide starting points for understanding his meaning.

There is another and more fundamental difficulty that confronts the educated reader of Aristotle and is not so easily remedied. It is identified by Aristotle as a general difficulty of the inquiry into truth, but it applies also to understanding the results of Aristotle's inquiries. "Perhaps, too, as difficulties are of two kinds, the cause of the present difficulty is not in the things but in us. For as the eyes of bats are to the blaze of day, so is the mind in our soul to the things which are by nature most evident of all" (*Metaph.* ii.1.993b7–11, after Ross). It is precisely the things that are by nature most evident of all that Aristotle is concerned to discover, and these are the things that our minds are ill-suited to apprehend. Aristotle's philosophy is intrinsically difficult for all of us, and this is a difficulty that I cannot remove. To overcome this difficulty requires sustained effort on the part of the reader; he is in effect the one carrying on the inquiry. Everyone who understands Aristotle has to go through a like process. I have done the best I can to make this book easy to understand, but it is still a very difficult book.

With this much by way of introducing the situation in which the book is written, what the book proposes to do, how it proposes to do it, and difficulties for the reader, I turn now to Aristotle's idea of scientific rationality conceived as the generative idea of his whole series of arts and sciences.

PART I. *Groundwork*

Chapter 1
ARISTOTLE'S ARTS AND SCIENCES

The great idea which we owe to the Greeks, and to Aristotle in particular, and which has transformed the world, is Aristotle's idea of scientific rationality. Other cultures and traditions have had ideas of rationality, but Aristotle's idea of scientific rationality has originated in no other culture or tradition. This chapter is concerned to examine this idea and its development in Aristotle's series of arts and sciences.

1. THE *ORGANON*

Scientific rationality is one form of rationality, and to understand what scientific rationality is, we can begin by considering what rationality is. Rationality requires reasoning, and reasoning is discourse in which, certain things being posited, something other than what is posited follows of necessity from these being so (*Prior An.* i.1.24b18–20). Reasoning in this sense is investigated in Aristotle's *Prior Analytics.* But reasoning is composed of propositions that can be either true or false, and thus presupposes that we know what true and false propositions are. Propositions as true or false are investigated in the treatise that immediately precedes the *Prior Analytics,* the *Peri hermēneias,* whose English title in the Oxford translation is *On Interpretation* but would be better translated as *On Expression,* for it is entirely concerned with expression and has nothing to say about interpretation.[1] True or false propositions are in turn composed of terms that designate things, and thus presuppose that we know what the terms that designate things are. Aristotle cannot explain all these terms individually, for their number is unlimited, but he can treat them by categories. The categories of terms that designate things are investigated in the treatise that immediately precedes *On Interpretation,* the *Categories,* which is the first treatise of the Aristotelian corpus. This corpus, as it has been traditionally handed down, includes a number of spurious works, but I shall understand the term to include only the genuine works. The starting point of the whole series of arts and sciences in the relation of words to things recalls Confucius's answer to the question, "What is the first thing to be done?" He replied, "What is necessary is to rectify names" (*Analects* 13.3). The first three treatises of the corpus constitute a formal logic by which a symbolic sequence can represent a necessary connection of things. Aristotle in the *Prior Analytics* uses letters to stand for terms when the particular term does not matter, and his logic is in this respect symbolic.

Following this account of reasoning or rationality in general, Aristotle in the *Posterior Analytics* treats *scientific* reasoning. We think we have unqualified scientific knowledge of a thing when we know the cause because of which the fact is, that it is the cause of that fact, and that it is not possible for the fact to be otherwise (*Post. An.* i.2.71b9–12). Book I of the *Poetics* provides examples of scientific reasoning. If the fact to be explained is that a plot should have a beginning, middle, and end, this is because the plot should be a whole, and a plot that is a whole has a beginning, middle, and end. If the fact cannot be otherwise, and the premises state the cause of the fact, the premises also cannot be otherwise. If the fact can be otherwise, we still have a hypothetically necessary series of terms; that is, if there is a tragic plot, it necessarily has a beginning, middle, and end. Thus a necessary sequence of terms in formal logic (subject—middle term—predicate), becomes in the science of poetics a necessary causal sequence (plot—whole—having a beginning, middle, and end). This hypothetical necessity makes poetics a science in a qualified sense, a poetic science, even though it is not a science in the strict sense because its objects, such as poetry and plots, can be other than they are.

The necessity of the causal connection requires that it result from what the connected terms essentially are and not from their accidental attributes (ibid., i.6). Nature does not present us with the distinction between essence and accident, for these are mixed together in our experience,[2] but the distinction is necessary if we are to discover the necessary connections of science. That a necessary connection of things depends on what they essentially are requires that the things connected belong to some underlying genus (ibid., i.7), which in the example just given is the tragic plot, which falls within the more general subject of tragedy. Because cause and effect must belong to the same genus, both are internal to the genus, which is in this way self-determining. Here we encounter for the first time another of Aristotle's *archai*, his reflexive principles, which require that scientific functioning be self-determined. This connection of scientific necessity with the self-determination of a subject genus is a distinctive feature of Aristotle's scientific rationality and is not generally accepted, but it is essential to the whole succeeding argument. An initial understanding of its meaning can be gained if one thinks about where in the world the necessary connections can be found that make it scientifically intelligible. Aristotle is saying that it is only *within* determinate genera, such as inanimate nature, or living things, or human actions, or poems. In this sense scientific knowledge always implies a self-determining genus.

Although knowledge of a single cause is already scientific, the complete science of a subject includes all of its causes. The number and nature of the causes is discussed in the following chapter. Independent sciences, each concerned to state all the ways in which the genus that defines its subject matter is self-determining, are a general feature of Aristotle's scientific rationality. Causes are discovered by inquiry, which is the subject of the second book of the *Posterior Analytics*. Aristotle's arts and sciences thus present the results of inquiries into the causal connections by which a genus is self-determining.

The conception of sciences as self-determined genera leads at once to the problem of what genera or domains can be subjects of a science. Not everything that happens can be the subject of a science, for not everything that happens is self-determined. The distinction of the different possible domains of a science illustrates the remaining component of Aristotle's archic profile, his disciplinary perspectives. The domains in which Aristotle established sciences are best considered in the order in which Aristotle placed them, which is the order determined by the works themselves, and for this reason can be called their proper order. This is for the most part the same as the traditional order of the corpus largely followed by Bekker in the Berlin edition of 1831–70. Bekker's order is followed by Ross and Smith in the Oxford translation of 1908–52. The principal corrections that need to be made to the Bekker order are placing Book Little Alpha (II) of the *Metaphysics* between the *Organon* and the *Physics* as a one-book preface to the theoretical sciences, placing Book Lambda (XII) of the *Metaphysics* after rather than before Books Mu (XIII) and Nu (XIV), placing Books VII and VIII of the *Politics* before Book IV, and transposing the *Rhetoric* and the *Poetics*. The reasons for these corrections are not directly related to the problem of interpreting the epitome, and I have therefore relegated them to an appendix, but the order that they establish will be presupposed in all that follows.

With the treatises in their proper order, we can see that in their procession the *Posterior Analytics*, as the science of science, occupies the place of a monarch. The three logical treatises that precede it, which have just been described, provide the preconditions for its rule. The two that immediately follow it support and protect it, and the rest, except for the last, are the sciences that, by conforming to its rule, achieve scientific knowledge of their respective domains. The last treatise, which is no longer a science but an art, has the role of making scientific knowledge effective in our lives. All the arts and sciences can in this way be understood as developing from Aristotle's conception of scientific rationality, and we now pursue the specifics of this development by running through the remaining arts and sciences of the corpus.

Not all reasoning is scientific reasoning. The forms of reasoning other than scientific reasoning are useful to the sciences in important ways, and before proceeding to the sciences themselves Aristotle instructs us in these other forms of reasoning. The *Topics* considers dialectical reasoning, which reasons from *endoxa*, or accepted opinions, rather than from premises that are true and primary. Though not itself a science, it is useful to the sciences because, as an art of examination, it holds the way to the principles of all methods[3] (*Topics* i.2.101b3–4), an important point to which we shall have occasion to return. The principles of the sciences can be discovered and supported by dialectical arguments, but they become known as scientific principles only when known in relation to their consequences in a subject matter. *On Sophistical Refutations* considers rationality in appearance only, and is useful in dealing with the relations of words to things in general and in avoiding fallacies in one's own reasoning (*Soph. Ref.* 16.175a5–12).

These first six treatises were grouped together in antiquity under the title *Organon*, or instrument, of the sciences. Their subject would today be called logic and the scientific method, but there were in Aristotle's time no Greek words corresponding to these concepts, for both logic and the scientific method were his discoveries (*Soph. Ref.* 34.184b1–3). The *Analytics* are themselves sciences in a sense, but sciences only of argument itself, not of the other things that we know by means of argument, and in this way the *Organon* is a science that is the instrument of itself and all the other sciences, each of which investigates some genus of being.

2. PREFACE TO THE THEORETICAL SCIENCES

The transition from the *Organon* to the sciences that are known by means of it is marked by the preface to the theoretical sciences that was mentioned in the previous section as a single book traditionally misplaced as Book Little Alpha (II) of the *Metaphysics*. It was also referred to in the Introduction for its statement of difficulties. It is relevant here in other respects. Its opening words state the concern of the subsequent corpus, the investigation of truth (*hē peri tēs alētheias theōria*). Truth is the concern of philosophy: "It is right also that philosophy should be called science of truth. For the end of theoretical science is truth, of practical science a work (*ergon*), and even if practical men view how things are, they do not investigate the cause in itself, but as relative and in the present" (*Metaph.* ii.3.993b19–23, after

Ross). Philosophy is not *the* science of truth, for there is no single science of truth, but it is rather science, or scientific knowledge, of the truth. A science requires a definite subject matter with respect to which it investigates the truth. Philosophy and science are the same thing, but, like politics and practical wisdom, their essence is not the same (*Eth.* vi.8.1141b23). When conceived as science of truth, it is philosophy, but when conceived as the science of a subject matter, it is a science. That the same thing can have different essences is a consequence of Aristotle's disciplinary perspectives, which are not in the things themselves but originate from the knower. The same thing can be defined in different ways depending on the perspective of the knower, and thus have different essences.

The concern of philosophy with truth leads to the division of philosophy into theoretical philosophy, in which truth is sought for its own sake, and practical philosophy, in which truth is sought for some further end. The concern of the sciences with subject matters, in contrast, leads to the three-fold division of the sciences into theoretical, practical, and productive, each with its own subject matter. This distinction by subject matters is stated in the *Metaphysics* (xi.1.1064a10); it is also recognized in accepted opinion (*Topics* vi.145a15, vii.i.157a10). Practical philosophy includes both the practical and productive sciences, for both seek the truth for the sake of a further end. Philosophy and the sequence of sciences begin with the theoretical sciences because they are concerned with the truth as such, not the truth as relative to some other end. In the proper order of the sciences, the first two of the theoretical sciences are mathematics and physics. Physics is here understood in the broad sense of natural science; in its narrow sense it is distinguished from biology. The preface indicates that mathematics and physics begin the series of sciences, for it ends with an educational prerequisite for physics, which is that the student understand the difference between the modes of mathematics and physics. "The minute accuracy of mathematics is not to be demanded in all cases, but only in the case of things that have no matter. Hence its mode is not physical (*phusikos*), for presumably all nature (*phusis*) has matter" (ibid., 995a12–17, after Ross).

3. MATHEMATICS

The first science in the series of sciences that investigate genera of being, then, is the familiar science of mathematics. Mathematics is the first science to emerge historically (*Metaph.* i.1.981b23–5), and the first in which the young can become expert (*Eth.* vi.8.1142a12). There are no mathematical works in the Aristotelian corpus, although mathematics figures prominently in the other works. It is one of the three theoretical sciences, and the objects of mathematics are discussed in the first three chapters of Book Mu (XIII) of the *Metaphysics*. Many of the examples Aristotle uses in the *Posterior Analytics* to explain what science is are taken from mathematics. If, therefore, there had been mathematical works in the corpus, there is little doubt that their proper place would have been following the *Organon* and preceding all the other sciences.

Mathematics is the leading example of scientific rationality, for we see the theorems of mathematics demonstrated from mathematical definitions, postulates, and axioms. Both the principles and the consequences belong to the domain of quantity, discrete or continuous, so mathematical demonstrations demonstrate the self-determination of quantity. Many examples of mathematical demonstration were known in Aristotle's time, but Euclid's *Elements*, composed after Aristotle, in the third century BCE, brought together the demonstrations of many geometrical theorems and became a paradigm for scientific reasoning in mathematics, as well as in other sciences, although the order of the demonstrations did not conform to Aristotle's standards (Apostle 1958).

Mathematics demonstrates necessary relations within the domain of quantity, and therefore can be used to discover and formulate necessary relations in all domains so far as they are quantitative. But pure mathematics, which depends only on the mathematical hypotheses from which the conclusions follow, is distinguished as a discipline from physics in Aristotle's introduction to the science of physics. He writes,

> The next point to consider is how the mathematician differs from the physicist. Obviously physical bodies contain surfaces and volumes, lines and planes, and these are the subject matter of mathematics.
>
> Further, is astronomy different from physics or a department of it? It seems absurd that the physicist should be supposed to know the nature of sun or moon, but not to know any of their essential attributes, particularly as the writers on physics do discuss their shape also and whether the earth and the cosmos are spherical or not.
>
> Now the mathematician, though he too treats of these things, nevertheless does not treat of them as the limits of a physical body; nor does he consider the attributes indicated as the attributes of such bodies. ...
>
> Similar evidence is supplied by the more physical of the branches of mathematics, such as optics, harmonics, and astronomy. These are in a way the converse of geometry. While geometry investigates physical

lines but not *qua* physical, optics investigates mathematical lines, but *qua* physical, not *qua* mathematical. (*Phys.* ii.2.193b22–194a12, trans. R. P. Hardie and R. K. Gaye)

Thus physical lines become mathematical when they are treated in abstraction from physical objects, and their properties then do not depend on physical measurements but on the definitions, axioms, and postulates from which they are proved. Mathematical lines again become physical when they are treated as the limits of physical bodies, and this application must be justified not only by mathematical proofs but by evidence that the mathematical lines exist in the physical situation. Euclidean geometry, for example, is a mathematical science, and the mathematical space resulting from its fifth postulate is infinite. The physical space of Aristotle's cosmos, determined by physical considerations, is finite, and the space of his cosmos is therefore non-Euclidean. It was not until the nineteenth century, however, that mathematicians, by denying Euclid's fifth postulate, developed the geometry of finite spaces.

4. THE PHYSICAL SCIENCES

Following mathematics, the next domain of scientific rationality is that of natural things, which are self-determining because they have within themselves a principle of motion or rest, such as mass or charge, or, in the case of living things, a soul. The domain of natural things is familiar to us as the domain of the natural sciences, or physics in the broad sense, and its subdivision into the domains of the physical and biological sciences is also familiar.

First come the physical sciences. Aristotle explains the orbital motion of celestial bodies and the falling motion of bodies at the surface of the earth as consequences of the internal principles of motion of these bodies taken in conjunction with the physical properties of the place where they are. There is no vacuum in the sense of a void without physical properties, and the inertial motion of a body after an external push is explained as a consequence of the continued action of the air in which it moves. No one today could take these explanations seriously, and to find something in our own experience in which these ideas are found we need to consider the history of explanations of inertial and gravitational motion.

Aristotle's explanations contrast with the earlier ones of Democritus, for whom space is a void without physical properties and the observable motions are necessary consequences of the inertial motions and impacts of atoms moving in the void. Modern physics began in the seventeenth century in a revolt against Aristotle. Newton writes, "The moderns, rejecting substantial forms and occult qualities [terms used for Aristotelian doctrines by their opponents], have endeavored to subject the phenomena of nature to the laws of mathematics" (Newton 1934, xvii). The subjection of nature to the laws of mathematics entails the rejection of the Aristotelian disciplinary distinction between mathematics and physics which we have just discussed. In the objective perspective of Democritus and Newton, there is only one space, which we know both from physical measurement and, more accurately, from the propositions and demonstrations of mathematics: "Geometry is founded in mechanical practice, and is nothing but that part of universal mechanics which accurately proposes and demonstrates the art of measuring" (ibid.). Newton rejects not only Aristotle's separation of mathematics from physics, but also his method of interdependent parts and wholes in favor of the Democritean method of explaining the whole by the parts. (The physical properties of place in Aristotle represent the influence of the whole on the parts.) Thus for Newton inertial motion is the continuation of the motion of a mass when taken in isolation, and this motion is in a straight line, in itself infinite. Gravitational motion results from the attraction between any two masses taken in isolation. These principles enabled Newton to construct a theory that enormously improves on Aristotle by uniting both celestial and terrestrial motion in a single theory that, with respect to the bodies moved, depends only on their masses and not on their substantial forms. Thus the motion of the moon in its orbit is the result of its continuing inertial motion in a straight line combined with a continual gravitational falling toward the earth. Aristotle's self-determination of moving bodies is preserved insofar as gravitational motion is determined by the distribution of the masses themselves.

Newton's theory includes, however, what are for Aristotle physical impossibilities, infinite space devoid of physical properties and infinite velocities for the transmission of physical effects. Newton's law of gravitation requires that the motion of any mass in the universe instantaneously affect all the other masses in the universe. For Aristotle, infinities are all right in mathematics, but in physics there are only potential infinities, such as the infinite number of different finite velocities, and no actual infinities, such as an infinite velocity. The theory is nevertheless almost perfectly accurate for small regions of the universe, such as the solar system, in which the curvature of space and communication times are negligible. In this respect it is like Euclidean geometry conceived as a physical geometry, for that, too, entails an impossible infinity and yet is almost perfectly accurate for measurements in small regions of physical space.

Einstein was able to remove the physical impossibilities in Newton's mathematical theory by returning to a physical theory that uses concepts like those of Aristotle, for he treats both the gravitational and inertial motion of a body as depending on its mass, which corresponds to Aristotle's internal principle of motion, together with the physical properties of the field in which it moves, which correspond to the physical properties of place in Aristotle, these properties being determined with finite speeds of communication by the other masses (including energy as a mass-equivalent) in a universe that is finite but unbounded. General relativity, with its generic self-determination of both gravitational and inertial motion by the masses of the things moved is thus an excellent and indeed a marvelous example of an Aristotelian physical science.

The theory of general relativity developed from the theory of special relativity and this from the new science of electricity, magnetism, and optics. From Maxwell's equations of the electromagnetic field can be demonstrated all the phenomena of electricity, magnetism, and electromagnetic radiation so far as they are properties of the electromagnetic field. This theory is thus also an excellent example of an Aristotelian science of a self-determining subject. The discovery of the laws of the electromagnetic field did not require the mediation of a Newtonian theory (although attempts at a Newtonian theory preceded the work of Faraday and Maxwell) because the lines of force of a magnetic field are far more sharply curved than those of a gravitational field and can be given visual representation by means of iron filings.

Quantum mechanics, through which we understand the motions and interactions of the smallest parts of things, illustrates Aristotle's conception of the relation of matter to form in physical things. Like any other science, quantum mechanics demonstrates necessary connections, but its necessary conclusions are interpretable physically only as the probabilities of actual occurrences. This result came as a shock to the Democritean scientific tradition, which supposes that "nothing comes to be at random, but all things for a reason and by necessity" (DK, Leucippus B 2, trans. Guthrie 1965, 2:386). It was, however, in accord with the Aristotelian scientific tradition, for which wholes are not simply consequences of their parts. Form as well as matter is an independent cause.

5. THE BIOLOGICAL SCIENCES

Thus when we move from inanimate nature to living things we encounter a new domain of necessary self-determination, the determination of the properties of living things by their forms, which are their distinctive powers: reproduction, metabolism, self-motion, sensation, and thought. These are treated by Aristotle in *On the Soul* and related treatises. The modern reader may be put off by the use of "soul" (*psuchē*) as a scientific term, perhaps particularly its application to plants, which, as living things, also have souls, but Aristotle prefers to give ordinary words technical meanings rather than invent new technical terms. Ordinary language has a wisdom that is respected in this approach. Sigmund Freud, like Aristotle, uses ordinary words in new meanings, including the German word for soul, "*Seele*," and its adjective "*seelisch*." His official translator, James Strachey, preferred to use new technical terms such as "cathexis" and "parapraxis," and mistranslates "*Seele*" and "*seelisch*" as "mind" and "mental," which does no service to his author and severs a strand of our cultural tradition.

Living things provide the most evident examples of Aristotle's *archai*—genera and species, the reciprocal determination of parts and wholes, and the self-determination of the whole—and Aristotle has always had a high repute as a biologist. Darwin says of him, "Linnaeus and Cuvier have always been my two gods, though in very different ways, but they were mere schoolboys to old Aristotle" (Darwin 1888, 3:252). Biology, unlike physics, did not require a Newtonian detour. The great achievement of seventeenth-century biology, William Harvey's discovery of the function of the heart, was made within an Aristotelian framework of seeking for the parts of animals functions that contribute to the whole. Unlike Newton's *Mathematical Principles of Natural Philosophy* (1687), which dismisses Aristotle in its opening sentence, Harvey's *Anatomical Studies on the Motion of the Heart and Blood* (1628) cites Aristotle ten times, always with the respect appropriate to a fellow scientist, usually in support of his own work, sometimes to note or explain a difference between himself and Aristotle. Aristotle's assignment of functions to the parts of animals and plants was in need of many corrections, and Harvey initiated them by taking from the heart the function that we now assign to the brain and assigning to the heart the more modest function of a pump that circulates blood throughout the whole body, including itself.

The great modern development in the foundations of biology, the theory of evolution, brings out a different kind of problem in Aristotle's biology. Charles Sanders Peirce, the American philosopher whose own system is evolutionary, tells us that Aristotle's system was, like all the greatest systems, evolutionary (Peirce 1935, 1:22). Peirce explains what he means by saying that Aristotle recognized "an embryonic kind of being, like the being of a tree in its seed, or like the being of a future contingent event, depending on how a man shall decide to act" (ibid). Evolution for Aristotle and Peirce thus proceeds from potentiality to actuality. Peirce's account of evolution is similar to Aristotle's, except that Peirce's account is metaphysical and applies to all things, whereas Aristotle's accounts are disciplinary and apply to particular subjects such as poetry or human communities.

Aristotle's sciences of animals investigate the parts of animals and the reproduction of animal species, but treat the species themselves as simply given. From the standpoint of a complete science as demonstrating all the ways in which a genus is self-determining, this is a shortcoming. But for Aristotle all science is based on experience (*Post. An.* ii.19.100a6–9), and the data available to him did not appear to support the mutability of living species. The data acquired by Darwin on his voyage to the Galapagos Islands led him to conclude that living species are mutable, and to the theory that the evolution of species is the result of natural selection (Darwin 1958, 174–82). The actual course of biological evolution is not a necessary consequence of either its antecedents (preformation) or its results (teleology), but an *epigenesis* in which what a species is and does at any given time contributes to what it becomes. It is thus a form of the self-determination of the subject genus, although not a necessary one. The genesis of poetic species as Aristotle describes it in the *Poetics* is such an epigenesis, but one in which art takes the place of chance and natural selection. The theory of evolution thus remedies an insufficiency in Aristotle's biology.

An analogous argument applies to cosmic evolution. We shall see that the evolution of poetry as imitation begins from imitation that is only potentially poetry. Similarly, the evolution of life begins from inanimate matter that is only potentially alive, and the evolution of the cosmos begins from a beginning in a big bang that is only potentially a cosmos. In both the physical and biological sciences, then, modern science, while going far beyond Aristotle's sciences, retains in important respects their philosophic foundations.

6. FIRST PHILOSOPHY

This brings us to the last of the great domains independent of us within which we seek principles of necessary self-determination, the universal domain that includes all things. All things are not a genus and its principles are only analogical unless there is something whose principles apply to all things. This is the supreme good, corresponding in some ways to, but very different from, common ideas of an anthropomorphic God. The divine is for Aristotle wholly self-determined and moves all things as an object of love. Its self-determination is that of thought thinking itself. We have been considering the self-determination of scientific genera, and this is the self-determination of the universe in which the self determination of God is self determination in its most complete form. The divine appears in physics as a first mover, in psychology as mind in its actuality—separable, impassive, and unmixed—and in ethics as something present in us in accordance with which we should strive to live.

The editor of the corpus in the first century BCE, Andronicus of Rhodes, called the science we are considering "metaphysics" (*tōn meta ta phusika*, "of the things following the physical things"). Aristotle himself refers to it in four ways. As knowledge of first causes and principles it is *wisdom*; as knowledge of being as being it is simply *philosophy*; as knowledge of what is most true it is *first philosophy*; as knowledge of first and immovable being it is *theology*. It corresponds to what is familiar to us simply as philosophy. Aristotle includes it among the theoretical sciences, however, whereas we generally group it with the humanities, and this calls for explanation.

Aristotle's philosophy is the culmination of the culminating phase of Hellenic philosophy, which bequeathed to all future philosophy archetypal forms of the different principles by which all things can be determined. All things can be determined by us who determine them (Protagoras, 485–411 BCE), or by the matter of which all things are composed (Democritus, born c. 460 BCE), or by the form of the whole (Plato, 428–347 BCE), or by their own activity or functioning, which is the end of the other principles (Aristotle, 384–322 BCE). Aristotle's philosophy is the culmination of Hellenic philosophy insofar as the principle that it adds to the source of motion, matter, and form is the functioning which is the end of the others and for which the others are required. His use of the doctrines of his predecessors to arrive at a philosophy that incorporated their principles did not, however, entail doing them historical justice. Thus Richard McKeon writes,

> Since the scheme of the four causes is the invention of Aristotle, this translation of his predecessors' speculations into the opposition of causes is a use of the history of philosophy, for philosophic purposes, in the schematism and to the ends of one philosophy. No philosophy (except Aristotle's) could be complete in such translation. Aristotle's treatment of his predecessors, therefore, does not do full justice to the intentions and scope of their philosophies; and historians of philosophy have followed the philosophers of antiquity and the Middle Ages in pointing out the faults of historical method and the injustice of judgment implicit

in Aristotle's historical information. He forces terms to meanings which those terms have in his own philosophy, improves on statements by supplying them with significances toward which he supposes their authors were vaguely groping, with supporting facts which their authors did not know, with basic principles they would have denied, and with arguments they would have combated; and he refutes doctrines because of consequences which no philosopher before him had drawn from such theories. This is bad history, in so far as history consists in doing justice to the men and positions which are treated. (McKeon 1949, 20)

It was not unreasonable for Aristotle to think that his philosophy had reached a truth to which his predecessors had not attained and that there was no need to try to do them historical justice. But the history of philosophy since Aristotle has made clear that the refutations of philosophers by one another depend on their own principles, as McKeon indicates in the case of Aristotle's refutations of his predecessors, as well as on advances in knowledge, and thus adequate philosophic principles are not refuted. The history of philosophy and of the use of philosophic principles in the sciences confirms rather than eliminates the plurality of philosophic possibilities. Although philosophy states principles that are true of all things, it is possible to do this in more than one way, for we do not know things as they are in themselves, but as they are within our human perspectives. As was said in distinguishing science from philosophy, the same thing may have different essences. Different philosophies are different formulations of the essence of all things. These differences give prominence to the human factor in philosophy, and for this reason it can be placed in the humanities. In the *Architectonics of Meaning* I have endeavored to show how the history of philosophy and culture since Aristotle leads to a pluralistic Aristotelian philosophy in which the properties of each philosophy are consequences of its own principles, and the principles of different philosophies are analogous and reciprocally prior to one another, which results in a pluralism of philosophies in which each can, in its own terms, rightly claim priority over all the others.

7. THE ORDER OF THE ARTS AND SCIENCES

The transition from the end of the *Metaphysics*, the last of the theoretical sciences, to the beginning of the *Ethics*, the first of the practical sciences, is the most dramatic of the entire series. The concluding sentence of the theoretical sciences looks backward to theoretical philosophy and forward to practical philosophy by means of a poetic analogy between the unifying principles of the two domains: "The rule of many is not good; one ruler let there be" (*Metaph.* xii.1076a4, trans. Ross), a quotation from the *Iliad*. The opening sentence of the *Ethics* is "Every art and every method, and similarly every action and choice, is thought to aim at some good, and for this reason the good has rightly been declared to be that at which all things aim" (*Eth.* i.1.1094a1, after Ross). The two sentences are alike insofar as they both concern the good or end of their respective domains, and they are opposite insofar as the first principle and end of all theoretical knowledge is something actually existing that lies at the end of all the theoretical sciences, whereas the first principle and end of all practical knowledge is something to be brought into existence that lies at the beginning of all the sciences that comprise practical philosophy.[4]

The transition from theoretical to practical philosophy is marked by a preface (*proöimion, Eth.* i.1, 1094b27) to the practical sciences that consists of the first three chapters of the *Ethics* and parallels the preface to the theoretical philosophy referred to earlier. Both prefaces treat the same three topics: (1) the end of the inquiry, either the truth or the good for man, with analogous hierarchies of truths and goods, (2) the existence of the subject to be investigated, and (3) the prerequisites for the student. The two prefaces differ in that the preface to the theoretical sciences is a separate book that is not part of any theoretical science, whereas the preface to the practical sciences is included in the *Ethics*. In the practical preface itself, the science to which it is a preface is referred to as politics. Politics for Aristotle has both a broad and a narrow sense. In its broad sense it includes both the *Ethics* and the work that we know as the *Politics*. Both the *Ethics* and the *Politics* are parts of a single method inquiring into the good for man. The *Ethics* treats this as the good of the individual person, the *Politics* as the good of a community of individuals. The preface to the method is properly placed within it, at its beginning. The theoretical sciences, unlike ethics and politics, are not complementary parts of a single method. They all aim at truth, but not at the same truth, for each science aims at the truth of its own subject matter. Therefore the preface to these sciences is not a proper part of any of them. The inclusion of the practical preface in the *Ethics* thus reminds us that ethics and politics are complementary inquiries aiming at the good for man, while the isolation of the only book in the corpus that belongs to philosophy but not to any science reminds us that philosophy's concern with truth is not limited to the truths of any particular scientific subject matters.

The two prefaces mark two new beginnings within the series of arts and sciences and divide it into three parts. Let us pause at this high point of the series, so to speak, where the first principles of theoretical and practical philosophy meet, to view the series as a whole. Its first part is the *Organon*, which differs from the other two parts in not being concerned with the truth of any kind of being, whether it is eternal or relative and in the present, but only with how the truth of either is to be known. Because of this difference, the three parts of the series are not species of a genus that might be used to give them scientific definitions. In the nonscientific arts of dialectic and rhetoric that deal with things as they are ordinarily understood, topics or places (*topoi*) take the place of scientifically defined terms. They are somewhat indeterminate in meaning and are often best understood through examples. If we consult the *Topics* for a set of three topics that correspond to the three parts of the series of arts and sciences, we find the following:

> Of propositions and problems there are—to comprehend the matter in outline—three divisions. Some are ethical propositions, some physical, and some logical. Ethical are such as whether one should obey one's parents rather than the laws when they disagree; logical such as whether contraries belong to the same science; physical, whether the universe is eternal or not. Likewise also with problems. The nature of each of the aforesaid kinds of proposition is not easily rendered in a definition, but we have to try to recognize each of them by means of the familiarity attained through induction, examining them in the light of the illustrations given above. For philosophy, we must treat of these things according to the truth, but dialectically relative to opinion. (*Topics* i.14.105b19–31, after Pickard-Cambridge)

When we view the series of arts and sciences as consisting of problems and propositions, it falls into three parts, logical, physical, and ethical. The *Organon* is concerned with logical problems of how we know things. Mathematics, physics, biology, and first philosophy are concerned with physical problems of how things are. Ethics, politics, poetics, and rhetoric are concerned with ethical problems of how things ought to be, either by way of acting or making. The distinction between science and the method of science and between what is and what ought to be are commonplace distinctions that everyone understands but are difficult to define. As we see, Aristotle explains them by examples rather than definitions. Although the parts of Aristotle's series of treatises are distinguished dialectically, the problems within each treatise can be treated either dialectically according to opinion or philosophically according to the truth.

Aristotle's division of propositions and problems into ethical, physical, and logical is the first formulation of a distinction that has played a major role in the history of philosophy in ordering individual philosophies and in relating the problems and propositions of different philosophies to each other. In the Hellenistic period the division of philosophy into physics, logic, and ethics was the accepted division of philosophy used by all the schools — Academic, Peripatetic, Stoic, Epicurean, Skeptic. In Latin it became the distinction between natural, rational, and moral philosophy. Augustine, beginning the Christian philosophy of the Middle Ages, attributes the distinction to Plato. Plato did not formulate the distinction or use it to order his dialogues, but Socrates says in the *Republic* that the idea of the good is the cause of knowledge and truth (vi.508e), existence and being are the result of it (vi.509b), and that it must be seen by anyone who would act wisely either in private or in public (vii.517c, translations by A. Bloom). Thus what for Aristotle are distinct parts of his works dependent on different principles are for Plato all dependent on different aspects of a single principle. Here is Augustine's account:

> Socrates is said to have excelled in active philosophy, while Pythagoras is said to have devoted himself to the contemplative with all the intellectual powers he possessed. Plato, thereupon, by joining these two together, is remembered for having perfected philosophy, which he divided into three parts: one *moral*, which is concerned chiefly with action; a second *natural*; which is assigned to contemplation; and a third *rational*, by which the true is distinguished from the false. (*City of God* viii.3, trans. McKeon 1943, vol. 1, III-C, p. 10)

Augustine grounded the distinction in the triune nature of God, much as it can be found in Plato's idea of the good, and ordered the parts of philosophy in accordance with it:

> For perhaps those who are remembered with greater renown for having understood more accurately and more truly, and for having followed, Plato (who is held in far higher esteem — and rightly so — than other philosophers of the pagans) think something such as this of God, that in Him is found both the cause of subsisting and the reason of understanding and the order of living, of which three it is understood that one pertains to the natural, the second to the rational, and the third to the moral part of philosophy. (Ibid., 11)

Locke, at the beginning of modern science, sees the triad as the proper division of science:

All that can fall within the compass of human understanding, being either, First, the nature of things, as they are in themselves, their
relations, and their manner of operation; or, Secondly, that which man
himself ought to do, as a rational and voluntary agent, for the attainment of any end, especially happiness; or, Thirdly, the ways and means
whereby the knowledge of both the one and the other of these is attained and communicated: I think science may be divided properly into
these three sorts. (Locke 1690, iv.21.1)

Kant, working in the Aristotelian tradition, uses the distinction to order
his own philosophy, and within that philosophy is able to give it a principled
formulation.

Ancient Greek philosophy was divided into three sciences: physics,
ethics, and logic. This division is perfectly suited to the nature of the
subject, and the only improvement that can be made in it is perhaps
only to supply its principle, so that there will be a possibility on the one
hand of insuring its completeness and on the other of correctly determining its necessary subdivisions.
All rational knowledge is either material and concerned with some
object or formal and concerned with the form of understanding and of
reason themselves and with universal rules of thought in general without regard to differences of objects. Formal philosophy is called logic.
Material philosophy, however, has to do with determinate objects and
with the laws to which these objects are subject; and such philosophy
is divided into two parts, because these laws are either laws of nature
or of freedom. The science of the former is called physics, while that
of the latter is called ethics; they are also called doctrine of nature and
doctrine of morals, respectively. (Kant 1994, 1)

Thus the distinction first formulated by Aristotle as a non-technical or
commonplace distinction and used to order his own works has had a distinguished history and been used by many other philosophers coming from
various schools.

8. THE PRACTICAL SCIENCES
The transition from the works of Aristotle that we have considered so far to
those we are about to consider is a transition from the sciences of what is to
the sciences of what ought to be. The rationality of the theoretical sciences
is found in the necessary determination of consequences by principles in

things that exist independently of us, while the rationality of the practical sciences is found in the necessary determination of consequences by principles in the things that we do. The first treatise of the practical sciences is the *Ethics*, which is concerned with individual action. The genus of action is self-determining through its end, which is happiness, itself an action or activity of a certain kind, namely, in accordance with virtue. The individual who acts ethically is rationally self-determining. Individuals act not only for their own good, however, but as rulers of communities such as the family or business or state, each of which is an organized whole that can be self-determined by its own good. The practical science of a group, like the practical science of the individual, is the science of its rational self-determination.

These sciences are necessary structures of value. They bring together into a self-determining whole all the different inquiries in which we engage that are concerned with what is better or worse in human action. This is not the way in which the sciences of action are commonly conceived, however. The primary examples of science have always been mathematics and the natural sciences, and since they are sciences of what is, not of what ought to be, it is commonly supposed that if the study of action is to become scientific, it must be value-free, not in the sense that it does not investigate values but in the sense that it does not make value judgments. The science of individual action so conceived is usually given the name of a natural science, psychology. Such a science, while it may succeed in a limited way, cannot give a scientific account of a domain characterized by the pursuit of what ought to be because it is not self-determined. If one attempts to understand action as a necessary consequence of its antecedents, one finds that its antecedents do not belong to one genus, but are highly heterogeneous, and, as heterogeneous, are not necessarily connected with the action. It does not help to bring in values simply as facts, as the apparent goods at which actions aim, because these, too, depend on antecedents that are heterogeneous. There is no escape from the fundamental fact that the universals in the domain of what ought to be, as philosophers as diverse as Aristotle, Augustine, Locke, and Kant have all recognized, are not laws of what is, but of what ought to be. The attempt to achieve a value-free science of action is always subject to the double criticism that it lacks relevance and is not scientific.

Freud has contributed much to the science of action, and has done so by investigating human behavior as if it were the proper subject of a natural science. This may seem to contradict what was just said about the impossibility of a value-free science of behavior. But the reason for this is not far to seek. What Freud was investigating was precisely those aspects of behavior that are not directly subject to choice and rational control because they depend on unconscious factors. We do not choose what we dream or what we say in slips of the tongue or what we do in actions that are contrary to choice. The investigation of such things has a place in Aristotle's *Ethics* insofar as they work against the rational self-determination of the individual. They are treated in Book VII of the *Ethics*, which begins, "Let us now make a fresh beginning and point out that of the states to be avoided there are three kinds — vice, incontinence, brutishness" (1145a15, trans. Ross). Incontinence and brutishness become in Freud psychoneurosis and psychosis, the one implying possession of a rational principle along with an element that opposes it (*Eth.* i.13.1102b13–18), the other the absence of such a principle.

Ethics as a practical science differs in a number of ways from a theoretical science. Both depend on experience, but what we experience as better or worse depends on our character, and since ethical universality lies in what is truly good, not in what people may think is truly good, one must begin with a character that enables one to perceive what is truly good. "Hence any one who is to listen intelligently to lectures about what is noble and just and, generally, about the subjects of political science must have been brought up in good habits. For the fact is the starting-point, and if this is sufficiently plain to him, he will not at the start need the reason as well; and the man who has been well brought up has or can easily get starting-points" (*Eth.* i.4.1095b4–8, trans. Ross). Rational argument alone does not suffice in ethics. The analogical argument for the definition of human good in Book I of the *Ethics* helps us to grasp its meaning and probability, but the apprehension of its truth depends on its capacity to order its whole domain, in this case the domain of the better and worse in human life, and how the better and worse are perceived depends on character, as was said. The dependence of ethical judgment on character is why we tend to attribute a firm and unshakeable adherence to what is right to upbringing or religious faith rather than simply to rationality. It is also one reason why we continue to pursue the chimera of a value-free science of behavior — we would like a science that does not depend on moral character.

Ethics is also less exact than the theoretical sciences. "Now fine and just actions, which politics investigates, admit of much variety and fluctuation of opinion, so that they may be thought to exist only by convention and not by nature. And goods also give rise to a similar fluctuation because they bring harm to many people; for before now men have been undone by reason of their wealth, and others by reason of their courage. We must be content, then, in speaking of such subjects and with such premises to be content to indicate the truth roughly and in outline" (*Eth.* i.2.1094b14–21, after Ross). Outline universals take the form of the definitions of the virtues as habits of choosing a mean that is right relative to the individual. All persons of practical wisdom can concur in thinking of the mean relative to the individual as what is right for that individual, though it need not be right for everyone.

Since what is truly good depends on the individual, ethics requires faculties of perceiving, understanding, and judging particulars. Aristotle in the *Ethics* introduces mind (*nous*) and three other intellectual virtues—judgment (*gnōmē*), understanding (*sunesis*), and practical wisdom (*phronēsis*)—that relate universals to particulars. He concludes,

> For all these habits with good reason tend to the same point, for when we speak of judgment and understanding and practical wisdom we credit the same people with having judgment and by this time mind and being practically wise and understanding. For all these faculties deal with the ultimates (*ta eschata*) and the particulars (*ta kath' ekasta*); and to be understanding and of good or sympathetic judgment is to be able to judge the things about which practical wisdom is concerned, for the equitable (*ta epieikē*) is common to all the good in relation to one another. Now all the things to be done are included in the particulars and ultimates, and the man of practical wisdom must know these, and understanding and judgment are about the things to be done, and these are ultimates. And mind concerns the ultimates in both directions, for both the first terms and the last are objects of mind and not of reason (*logos*)—in demonstrations it apprehends the unchangeable terms and first premises (*ta prōta*), and in practical affairs the last and variable term and the other premise (*hē hetera protasis*), for these are beginnings (*archai*) of the end, for from the particulars, the universal; of these, then, there must be perception (*aisthēsis*), and this is mind (*nous*).[5] (*Eth.* vi.11.1143a25–b6)

Mind, in apprehending both the first and the last premises of demonstration, encloses demonstration. The problem of the domains within which demonstration is possible, which we are considering here, is itself a problem of mind rather than demonstration. Recent research suggests that mind and demonstration make principal use of different hemispheres of the brain. Mind is the intellectual ability in which Aristotle himself excelled, and it is particularly with respect to mind or *intellectus* that Peirce can reasonably say, "Aristotle was by many lengths the greatest intellect that human history has to show" (Peirce 1935, 6:96).

Ethics thus differs from a theoretical science in its dependence on character, in being less exact in its subject matter and thus admitting of only outline formulation, and in requiring apprehension by mind of the particulars with which action is concerned. Finally, in an unqualified sense it is not even science at all. "What science is, if we are to speak exactly and not follow similarities, is plain from what follows. We all suppose that what we know is not even capable of being otherwise; of things capable of being otherwise we do not know, when they have passed outside our observation, whether they exist or not. Therefore the object of scientific knowledge is of necessity. Therefore it is eternal; for things that exist of necessity in the unqualified sense are all eternal; and things that are eternal are ungenerated and imperishable" (*Eth.* vi.3.1139b18–24, after Ross). If we speak exactly and do not follow similarities, practical wisdom and the arts, although they may be similar to sciences in demonstrating necessary consequences within a subject genus, are not sciences in the strict sense because the existence of what is demonstrated is not necessary. They are sciences only in a qualified sense, that is, practical or productive sciences. This usage corresponds to our own, for when we speak of science in the unqualified sense, we think of the natural sciences, and if the social and behavioral sciences are thought to be sciences at all, it is only in virtue of a similarity and in a qualified sense. As for our present subject, poetics, we do not speak of it as a science at all, and neither did any of Aristotle's predecessors.

An Aristotelian science of the family is well illustrated by the popular television series *Supernanny*, which began in the United Kingdom in 2004 and in the United States in 2005. It shows Jo Frost as the supernanny who in each episode comes to the rescue of a family that is having problems with its children that it has been unable to solve. In many episodes the first step is simply to establish the rational authority of the parents over their children. One of the techniques Jo Frost uses for doing this has become generally familiar as the "time-out." It uses the physical strength of the parent to establish parental authority in a way that is never physically punitive or verbally abusive and always respects the capacity of the child to understand and voluntarily follow a right rule, and in this way is a training in rational action. After violating a rule which he knows, and having been warned once not to do so, the child is simply returned to a given place and told why he is being placed there and that he must remain there for a number of minutes equal to his age in years. When he has completed the time-out, he is again told why he was placed there and is asked to apologize for the wrong that he has done. The first time the parent tries this technique the child is almost sure to leave the place immediately and continue to do so many times, but if he is always calmly and firmly returned to it by the parent, he eventually remains voluntarily. When he remains for the given time and apologizes for what he has done, the episode ends with joy and loving embraces. This is of course only the first step in establishing parental authority and ultimately the rationality and good habits of the child, but this authority is a precondition for further progress. It gives to the moral law an unconditional force analogous to a natural law. Jo Frost goes on to show her practical wisdom in many other ways, such as her ingenuity in devising activities appropriate to the particular family in which parents and children can happily engage together.

Let us note the ways in which this example illustrates the fundamental features of an Aristotelian practical science. First of all, right and wrong are real, not simply matters of opinion. Sometimes when Jo Frost is on her way to help a troubled family we view with her a videotape of the children engaging in destructive or injurious behavior, and she will look at us as if in expectation of our assent that this is wrong and must stop. Moreover, her perception of what is right and wrong is not simply an intellectual perception, but is rooted in the person that she is. Sometimes when a mother is admonishing a child with insufficient conviction of her own moral authority, Jo Frost will admonish the child herself in order to show the mother how to speak with the moral authority that she in fact possesses. Again, each household has its own problems, and each problem is resolved in a way appropriate to that problem, but the principles are universal. Every household needs rules, but Jo generally asks each family to draw up its own set of rules. Again, the end at which the household aims is attained through its rational self-rule. To attain the end, it is not enough to know what to do; it must be done. In each episode Jo goes away for several days so the parents can themselves take responsibility for enforcing the rules they have drawn up by using the means she has been teaching them, and in this way the household becomes self-determining and no longer in need of her help.

We come finally to the political community and its rule over equals. Since the end of all action is individual happiness, the good of the state lies in the happiness of its citizens. The interdependence of parts and wholes implies that the difference between what is right and wrong in politics is simply the difference between what is in the common interest and what is in the interest of a faction. What is right and wrong with respect to the immediate issues of the day can often be determined simply by asking which of the conflicting sides represents the common interest and which a factional interest. The legislative wisdom treated in Aristotle's *Politics* concerns how to establish a government that rules in the common interest. A right (*orthos*) constitution or government rules for the common advantage (*to koinon sumpheron*), as distinguished from deviations (*parekbaseis*) from this that rule for the private advantage (*to idion sumpheron*) of the sovereign or ruler (*Pol.* iii.7.1279a25–31). Rule in the common interest is in general best achieved by laws rightly laid down (11.1282b2), for law is reason without desire (16.1287a32). The rule of law can in general best be achieved through the separation of legislative, executive, and judicial powers (iv.14, 1297b32–1298a4). The basic source of factional interests which oppose the common interest within states is the opposition between wealth and poverty, with corresponding oligarchic and democratic factions. The best constitution and way of life for most states is accordingly the polity (*politea*), which is a mean between oligarchy and democracy achieved through the middle class (iv.11.1295b35).[6] It is easiest for a person in a middle position with respect to the goods of fortune to be obedient to reason (1295b5). A rational politics establishes rationality within the political community itself so that it becomes rationally self-determining.

All of this is well illustrated by the Constitution of the United States. The mix of oligarchic as well as democratic elements in the original Constitution can be seen in its assigning to the people as a whole no power whatsoever. In the election of senators and the president, the power of the people is checked by intermediate electors interposed between the people and the election. These intermediate electors were intended to insure that the Senate and the presidency would belong to the "natural aristocracy" of "people of virtue and ability" (McCullough 2001, 377), an end as desirable as it is difficult to secure. The device of intermediate electors, however, proved vulnerable to partisan appropriation and did not achieve its desired end. By 1832 all the states except South Carolina had assigned the power of choosing presidential electors directly to the people of the state, and the Seventeenth Amendment (1913) provided for the direct election of Senators by the people of each state. The constitution thus became more democratic and less oligarchic than the founders intended. But without effective checks by the natural aristocracy of people of virtue and ability, the government became more vulnerable to unwise actions by the people and to demagogic manipulation of the people by the wealth of the oligarchs.

The great change in the subject matter of politics since Aristotle's time has been the emergence of an international community, and many of the great problems that confront us today, such as climate change, ecological degradation of land and sea, over-population, the proliferation of nuclear weapons, regional conflicts, and international terrorism, require international action for their solution. An Aristotelian approach to this new situation would seek to establish, in matters that require international action, a self-determining international community under the rule of law. A wrong approach, on the other hand, based simply on a supposed factional interest, is formulated in the neoconservative "Project for the New American Century" (available on the Internet). It sees the great power of the United States as an opportunity to dominate the world for the indefinite future, unrestrained by law or the collective wisdom of all nations or any opposing power. Among the signatories of this project were a number of those who soon came into power as leading members of the Bush administration, including the Vice President and the Secretary of Defense, and had the opportunity to put its principles into practice, with the consequences that we have seen and continue to see.

9. THE PRODUCTIVE SCIENCES: POETICS

The productive sciences are concerned with rationality in the things that we make. They are sciences in the sense that they demonstrate the necessary consequences of principles in the things that we make, and also arts because their ends are realized in the things made. The only scientific art for which Aristotle offers a formulation is poetics, which is our concern here.

The self-determination of poetry is illustrated in *Poetics* I at both the generic and specific levels. At the level of poetry in general we see the properties of poetry determined by imitation and its consequences, which include the various forms or parts common to all poetry and the generic treatment of how they ought to be constructed. At the specific level of tragedy we see the properties of tragedy determined by its definition.

Both of these accounts are, however, incomplete. The generic account is incomplete because there is no statement of the generic end of poetry beyond saying that it is a pleasure, and this is indeterminate unless what it is that is pleasant is specified. We already know this much about the generic end of poetry as a science, that it must belong to the same genus as that of which it is the end, and thus make its subject self-determining or autonomous. The incompleteness of the specific end of tragedy is of an opposite kind, for it is stated as the catharsis of emotions such as pity and fear, but the statement is without justification or explanation, as if from nowhere or as an alien intrusion from another realm. Gregory Scott has recently argued that athetizing the catharsis clause, that is, removing it from its place, "would not only help purify the definition of tragedy but also clarify Aristotle's aesthetics" (Scott

2003, 262). The absence of an explanation of catharsis and the absence of a generic account of the end of poetry suggest that all discussion of the end of poetry is relegated to *Poetics* II. That there is a full discussion of the generic consequences of what poetry is as imitation in *Poetics* I leads to the supposition that Aristotle was conceiving poetry as the union of two heterogeneous components, its imitative materials and their poetic end, each of which has generic consequences, and that he accordingly divided his *Poetics* into two books, the first taking its starting point from the imitative materials and the second from their poetic end. *Poetics* I begins from poetry as imitation and from the differentiae of imitation. We thus have reason to expect *Poetics* II to begin with a reorientation of poetic inquiry to the ends of poetry.

Poetics is the last and least of Aristotle's sciences, although it is also, perhaps, like Cordelia, not less dear to us. Poetics is the last of the sciences because of its dependence on all the others. It derives its scientific form from the *Posterior Analytics*, the theory of causes by which it is organized from the natural sciences and philosophy, the moral distinctions by which it discriminates characters from the *Ethics*, and the political order that it presupposes from the *Politics*. Aristotle does not discuss this last point, presumably because there is no political order that is proper to poetics. Both tyrannies and ideal states are appropriately found in poetry. For a discussion of the political order favored by Shakespeare and how politics functions in Shakespeare's plays, see Richard Levin's "Who Do the People Love?" (2008). Poetics contributes to rhetoric the analyses of diction and jokes and makes use of it for the thought of its characters.

Poetics is the least of the sciences because it is the least exact. The practical sciences are less exact than the theoretical sciences, and the arts less exact than the practical sciences: "Virtue is more exact and better than any art, as nature also is" (*Eth.* ii.1106b14, trans. Ross). Poetics is less exact than virtue because there is a single set of virtues that can be formulated, even if only in outline, for all individuals. If poetry were like virtue, all poems would be different versions of one poem. But since this is not the case, it is not possible to treat poetry even by means of outline universals. Universal formulations of poetic virtues, at least in Book I, are given only for the parts of poetry, as the virtue of diction is to be clear without being commonplace.

As in the practical sciences the demonstrations of science cannot tell us what it is best to do in individual cases, but only provide a foundation for determining this, so in poetics the demonstrations of science cannot produce a good poem, but only provide a foundation for producing one. Computers cannot write good poetry except by accident. Because of the inexactness of the subject matter it is more dependent on intuitive mind than the other sciences, and the sequence of scientific determination within poetics or within a poem is not long. To illustrate the limits of scientific determination in poetics, let us complete the sequence that was used at the outset to illustrate the definition of science given in the *Posterior Analytics*. Aristotle's definition of tragedy requires that it imitate a complete action, and as complete the action must be a whole with beginning, middle, and end, and this in turn requires the incidents to be connected by probability or necessity, and this in turn requires that they have universality. After only four steps from the definition the reasoning ends, and the determination of universality in the actions of poetry is left to intuitive mind rather than to laws of human behavior.

10. RHETORIC

The final work in Aristotle's series of arts and sciences is the *Rhetoric*, and its cryptic opening sentence, "Rhetoric is converse (*antistrophos*) to dialectic," requires us to look back over the entire series and conceive it as a functioning group. The strophe and antistrophe of a chorus or race traverse the same ground in opposite directions. The common ground of both dialectic and rhetoric is such things as it belongs to all in some manner to know, and not to any special science (*Rhet.* i.1.1354a1–3). The sense in which they proceed in opposite directions over this common ground follows from the earlier statement that dialectic holds the way to the principles of all methods. Thus the scientific arguments of all the sciences are preceded by dialectical arguments which, except for the *Organon* and the *Poetics*, which Aristotle founded, occupy a whole book.[7] Book I of the *Physics* is a dialectical inquiry into the principles of all natural motion and change. Book I of *On the Soul*, the first of the biological treatises, is a dialectical inquiry into the first principles of all living things. Book Alpha (I) of the *Metaphysics* is a dialectical inquiry into the first principles of all things. Book I of the *Ethics* is a dialectical inquiry into the first principle of all action. Book II of the *Politics* is a dialectical inquiry into the best constitution. (Book I concerns the household, and discussion of legislation for the political community begins in Book II.) From these examples it is evident that dialectic ends with the principles from which the sciences individually begin. Rhetoric in its right use, on the other hand, begins from the conclusions with which the sciences end. In this respect dialectic proceeds from opinion to science, and rhetoric in its right use from science to opinion. If we take the sciences collectively rather than individually, we see that in their proper order they all lie between dialectic and rhetoric. Instead of Plato's single science of dialectic, we have a functioning group of independent sciences and arts each contributing to the common good in its own way.

The rational self-determination that belongs to rhetoric is the determination of the speech by its end in persuasion. Rhetorical persuasion is a self-determination of the mind of the audience by which it arrives at a new conclusion. As the art of persuasion, it can be used to persuade people either of the true and the just or the false and the unjust. But those who use it to persuade people of what is false and unjust must take it in isolation from the other sciences. As Aristotle says, "we must not make people believe what is wrong" (*Rhet.* i.1.1355a31, trans. Roberts). The right use of rhetoric depends on all the other sciences, and particularly on ethics and politics, and rhetoric comes after them all in the proper order of the works. This of course does not prevent unscrupulous rhetoricians from using rhetoric to persuade people of what is false and unjust. In recent years we have witnessed the power of wealth to utilize charismatic radio and television commentators to persuade large numbers of people of what is false and contrary to the common interest. For Aristotle, such misuse of rhetoric is one reason why rhetoric is needed. Since the true and the just naturally tend to prevail over their opposites, if decisions are not what they ought to be, the defeat must be due to the advocates of the true and the just, who in this respect deserve blame (i.1.1355a21–3). Scientific arguments do not suffice for persuasion, for they are not effective with everyone. Scientific argument belongs to instruction (*didaskalia*), which may not be possible, but persuasions and arguments must be made by means of commonplaces, as is said also in the *Topics* about encounters with the many (*Rhet.* i.1, 1355a21–29; *Topics* i.2.101a30–4). Instruction in the sciences presupposes education (*paideia*), and, for those who can be educated, education is the alternative to rhetoric.

The domain of rhetoric is the domain of persuasion rather than instruction, and what is persuasive depends on the circumstances and, like dialectic, is treated by means of topics rather than universals and is the subject of an art but not a science. Mathematics and rhetoric are at opposite extremes with respect to exactness: "It is evidently equally foolish to accept probable reasoning from a mathematician and to demand from a rhetorician scientific proofs" (*Eth.* i.3.1094b25–7, trans. *Ross*). Mathematics first escapes from opinion into science by the precision made possible when quantity is abstracted from matter, and rhetoric returns to opinion as the subject of the art of persuasion by which, when rightly used, opinion can be brought into accord with all that the sciences have discovered.

11. SCIENTIFIC RATIONALITY AS A GUIDING IDEA

Aristotle's philosophy transforms philosophy into a series of sciences in which the idea of scientific rationality can be realized. In the theoretical domains, we find that the sciences that he distinguished are flourishing on his principles and without any need for Aristotle, while in the practical domains we find that his principles have been incorporated in our lives and institutions, and the better and the worse that he distinguished are present in our modern world, but both the scientific status and the practical relevance of our social and behavioral sciences could be furthered by the union of science and practical relevance in a scientific knowledge of what is best.

Aristotle's organization of the sciences can be viewed as constituting a program for the development of scientific rationality. Aristotle himself developed the sciences on the basis of ordinary observation and experience. His works can, as foundational works, hold their own against any more recent formulations. But all science is for Aristotle based on experience, and as we have acquired data from domains that lie outside of ordinary experience, either by reason of their minuteness or remoteness in space or time or because we conceal them from ourselves, we have acquired knowledge of the atomic and subatomic constitution of matter, of the evolution of the cosmos and of life, and of the unconscious mind. The difference between the culture of Aristotle's time and that of our own is largely a consequence of the development of scientific rationality as Aristotle conceived it in the various domains that he distinguished. The great success of Aristotle's program has led to new problems such as the danger of climate change, nuclear catastrophe, and the other trans-national problems already mentioned. Although these problems are the result of the development of science, their solution does not lie in the abandonment of scientific rationality, but rather in its use to solve them, and in particular on its use in the domain of international politics. The program of scientific rationality represents an ideal never fully realizable but always providing guidance as to the best way to resolve new problems to which its successes lead. Scientific rationality is the progressive element in history, and historical progress is ultimately limited only by the subjects of the arts and sciences themselves. "Probably each art and each science has often been developed as far as possible and again perished." (*Metaph.* xii.8.1074b10, trans. Ross) This statement can be understood as referring to the development of scientific rationality throughout the universe.

Chapter 2
CAUSES

Scientific knowledge is knowledge of causes (*aitia*), and the problem with which this chapter is concerned is, given the different scientific subjects that have been distinguished in the preceding chapter, what are the causes from which their properties can be explained? Since the causes must belong to the same genus as their effects, they are principles of the self-determination of the genus. If there are different kinds of causes, they correspond to different modes of self-determination within a genus. We noted earlier that the self-determination of a science illustrates Aristotle's reflexive principles, and the causes, as different modes of the self-determination of a genus, illustrate different kinds of reflexive principles. There is no single science of causes, but Aristotle discusses them in the context of four successive sciences, beginning with the *Posterior Analytics* and ending with the *Metaphysics*. We shall consider these discussions separately and then the series as a whole.

The first account of the causes presents them as questions for inquiry: "We think we have scientific knowledge when we know the cause, and there are four causes: one the 'what was it to be?' (*to ti ēn einai*), one the 'from what things is it a necessity that this be?' (*to tinōn ontōn anagkē tout einai*), another the 'what first moves?' (*hē ti prōton ekinēse*), and fourth the 'for the sake of what?' (*to tinos heneka*)" (*Post. An.* ii. 11.94a21–23). The use of the imperfect tense for the first cause, "what it was to be," rather than the present tense, "what it is to be," is because what is intended is not the momentary state of the thing, but the form that belongs to it throughout its existence, as the oak tree is an oak tree at all stages of its life. English has derived from Latin a word that conveniently translates the "what it was to be" of a thing as its "essence," and I shall use the two interchangeably. This first formulation of the causes as questions is appropriate to its context, for the second book of the *Posterior Analytics* is concerned with inquiry, and a cause is what is sought in inquiry.

The next discussion of the causes is in Book II of the *Physics*. It is the definitive formulation of the nature and number of the causes. Most of it is repeated almost verbatim as the account of cause (*aition*) in the lexicon that constitutes Book Delta (V) of the *Metaphysics*. It is too long to quote in full, but three excerpts will suffice for the present purpose:

These things being determined, we must next consider the causes, their nature and number. Since the end of this treatise is to know, and we do not think we know a thing until we have grasped the "why" of it (*to dia ti peri hekaston*), and this is to grasp its first cause, it is clear that we must also do this with respect to generation and destruction and all physical change, so that knowing their principles we may try to refer to them each of the things being inquired into.

In one sense (*tropos*), then, a cause is said to be that out of which a thing comes to be and is present in it (*to ex hou gignetai ti enhuparchontos*), as the bronze of the statue and the silver of the bowl and the genera of these; in another the form and the paradigm (*to eidos kai to paradigma*), and this is the formula of the essence and its genera (*ho logos ho tou ti ēn einai kai ta toutou genē*), such as of the octave the ratio of two to one, and generally number, and the parts in the definition. Again, whence the first beginning of the change or rest (*hothen hē archē tēs metabolēs hē prōtē ē tēs ēremēseōs*), such as the man who gave advice is a cause, and the father of the child, and in general the maker of the made and that which changes of that which is changed. Again, as the end (*to telos*), and this is the "for the sake of which" (*to hou heneka*), such as of walking, health—why does he walk? We say, "For the sake of health," and speaking thus we think we have assigned the cause. . . .

Causes, then, have perhaps this many senses, and since causes are spoken of in several senses, it follows that there are several causes of the same thing, and not accidentally; for example, of the statue both the sculptor and the bronze are causes, and not in virtue of something else the statue may be, although not in the same sense, the one as matter (*hulē*), the other as whence the motion (*hothen hē kinēsis*). . . .

All the causes now mentioned fall into four most evident modes (*tropoi*): (1) the letters are causes of the syllable, and the matter of artificial products, and fire and the like of bodies, and the parts of the whole, and the hypotheses of the conclusion, as the "out of which" (*to ex hou*) is a cause; of these pairs one is a cause as the substratum, such as the parts, the other (2) as the essence—the whole and the synthesis and the form; (3) the seed and the doctor and the man who gave advice and in general the maker, all "whence the beginning of the change or stationariness" (*hothen he archē tēs metabolēs ē staseōs*); and (4) things as the end and the good of the others, for the "for the sake of which" (*to hou heneka*) means to be best and end of the others; it makes no difference whether we say the good itself or the apparent good. (*Phys.* ii. 3.194b16–195a26)

This account is appropriate to the first subject-matter science in the corpus because we need to know what the causes are in order to be able to refer to their principles each of the things being inquired into. This indicates that we may expect the internal organization of a science to correspond to the different kinds of principles to which the inquiries of the science are referred, that is, to the four causes. Because this account of what the causes are precedes the science, however, the examples of the causes are taken for the most part not from the sciences themselves but from ordinary knowledge. The two more technical examples, the ratio of two to one as the formula of what it is to be an octave, and the hypotheses as the "out of which" of the conclusion, are mathematical or logical, and logic and mathematics are the sciences that precede physics. In subsequent discussions, the causes are exemplified as principles within the sciences.

The way in which the things being inquired into are referred to their principles in the physical sciences is indicated at the beginning of the last of them, the *Meteorology*:

[1] The first causes of nature and of all natural motion, also [2] the stars arranged according to the heavenly motion, and the elements of bodies, how many and of what kinds they are, and their changes into one another, and [3] generation and perishing in general, have already been spoken of. Still remaining to be considered is [4] a part of this method which all our predecessors have called meteorology. It is concerned with events that are natural, though their order is less perfect than that of the first of the elements of bodies; they take place in the region nearest to the motion of the stars.

There is no need to mention here the four causes as such, since we already know what they are, and are referring the four physical treatises to them. (1) The *Physics* treats the first causes of all natural motion, and these are themselves unmoved but move as a "for the sake of which." (2) *On the Heavens* treats the stars, composed of what is here referred to as the first of the elements of bodies, and it also treats the other elements of bodies, how many and of what kinds they are, and how they change into one another, and thus it refers its inquiries to the "out of which" of all natural things. (3) *On Generation and Corruption* treats generation and perishing in general, and this is the source of the natural things in which all natural motions have their beginning. There remain to be treated (4) the events beneath the moon, a part of the method that all Aristotle's predecessors have called meteorology, but which would most closely approximate to what we call chemistry, and the principle to which these events are then referred is the remaining cause, the form, or ratios and structures of composition, by which these events are explained. The four parts of the method thus correspond to the principles to which the inquiries are respectively referred, and these correspond to the four sense of causation.

The third discussion of the causes is at the beginning of *On the Generation of Animals*, the last of the biological treatises, and thus in the same relative place in the biological sciences as the quotation from the *Meteorology* is in the physical sciences.

The other parts, of the parts belonging to animals, have been spoken of, both in common, and separately, according to each genus as proper to that genus. It has been said in what way each part exists through a cause—I mean the "for the sake of what?" (*to heneka tou*), for four causes are presupposed, the "for the sake of which" (*to heneka hou*) as end (*telos*) and the formula of the substance (*to logos tēs ousias*), which may indeed be taken as almost one thing, third and fourth the matter (*hulē*) and "whence the beginning of the motion" (*hothen hē archē tēs kinēseōs*). The other causes, then, have been spoken of, for the formula and the "for the sake of which" as end are the same, and the matter of animals is their parts, of the whole animal in its totality the heterogeneous parts, and of these the homogeneous parts, and of these the so-called elements of bodies. There remain, then, of the parts, the parts that together have as their end the generation of animals, about which nothing has so far been determined, and, of the causes, the moving cause, what it is. The investigation of this and of the generation of each animal are in a way the same, and therefore our discourse has brought them together into one: in what concerns the parts, the parts of generation last, and in what concerns generation, a beginning preserving the order of the parts.

Here the kinds of causes have been made explicit in order to explain how the parts of the method relate to the causes. There are two unusual circumstances in biology that interfere with the simple one-to-one correspondence of parts of the method to the causes that obtains in the physical sciences. First, the "for the sake of which" as end and the formula of the substance are almost one thing. The formula of the substance is the definition of the soul. As the first actuality of a natural organized body it differs from the end or functioning only in being the first rather than the second actuality of the same body. That is, a living body differs from the same body without life in being able to function even if it is not actually functioning, and this is its first actuality, while its actual functioning is its second actuality. As subjects of science, both actualities are treated together in *On the Soul*. The particular functioning of animals depends on the circumstances in which they function, which are contingent rather than necessary, and the lives of animals are treated in the history of animals rather than a science of animals. Thus, contingency in the functioning of animals results in the incorporation of the scientific treatment of animal functioning into the same treatise as the formal treatment of the capacity to function. The second unusual circumstance in biology is that the parts of animals, which are their matter, are referred to different causes and treated in different treatises, for the parts of generation are referred to "whence the beginning of the motion," whereas the other parts are treated in *On the Parts of Animals* as the "out of which."

We also see here a feature of the causes that we might expect but that so far has not been made explicit, and this is that the causes themselves may have causes. That is, each of the parts of animals (matter) has been referred to a "for the sake of which" (end of matter), and also the parts of the whole animal, which are the heterogeneous parts (matter), themselves have parts, which are the homogenous parts (matter of matter), and these in turn have parts, which are the elements of bodies (matter of matter of matter). Thus we can expect a recursive use of the causes to organize the subordinate parts of a science.

The fourth and final discussion of the causes is in Book Alpha (I) of the *Metaphysics*. After a preface concerned with the nature and end of wisdom, Aristotle says,

Evidently we have to acquire scientific knowledge of the original causes (*ta ex archēs aitia*) (for we say we know each thing only when we think we recognize its first cause), and causes are spoken of in four senses. In one of these we mean the substance and the essence (*hē ousia kai to ti ēn einai*) (for the "why" (*to dia ti*) leads up to the ultimate definition, and the first 'why' is a cause and principle); in another the matter and the substratum (*hē hulē kai to hupokeimenon*), in a third whence the beginning of the motion (*hothen hē archē tēs kineseōs*), and in a fourth the cause opposed to this, the for the sake of which and the good (*to hou heneka kai t'agathon*) (for this is the end (*telos*) of all generation and motion). We have studied these causes sufficiently in our works on nature, but yet let us call to our aid also those who have come to the investigation of being and philosophized about the truth before us, for obviously they speak of certain principles and causes. To go over their views, then, will be of profit to the present method, for we shall either find another kind of cause, or be more persuaded of those now spoken of. (*Metaph.* i.3.983a24–b6, after Ross)

Aristotle concludes this inquiry by saying, "That all men seem to seek the causes named in the *Physics*, and we cannot name any beyond these, is clear even from what was said before; but they seek these as it were in the dark, and though in a sense they have all been described before, in a sense they have not been described at all" (*Metaph.* i.10.993a11, after Ross).

What is said about the causes in the *Metaphysics* differs from what is said about them in the physical and biological sciences because in the latter it was a matter of referring inquiries to the causes, whereas in the *Metaphysics* the causes themselves are the subject of inquiry, and this entails an inquiry into the whole history of thought about principles and causes. After the *Metaphysics*, there is no further discussion of the four causes as such.

If we take the series of discussions of the causes as a whole, the four discussions can be conceived as parts of a single inquiry into causes in general, each of the parts being concerned with a different aspect of the causes. That is, the successive discussions are concerned respectively with (1) the origin of the causes in questions to be investigated, with (2) what the causes are, with (3) anomalies in their application to a particular subject matter, and with (4) the finality of the set. Thus the different aspects of the causes can themselves be referred to the four causes. Similar examples of separate discussions of a single subject that can be referred to the four causes are found within a particular treatise, as the four separate discussions of pleasure in the *Ethics* (i.8.1099a7–31, ii.3, vii.11–14, x.1–5) can be conceived as parts of a single inquiry into pleasure.[1]

The number of the causes is always four, but they are designated not by a fixed set of technical terms, but by varying words or phrases from ordinary language. The phrases and examples vary with the science in which the discussion occurs. The *Posterior Analytics* gives a formulation of the "out of which" that is not found elsewhere, the "from what things is it a necessity that this be?" or the antecedents that necessitate a consequent. This is a formulation appropriate to logic and mathematics, the first sciences in the sequence. It appears in the comprehensive account in the *Physics* only as an example, "the hypotheses that cause a conclusion." In the sciences other than logic and mathematics the necessity generally runs the other way—not, "if the cause, then necessarily the effect," but rather, "if the effect, then necessarily the cause." But even though the direction of the necessity is different, the analogy between the "out of which" and what is necessarily connected with it still holds. It is essential to science that there be some necessity in the connection, but the necessity can run either way, from cause to effect or from effect to cause, or both at once. Again, the definition of the "whence the beginning of the motion" in the *Physics* is the only one that adds "or rest" or "or the stationariness," for in physics forces produce both acceleration and deceleration. Again, the account quoted from *The Generation of Animals* is the only one to say that the end and the formula of the essence can be taken as almost the same thing. Again, the account of the causes at the beginning of the *Metaphysics* is the only one besides the one in the *Physics* to include, along with the "for the sake of which," the good (*to agathon*), for this science is concerned with the supreme good of all things. All this indicates that what the four causes are as universals is indeterminate, and they become determinate only as causes of definite things.

We need to consider more closely what the universal causes are. Taking the "out of which" as an example, we can say that letters of the alphabet, bronze, the parts of animals, and hypotheses all fall under it. Yet what do they have in common? Nothing, except that they have a similar analogical relation to something else. As the letters are to the syllable, so is the bronze to the statue, the parts of animals to the animal, and the hypotheses to the conclusion. As Aristotle says, "The causes and the principles of different things are in a sense different, but in a sense, if one speaks universally and analogically, they are the same for all" (*Metaph.* xii.4.1070a31, trans. Ross). That is, when one speaks of the causes universally, one is speaking only of analogies, and analogies are always obscure (*Topics* vi.2.139b34). This is why Aristotle designates the causes by varying phrases of ordinary language rather than by technical terms. The closest he comes to standard formulations is in the phrases and single words he uses most often: the "out of which" (*to ex hou*), the "what it was to be" (*to ti ēn einai*), "whence the beginning of motion" (*hothen he archē tēs metabolēs*), and the "for the sake of which" (*to hou heneka*). Three of these can be expressed in single words: matter (*hulē*), form (*eidos*), and end (*telos*). Technical terms presuppose a definite subject genus, but there is no definite subject genus of the universal causes. Technical terms for the causes were introduced in the Latin tradition, however, and their cognates have been used in the Oxford translation, which refers to the causes as efficient, material, formal, and final. These terms are very useful in designating unambiguously what is in its own nature ambiguous, but they may give the impression that what is being designated has a definiteness that it does not have.[2]

The kind of importance the causes have is easily misunderstood. Since Aristotle uses the causes to organize his sciences but does not, after the natural sciences, tell us what the universal causes are under which the particular causes fall, it is sometimes supposed, overestimating their importance, that this is an esoteric wisdom that Aristotle is keeping from us, or, underestimating their importance, that he is not really using the causes to organize his sciences. But in his four discussions of causes Aristotle has said what there is to say about the causes in general, and if he does not make explicit what the four causes are in each science it is not because he has an esoteric wisdom that he is keeping from us, or because he is not using the causes to organize his sciences, but because a statement that this or that particular cause falls under this or that universal cause is not a scientific statement at all. Scientific statements predicate literal terms of the underlying genus. To say that a particular cause falls under one of the universal causes is only to say that what is being said about this particular cause is analogous to what is said about other particular causes in this and countless other works. To understand a particular cause is to understand something definite, but to understand a particular cause as an instance of a universal cause adds nothing definite with respect to the subject matter. It cannot be otherwise, for just because the universal causes are universal and analogical, they say nothing definite about the particular subject matter.

Freud's *The Interpretation of Dreams* can be taken as an illustration of this. After a dialectical chapter on the scientific literature dealing with the problems of dreams, the next three chapters lead to the discovery of the opposed psychic forces operative in the production of dreams, the next concerns the material and sources of dreams, the next concerns the dream-work by which dreams acquire their form, and the last is on the psychology of the dream-process and examines the function of dreams. Freud was founding a complete science of dreams, and so was naturally led to their four causes. But in saying this I have not made a contribution to the science of dreams; I have only used Aristotelian terms to call attention to an analogy between *The Interpretation of Dreams* and many other works.

Hunting for the four causes in a special science does not contribute to knowledge of its subject matter and tends to take us away from the determinate subject matter into indeterminate analogies, and for this reason it is best to follow Aristotle's example and not refer parts of a science to the universal causes unless there is a problem as to the organization of a science or its parts. In the present case, the organization of the *Poetics* is critical to determining what to expect in Book II, and so I shall be concerned to refer what is said in the *Poetics* to the universal causes.

Since Aristotle discusses the use of the causes to organize his sciences only in the physical and biological sciences, it may be doubted whether he does so in the *Poetics* also. To make the strongest possible case that he does use the causes to organize the *Poetics*, I need to show that he uses the causes to organize not only the physical and biological sciences, but also the other sciences and arts. To do this adequately would require a thorough examination of each science that would be out of place here. What I can do is simply state without argument what I take to be the causal organization of each of these arts and sciences. I should say, however, that there is at present no agreement on these matters, again because of the analogical nature of the causes. The respects in which a thing may or may not be analogous to something else are indeterminate, and therefore it is possible to pair off with some plausibility almost any set of four things with the four causes. If you can divide one of Aristotle's treatises into four parts in some plausible way, you can be pretty sure of finding a reasonable way to match them to the four causes. This is not to say, however, that these questions are not subject to definitive settlement by further argument.

For the purpose of showing how I refer the principal parts of a science to the causes, it is convenient to make use of the Latinate technical terms, which I shall abbreviate as *mat.*, *for.*, *eff.*, and *fin.* This usage should not, of course, be taken to imply that these terms designate more than analogies. The analysis of the causal organization of the *Metaphysics* and the *Politics* presuppose what is said in the appendix about the books that belong in them and their proper order.

The domain of the *Metaphysics* is all things, but all things are not a definite kind of thing, and therefore this work, unlike the special sciences, has initially no defined subject genus to which the causes can be referred. The initial definition is the definition of the human virtue of wisdom as the science of first causes and principles. But man and his desire to know turn out to be only the originative source (*eff.*) of this wisdom, and this human contribution to wisdom is treated in Books Alpha (I) and Beta (III). What this wisdom is about is being (*mat.*), and Books Gamma (IV) and Delta (V) deal with the axioms and definitions that belong to being as being. "Being," however, has various senses (*for.*), including first being or substance, and these are discussed in Books Epsilon (VI) through Iota (X). Books Mu (XIII) and Nu (XIV) and Lambda (XII) concern first or immaterial substance (*fin.*), which is the good and the end of the other inquiries, and provides philosophy with a determinate genus of being. Philosophy is thus an inquiry unified by the end at which it aims rather than by an initially defined subject genus. It begins from our desire to know and ends with knowledge of what is most true in the nature of things, distinguishing the subject genera of the special sciences along the way.

Book I of the *Ethics* is a dialectical inquiry into the end of action, and the remainder is scientific, dealing with character (*eff.*), from which action begins (II–V); with thought (*for.*), which informs action (VI); with unregenerate human nature (*mat.*), which may either impede or assist right action (VII); and with the activity (*fin.*) that is the end of action (VIII–X). The *Politics* deals with the parts (*mat.*) of the state (Book I); the finality of the state in the best state (*fin.*), first dialectically (II) and then scientifically (III, VII–VIII); the constitution (*for.*) as the form of the state (IV); and the causes of changes (*eff.*) in states (V–VI). The *Rhetoric* deals with the opinions (*mat.*) that are the materials of persuasion (Book I), motivation (*eff.*) for persuasion in character and emotion (II, chapters 1–18), the forms of persuasive argument (*for.*) (II, chapters 18–26), and the end of persuasion in the persuasive speech (*fin.*) (III). (The reference of both the principal and subordinate parts of the *Rhetoric* to the causes is worked out in Watson 2001, pp. 391–9, although without the use of Latinate terms.)

All of these sciences and arts, then, confirm what we would expect on general grounds and from the examples provided by the physical and biological sciences, that the parts of a science or an art can be referred to the different causes of its subject genus.

PART II. *The Symbolon Argument*

Chapter 3
CAUSES IN THE *POETICS*

The preceding account of the causes in general was undertaken for the sake of its application to the *Poetics*. We can expect the whole *Poetics* to be organized by the causes to which its inquiries can be referred. What causes to expect in Book II can be determined if we know what causes are to be treated in the whole poetics and which of them are treated in Book I, for if we subtract from the causes treated in the whole those treated in Book I, the remainder should be those treated in Book II. Since we must infer the causes to be treated in the whole from those treated in Book I, we must begin by determining the causes treated in Book I.

The first thing we must do is distinguish the treatment of the generic causes that apply to all poetry from the treatment of specific causes that apply only to particular species of poetry. In our review of Aristotle's accounts of the causes, we skipped the second part of the account in the *Physics* as not needed to determine their nature and number, but it is needed here. The first part of the account is concerned with what the causes are and the number of their kinds, and the second with the modes (*tropoi*) of the causes, where the modes are variations or differences that may characterize any kind of cause. The principal modes depend on whether the causes are general or particular, proper or incidental, potential or actual. Only the first of these is our concern here. This is what Aristotle says about it, beginning at the point where he turns from the kinds of causes to their modes:

> These, then, are the causes and the number of their kinds, but the modes of causes are many in number, although when brought under heads they also are rather few. Causes are spoken of in many senses, and of causes of the same kind, some are causes in a prior and others in a posterior sense, as both physician (*iatros*) and man of art (*technitēs*) are causes of health, and both the ratio 2:1 and number are causes of the octave, and always what is inclusive is prior to what is particular (*Phys.* ii.3.195a26–32). . . . Similarly, what has been said about the causes may also be said about the things of which the causes are causes, as the causes may be causes of this statue or of statue or of image in general, or of this bronze or of bronze or of matter in general (ibid. b6–9). . . . Further, we should seek generic causes of genera, but

particular causes of particulars, as sculptor of statue, this sculptor of this statue. (Ibid., 25–27)

From this it is plain that generic causes are not the same as specific causes, that generic causes are prior to specific causes in the sense of being more inclusive, that both may be of any of the four kinds, and that we should seek generic causes of genera and specific causes of species. In the present case, this means that we should expect in the *Poetics* both the causes of poetry itself and the causes of its species.

Kenneth Telford (1961) analyzed the causes in *Poetics* I on the supposition that they were a complete set of the causes of tragedy, whereas we have argued that the final cause of tragedy, the catharsis of emotions such as pity and fear, is left for Book II. He also did not distinguish generic from specific causes. We can use his analysis to discover how the treatment of generic causes is combined with the treatment of specific causes in *Poetics* I by noting with respect to the account of each of the causes of tragedy what is specific to tragedy and what is generic, as well as anything that is neither a specific nor a generic cause of tragedy. This argument is unavoidably technical, and more technical than is appropriate to a book intended for educated readers in general, and, although it is necessary for establishing its conclusions, it is fortunately not necessary for understanding the rest of the book. Those who wish to can therefore skip directly to the reason for the division of the *Poetics* into two books, stated in the long paragraph that begins on page 62, and from this go directly to the brief concluding paragraph at the end of the chapter.

Telford divides *Poetics* I into three principal sections. The first section, chapters 1–5, Telford says concerns the genesis or efficient cause of tragedy. Chapter 4 does indeed give an account of both the generic and specific genesis of tragedy, but what precedes this in chapters 1–3, the differentiae of poetry in general as imitation, is not about genesis at all, and what follows it, in chapter 5, is specific to comedy. Thus we have here, in addition to the specific account of the genesis of tragedy, a generic account of the materials and genesis of poetry up to the emergence of poetic species, and a specific account of the genesis of comedy.

The second section of the *Poetics* is said by Telford to be concerned with tragedy as a composite whole or quasi-thing (chapter 6), and to have two parts, concerned respectively with plot as the formal cause of tragedy (chapters 7–18), and with diction as the material cause of tragedy (chapters 19–22). This form-matter analysis of tragedy, like the account of its genesis, includes both generic and specific components. What the plot should be as the result of the fact that the action imitated is complete applies to all plots and not to the plot of tragedy only, whereas what the plot should be in order to arouse pity and fear applies only to species whose end is a catharsis of emotions such as pity and fear. When Aristotle comes to discussing character in chapter 15 he returns initially to a generic account. To make this clear we must first interchange Telford's assignment of causes to chapters 14 and 15, for he supposes chapter 14 to be concerned with *hamartia* (error, mistake) as the efficient cause of tragedy's function and chapter 15 to be concerned with character as the material cause of tragedy's function. But chapter 14 is not concerned specifically with *hamartia*, which is never mentioned, but with the arousal of pity and fear by the spectacle and incidents. This is the cause of a piteous and fearful plot as an "out of which," or material cause. Chapter 15 is indeed about character, but about character as the cause of a plot in the sense of the source of the beginning of action, or an efficient cause. But since it has this same function in any plot, whether or not it is made piteous and fearful by a mistake, Aristotle has here returned to a generic account.

Turning now to Telford's material cause of tragedy, we find that the beginning of chapter 19 gives a generic referral of what thought should be to the *Rhetoric*, as well as a specific mention of four rhetorical forms or ideas (*ideai*) that are particularly appropriate to tragedy. Most of the treatment of diction is generic, applying not only to poetic diction, but to all diction. (This corresponds to the treatment of English composition in our departments of English, for this, too, concerns all diction, that is, expression in language.) In the conclusion of the section on diction Aristotle considers the fitting use of diction in different kinds of composition distinguished according to their meter, both tragedy and comedy being included under iambic poetry. Metaphors are most suited to iambic poetry, and Aristotle has already explained that both augmented words and metaphors can be either serious or laughable.

There is thus a generic discussion of each of the parts except melody and spectacle, followed in each case by a specification to tragedy. There is also a specific discussion of tragic character and spectacle in relation to the end of tragedy, for it is said of tragic character that it should evoke pity and fear, and of tragic spectacle that it should be fearsome (*phoberos*) rather than monstrous (*teratōdēs*).

The final section of the *Poetics* Telford says is concerned with the expression of a poetic argument as the final cause of tragedy. Although this section does not give us the final cause of tragedy, Telford's "expression of a poetic argument" indicates the respect in which this section is concerned with finality, for it considers tragedy and epic as functioning wholes, not in every respect, but as imitations. This is made explicit at the beginning of the final chapter, which asks not whether epic or tragic *poetry* is better, but whether epic or tragic *imitation* is better. The question as to which species better achieves its specific end is raised at the very end of the chapter, but is left unanswered. When Aristotle in chapters 23 and 24 discusses epic poetry by comparing it with tragedy, he compares them as completed imitations, that is, in their finality as imitations. In chapter 25, when Aristotle treats problems of imitation and their solutions, he returns again to a generic account, as he did at the beginning of his treatment of each of the parts. This is evidently because the resolution of problems with respect to imitation is largely independent of the particular species of imitation, and, to the extent that it does depend on the species, the resolution can still be stated generically by referring to the end of the species. Thus, an impossibility may be justified if it happens to serve the end of the art. If the end is as stated in the definition of tragedy, the impossibility will be justified if it makes either this or some other part more terrifying (25.1460b24).

Let us now bring together all that we have found to be generic in *Poetics* I: (1) the differentiae of imitation, (2) the genesis of poetry up to the emergence of definite species, (3) the six parts or forms, and the generic account of what four of them should be, (4) problems and solutions with respect to poetic imitation. These can evidently be referred to the four generic causes of poetry as imitation: the differentiae of imitation are a matter, out of which nature, character, and art as efficient causes generate the species of poetry, of which the parts are the forms assumed by the differentiae, and whose end is the perfection of poetry as imitation in a faultless imitative whole. Thus the primary organization of *Poetics* I is determined by four generic causes of poetry, but of poetry only *as imitation*.

Poetry as imitation is one source of its generic causes, but poetry, unlike the subject of any other science, unites two heterogeneous sources, antecedent materials and an artistic end. The antecedent material is found in imitation with its three differentiae, the "in what," "of what," and "how" of imitation, which are three of the causes of poetry. The fourth cause, the end of the imitation, is not a differentia of imitation in general, but only of poetic imitation, for imitation in general has no proper end, but can be used for many heterogeneous ends, such as learning or mockery or flattery, as well as for properly poetic ends. The generic properties of poetry may result from either its materials or its end, and, since these are heterogeneous, the analysis of the generic causes of poetry, unlike the analysis of generic causes in any other science, is divided into two analyses, the generic analysis of poetry as imitation and the generic analysis of the end or ends of poetry. It is evidently this difference that divides the *Poetics* into two books, as we were led to expect in the discussion of poetics in chapter 1. Book I begins from the generic causes of poetry as imitation, and we can expect Book II to begin from the generic end or ends of poetry. The reason for the division of the *Poetics* into two books thus turns out to be something simple, fundamental, and even obvious, once it is recognized that poetry has two generic sources that are only artificially united, the materials of imitation and the poetic end. It follows that we can expect at the beginning of *Poetics* II a fundamental shift from the analysis of poetry as imitation to the generic analysis of the end or ends of poetry.

Let us now turn to the specific causes. For the specific causes of tragedy in Book I, we can follow Telford's analysis. The genesis of poetry begins generically with pre-poetic imitation, splits at the beginning of poetic imitation into the precursors of tragedy and comedy, which are the works of the graver poets on the one hand and more frivolous poets on the other, and becomes specific with the appearance of tragedy and comedy. The account of the specific genesis of tragedy distinguishes the successive innovations through which it acquired its form, attributed where possible to particular poets. This account can be referred to the efficient cause of tragedy, which is the art of the tragic poet. The genesis is an epigenesis in which each advance depends on what the poetry already is. It is the art of tragedy generating itself.

The account of the genesis of tragedy is followed in Book I by an analysis of its plot, which is partly generic, partly specific, and includes the account of character, from which the actions of the plot begin. The analysis of the plot can be referred to the formal cause of tragedy, as we have said, for the plot is as it were the soul of tragedy. Next comes the consideration of thought and diction. For thought we are referred to the *Rhetoric*. Rhetorical ideas and diction can be referred to the material cause of tragedy as that out of which tragedy comes to be and is present in it. The expected account of tragic catharsis can be referred to the remaining cause, the final cause.

In referring the parts of tragedy to its causes, there is a problem with respect to spectacle. We have said that what spectacle ought to be in tragedy is referred to the end of tragedy, but spectacle itself, unlike any of the other parts of poetry belonging to tragedy, has not been referred to any of its causes. Let us consider why this is so. The form of tragedy is referred by Aristotle to the object of imitation, the matter of tragedy to the means of imitation, and spectacle to the manner of tragedy, which is an efficient cause in the sense of the mode of authorial presence in the work. Spectacle is therefore concerned with an efficient cause, but the efficient cause not of the tragic poem, but of its stage production. The stage production does not belong essentially to the art of the tragic poet, but rather to a group of auxiliary arts that present on the stage what he has composed. The stage production depends on the arts of the scene painter (1449a18), the costume maker (6.1450b20), the choral directors (14.1453b8), and the art of elocution (19.1456b10). These would fall under the art of the director, who would be either the poet himself or whoever takes his place in the stage production. His art is not mentioned as such in the *Poetics*, but may have been treated in Aristotle's published writings, to which he refers us in connection with the stage presentation of character (15.1454b15–18). The art of the tragic poet produces tragedy up to a point, and in doing so generates the need for the auxiliary arts that are required for the final stage of its production. The disappearance of authorial presence from dramatic works is well expressed by James Joyce, an author in the Aristotelian tradition, in the account of the development of poetry that he puts into the mouth of Stephen Dedalus:

> The personality of the artist, at first a cry or a cadence or a mood and then a fluid and lambent narrative, finally refines itself out of existence, impersonalizes itself, so to speak. The esthetic image in the dramatic form is life purified in and reproduced from the human imagination. The mystery of esthetic like that of material creation is accomplished. The artist, like the God of the creation, remains within or behind or beyond or above his handiwork, invisible, refined out of existence, indifferent, paring his fingernails. (Joyce 1916, 211–15)

The result of this chapter is a short but important list of the causes that remain to be discussed in *Poetics* II. Of the generic causes of poetry, its generic end or ends remain to be discussed. Of the specific causes of tragedy and epic, their specific end or ends remain to be discussed. Of the specific causes of comedy, its specific form, matter, and end remain to be discussed.

Chapter 4
POETIC IMITATION

1. THE ANALYSIS OF POETIC IMITATION

We can derive further expectations of *Poetics* II from what is said in *Poetics* I. Of particular interest is the sequence of the inquiry into poetry as imitation, for if it is not complete, we can expect it to be continued and completed in *Poetics* II.

Aristotle ends the first sentence of the *Poetics* with the statement of how he proposes to begin: "beginning, in accordance with nature, first from first things." There are two unusual features in this statement. The first is the adverb "first" modifying "beginning." It makes no sense to speak of a first beginning unless there is more than one beginning, and that there will be in *Poetics* II a new beginning from the end of poetic imitation confirms what we have concluded from the analysis of the causes in the *Poetics*.

A second unusual feature of Aristotle's statement is that this first beginning is from first things, a plural where one would expect a singular. The beginning itself is as follows: "Epic poetry and the production of tragedy, and also comedy and the art of producing dithyrambs, and the art of the flute for the most part and of the lyre, all happen to be imitations when taken as a whole." This beginning is from two wholes, the inclusive whole that is poetry and the specific wholes of which it is composed, all of which are imitations. What exactly the specific wholes are requires further consideration. All the arts mentioned are performance arts. Epics were recited by bards or rhapsodes, dramatic poets did not simply write their plays but initially acted in them (*Rhet.* iii.1403b23) and later directed their performance, dithyrambs were sung by choruses of fifty, and the arts of the flute and the lyre were arts of playing these instruments. This is not to say that poetry that does not aim at public performance is not imitation, but only that what is meant by poetic imitation here can best be understood by thinking of the arts in their fullest realization, that is, if they are performance arts, in their performance. Aristotle is speaking here at the level of generality of a species, so the performance will be the kind of performance characteristic of a species, not the performance in its unique individuality. This kind of performance, taken as a whole, is what is said to be an imitation. Since the performances are perceived by the senses, this beginning is from poetry as perceived by the senses.

Aristotle in the *Posterior Analytics* distinguishes two kinds of priority that are relevant here, each determining a kind of firstness: "Now 'prior' and 'more knowable' have two senses, for what is prior in nature is not the same as what is prior for us, nor is what is more knowable the same as what is more knowable to us. I mean by what is prior and more knowable for us what is closer to sense-perception, and by what is prior and more knowable without qualification what is further from sense-perception" (*Post. An.* i.2.71b35–72a). Scientific demonstration begins from what is prior and more knowable in nature; scientific inquiry begins from what is prior and more knowable to us. The perceived performances characteristic of a species are therefore the natural beginning of an inquiry into poetry.

We may note that no one today would begin by saying that poetic performances are imitations, but would rather say they are performances or enactments or expressions or communications or something else of this sort. This is a difference in the mode of philosophizing characteristic of the Hellenic epoch, in which poetry is a thing, and the mode of philosophizing characteristic of the present epoch, in which poetry is an expression. We shall have more to say about the modes of philosophizing as we proceed.

Inquiry begins from what is prior and more knowable to us, and seeks to discover causes, which are prior and more knowable in nature. How do we advance from the one to the other? The procedure is illustrated in what Aristotle does, but it is helpful to have a general formulation to tell us what to look for. There is no such formulation in the *Poetics* itself, presumably because it has been formulated in an earlier science in the series. We find it in fact at the very beginning of the subject-matter sciences, in the first chapter of the first book. Aristotle says, "Now what is clear and distinct to us at first is rather the confused wholes, and from them their elements and principles become known to us later by making distinctions within them. Therefore we must advance from universals to particulars, for the whole is better known from sense perception, and the universal is a kind of whole, for it comprehends many things as parts. The same thing also happens in a way to names in relation to the definition; the name 'ring' (*ho kuklos*), for example, designates in an undifferentiated way a sort of whole which its definition distinguishes into the particulars. And children begin by calling all men 'father,' and all women 'mother,' but later on distinguish each of them" (*Phys.* i.1.184a21–b14). (To avoid confusion, the reader should note that in making this statement Aristotle is at the same time illustrating it by using the words "whole" and "universal" not in a technical sense, but in their ordinary nontechnical senses in which they mean many different things which are left undistinguished.)

"Poetry" and "imitation" at the beginning of the inquiry similarly designate the confused wholes of sense perception which include many different kinds of things that will subsequently be distinguished. This is what Aristotle begins to do immediately in the third sentence of the *Poetics*. He distinguishes the "in what," "of what," and "how" of poetic imitation and the possibilities with respect to each. *Poetics* I develops the consequences of these distinctions. But the process of making distinctions within poetic imitation to discover its causes is not completed in *Poetics* I, for we have no distinctions that enable us to formulate either the end or ends of poetry or the proper subject of poetics. Thus we can expect *Poetics* II to make a second beginning by making distinctions within poetic imitation that enables us to formulate its end or ends and define the proper subject of poetics.

2. THE SCOPE OF POETIC IMITATION
In the course of formulating distinctions within the means of imitation, Aristotle encounters the problem of how meter is related to poetry. Both in ancient Greece and today we see that anything in verse is commonly called poetry. But the requirements of an art of poetry may conflict with this popular usage, and Aristotle deals with this problem at the beginning of his poetics. The question is of importance for the interpretation of the epitome because the defenders of its authenticity have been led to suppose that the nonimitative poetry with which it begins is nonimitative verse which is called poetry because it is in verse. Aristotle writes,

> The art that uses only bare speech and meters, and if meters either some one kind or several kinds mixed with one another, happens to be nameless up till now. For we have no common name for the mimes of Sophron and Xenarchus and a Socratic discourse, nor would we have one if the imitation were made by means of trimeter or elegiacs or something else of this sort, if it were not that people, connecting poetry to the meter, name men elegiac poets and epic poets, calling them poets not by virtue of the imitation but by virtue of the meter, without distinction between what is imitative and what is not. For if a man brings out something medical or physical in meter they are accustomed to calling the man a poet. Yet there is nothing except the meter that is common to Homer and Empedocles, and on this account it is just to call the former a poet, the latter a natural philosopher (*phusiologos*) rather than a poet. In the same way, even if a man were to produce an imitation by mixing all meters, as Chairemon produced *The Centaur*, a

mixed rhapsody of all meters, he must still be called a poet. About these things, then, let it be determined in this manner. (*Poet.* 1.1447b1–24, after Telford)

The first sentence tells us that there is one art that imitates in speech, whether in bare speech or meters. Aristotle is here considering the means of imitation used in existing arts. Since prose and verse differ in their means of imitation, verse adding rhythm to speech (4.1448b21), we might expect there to be separate arts of prose and verse, but Aristotle takes for granted that they belong to one art and does not at first give a reason for this. That we also have a single art of prose and verse, which in Aristotle's time was nameless, but which we would call the art of literature, is evident from the academic departments of our contemporary colleges and universities, for we have departments of literature, but not separate departments of prose literature and verse literature. If Aristotle in his initial formulation of poetics has truly hit upon a primary domain of scientific rationality, that is, a domain within which there is an extensive determination of consequences by principles, then we would expect his account to be confirmed by the departmental organization of our modern universities. For departments will naturally be led to include within their domain whatever follows from the principles they are in fact using, and to formulate as principles of their domain whatever determines the subjects they are in fact investigating, and so will tend toward a conception of their domain as a domain within which consequences are determined by principles belonging to that domain, that is, as the domain of a science in Aristotle's sense. Even that component of the work of departments of English that is most remote from the professional interests of most of its professors, English composition, has, as we noted earlier, its counterpart in the *Poetics* in the discussion of diction, or expression in language.

How is the nameless art of literature related to poetics? Aristotle has not yet identified the means of imitation used in the art of poetics, but only one more needs to be added to language and rhythm, namely, melody. Poetics includes in its subject matter all that is included in the art of literature, and includes in addition literary works accompanied by melody. Melody is one of the six parts of tragedy, but, as we have seen, it is not discussed in *Poetics* I. Melody is discussed in the epitome, and what is said is, "Melody is proper to music, hence one will need to take from music its starting points complete in themselves" (§ 15). Thus poetics differs from the art of literature only in including in its subject matter literary works accompanied by melody, and for the technical analysis of melody we are referred to the art of music. In terms of its own artistic content, it does not differ from the art of literature. There is thus no need for a separate name for the nameless art of literature or a separate discussion of this art, for its essential content is that of poetics.

The inclusion of the art of literature within poetics has, however, an important and perhaps unexpected consequence: poetics includes the study of imitative prose. This accords with the epitome, which places the prose mimes of Sophron and Xenarchus under dramatic poetry alongside tragedy, comedy, and satyr plays, and provides a place for the other recognized form of prose literature, Socratic discourses, under educational poetry. These were the only forms of prose imitation that had evolved in Aristotle's time (Janko 1984, 134). It sounds odd to say that imitative prose is a form of poetry, but this is another reminder that the requirements of art need not conform to popular usage. Aristotle, as we have said, prefers to use old words in new meanings rather than coin new words. In the technical sense of poetry, imitative prose is poetry.

The art of literature is said to be nameless up till now, and the "up till now" suggests that it is nameless because of its recent origin. The "for" in the following sentence suggests that this sentence will explain why the general art of literature is nameless. What this sentence actually says is that the prose arts are as a group also nameless, and the implied reason why they are nameless is their recent origin. This also explains why the art of literature is nameless, for it is because it includes prose literature that it is nameless. Imitation in verse had of course long existed and its name was poetry, *poiēsis*. In pre-literate times any enduring verbal work is in meter, for meter is needed as an aid to memory, and it is only with the development of writing that a tradition of prose literature becomes possible. The name "literature" reminds us of its origin in letters. With the development of writing, bards lose their ability to recite whole volumes of poetry, and we marvel at a human ability that is no longer needed and not a part of our experience.

Just as the technique of writing made it possible to record the forms of poetry that preceded it, and led to the development of prose literature, so in our own time new techniques of recording and transmitting sounds and sights make it possible to record performances of the forms of poetry that preceded them, and have led to further developments in the art of poetry. While the arts of calligraphy and typography do not enter into the making of poetry as poetry, the same is not true of the arts of sound recording and cinematography that enter into films. Although the choral odes of Greek drama are comparable to background music, sound recording leads to a more varied and extensive use of melody than is found in Greek drama and to a closer integration of melody and action. Cinematography goes far beyond simply recording performances as they could be seen before its invention, and leads to works which are first produced in their recorded form, as films or digital recordings. Cinematography thus becomes a poetic art, an art of spectacle. Spectacle is not limited to particular sets and costumes and a more or less fixed perspective on the action, but can range freely over the whole domain of visible objects, and can view whatever it selects from any perspective and in any light, and thus becomes a more significant part of the performance. Other arts and sciences can be used to produce special effects that would otherwise never be seen at all. Painting and comic books used successions of drawn figures to imitate action before the invention of the cinema, but the cinema gave new life to such figures, although of course animated films are only a small part of cinematic works. The implementation of these technical advances involves large numbers of people in various ways, and their names appear under many headings in the long lists of credits that now follow a film.[1] This may be contrasted with the single author whose name appears on the title page of literary works. The film is not the production of a single poet or a single art, but the work of many persons and many arts under the overall direction of the director, in a way comparable to the very first dramatic poets, who acted in and directed their own works. We now have a new architectonic art, the art of the film director, who becomes the principal poet, while the writer is only the poet of the script. None of these changes, however, or the transmission of their results through television, or live television, introduces any new means of imitation or removes films and television from the domain of poetics. We have up till now no common name for the arts of literature and the arts of cinema and television, but just as Aristotle, in accordance with the requirements of scientific rationality, extends the scope of poetry to include prose as well as verse, let us extend it yet further to include cinematic as well as literary poetry, both belonging to the art of poetics as Aristotle conceived it.

Aristotle continues the quotation we are considering by saying that even if the new prose arts had something in common such as meter, this would still not have provided a name for them, were it not that people, connecting poetry to the meter, name the kinds of poets according to their meter. The argument against this way of naming arts culminates in the statement, referred to by Bernays, that since Homer and Empedocles have nothing in common except the meter, it is just to call one a poet and the other a natural philosopher. But why should a common trait be insufficient to justify a common name? Here we must call upon the conception of scientific rationality that was sketched in the first chapter. A science requires a domain within which there is a determination of consequences by principles. If one begins from poetry as imitation, a host of consequences follow, but if one begins from poetry as metrical speech, nothing follows but the division of poetry according to meter, and whatever follows from the meter. This is why there is a single art of prose and verse. Imitation and meter are at opposite extremes with respect to the determination of consequences by principles; one belongs at the beginning of the science, the other at the end. David Grene in his teaching of *Othello* suggested as a possible essay topic the use of prose and verse in that play, a topic that in itself indicates the subordination of questions of prose and verse to a single poetic art. All of Shakespeare's plays use both prose and verse, but we do not account for character and incident as consequences of their appearance in prose or verse, but rather account for the use of prose or verse by character and incident, while from the use of prose or verse little or nothing follows with respect to the rest of the play. Thus while imitation can rightly be used as the genus of poetry, verse cannot.

The final argument in the quotation relates to works written in more than one meter. If poetry is to be differentiated by meter, works written in a medley of meters are not proper species of poetry, and yet a work such as Chairemon's *Centaur* must still be called poetry.

The conclusion is an injunction, "About these things, then, be it determined in this manner." "These things" are how each of the three possibilities with respect to meter—no meter, one meter, or more than one meter—relate to poetry. All three things have been determined in one manner; namely, what is poetry is determined by imitation and not by meter. Imitative prose is poetry, but nonimitative verse is not. The scope of the injunction that these things be determined in this manner is that of poetics, but not beyond, for the determination depends on the requirements of poetics. Even though Aristotle may use poetry in the popular sense of verse in the *Rhetoric* and in his nontechnical writings, the "nonimitative poetry" in the sense of nonimitative verse with which the epitome begins has no place in poetics.

3. THE EVOLUTION OF POETIC IMITATION

Poetics I begins, as we have said, by distinguishing the three differentiae of poetic imitation, its "in what," "of what," and "how," but says nothing about its end. Although its end is a differentia of poetic imitation, it is not a differentia of imitation. When *Poetics* I then goes on to sketch the evolution of poetic imitation, it treats it only in terms of the differentiae of imitation, even though there are obviously differences at each stage in the end as well. These differences are left for *Poetics* II.

The evolution has three stages. The first is imitation before it becomes poetry, the second is imitation which is poetry but not yet the self-determining or autonomous poetry that can be the subject of a science, and the third is imitation which is poetry in this fully realized or technical sense. One might well ask why imitation which is not yet poetry should be included as the first stage in the evolution of poetry, and here Peirce and his view of Aristotle's philosophy as evolutionary provide an answer. Potentiality, too, is a kind of being, as illustrated by the difference between a seed that is viable and one that is not. Imitation is like a seed that has the potentiality to become poetry even though it is not actually poetry, just as an acorn has the potentiality to become an oak tree even though it is not actually an oak tree.

In the first stage of its evolution imitation is a natural activity whose principle is nature. Natural imitation seeks to make makes exact likenesses of the objects it imitates. Imitation at this stage is wholly heteronomous in the sense that its form depends wholly on the object which it imitates. The pleasure that we take in imitation at this stage is the pleasure of learning:

> "For we delight in the most exact likenesses of things which are in themselves painful to see, e.g., the shapes of the most dishonored beasts and corpses. The cause of this is that learning is most pleasant, not only to philosophers, but to others as well, however little they may share in it. For men delight in seeing likenesses because in contemplating them it happens that they are learning and reasoning out what each thing is, e.g., that this man [in the imitation] is that man [previously seen], for if by fortune one has not previously seen what is imitated, the likeness will not produce the pleasure as an imitation, but because of its execution or coloring or some other cause of this sort." (*Poet.* 4.1448b10–19, after Telford)

Because Aristotle leaves the discussion of the ends of poetry to Book II, and in Book I says only that the end of each species is its proper pleasure and that the end of tragedy is to achieve a catharsis of emotions such as pity and fear, those seeking a better understanding of what he means by proper pleasure or catharsis have naturally been led to look for guidance in what is said about imitation in its first stage. But imitation is said to become poetry only in its second stage (4.1448b23), and becomes the proper subject of poetics only in the third stage when it is self-determined by its own end in accordance with the general requirement for the subject of a science. Thus whatever is said of imitation in its first stage is not necessarily true of poetry in general or of poetry proper.

When I was a graduate student the great objection to poetry as imitation was that imitation is copying and poetry is not copying (see, e.g., McKeon 1954, 277n247). That imitation is copying before it is poetry is clear from the preceding quotation, and if it did not evolve, poetic imitation would remain copying. More recently, the difficulties that result from a failure to recognize the evolution of imitation into poetry and poetry proper have led some translators of the *Poetics* to translate *mimēsis* not as "imitation" but as "representation," a word that to some extent bridges the gulf between the initial and final stages of the evolution. This seems innocuous enough, but it is not an accurate translation and it takes a step in the wrong direction, for inquiry advances by discrimination but is retarded by conflation. Other translators leave *mimēsis* untranslated, which is unnecessary, since we have an accurate English equivalent, and it obscures the problems that arise from the evolution of *mimēsis* into poetry and the solution to these problems. The same basic mistake has also led in recent years to a rash of cognitive interpretations of catharsis and the function of tragedy. A reader of the manuscript of the present book who chooses to remain anonymous faults it for not addressing the "recent momentum toward a cognitive interpretation of catharsis. The core meaning of catharsis in this cognitive theory has been recently expressed by Christopher Shields (Shields 2007, 396) as follows: "The function of tragedy is not—and this cannot be over stressed given the endemic contentions to the contrary—catharsis. Nor is it pleasure, nor diversion, nor titillation or escape. Rather the function of tragedy, as a form of imitation or *mimēsis*, says Aristotle in his characteristically intellectualist fashion, is 'learning, that is, figuring out what each thing is' (*Poet.* 1448b16–17)." Once the evolution of imitation is recognized, this argument is an obvious case of the logical fallacy which Aristotle identifies in *On Sophistical Refutations* as the fallacy of taking what is said in a certain respect as if it were said without qualification (*haplōs, simplicter*) (*Soph. Ref.* 5.166b38–167a20, after Forster), like saying an Ethiopian is white because he has white teeth. Shields takes what is said about imitation in the first stage of its evolution as if it were said of imitation without qualification. Shields rightly recognizes that if the function of tragedy is learning, it is not a catharsis of emotions, but his view then runs into the difficulty that the definition of tragedy says that it achieves through pity and fear a catharsis of such emotions, which certainly looks like a statement of its function. Leon

Golden, who holds that tragic catharsis is "intellectual clarification," bases this theory on the core meaning that is found in Shield's theory and deals with the inconsistency between "intellectual clarification" and Aristotle's "catharsis of emotions such as pity and fear" by translating "pity and fear" as "pitiable and fearful incidents" (Golden 1968, 21). This is a category mistake, for pity and fear are emotions and in the category of undergoing (*paschein*), whereas incidents (*pragmata*) are in the category of doing (*poiein*). There is indeed poetry whose function is cognitive clarification—*Paradise Lost*, for example—and that this kind of poetry is not recognized in Book I is another indication of the need for Book II.

The second stage of the evolution begins when the imitation becomes poetry. "Imitating, then, is in accordance with our nature, as also are harmony and rhythm (for it is apparent that meters are parts of rhythms), and from this natural beginning, advancing mostly by small steps, men generated poetry (*poiēsis*) out of their improvisations" (*Poet.* 4.1448b20–24, after Telford[2]). The new principle that enters into imitation at this second stage and which makes it poetry rather than a natural activity is the character of the poet: "Poetry was drawn asunder by the poets' own characters, for the graver poets imitated noble actions and the actions of those of their sort, while the more frivolous poets imitated the actions of base men, producing invectives at first as the former produced hymns and encomia" (4.1448b24–27). The shift from nature to character is a shift from the theoretical domain whose principles are independent of us to the productive domain whose principles are those by which we make things. "In the case of things made, the principle is in the maker—it is either mind or art or some faculty" (*Metaph.* ii.1025b22, after Ross).

The Greek word for poetry, *poiēsis*, is an ordinary Greek word that has two senses, a broad sense in which it means making or production in general, and a narrow sense in which it means poetry. It is used in the *Poetics* in the narrow sense for the first time in the sentence quoted above that speaks of the generation of poetry. Imitation whose principle is character is a *poiēsis* in the sense of a making because character is in the maker, and it is a *poiēsis* in the sense of poetry because what is made is an imitation. Aristotle, in accordance with the principle of his division of the *Poetics* into two books, does not mention the pleasure accompanying imitation at this stage. Presumably the pleasure accompanying hymns, encomia, and invectives is the pleasure in seeing moral agents, men or gods, get the praise or blame which they deserve. The pleasure in the recognition of who is being imitated necessarily accompanies the pleasure of this stage, but is subordinated to seeing that individual praised or blamed. Poetry at this stage escapes from the complete heteronomy of the first stage because its form depends on the character of the poet as well as on the object imitated, but it remains heteronomous because both of these are external to the art of poetry.

The third and final stage of poetic evolution is represented by tragedy, comedy, and epic poetry, and the principle of such poetry, which I call poetry proper in order to distinguish it from the poetry of the second stage, is art rather than nature or character. The transition to the third stage was made by Homer. "And just as Homer was the most important of worthy (because he not only produced these well, but also in dramatic imitation), so also he was the first to show the patterns of comedy by producing dramatically not an invective, but an imitation of the laughable (*Poet.* 4.1448b34–8, after Telford). Homer is of course a narrative poet (3.1448a21–2), and the reference to the dramatic character of his imitations must be understood to refer to the dramatic component within his narration. Aristotle later says that Homer alone, of all the poets, understood the role of the poet himself in his poems, and spoke in his own person the least of all (24.1460a6–11). If Homer wrote both serious and comic poetry, as Aristotle thought, this would imply that the principle of his poetry is art rather than character, for "a faculty or a science which is one and the same is held to relate to contrary objects, but a state of character which is one of two contraries does *not* produce contrary results" (*N. Eth.* v.1.1129a3, trans. Ross). What Aristotle here says of Homer—that he excelled in both kinds of poetry, that his serious poetry stood alone in literary excellence and the dramatic character of his imitations, and that in comic poetry he produced dramatically not an invective but an imitation of the laughable—can be understood as consequences of the principle of his poetry being the art of poetry rather than character or nature.

The object of imitation at the third stage shifts from the individuals of the preceding stages to universals. Invectives imitate particular persons, but the ridiculous or laughable is independent of any particular person. The parallel point with respect to serious poetry is implied by the praise of Homer's serious poetry as dramatic, and is made later in the *Poetics* as the contribution of the poet to the formal structure of the plot: "The work of the poet is not to speak of things that have happened, but rather of such as might happen and are possible either as probable or necessary" (9.1451a36–8). Thus poetry in the third stage imitates the world in its universality, either as conforming to universal causes of the laughable or as conforming to universal probabilities or necessities.

Poetry proper, like the poetry of the second stage, is presented without a name or a defined end. The ends of poetry in the first and second stage depend on recognizing historical individuals, but poetry proper no longer imitates historical individuals, and the pleasure in recognizing that the individual imitated is one previously seen becomes a pleasure in recognizing the universality of what is presented, which is learning in a stronger sense than the learning involved in recognizing the individual who is imitated. But this pleasure in learning is subordinated in tragedy to the pleasure of witnessing the terrible and pitiable consequences suffered because of universal probabilities or necessities. The emotional response to people getting what they do or do not deserve, when subordinated to the required pity and fear of tragedy, leads to the tragic hero as a person like us or somewhat better who suffers misfortune not because of vice (*kakia*) or wretchedness (*mochthēria*) but because of some error (*hamartia*).

We have said that what is missing from the account of poetry proper in *Poetics* I is its generic end and that this end must belong to the same genus as that of which it is the end and thus make poetry self-determining or autonomous. We have seen that the evolution of poetic imitation is from an end external to the art of poetry to an end proper to the art of poetry itself. In the full realization of the possibilities of poetic imitation as poetry proper nothing in the poem is merely copied, for everything in the poem must be justified by its contribution to the poetic end. What is simply copied without relation to the poetic end is no part of poetry proper. Similarly, if we look at the final stage from the standpoint of its emotional end, emotions that are not adequately embodied in the materials of imitation are sentimentalities that have no place in poetry proper. In poetry proper, materials and end are united in a new self-determined or autonomous object.

To sum up the differentiations in imitation that result from the generic history of poetry, we have, in addition to the imitation before it is poetry, two kinds of imitation that are poetry: the heteronomous imitation of the second stage and the autonomous imitation of the final stage. Neither of these is given a name or a formulated end. We can expect both their names and the formulations of their ends in Book II.

We conclude this account of poetry as imitation by considering the art which has as its subject genus poetry proper. The art of *poiēsis* is *poiētikē*, the feminine singular of the adjective "poetic" used as a noun, as in English also the art of poetry is sometimes called "poetic," although it is customary to translate it as a plural noun with a singular meaning, "poetics." This avoids confusion of the noun with the adjective, which is more of a problem in English than in Greek because English does not have three genders for its adjectives. The singulars "poetic," "physic," "ethic," and "politic" do not unambiguously designate arts, as do the plurals "poetics," "physics," "ethics," and "politics" along with the singulars "arithmetic" (accented on the second syllable, not the third), "logic," "dialectic," "rhetoric," and "music."[3]

If *poiēsis* is taken in its broad sense, *poiētikē* means the art of making or production in general, and if *poiēsis* is taken in its narrow sense, *poiētikē* means the art of poetry. Aristotle uses *"poiētikē"* in the narrow sense as a name for his new art, and it thus becomes a technical term whose meaning is determined by the requirements of the art. Before Aristotle, the surviving texts show the word used only twice as a noun designating an art. In Plato's dialogues the word is used in a broad sense by the Eleatic Stranger in the *Sophist* (265b) and in a narrow sense by Socrates in the *Gorgias* (501d–502c).

The Eleatic Stranger gives the name *poiētikē* to the general art of production, as distinguished from the general art of acquisition. This art corresponds to Aristotle's productive (*poiētikē*) science or art, but for Aristotle this is not one science or art, but a group of them. The art of producing imitations is for the Eleatic Stranger a subdivision of the general art of production, whereas for Aristotle, although poetics is a productive science, the genus of poetry is not production but imitation. The genus of poetry is not production because production involves two heterogeneous components, materials and an end, and production is not a genus that can be differentiated into species. One needs some genus in which the two are united. In the case of poetry in the narrow sense, this is clearly imitation, for all poetry is imitation. This can be differentiated by its "in what?," "of what?," and "how?" and the resulting differentiations, together with an end, can be used to define the species of poetry, and the properties of each species can be demonstrated from its definition.

Socrates in the *Gorgias* calls by the name *poiētikē* the art that includes the arts of flute playing and lyre playing, the instruction of choruses and the production of dithyrambs, and the production of tragedy. This list of poetic arts is strikingly similar in content and wording to Aristotle's list of imitative arts in the second sentence of the *Poetics*, which we quoted earlier, except that Socrates's list does not include comedy and epic poetry. Presumably comedy is omitted because it obviously aims to please a popular audience, which is what Socrates is arguing that all of these arts do, and epic poetry is omitted for the opposite reason, that it does not aim to please a popular audience. Socrates's art of poetics thus excludes epic poetry and treats the other poetic arts as forms of rhetoric aimed at pleasing a popular audience. Epic poetry for Aristotle does not belong to a genus different from that of the other poetic species because the properties of both epic poetry and tragedy follow from their definitions as imitations. Since all the parts of epic poetry are also parts of tragedy, the parts of epic poetry are treated in treating the parts of tragedy. The similarities and differences of the two species are discussed in chapters 23 and 24 of the *Poetics*. The alleged vulgarity of tragedy as compared with epic, Aristotle argues in chapter 26, is not the result of what it is, but of the way in which it is performed.

The difference between Plato and Aristotle with respect to poetics illustrates the general difference between a philosophy which identifies science and dialectic and one which distinguishes them. For Plato, one is free to assign to "poetics" any meaning accepted by an interlocutor in a dialogic context and pursue its consequences, whereas for Aristotle there is a single meaning corresponding to the real causal connectedness within an underlying genus. (For more on Plato's method, see Watson 1995.)

Chapter 5
EXPECTATIONS OF *POETICS* II

A final source of expectations of *Poetics* II is the references of Aristotle and others to what is in the *Poetics*. The principal such source is the opening sentence of the *Poetics*, which states what Aristotle proposes to do in this work. "We propose to speak about both poetics itself and its species, what the power of each species is, how plots ought to be constructed if the making is to be done well, and also from how many and what sort of parts, and similarly about whatever else belongs to the same method." This program is an open-ended dialectical list of topics to be discussed, not a scientific statement of the causes of its subject, poetics itself, for we do not yet have a definition or even a name for this subject, nor do we get one until the beginning of Book II. The program is nonetheless useful for our purposes because we can expect Book II to discuss any of the proposed topics that are not discussed in Book I.

The first topic proposed is poetics itself. Poetics and poetry are related as the art to its subject, and the art is relative to the subject, which implies that poetics is to be explained by poetry (*Cat.* 7.6a36–b11). There will not be two analyses, one of poetics itself and another of its subject, which, for want of a better name we have been calling poetry proper, but a single analysis of poetry proper, which is at the same time an analysis of poetics itself. Poetry proper designates the poetry that includes tragedy, comedy, and epic poetry, but not the invectives, hymns, and encomia mentioned in passing in Book I. Poetry proper as imitation is discussed in Book I, leaving a discussion of its end for Book II.

The next topic proposed is the species of poetics itself. The genesis of epic poetry is discussed in chapter 4 of Book I, and of comedy and tragedy in chapter 5. The program for their further analysis is stated at the beginning of chapter 6: "Of imitative art in hexameters [the meter of epic poetry], and of comedy, we will speak later. Let us now speak of tragedy . . ." Thus we can expect the *Poetics* to provide a full analysis of only epic poetry, tragedy, and comedy. No reason is given for limiting the *Poetics* to these three, but perhaps this will be provided by the epitome.

Tragedy and epic poetry, apart from their end, are analyzed in Book I, leaving comedy, apart from its genesis, for Book II. The *Rhetoric* has three references to what has been said in the *Poetics* that do not correspond to anything said in Book I, and therefore must refer to what has been said in Book II. The *Rhetoric* says that "distinctions with respect to the laughable have been made separately in the *Poetics*" (i.11.1372a1–2), that "it has been said how many forms of the laughable there are in the *Poetics*" (iii.18.1419b5–6), and that what homonyms and synonyms are has been said in the *Poetics* (iii.2.1404b37–1405a6). We may therefore expect Book II to speak about comedy (its genesis being presupposed) and in particular to distinguish the forms of the laughable and to define homonyms and synonyms.

The next three topics listed in the opening sentence are problems with respect to poetry proper and its species whose resolution will constitute the science of poetics. Two of the problems, the problem of how the plot should be constructed if the making is to be done well, and from how many and what sort of parts, are treated in the course of the discussion of tragedy in *Poetics* I. The problems of the plot and the parts are problems of making, and thus differ from the remaining problem, what the power of each species is, which as stated as a problem, not of making, but of the power possessed by the poems of each species once they are made. Further, the first two problems are stated universally, whereas the third is stated only as a problem for each species, from which we can infer that the generic treatment of the ends of poetry will be limited to distinguishing the ends of the various kinds and there will be no account of generic properties deriving from the generic end comparable to the analysis of the plot and the parts as deriving from the differentiae of imitation.

The power of tragedy is stated in the definition of tragedy to be the power to effect a catharsis of emotions such as pity and fear, but without any explanation of what catharsis means. The use of the word without explanation echoes an earlier use of the word in the *Politics*. Just before discussing catharsis as an end of music, Aristotle says, "What we mean by 'catharsis' we now leave simply to the word, but when we return to it in the *Poetics* we will say more clearly" (*Pol.* viii.7.1341b38–40). Aristotle uses the word again here but defers the explanation, as relating to the end of poetry, to Book II. We can expect in Book II an account of tragic catharsis that will also explain what is common to tragic and therapeutic catharsis.

What are the species of poetry proper whose powers we may expect to be analyzed? If Aristotle is taking the three species, tragedy, epic, and comedy, as sufficient for his analysis of the problems of poetics itself, Aristotle would need to analyze no more than the powers of these three species. That the powers of tragedy and epic are the same follows from the conclusion of the comparison of tragedy and epic in the final chapter: "If, then, tragedy is superior in all these respects, and also with respect to the function of the art (for tragedy and epic poetry ought not to produce any chance plea-sure, but rather what has been said) it is clear that it is superior if it is more achieving of the end than epic poetry" (26.1462b12–15, trans. Telford). All that has been said about the proper pleasure of tragedy and epic poetry is that tragedy achieves through pity (*eleos*) and fear (*phobos*) the catharsis of such emotions, and the subsequent discussions of what is piteous (*eleeinos*), fearsome (*phoberos*), or terrifying (*ekplētikos*). Since nothing is said of any proper pleasure of epic as distinct from that of tragedy, and since both aim at the proper pleasure that has been said, we must conclude that both have the same proper pleasure. This conclusion is confirmed by the fact that Aristotle treats even that part of the analysis of plot that depends on the specific end of tragedy as adequate also for epic, for in the subsequent discussion of the epic plot in chapter 23 there is nothing that depends on an end peculiar to epic. Thus we should expect in *Poetics* II an analysis of the ends of tragedy and comedy, but no separate analysis of the end of epic poetry.

Since the question whether tragedy is more achieving of the end than epic poetry is left unanswered, we can expect it to be answered in Book II.

The last item in the opening sentence is "whatever else belongs to the same method." The method of poetics is defined by its subject genus, poetry proper, and the most obvious candidate for the "whatever else" would be whatever poetry is not poetry proper, such as invectives, hymns, and enco-mia. Insofar as the kinds of poetry other than poetry proper make use of the science of poetry proper, they would belong to the method of poetry proper even though they are not species of poetry proper. This completes our list of expectations derived from Aristotle's references to an implied second book.

Two other expectations derive from later authors who report what was in the second book. From Simplicius we expect a definition of synonymy, also expected from what is said in the *Rhetoric*, and from the Anti-Atticist the word *kuntotaton*.

We have derived expectations of Book II from the general nature of sci-ence and of poetry, from the causal structure of the poetics, from the order of inquiry and the evolution of imitation in *Poetics* I, and from the references to an implied second book in Aristotle's existing works or in later authors. For the purpose of comparison with what is in the epitome, let us now bring together the expectations from all these sources and list them according to their probable order of treatment in the second book. We can expect what is generic to be treated before what is specific and the completion of the account of tragedy before the beginning the account of comedy. In the absence of any reason to suppose that the causes of comedy will be treated in a different order from those of tragedy, we shall tentatively list them in the same order. Here then are our expectations of *Poetics* II.

Expectations with Respect to Poetry in General
1. A return to poetry as a confused whole with which *Poetics* I began in order to make a fresh beginning from a new kind of distinction within it, a kind of distinction that depends not on the differentiae of imitation, but on the ends of the different kinds of poetry.
2. An initial formulation of the end of poetry proper and a name for the poetry distinguished by this end.
3. The end of the poetry that includes the hymns, encomia, and invectives that were mentioned in passing in Book I, and a name for such poetry.
4. A determination of whether tragedy or epic is more achieving of their common end.

Expectations with Respect to Tragedy
5. An account of the power or function of tragedy.
6. A definition of catharsis.
7. An explanation of how therapeutic and tragic catharsis can be the essentially the same and yet different.

Expectations with Respect to Comedy
8. An account of the forms of the laughable.
9. Definitions of homonymy and synonymy.
10. The word *kuntotaton*.
11. An account of the matter of comedy.
12. An account of the end of comedy.

Chapter 6
THE EPITOME OF *POETICS* II[1]

1. Poetry is (*tēs poiēseōs*)—
   —either nonimitative[2] (*hē men amimētos*)—
   —historical (*historikē*)
   —educational (*paideutikē*)—
   —guiding (*huphēgētikē*)
   —theoretical (*theōrētikē*)
2. —or imitative (*hē de mimētikē*)—
   —either narratable (*to men apangeltikon*)
   —or dramatic and actable (*to de dramatikon kai praktikon*)—
   —comedy (*kōmōidia*)
   —tragedy (*tragōidia*)
   —mimes (*mimous*)[3]
   —satyr plays (*saturous*)
3. Tragedy removes the fearful emotions of the soul (*hē tragōidia huphairei ta phobera pathēmata tēs psuchēs*) by compassion and dread[4] (*di' oiktou kai deous*); it aims to have a symmetry[5] of the fearful (*summetrian thelei echein tou phobou*); it has as its mother pain (*echei de mētera tēn lupēn*).
4. Comedy is an imitation of action laughable and with no share in magnitude (*kōimoidia esti mimēsis praxeōs geloias kai amoirou megethos*), complete (*teleios*), in speech made pleasing in each of the parts separately in its forms (*<hēdusmenōi logōi>*[6] *chōris hekastōi tōn moriōn en tois eidesi*), by actors and not by narration (*drōntōn kai <ou> di' apaggelias*), through pleasure and laughter achieving the catharsis of such emotions (*di' hēdonēs kai gelōtos peirainousa tēn tōn toioutōn pathēmatōn katharsin*). It has as its mother laughter (*echei de mētera ton gelōta*).
5. Laughter arises (*ginetai ho gelōs*)—
   —from the diction (*apo tēs lexeōs*)—   —from the incidents
     (*apo tōn pragmatōn*)
   —from homonymy (*kata homōnumian*)
   —synonymy (*sunōnumian*)
   —repetition (*adoleschian*)
   —paronymy (*parōnumian*)—
     —by addition and subtraction (*para prosthesin kai aphairesin*)

83

—a diminutive (*hupokorisma*)
—alteration (*exallagēn*)
—parody (*parōdian*)
—transference (*metaphoran*)—
—by sound (*phonēi*)
—by homogeneous attributes (*tois homogenesi*)
—form of diction (*schēma lexeōs*).

6. The laughter from the incidents (*ho ek tōn pragmatōn gelōs*)—
   —from deception (*ek tēs apatēs*)
   —from assimilation (*ek tēs homoiōseōs*), used (*chrēsei*)—
   —toward the better (*pros to beltion*)
   —toward the worse (*pros to cheiron*)
   —from the impossible (*ek tou adunatou*)
   —from the possible and inconsequential (*ek tou dunatou kai anakolouthou*)
   —from things contrary to expectation (*ek tōn para prosdokian*)
   —from accoutering the personages toward the wretched (*ek tou kataskeuazein ta prosōpa pros to mochthēron*)[7]
   —from using vulgar dancing (*ek tous chrēsthai phortikēi orchēsei*)
   —when someone having the resources (*hotan tis tōn exousian echontōn*) lets slip the greatest things in order to take the most paltry (*pareis ta megista ta paulotata lambanēi*)
   —when the speech is disconnected (*hotan asunartētos ho logos*) and lacking any consecution (*kai mēdemian akolouthian echōn*).

7. Comedy differs from abuse (*diapherei hē kōmōidia tēs loidorias*), since abuse recounts without concealment the bad attributes (*epei hē men loidoria aparakaluptōs ta prosonta kaka diexeisin*), whereas comedy has need of indirection[8] (*hē de deitai tēs kaloumenēs emphaseōs*).

8. The mocker aims to reproach wrongness of the soul or of the body (*ho skōptōn elenchein thelei hamartēmata tēs psuchēs kai tou sōmatos*).

9. There aims to be a symmetry of fear in tragedies (*summetria tou phobou thelei einai en tais tragōidiais*) and of the laughable in comedies (*kai tou geloiou en tais kōmōidiais*).

10. The matter of comedy (*kōmōidias hulē*[9]): plot, character, thought, diction, melody, spectacle (*muthos, ēthos, dianoia, lexis, melos, opsis*).

11. A comic plot is one having its construction around laughable actions (*muthos kōmikos estin ho peri geloias praxeis echōn tēn sustasin*).

12. The characters of comedy (*ēthē kōmōidias*): the buffoonish, the ironical, and the boastful (*ta te bōmolocha kai ta eirōnika kai ta tōn alazonōn*).

13. Thought has two parts, maxim and persuasion (*dianoias merē duo gnōmē kai pistis*). Persuasions are five (*pisteis pente*): oaths, contracts, witnesses, tortures, and laws (*horkoi sunthēkai, marturiai, basanoi, nomoi*).

14. Comic diction is common and popular (*kōmikē esti lexis koinē kai dēmiōdēs*). The comic poet should give their native idiom to his characters (*dei ton kōmōidopoion tēn patrion autōn glōssan tois prosōpois peritithentai*), and the local idiom to himself (*tēn de epichōrion autōi ekeinōi*).

15. Melody is proper to music (*melos tēs musikēs estin idion*); hence one will need to take from music its starting points complete in themselves (*hothen ap'ekeinēs tas autoteleis aphormas deēsei lambanein*).
    The spectacle supplies a great service to dramas when in harmony with them (*hē opsis megalēn chreian tois dramasi tēn sumphōnian parechei*).[10]

16. Plot, diction, and melody are observed in all comedies (*ho muthos kai hē lexis kai to melos en pasais kōmōidias theōrountai*), thoughts, character, and spectacle in not a few (*dianoiai de kai ēthos kai opsis en <ouk> oligais*).

17. The parts of comedy are four (*merē tēs kōmōidias tessara*): prologue, choral part, episode, exode (*prologos, chorikon, epeisodion, exodos*).
    Prologue is the part of comedy up to the entrance of the chorus (*prologos estin morion kōmōidias to mechri tēs eisodou tou chorou*).
    Choral part is the song sung by the chorus when it has sufficient magnitude (*chorikon esti to hupo tou chorou melos aidomenon hotan echē megethos hikanon*).
    Episode is the part between two choral songs (*epeisodion esti to metaxu duo chorikōn melōn*).
    Exode is the part at the end spoken by the chorus (*exodos esti to epi telei legomenon tou chorou*).

18. Comedy is (*tēs kōmōidias*)—
    —old, which goes to excess in the laughable (*palaia, hē pleonazousa tōi geloiōi*);
    —new, which, abandoning this, inclines toward the solemn (*nea, hē touto men proïemenē, pros de to semnon hrepousa*);
    —middle, which is a mixture of both (*mesē, hē ap'amphoin memigmenē*).

Chapter 7

COMPARISON OF THE EPITOME WITH OUR EXPECTATIONS

Now we come at last to the comparison of the epitome with our expectations, which completes the symbolon argument. The epitome begins with a distinction between nonimitative and imitative poetry. The Greek terms can also be translated as nonmimetic and mimetic, and I shall use the two translations interchangeably. This distinction confronts us at the outset with the great problem which, more than any other, has kept the epitome for so long in scholarly limbo. From Bernays on, it has been seen as prima facie evidence of inauthenticity. Jonathan Barnes writes, "The problem is this: TC begins with a formal *diairesis* [division] of poetry which is overtly inconsistent with Aristotle's formal account of poetry in the *Poetics*. If TC represents Aristotle accurately, then we must suppose that he began *Poetics* II by flagrantly contradicting *Poetics* I" (Barnes 1985, 106). As was said in the discussion of the scope of poetic imitation, those who have sought an Aristotelian meaning for the distinction have supposed it to be a distinction between poetry that is called poetry because it is imitative and poetry that is called poetry because it is in verse. Lane Cooper (1922, 12–13) cites the verse of Solon and of Aristotle himself as examples of nonimitative poetry. Elder Olson (1950, 63; 1976, 137) asserts that nonimitative poetry "stands for any works which, although nonimitative, involve devices or characteristics especially associated with mimetic poetry." Of these devices or characteristics, verse is the most conspicuous. Janko (1984, 123–4) writes, "Whereas popular usage distinguished poetry by the formal criterion of versification, A. [Aristotle] offered an alternative, namely *mimesis* [imitation]. . . . In *Poet.* A. restricts the discussion to poetry definable by both criteria, *mimesis* and verse." All three of these interpreters thus make nonimitative verse poetry, contrary to Aristotle's definitive determination at the beginning of the *Poetics*, which we examined at length in chapter 4, that whether or not a literary work is poetry depends wholly on whether it is imitation and not at all on whether it is in verse.

But now that we have devoted the first five chapters to determining what to expect in Book II, it is not difficult to see how the whole problem can be solved. The extensive preparation perhaps begins to look like overkill and the only surprise that remains is that the solution was not seen long ago.

We expected that Book II would be a fresh beginning, and this we see in the contrast between the opening words of Book I, "About poetics itself . . ." and the opening words of the epitome, "Of poetry . . ." Poetics and poetry are correlative terms, one designating the art, the other its products. In a sense they designate the same thing, the one as a potentiality, the other as an actuality. But as starting points of inquiry, they are opposites. Poetics is prior to poetry in the sense that it brings poetry into existence, but poetry is prior to poetics in the sense that poetics is for the sake of poetry. Book I traces the genesis of poetry and its species, whereas Book II begins from poetry as already in existence, and considers the ends which it realizes.

We expected that Book II would begin by naming and defining the subject genus of poetics itself, which we tentatively referred to as "poetry proper." We can now use the more meaningful name "imitative poetry." We expected that the difference between this and the other kinds of poetry would depend on their ends. We know already from chapter 1 that the end of imitative poetry must belong to the same genus as that of which it is the end, thus making it poetry for its own sake, or poetry which has its end in itself, and is thus self-determined or autonomous. All other poetry, which the epitome calls nonimitative, must be for the sake of something other than itself, or take its end from something other than itself, and is thus heteronomous.

We expected that Book II would begin by continuing and completing the process of making distinctions within the ordinary meaning of imitation, and this is exactly what has been done. All poetry is imitative, but only imitative poetry has its end in the imitation itself. This is why it is properly called imitative poetry. In the ordinary sense of imitation, all poetry is imitative, but in the technical sense of imitation which is now defined, only imitative poetry is imitative. The distinction is here formulated for the first time, but it was already present in the opening sentence of the *Poetics* as the distinction between poetics itself and its species, which define the method of poetics, and whatever else belongs to the same method.

The name "imitative poetry" makes the words "imitative" and "imitation" ambiguous, but it is just the usual ambiguity between the ordinary and technical meanings of a term. We do not think of poetry as imitation, and consequently would not call poetry for its own sake imitative poetry. But if we think of poetry as the product of the imagination, we might well call poetry for its own sake imaginative poetry in order to distinguish it from other kinds of poetry. Similarly, if we think of poetry as expression, we might well for the same reason call poetry for its own sake expressive poetry. The ambiguity is less troublesome than it might seem. In Book I, "nonimitative" is not used at all, and "imitative" is predicted of animals, people, and arts, but never of poetry, and therefore the alleged contradiction is not overt and the inconsistency not flagrant, but rather both are contrived.

What does not accord with our expectations is that the epitome does not tell us the ends of the different kinds of poetry, but only names the kinds, which means that the epitomist has here neglected his proper work. A further clue that this is the case is the name "nonimitative poetry," which is not an Aristotelian name. A negative term is indefinite in its meaning and therefore cannot designate either a genus (*Topics* i.5.102a31; *Parts of Animals* i.3.642b21–643a7) or a species (*Topics* vi.6.143b11–23). While all nonimitative poetry is doubtless not imitative, the name "nonimitative poetry" reifies this shared negation into a kind of poetry that does not exist as a determinate kind. If the term for nonimitative, *amimētos*, were translated with the meaning that it has elsewhere in the corpus (*Problems* xxix.10.951a6), nonimitative poetry would be inimitable poetry, which is obviously not a well-defined species of poetry. This is a technical point, but it is important for the present purposes because the epitomist could easily have overlooked it, whereas Aristotle himself would certainly not have overlooked it.

The epitomist's need for a negative term at this point in the schema enables us to determine the formal relations among poetry and its three principal kinds. Since nonimitative poetry is not a species, poetry is not a genus with two species, imitative and nonimitative, but an ambiguous term used to designate two heterogeneous kinds of things that are both called poetry. Similarly, since nonimitative poetry is not a genus, historical and educational poetry are not species of a genus, but two heterogeneous kinds of things that are both called poetry. Taken together, the three kinds of poetry have no genus-species relationships, but are three heterogeneous kinds of things that are all called poetry.

These formal relations represented by the schema are evidently very different from the relations represented by the schema in its other parts, and in this we can see a second non-Aristotelian element in the epitome. This is the use of a single schematic form to represent different kinds of relations. It first represents heterogeneous things having the same name, as was said. The division of educational poetry into guiding and theoretical, on the other hand, appears to represent a division of a genus into species. The subdivisions of mimetic poetry do not appear to present either the meanings of an ambiguous term or the complete species of a genus, but a selection of species made for a non-taxonomic purpose. This enables us to see that what the epitomist has done is to take the kinds of poetry that were mentioned by Aristotle in different contexts and for different purposes and put them into a single schema of the kinds of poetry, and this required him to introduce a nonexistent kind of poetry in order to have a place in his schema for historical and educational poetry as both different from imitative poetry. Getting all the kinds of poetry into a single schema would doubtless be a desideratum for the epitomist, perhaps even a sort of Holy Grail, and he may have been quite proud of what he had done, even though it required him to introduce a name that was not in the text he was epitomizing and a schema of the kinds of poetry that was also not in the original. The art of epitomizing is an extension of the art of copying: it copies selected portions of a text. Epitomists do not, in general, introduce into their epitomes terms that are not in the original. We have no reason to think that the epitomist would introduce any further term that was not in the original unless it were only by doing so that he could achieve an epitomizing aim comparable in importance to that of getting all the kinds of poetry into a single schema.

There is another anomaly in the schema which shows both the epitomist's concern to use the words of the original and the two different parts of the text which the epitomist has combined into one. The names of mimes and satyr plays are in the accusative case, the case of grammatical objects, rather than, like the names of all the other kinds of poetry, in the nominative case, the case of grammatical subjects. Naming the kinds of poetry and distinguishing them by their ends calls for putting their names in the nominative case, but statements about them could well be made in the accusative case, as "We can dismiss mimes and satyr plays from consideration because, etc." The fusion of the two different contexts is achieved by giving to the word "imitative" the double function of completing the kinds of poetry distinguished in section 1 and serving as a starting point for the divisions of section 2.

A statement of the ends of poetry would have been called for in the first context only, not the second, and this enables us to see why the ends of the three principal kinds of poetry have been omitted. It would spoil the homogeneity of the schema to have attached ends to some of the kinds of poetry and not to others. Also, if one looks at the schema in the photographs of the manuscript that Janko has provided (1984, following p. 6), one can see that attaching ends to the principal kinds of poetry would not have been possible without confusing the whole presentation. The ends could have been stated in a separate part of the epitome, but this would involve repeating the names of the kinds of poetry and enlarging the epitome, and, as Barnes has pointed out, this epitomist values brevity more than most. Thus the missing ends can be seen as a casualty of the epitomist's pursuit of an epitomizing purpose of his own, a purpose that was not Aristotle's. It is probable that Book II began with something like, "Of poetry, some is for the sake of itself, and some for the same of something else" and the epitomist has given the indefinite "for the sake of something else" the appearance of definiteness by using it as if it defined a kind of poetry.

Let us now turn to the subdivision of nonimitative poetry into historical and educational. We expected there would be a name and definition for the kind of poetry mentioned in passing in *Poetics* I that includes hymns, encomia, and invectives, and this is evidently what the epitome calls historical poetry. This is an appropriate name for this kind of poetry insofar as it imitates historical individuals.

Educational poetry we did not expect, but this is because we were basing our expectations on the surviving works of Aristotle, in which there is no mention of such a kind of poetry. If we had enlarged the basis for our expectations to include not only what Aristotle himself says, but what Aristotelian critics and theorists have said, we would have had good reason to expect this kind of poetry, for the so-called Chicago school of criticism[1] made much of a kind of poetry that they called didactic poetry, which would be educational poetry under another name. The importance of didactic poetry in their work, as well as a division within the school as to whether it is Aristotelian, can be seen from Wayne Booth's account of his experience in preparing an exam on the theory of fiction at the University of Chicago:

> I was once "ordered" by the founder of the Committee on Ideas and Methods, Richard McKeon, to prepare an examination on theory of fiction for a graduate student. Almost automatically, and a bit blindly as I look back on it now, I shaped all the questions in a way that relied on the didactic/mimetic distinction. When McKeon reviewed my questions, he rejected them flatly (in his daunting, not to say terrifying style), saying, 'I've never been able to figure out how Ronald and Elder thought they could find that distinction in the *Poetics*.'" (Booth 1995, 11)

We can now see that Wayne Booth, Ronald Crane, Elder Olson, and the others who used the didactic/mimetic distinction were right in thinking it was required in an Aristotelian poetics, and that McKeon was right in thinking that it could not be found in Book I.

It is not only the Chicago school that has felt a need for educational poetry. The recent momentum toward cognitive theories of catharsis referred to in chapter 4 also manifests the need for a concept of such poetry. To make the end of imitative poetry cognitive, however, eliminates Aristotle's imitative poetry altogether, and with it poetics as a self-determining discipline.

It is not difficult to understand why educational poetry is never mentioned in Book I. In Book I, poetry is distinguished according to the differentiae of imitation. Historical poetry as imitation can be distinguished from imitative poetry because it imitates particulars. But educational poetry cannot be distinguished in this way from imitative poetry because, as educational poetry, it presumably, like imitative poetry, speaks more of universals. It would thus have the same objects of imitation as imitative poetry, and there is no reason to think it could be distinguished by its means or manner of imitation. It appears as distinct from imitative poetry only when the ends of poetry are taken into account.

If the kinds of poetry are distinguished by their ends, and imitative poetry has its end in itself, what are the ends of historical and educational poetry? In the case of historical poetry, the obvious answer is that it derives its end from history. This fits the ends attributable to hymns, encomia, and invectives, for they aim to praise or ridicule particular historical individuals, and in this way derive their ends from history.

What is the end of educational poetry? We should note first that if Aristotle's division of poetry into imitative, historical, and educational poetry is to be acceptable, it must exhaust the subject and divide it into mutually exclusive parts. It therefore must depend upon some exhaustive and disjunctive triad. The sources of the ends of the first two kinds of poetry are history and poetry. These are two parts of the well-known triad of Book I: history, poetry, and philosophy. This is an exhaustive and disjunctive triad because it depends on the distinction between particulars, universals, and what we may call particularized universals or universalized particulars. Thus, if the three kinds of poetry distinguished in Book II depend on whether the poetry derives its end from history, poetry, or philosophy, educational poetry will derive its end from philosophy, and the distinction of the three kinds of poetry will be exhaustive and disjunctive. Why this third kind of poetry is called educational rather than philosophic will be taken up in the detailed interpretation, but we can say here that educational poetry must, as imitation, present particularized universals rather than universals as such, and thus cannot be philosophic (or didactic) in a strict sense, but such poetry can nevertheless take its end from philosophy, and, if so, it will appropriately be called educational poetry.

We expected the distinction between imitative, historical, and educational poetry to depend upon their ends, but we can now speak more precisely, and say that the distinction among their ends lies in the *sources* of their ends. A little reflection shows why this must be so. The generic properties of poetry depend on what each of the two generic sources of poetry—the differentiae of imitation and its end—is in itself and not on what may result from its union with the other generic source in the specific forms of poetry. They are possibilities only, not the actualities that result from the work of poets in uniting its two generic sources. The generic possibilities for the ends of poetry result from their possible sources, just as the generic possibilities for poetry as imitation result from the possibilities for the differentiae of imitation. The generic differences of ends, however, lead only to the three different kinds of poetry, whereas the differentiae of imitation lead to the generic parts of poetry, some or all of which are found in all poetry.

We thus reach the conclusion that the beginning of the epitome epitomizes an exhaustive and disjunctive division of all poetry, according to the source of its end, into historical, educational, and imitative poetry. This is a distinction of great simplicity and power that is new to the modern world, and it will be examined in detail in the following chapters.

Section 2 of the epitome, with its initial division of poetry into narratable and actable, evidently corresponds to our expectation that there would be a resolution of the unresolved question of whether tragedy or epic is more achieving of their common end. We can now see why it was not resolved in the specific comparison of tragedy and epic in Book I, for it is appropriately resolved at the more general level of the difference between narratable and actable poetry. The question is apparently being dealt with here in order to determine which poetic ends require a full analysis, and from what follows it is clear that there are only two, the ends of tragedy and comedy, and that narratable poetry, mimes, and satyr plays are introduced only in order to be dismissed from further consideration.

Section 3 evidently corresponds to our expectations with respect to the end of tragedy. We expected Book II to state more clearly what is meant by catharsis, and this is done in the first part of section 3, which states what catharsis itself is, which is a removal defined by what is removed, from what, and by what. We also expected a distinction between the therapeutic catharsis of the *Politics* and the poetic catharsis of the *Poetics*, and this is done in the remainder of section 3. Poetic catharsis aims at symmetry, whereas therapeutic catharsis would presumably aim at the psychic health resulting from the removal of excessive emotion. Poetic catharsis has as its mother pain, whereas therapeutic catharsis would presumably have as its mother the excessive emotion. There remain interesting problems as to why the emotions of catharsis are differently named in the two books of the *Poetics* and why Aristotle, like Nietzsche, here speaks metaphorically of the mother of tragedy, but these must be left for the detailed interpretation.

Section 4 is the definition of comedy, which was not included among our expectations, but would have been if the question had come up, for we expected the scientific treatment of comedy in *Poetics* II, and the scientific treatment of comedy would, like the scientific treatment of tragedy, begin from its definition. The definition parallels the definition of tragedy in chapter 6 of *Poetics* I. That the action of comedy has no share in magnitude speaks to an unsolved problem of Book I, how a whole action can lack magnitude. The mother of comedy was not expected, and the repeated metaphor emphasizes the need for an explanation of the use of metaphor.

Sections 5 and 6 state the sources of laughter, which evidently distinguish the forms of the laughable. We see that these include homonymy and synonymy and a place for *kuntotaton* as a paronym by addition of *kuntaton*. Thus our most specific expectations with respect to the account of comedy are met.

Sections 7–9 distinguish the indirect manner of comedy from the direct manner of abuse, identify the subject of mockery as wrongness of soul or body, and distinguish the symmetry of comedy from that of tragedy. These, together with the forms of the laughable, appear to be a four-cause analysis of the laughable; this must be investigated in the interpretation. Symmetry qualifies as another major surprise, for it is not so much as mentioned in *Poetics* I. This is evidently because it derives wholly from the end of poetry and not from what poetry is as imitation. The meaning of symmetry is a major problem for interpretation, and perhaps it would have been better if all the energy that went into interpreting the meaning of catharsis could have been devoted to this. The initial sundering in which poetry had its origin was based only on the character of the poet, not on any requirement of the art of poetry. Symmetry, as the final end of both comedy and tragedy, seems to be the way in which the art of poetry transcends the initial split that was required for the development of its two great alternative forms. The full enjoyment of either form is impossible unless it incorporates in its own way emotions like those that are dominant in the other.

Sections 10–16 correspond to the expected treatment of the matter of comedy. All the parts of comedy, even the plot, are here called *matter*, whereas in Book I they were all *forms*, an apparent inconsistency which Bywater noted and Janko removed by emending *hulē* (matter) to read *eidē* (forms). This is a particularly clear illustration of how comparisons of what Aristotle says in different contexts without taking the contexts into account lead to apparent inconsistencies that disappear when the context is taken into account. In the light of what has been said about the different starting-points of the two books of the *Poetics*, we can see that this is another instance of the same thing having different essences. In relation to the differentiae of imitation with which Book I begins, the parts are all forms taken on by these as matter, but in relation to the ends of poetry, from which Book II begins, they are all matter for the realization of these ends. The different terms for the parts are thus evidence of the epitome's authenticity rather than of either inauthenticity or garbling.

When we look at what is said about the particular parts, we find, as we might have expected, that the sections on the first four parts specify to comedy the generic accounts of these parts given in Book I. But when we come to the last two parts, melody and spectacle, we find as a welcome surprise that their treatment is generic, explicitly so in saying that the service of spectacle is to *dramas* rather than only to *comedy*. We could have expected this if we had thought more about it, for Aristotle promises in the opening sentence of the *Poetics* to speak of what the parts should be, and Book I does this generically for only four of the six parts, leaving the other two for *Book* II. The appearance of the generic account of these two parts, music and spectacle, in *Poetics* II rather than *Poetics* I confirms the reason we have given for the division of the *Poetics* into two books, for what these two parts should be in general depends not on what they are as imitative, but on their contribution to the emotional end of the poem, as the specifically tragic spectacle ought to arouse pity and fear (14.1453b10).

This interlocking of the two books in their generic treatment of the parts of poetry is a striking example of the symbolon fit that we are seeking. It is like the discovery of a piece in a jigsaw puzzle that connects two large regions of the puzzle that have already been assembled, so that a larger pattern emerges for the first time. The larger pattern that emerges here corresponds to what we have said about the two books of the *Poetics* as concerned respectively with poetry as imitation and with its emotional end.

Section 17 defines the quantitative parts of comedy. We did not expect this, but there is no reason why the quantitative parts of comedy should not be different or play different roles in comedy and tragedy. The same terms, however, are used for both, and they have been defined in Book I and are here defined again. This implies that the meaning of the terms varies with the kind of drama to which the parts belong.

Section 18 provides us with a final surprise, since its comparison of old, new, and middle comedy was unforeseen. Yet perhaps something like this might have been expected, for this section evidently corresponds to the comparison of the different kinds of serious poetry in the concluding part of *Poetics* I, as Janko has pointed out (Janko 1984, 58, 250). Both the comparison of tragedy with epic and the comparison of old, middle, and new comedy are standard topics in the history and criticism of poetry. Both depend on considering poetic works as wholes, one viewing the whole in relation to the differentiae of imitation, the other in relation to its end. We said that the concluding part of *Poetics* I concerned the final cause of the different kinds of serious poetry, or, in chapter 25, poetry in general, considered as imitation. The concluding section of the epitome similarly compares the different kinds of comedy considered as realizing their common end.

If this concluding section can be referred to the final cause of comedy, we have a way of referring what is said about comedy to its different causes that corresponds exactly to our expectations. The genesis of comedy having been discussed in Book I, its other three causes are discussed in Book II. The discussions of the matter and parts of comedy (sections 10–17) can be referred to its material cause. The discussion of the laughable (sections 5–9) can be referred to its formal cause. This accords with the laughable being the object of imitation in comedy (5.1449a34) and the object of imitation as providing the form of the species.

This concludes the symbolon argument. We have found an excellent fit between what can be expected in Book II and what the epitome tells us was in it. Everything that we expected is there except the ends of the three kinds of poetry, and we have explained why they are missing. There are also many surprises. McKeon once remarked that when we come to a new text by a great philosopher whose work we know well, and attempt to anticipate what he will say, we shall be surprised. As contributions to the science of poetics, it is the surprises, and not what is expected, that are most valuable. They can also be evidence of authenticity insofar as a reconstructor or impostor would be unlikely to have thought of them—symmetry, for example. They must, of course, be consistent with the rest of Aristotle's work. In retrospect we can see that there was in fact reason to expect most of them, and none appear to be inconsistent with *Poetics* I or Aristotle's other works. For the two big surprises that there was no reason to expect, educational poetry and symmetry, we have instead reasons why there was no reason to expect them.

The Barnes conditions for reliability are largely met. Three vital points of Aristotle's arguments were indeed missing—the ends of the three kinds of poetry—but we were able to supply them. Two non-Aristotelian items were added, nonimitative poetry and the grand schema of the kinds of poetry, but we were able to understand why they were added and use them as evidence for what should have been there. One word had appeared to be garbled, the parts of comedy as *matter*, but this turned out not to be garbling, but the result of the different starting-points of the two books. There may be other real or apparent errors, but these instances show that it is possible to detect and correct them. The causal structure found in the epitome provides a guarantee that all the principal causal parts of *Poetics* II are represented in the epitome and none is missing. If the accounts of the function of tragedy and the laughable turn out to have complete causal structures, this will be evidence that the causal parts of these are complete and none is missing. A number of problems remain to be solved, but we can, I think, proceed to their solution with confidence in the epitome's general reliability.

PART III. *The Kinds of Poetry*

Chapter 8
IMITATIVE POETRY

1. THE AUTONOMY OF IMITATIVE POETRY

Poetry is either nonimitative or imitative. (Here and in what follows, passages from the epitome that are to be interpreted, together with passages from *Poetics* I quoted for comparison, are quoted in boldface italics.)

We have argued in the preceding chapter that Aristotle is here making a fresh beginning by returning to the initial meaning of imitation as a confused whole and making a distinction with respect to a new aspect of it, its end. The fresh beginning of *Poetics* II is both a beginning from the end of poetic imitation rather than the differentiae of imitation and a beginning from poetry rather than poetics. Poetry is the more inclusive term, since it includes both the poetry that is for the sake of itself and poetry that is for the sake of other ends, but the treatment of both belongs to the same method. The initial distinction of *Poetics* II is the distinction between poetry that is autonomous because it is for the sake of itself and poetry that is for the sake of something else. This distinction adds to the generic distinctions in the differentiae of imitation a generic distinction in its end which makes iimitation the autonomous subject of an autonomous art.

2. THE AUTONOMY OF ARISTOTELIAN DISCIPLINES

Fresh beginnings are characteristic of Aristotle's work. They result from his disciplinary perspectives, which are the contribution of the inquirer to the inquiry. They include not only the perspective that defines the discipline as a whole, but also the subordinate perspectives determined by the causes sought and the method, dialectical or scientific, by which they are sought. The fresh beginning in the second book of the *Poetics* resembles the fresh beginning in Book VII of the *Ethics*, to which we referred earlier, for both begin the investigation of a new cause that was not mentioned in the first beginning and which enlarges the scope of the inquiry.

The fresh beginning of *Poetics* II also resembles the fresh beginning of *Physics* II, for both begin the scientific treatment of the ends of their respective subjects. Since the initial distinction between an internal and an external source of the end is a consequence of the general requirement that the end of any scientific subject matter belong to the same genus as its other causes, we can expect an analogous beginning of the scientific treatment of the ends of natural objects. An analogy between the two fresh beginnings would confirm our interpretation of the initial distinction of the epitome and its basis in Aristotle's conception of science.

Both fresh beginnings begin the second book of their respective treatises, but for different reasons. The end of poetry is the outcome of an evolutionary process, and therefore Aristotle treats the evolutionary process before treating its result, and begins the second book with the result. Since, as we have said, the evidence available to Aristotle did not appear to support the evolution of the cosmos or of living things, he investigates them first as functioning wholes. Generation and destruction within the cosmos are explained as consequences of what the cosmos already is, and the genesis of living things is explained as a consequence of what living things already are. But since, as was also said, physics, unlike poetics, was not a new science in Aristotle's time, the scientific treatment of natural things in Book II of the *Physics* is preceded by a dialectical examination in Book I of the principles of previous natural scientists. The fresh beginning in the second book of the *Physics*, like the fresh beginning in the second book of *On the Soul*, is a fresh beginning because it shifts from a dialectical to a scientific approach.

Physics II begins, "Of the things that exist, some exist by nature, some from other causes" (*Phys.* ii.192b8, trans. Hardie and Gaye). A formally exhaustive division of a non-generic totality (the things that exist) marks off by a negation (existing from other causes) the genus to be investigated (the things that exist by nature). This leads to the definition of natural things as possessing a distinctive power, the power to move from an internal principle, as contrasted with other kinds of things, artificial things and chance things, which exist from external causes. This definition leads in turn to the discussion of motion, which is the finality of nature.

This beginning is exactly analogous to the fresh beginning we find in the epitome, in which a formally exhaustive division of a non-generic totality (poetry) marks off by a negation (nonimitative) the genus to be investigated (imitative poetry). This implies a definition of imitative poetry as possessing a distinctive power, the power to function from an internal principle, as contrasted with other kinds of poetry, historical poetry and educational poetry, that function from external principles. We see from section 3 of the epitome that this leads in turn to the discussion of emotional catharsis, which is the functioning or finality of poetry and the analogue of motion in the natural world.

3. AUTONOMY OF ART IN THE ARISTOTELIAN TRADITION

Aristotle's view that imitative poetry is poetry for its own sake is not unique to Aristotle. In the absence of Poetics II, the idea of poetry for its own sake has been thought by some to be a modern idea which the Greeks would not have understood. In order to understand better its significance as the archetypal beginning of a major tradition in poetic theory, let us consider briefly what happens to Aristotle's principle of poetry for its own sake when it reappears in other contexts.

If the Aristotelian tradition were limited to those who share Aristotle's archic profile, there would be no Aristotelian tradition in philosophy, for no other major philosopher has his profile. But if we define the Aristotelian tradition to include those who share with Aristotle three of their four *archai*, the 3–1 Aristotelians as distinguished from the 4–0 Aristotle, we get a more interesting result. The Aristotelian tradition in philosophy then includes St. Thomas Aquinas, Kant, Peirce, Dewey, and McKeon. It was Peirce who, having "devoted two hours a day to the study of Kant's *Critic of the Pure Reason* for more than three years" (Peirce 1935, 1.4), brought the Aristotelian tradition to America, where it has flourished. These philosophers are Aristotelian in a qualified sense, and the qualification can be expressed by adding to "Aristotelian" an adjective naming the non-Aristotelian component in their archic profiles. Thus Aquinas and Kant are noumenal Aristotelians, where "noumenal" means that their primary reality transcends the world of the senses. Peirce is an objectivist Aristotelian, where "objectivist" means that he seeks to know things as they are independently of the mind that knows them, without Aristotelian disciplinary perspectives. Dewey is a creative Aristotelian, where "creative" means that the way things are depends upon us. McKeon can be called an agonistic Aristotelian, where "agonistic" does not mean that his method requires him to antagonize everyone else, but that it requires him to test alternatives against each other.

In addition to such differences in individual profiles, there are also cyclic differences within all traditions and the culture as a whole. These are differences in the mode of philosophizing, which moves from an ontic phase, concerned with how things are, to an epistemic phase, concerned with how we know the things that are, to a semantic phase, concerned with how we express in words and actions what we know about the things that are, and then makes a new beginning in an ontic return to the investigation of things. Ontic returns are motivated by radical novelties in the cultural circumstances and also, like the other two phases, by the exhaustion of the possibilities of the previous phase (Watson, forthcoming). For the present purpose, I limit myself to three examples of the autonomy of art in other contexts, two to illustrate how the different phases of the cycle affect its formulation and one to illustrate the consequences of a difference in one of the *archai*.

We can see the autonomy of art in the autonomy of the judgment of taste in Kant's *Critique of Judgment*. In an epistemic mode, the analogue to a principle of imitation is a principle of esthetic judgment. The judgment of taste is a reflective rather than a determinate judgment, that is, it does not subsume a particular under a universal, but is given a particular for which a universal is sought, just as poetics for Aristotle does not prescribe particular ends to poetry, but finds such ends in what poets create. All that can be said about the ends of poetry a priori is that they must have their source in poetry and thus make it self-determining in this respect. Similarly, the a priori principle of the judgment of taste in Kant is simply the purposiveness of the object for the faculty of judgment itself. Both principles are principles of autonomy or self-determination, either of poetry or of the esthetic judgment, and neither is a matter of a cognitive subsumption of art under universals of the kind found in the theoretical sciences.

John Dewey seeks principles neither in things, like Aristotle, nor in the mind, like Kant, but in the interaction of mind and things in experience. Dewey's three-stage account of the development of art as experience parallels Aristotle's three-stage account of the development of poetry as imitation. In both developments there is first a biological stage, then a stage in which poetry or the esthetic first appears but is not yet imitative poetry or the distinctively esthetic, and finally the third stage at which the poetic or esthetic principle becomes dominant and controlling. Thus in the following quotation *an* experience, as experience with esthetic quality, is analogous to the nonimitative poetry of Aristotle's intermediate phase in which it is poetry but not yet imitative poetry, while distinctively esthetic experience is analogous to imitative poetry in its technical sense.

The considerations that have been presented imply both the community and the unlikeness, because of specific emphasis, of *an* experience, in its pregnant sense, and esthetic experience. The former has esthetic quality; otherwise its materials would not be rounded out into a single coherent experience. It is not possible to divide in a vital experience the practical, emotional, and intellectual from one another and to set the properties of one over against the characteristics of the others.

The emotional phase binds parts together into a single whole; "intellectual" simply names the fact that the experience has meaning; "practical"
indicates that the organism is interacting with the events and objects
which surround it. The most elaborate philosophic or scientific inquiry
and the most ambitious industrial or political enterprise has, when its
different ingredients constitute an integral experience, esthetic quality.
For then its varied parts are linked to one another, and do not merely
succeed one another. And the parts through their experienced linkage
move toward a consummation and close, not merely to cessation in
time. This consummation, moreover, does not wait in consciousness for
the whole undertaking to be finished. It is anticipated throughout and
is recurrently savored with special intensity.

Nevertheless, the experiences in question are dominantly intellectual or practical rather than *distinctively* esthetic, because of the interest
and purpose that initiate and control them. In an intellectual experience, the conclusion has value on its own account. It can be extracted
as a formula or as a "truth," and can be used in its independent entirety
as factor and guide in other inquiries. In a work of art, there is no such
single self-sufficient deposit. The end, the terminus, is significant not
by itself but as the integration of the parts. It has no other existence.
A drama or novel is not the final sentence, even if the characters are
disposed of as living happily ever after. In a distinctively esthetic experience, characteristics that are subdued in other experiences are dominant; those that are subordinate are controlling—namely, the characteristics in virtue of which the experience is an integrated complete
experiences on its own account. . . .

An object is peculiarly and dominantly esthetic, yielding the enjoyment characteristic of esthetic perception, when the factors that determine anything which can be called *an* experience are lifted high above
the threshold of perception and are made manifest for their own sake.
(Dewey 1934, 55, 57)

Henry James is an existential Aristotelian, by which I mean that he shares
his archic profile with Aristotle except that his primary reality is the reality of individuals as individual rather than as universal. His principles, like
Kant's, are faculties of the mind rather than things or expressions. As existential, his art of poetry takes the form of prefaces to his novels, rather than
a poetics, the origin of his novels lies in individual germs rather than uni-

versal arguments (*logoi; Poet.* 17.1455a34), and his account of poetic germs takes the form of an account of the germ of *The Spoils of Poynton*, given in its existential particularity.

It was years ago, I remember, one Christmas Eve, when I was dining with friends: a lady beside me made in the course of talk one of those allusions that I have always found myself recognizing on the spot as "germs." The germ, wherever gathered, has always been for me the germ of a "story," and most of the stories straining to shape under my hand have sprung from a single small seed, a seed as minute and wind-blown as that casual hint for "The Spoils of Poynton" dropped unwittingly by my neighbor, a mere floating particle in the stream of talk. What above all comes back to me with this reminiscence is the sense of the inveterate minuteness, on such happy occasions, of the precious particle—reduced, that is, to its mere fruitful essence. Such is the interesting truth about the stray suggestion, the wandering word, the vague echo, at touch of which the novelist's imagination winces as at the prick of some sharp point: its virtue is all in its needle-like quality, the power to penetrate as finely as possible. This fineness it is that communicates the virus of suggestion, anything more than the minimum of which spoils the operation. If one is given a hint at all designedly one is sure to be given too much; one's subject is in the merest grain, the speck of truth, of beauty, of reality, scarce visible to the common eye—since, I firmly hold, a good eye for a subject is anything but usual. Strange and attaching, certainly, the consistency with which the first thing to be done for the communicated and seized idea is to reduce almost to naught the form, the air as of a mere disjoined and lacerated lump of life, in which we may have happened to meet it. Life being all inclusion and confusion, and art being all discrimination and selection, the latter, in search of the hard latent *value* with which alone it is concerned, sniffs round the mass as instinctively and unerringly as a dog suspicious of some buried bone. The difference here, however, is that, while the dog desires his bone but to destroy it, the artists finds in *his* tiny nugget, washed free of awkward accretions and hammered into a sacred hardness, the very stuff for a clear affirmation, the happiest chance for the indestructible. It at the same time amuses him again and again to note how, beyond the first step of the actual case, the case that constitutes for him his germ, his vital particle, his grain of gold, life persistently blunders and deviates, loses herself in the sand. The reason is of course that life has no direct sense whatever for the subject and is capable, luckily for us, of nothing but splendid waste. Hence the opportunity for the sublime economy of art, which rescues, which saves, and hoards and "banks," investing and reinvesting these fruits of toil in wondrous useful "works" and thus making up for us, desperate spendthrifts that we all naturally are, the most princely of incomes. (James 1950, 119–20)

We see operating throughout this account the difference between art and life. Life is what Aristotle means by history, what actually occurs, and there is no need for James to bring in philosophy separately, since for him it would exist only as actually occurring and included in life. The initial germ that pricks the imagination is suggestive by virtue of its fineness, unencumbered by the context of life in which it occurs. Even though it is initially needle-like, the first thing to be done for it is to reduce it further, almost to naught, to its latent *value*. And in the development of the germ, the artist is amused to note how life persistently blunders and deviates, loses herself in the sand. In all three phases of the history of the germ—the initial recognition, the reduction to its latent value, and the subsequent development—what is critical is the distinction between art and life. The intellectual faculty required to recognize the germ is a good eye for a subject, and, for its development, a sense of the subject. These for Aristotle would both belong to the same intellectual virtue, art, and James's distinguishing them as a good eye for a subject and a sense for the subject rather than as different aspects of one intellectual virtue is another illustration of his existential reality.

In summary, then, we can understand the opening distinction of the epitome to set forth the definitive character of imitative poetry in the technical sense as poetry having the source of its end within itself and distinguished in this way from other poetry. This beginning is required by Aristotle's conception of scientific rationality as the self-determination of a subject genus. The self-determination of imitative poetry is analogous to the self-determination of natural objects in Aristotle, to the self-determination of the esthetic judgment in Kant, to the self-determination of the distinctively esthetic in Dewey, and to the self-determination of art in the process by which Henry James wrote his novels. Thus the opening distinction establishes a fundamental conception of works of art analogous to Aristotle's conception of natural objects and one that has continued to exist in subsequent theories of art and literature.

Chapter 9

HISTORICAL, EDUCATIONAL, AND IMITATIVE POETRY

Poetry is either nonimitative or imitative; nonimitative poetry is either historical or educational.

Aristotle's conception of imitative poetry as poetry for its own sake runs through the whole Aristotelian tradition, but the same is not true of the distinction beween imitative, historical, and educational poetry. Wellek and Warren in their *Theory of Literature* (1949), for example, discuss extensively what others have said about literature, but there is no mention of this distinction or anything like it. Yet the distinction is of the highest importance, for without a clear conception of the ends of literature that is not for its own sake we have no basis for analyzing and judging it. The common distinction between fiction and nonfiction is no help, for both historical and educational poetry combine the two, fictionalizing nonfictional history or philosophic truth.

We can get an initial idea of the power of Aristotle's distinction by applying it to critcism rather than poetry. Some critics treat poetry as if it were social criticism, concerned with the historical realities in which and about which it is written. Others treat poetry as if it were philosophy, concerned to present a view of the world and of human life or some aspect of these. A third kind of critic, conspicuously represented by the Chicago school, treats poetry as primarily neither social criticism nor philosophy, but as having ends of its own proper to it as poetry. Yet poetic works generally reflect contemporary realities and embody philosophic lessons, so when the threefold distinction is applied to poetry, we must consider the end as the organizing principle of the poem as a whole. That is, everything in the poem should contribute to its end. To distinguish the kinds of poetry on this basis, we must ask, are all the parts of the poem organized with a view to what they say about historical realities, or with a view to a philosophic lesson, or with a view to a poetic end? Aristotle is here distinguishing the three great kinds of poetry not by their ends as such, but by the source of these ends, the ends being understood as what organizes the whole poem into a unity. While any poem can be read as either history or poetry or philosophy, which is why critics can base their criticism on any of the three, the kind of poetry that it is depends on which of the three is the source of the end or organizing principle of the poem.

Sheldon Sacks, a second-generation member of the Chicago school of criticism, is the only one I know of who has approximated to Aristotle's distinction, and he was able to do so by seeking the organizing principles of different types of prose fiction. He summarizes his results in *Fiction and the Shape of Belief* (1964):

> A satire is a work organized so that it ridicules objects external to the fictional world created in it.
>
> An apologue is a work organized as a fictional example of the truth of a formulable statement or a series of such statements.
>
> An action is a work organized so that it introduces characters, about whose fates we are made to care, in unstable relationships which are then further complicated until the complication is finally resolved by the removal of the represented instability (Sacks 1964, 26).

Satire corresponds to what Aristotle calls *iambos*, which I have followed Telford in translating as "lampoon," but which could equally well be translated, following Thomas Twining (1789), as "satire," and is one form of historical poetry. The requirement that satire be organized so as to ridicule objects external to the fictional world created in it combines Aristotle's requirement that it derive its end from objects external to the fictional world created in it, which makes it historical poetry, with the requirement that these objects be ridiculed, which distinguishes satire from other forms of historical poetry such as those which, like encomia, praise their objects. Thus Sacks's satires are a principal kind of historical poetry, although not the only kind.

The word "apologue" is usually applied to moral fables, but Sacks is evidently thinking of it broadly in a way that corresponds to Aristotle's educational poetry or what others in the Chicago school called didactic poetry. Both theoretical and guiding poetry provide fictional examples of truth, for theoretical poetry teaches theoretical truth and guiding poetry teaches practical truth. Sacks's formulation of apologue as a work organized as a fictional example of the truth of a formulable statement or a series of such statements contains, however, an unnecessary restriction of truth to formulable statements, for practical truth is not merely a matter of what is formulable but of what is equitable, which we certainly should not wish to exclude from educational poetry.

Sacks's definition of action in terms of characters about whose fates we are made to care in plots of complication and resolution states the organizing principle of action in terms of internal characteristics of the action, and thus derives its power from the imitation itself. The principle is stated, however, in terms of imitation rather than its end, and so lacks the generality of Aristotle's formulation of it as having its end in itself, but despite this and Sacks's restricted conceptions of historical and educational poetry, Sacks's organizing principle for satire has its source in historical particulars, his organizing principle for apologues has its source in universal truth, and his organizing principle for action has it source in poetry itself, and he has thus recovered within the field of his own inquiries into prose fiction Aristotle's threefold distinction between historical, educational, and imitative poetry. This is a remarkable achievement, and I would gladly incorporate the whole of the first chapter of Sacks's book within the present work, for it provides clear examples of how the principles determine consequences within each type of poetry. The first chapter uses Jonathan Swift's *Gulliver's Travels* as an example of satire, Samuel Johnson's *Rasselas* as an example of apologue, and Samuel Richardson's *Pamela* as an example of action. Dialectical arguments (in Aristotle's sense) such as I have been giving may make principles probable, but they cannot be apprehended as scientific principles until we understand them as adequate to their subject matter. Sacks's book thus provides an essential complement to what is here being said about the three kinds of poetry.

In the words of Wayne Booth, "Sheldon Sacks's distinction of the didactic into satire and apologue proved useful, I think, to everyone who ever paid full attention to it; one might say that regardless of how we read Aristotle, to distinguish 'actions,' 'satires,' and 'apologues' proves astonishingly helpful, especially in rescuing works of the second and third kind from attacks by critics who want to claim that genuinely 'literary' works should aspire only to the condition of the first kind: powerfully plotted actions" (Booth 1995, 11). Sacks's distinctions are astonishingly helpful because they are distinctions in the organizing principles of the work, and these principles determine a host of consequences within the work. In their general form, as apprehended by Aristotle, they are still more helpful, because they now cover the entire domain of poetry. Since poetry includes these three heterogeneous kinds, an initial distinction among them is essential to the analysis or evaluation of a work of any of the three kinds. If Book II of the *Poetics* had survived, the distinction might well be a commonplace, but as things are, we lack any such inclusive and exhaustive distinction among the kinds of poetry. One important contribution of the epitome to literary theory and to popular culture is its first distinction among the kinds of poetry or imaginative literature, one that is indispensable to the analysis of any of its kinds. Let us now consider each of these kinds.

Chapter 10
HISTORICAL POETRY

1. HISTORY OF THE PROBLEM

About historical poetry the epitome tells us only its name and that it is non-imitative. We have in the preliminary interpretation in chapter 7 concluded that these two things mean that in Poetics II it was said to derive its end from history. Unlike educational and imitative poetry, historical poetry has no subdivisions. The reason for this is presumably that history, unlike imitative poetry and philosophy, has no end proper to it, for the ends that have their source in history are indefinitely various. Historical poetry is therefore not a genus with species, but a heterogeneous collection, and the epitome leaves it without subdivisions. Further statements about what it is in general can therefore be made only by saying what it is not, which we shall do, but first let us try to get a better idea of what it is by considering examples of it, beginning with those provided or suggested by the *Poetics*.

Three kinds of historical poetry are mentioned in Book I: invectives, hymns, and encomia. The distinction among these three depends on the distinction between gods and men as objects of imitation and the distinction between praise and ridicule as ends of imitation. These two distinctions give rise to four possibilities, of which one, ridicule of the gods, is an empty class, for it is men's beliefs about the gods, not the gods themselves, that are subject to ridicule. Aristotle at this point in his account of the genesis of poetry is introducing the influence of the character of the poet on poetry, and the distinctions of agents imitated as divine or human, and of praise or ridicule as ends determined by the character of poets, are appropriate to this context, but should not be taken as essential to historical poetry in general. The context in *Poetics* I is not that of historical poetry itself as a kind of poetry, but of imitation as having its source in the character of the poet, as distinguished from imitation that has its source in nature or in art. This is why historical poetry is not mentioned as such in Book I, and also why what Book I says of this poetry, that its imitation has its source in the poet's character, cannot be taken as true of historical poetry generally. All that we know about historical poetry itself from this passage is that it includes invectives, hymns, and encomia, and that among the invectives is the *Margitēs*, or *Madman*, which Aristotle attributes to Homer.

The historical source of the power of the *Margitēs* is the works of other poets, whose influence is presumably exhibited in the words and actions of the madman, much as *Don Quixote*, whose hero might also be called a madman, exhibits the influence of Spanish chivalric romances. Aristotle says that the author of the *Margitēs* was the first to show the forms (*schēmata*) of comedy by producing dramatically, not invective, but the imitation of the laughable (1448b33), but he nevertheless calls the work an invective (4.1448b30). This can be understood to mean that it uses the universal forms of the laughable to make fun of particular poets. It is what might be called comic invective.

The *Margitēs* is one example of the early poets lampooning each other. Aristotle later cites Xenophanes (sixth century BCE) for his criticism of what Homer and Hesiod say about the gods (25.1460b37). Xenophanes says, "Homer and Hesiod have ascribed to the gods all deeds that among men are a reproach and a disgrace: thieving, adultery, and mutual deception" (*DK*, Xenophanes B 11, trans. Guthrie 1985, 1:371). This particular statement is not itself poetry, although it is in hexameters, for it is not imitative. Xenophanes also says about Homer, "From the beginning, all men have learned in accordance with Homer" (*DK*, Xenophanes B 10). This suggests that if Xenophanes had put his criticism of Homer and Hesiod into imitative form, as historical poetry, it would have been cultural criticism, not unlike, for example, Jonathan Swift's *Gulliver's Travels*.

We have another fragment of Xenophanes, this time in elegiacs, that is imitative: "They say that once when a puppy was being whipped, Pythagoras, who was passing by, took pity on it, saying, 'Stop! Do not beat it! It is the soul of a friend; I recognize his voice!'" (Diels-Kranz, Xenophanes B 7, trans. Robinson 1968, 61). This is poetry, for it is imitative, and historical poetry, for it ridicules a doctrine of his contemporary, Pythagoras. The action imitated is not an action ever performed by Pythagoras, but one invented by Xenophanes in order to ridicule Pythagoras's doctrine of the transmigration of souls. This technique offers opportunities for poetic invention while still maintaining a tie to historical reality, as we see also, for example, in Voltaire's *Candide*, which uses fictitious characters and actions to ridicule Leibniz's doctrine that this is the best of all possible worlds.

Xenophanes is also said to have written two historical epics, one on the founding of Colophon, his native city, and another on the settlement of a colony from it at Elea, in Italy (Diogenes Laertius ix.20). These epics would be historical poetry rather than history if they aimed, as they probably did, not merely to present the historical facts about the founding of his city and its colony, but to do so in a way that would make it a good story, in the manner of a Ken Burns documentary. We may note in passing that since Xenophanes wrote both lampoons and serious poetry, it is clear that his poems, like Homer's, originated from art rather than character. Historical poetry itself, as we said, has no particular relation to character.

This is a rather meager list of examples, so let us add a few more from our own experience. One familiar form of historical poetry is the everyday art of the raconteur. We begin from something that has happened to us, and endeavor to make it a good story. The endeavor to make a good story out of the actual events introduces the new principle that makes the story historical poetry rather than history. How many times did Casanova tell the story of his escape from the Venetian prison before it acquired the form that it has in his memoirs? What we call good stories tend to take two forms. In their comic form they are either a joke producing a single burst of laughter at the end, or a narration in which the comic complications build upon one another through a series of laughable incidents until the final resolution. In their more serious form, they tend to be stories of wonders, or of difficulties and perils about whose outcome we are held in suspense until the final resolution. One is reminded here of the stories that Othello tells to Desdemona. In their dramatic context they must be taken as historical poetry, as having their origin in actual events, for otherwise Othello is a con man and Desdemona a dupe, and the tragedy is ruined.[1] The principle that historical poetry must tell a story was used by Don Hewitt to develop the highly successful television program *60 Minutes*. What he asked of those who worked on the program was, "Tell me a story." Each program orders the materials of current events to tell one or more stories, generally three fifteen-minute stories. The program of January 25, 2010, told the story of Hewitt's achievement.

Stories of a whole life may be ordered to a poetic rather than a historical end. A *New York Times* book reviewer writes, "Any decent biography is a work of drama" (Vollmann 2005, 8). In support of this, one might cite David Hume's "My Own Life," of which Hume says, "This Narrative shall contain little more than the History of my Writings" (Hume 1987, xxxi). But, since, as he tells us, his ruling passion was the love of literary fame, the history of his writings has a dramatic structure in which failures and disappointments are met with the persistence of a naturally cheerful and sanguine temper, and at the end of his life he can see his literary reputation breaking out at last with additional luster. It is thus a history that is also dramatic. In the more usual case, however, the biography is not history but historical poetry, as

St. Augustine's *Confessions* is a praise of God, not a history but a hymn, in Aristotle's terms.

A principal field for historical poetry today is the documentary film. A documentary film may of course be merely historical, but its interest for us and our enjoyment of it can be increased by selecting and ordering the material for a poetic end. Ken Burns's documentary *Not for Ourselves Alone: The Story of Elizabeth Cady Stanton and Susan B. Anthony* (1999), for example, unites biography and cultural history to make an emotionally engaging story of the struggle for women's right to vote. Michael Moore in his successive documentaries—*Roger and Me* (1989), *Bowling for Columbine* (2002), *Fahrenheit 9/11* (2004), *Sicko* (2007), and *Capitalism: A Love Story* (2009)—successfully exploits the possibilities of invective in the new medium. As he says, "Although I'm trying to say things I want to say politically, I primarily want to make an entertaining movie. If the art of the movie doesn't work, the politics won't get through" (*New York Times*, September 20, 2009). *Man on Wire* (2008) documents Philippe Petit's high-wire walk between the World Trade Center towers, with all the preparation and difficulties that preceded it. The prospect of the walk at the end holds us in suspense throughout, like the blowing up of the bridge in Hemingway's *For Whom the Bell Tolls. In the Valley of the Wolves*, a PBS Nature documentary, uses only footage of Yellowstone National Park, but organizes it into a plot in which a particular pack of wolves inhabits a valley, is driven out by another pack, and eventually returns, a plot which is accompanied by a number of subplots and vignettes. Another program in the same series, *The Gorilla King*, first shown on April 20, 2008, follows the life history of an unusually able and successful mountain gorilla through its various phases and transitions. Documentaries of animal life generally take advantage of the similarity of animals to people to give the works human interest. This is carried to an extreme in Luc Sacquet's *The March of the Penguins* (2005). It is a natural history of the reproductive cycle of the emperor penguin, except that the material is ordered to bring out the similarity of the penguins to ourselves. For example, we never see them beside a human being or anything else that would give us an idea of their true size and thus interfere with thinking of them as like ourselves. Behavior that is recognizably similar to that of people is emphasized, and the threat of predatory seals is made humanly terrifying by fearful jaws flashing across the screen. In the original French version the penguins were even represented as speaking to one another, but this went too far, for the power of the work as historical poetry depends upon its being true to the facts in its presentation of penguin life.

More examples can be supplied by the reader, for historical poetry includes a vast array of heterogeneous forms—invectives, satires, parodies, hymns, encomia, eulogies, memoirs, confessions, true romances, true adventures, historical novels, documentary films, reality television, YouTube, and many more.

Let us now turn to what can be said about historical poetry in general by saying what it is not, that is, by distinguishing it from the three things it most nearly resembles: history, imitative poetry, and rhetoric. This will not only clarify the nature of historical poetry, but will help to show the viability of this whole set of Aristotelian distinctions. We begin with the difference between historical poetry and history.

2. HISTORICAL POETRY AND HISTORY

We first need to say what, for Aristotle, history is. History for Aristotle is well characterized by the memorable words of Jack Webb in *Dragnet*, "Just the facts, Ma'am." If the cause of a homicide is to be discovered, what the investigator needs to know are the relevant facts. The same is true of the discovery of causes in Aristotle's sciences. Aristotle says, "For if none of the attributes that truly belongs to the things was omitted from the history, what is demonstrable of each thing we shall be able to discover and demonstrate, and what is not in its nature demonstrable we shall be able to make clear" (*Post. An.* i.30.46a24). History states the facts, and from them the investigator is able to discover their causes, and thus to establish sciences. If the history of a subject is complete, the science of the subject can be complete. Two of the histories that Aristotle used in establishing his sciences have survived. One is the *History of Animals*, by far the longest work in the corpus, which records facts that are relevant to the sciences of animals (cf. *Parts of Animals* ii.1.646a6). The other is the *Constitution of Athens*, one of 158 histories on which Aristotle's *Politics* is based. Such histories aim to be an accurate record of the attributes belonging to each subject of investigation.

In distinguishing poetic from natural imitation at the beginning of chapter 4 we cited the statement from the *Metaphysics* (vi.1.1025b22) that in the case of things made, such as poetry, the principle is in the maker, and is either mind or art or some faculty. This statement should also distinguish poetry from history. It might be argued, however, that the statement does not distinguish poetry from history because history is also a thing made. To this it can be replied that history is indeed a thing made in the sense of a verbal expression, and Aristotle treats verbal expression as common to all the disciplines in the *Peri hermēneias,* or *On Expression.* Poetry and the other arts and sciences are distinguished from history not by being expressions, but by what they express. What poetry expresses is what the poet has made it express, whereas what history expresses, the facts of history, is not made by the historian. Poetry is a thing made because its end or organizing principle comes from the poet.

To this it may be objected that this still does not distinguish poetry from history because just as the end or organizing principle of poetry comes from the poet, so the end or organizing principle of history comes from the historian. To this it can be replied that for Aristotle the historian expresses just the facts, and even the principle according to which the facts are organized must also be a fact and not an invention of the historian. For Aristotle, histories are organized by principles such as subject and chronological order, for these, too, are facts. Such principles are those of history and not poetry, and Aristotle is critical of poets who fail to appreciate this. "A plot is not a unity, as some suppose, by being about one agent, for many and indefinite things happen to one agent, some of which do not make a unity" (8.1451a16, trans. Telford). A plot unified as being about one agent confuses poetry with the history of a person, or biography. "And it [the plot] ought not to put down anything similar to our customary histories, in which, of necessity, it is not a single action which is made evident, but a single time and whatever happens in that time, to one character or to many, each incident being related to the others as it happened" (23.1459a21, trans. Telford). A plot unified in this way confuses poetry with the history of a time.

Thus we can say that historical poetry, like all poetry, differs from history because its organizing principle or end comes from the poet. But to this it may be objected that now we are contradicting ourselves, for we said a moment ago that the end or organizing principle of historical poetry comes from history, and now we say that it comes from the poet. But to say that the end comes from the poet is true of all poetry, not historical poetry only, and does not specify from what source the poet derives his end, which may be history or poetry or philosophy. Thus historical poetry differs from history in being made by the poet, and from educational and imitative poetry because the source from which the poet derives the end of the poem is history rather than poetry or philosophy.

The relation of history to historical poetry can be illustrated by Sir Walter Raleigh's *The Last Fight of the Revenge* and Tennyson's "The Revenge: A Ballad of the Fleet." Raleigh's account begins, "Because the rumors are diversely spread, as well in England as in the low countries and elsewhere, of this late encounter [in 1591, not the better known encounter of 1588 off the coast of England] between her Majesty's ships and the Armada of Spain; and that the Spaniards, according to their usual manner, fill the world with their vain-glorious vaunts, making great appearance of victories, when on the contrary themselves are most commonly and shamefully beaten and dishonored, thereby hoping to possess the ignorant multitude by anticipating and forerunning false reports: it is agreeable with all good reason (for manifestation of truth, to overcome falsehood and untruth), that the beginning, continuance, and success of this late honorable encounter of Sir Richard Grenville, and other of her Majesty's captains, with the Armada of Spain, should be set down and published without partiality or false imagination."[2] Raleigh is proposing to write, in Aristotle's terms, a history of the encounter. He is careful to specify his sources, and to include unconfirmed reports only as unconfirmed, as when he says of what happened to the great *San Philip* after its first encounter with the *Revenge*, "Some say that the ship foundered, but we cannot report it for truth, unless we were assured." Again, as to when Sir Richard was wounded, he writes, "Some write that Sir Richard was very dangerously hurt almost in the beginning of the fight, and lay speechless for a time ere he recovered. But two of the *Revenge's* own company brought home in a ship of Lime from the islands, examined by some of the Lords and others, affirmed that he was never so wounded as that he forsook the upper deck, till an hour before midnight; and then being shot into the body with a musket, as he was a-dressing [as his wound was being dressed] was again shot into the head, and withal his surgeon wounded to death. This agreeth also with an examination, taken by Sir Francis Godolphin, of four other mariners of the same ship being returned, which examination the said Sir Francis sent unto master William Killigrew, of her Majesty's Privy Chamber."

Tennyson, unlike Raleigh, is not concerned to establish the facts, but rather to make a poem out of them. He is writing, in Aristotle's terms, an encomium on the actions of Sir Richard and his shipmates. His poem begins:

I
At Flores in the Azores Sir Richard Grenville lay,
When a pinnace, like a fluttered bird, came flying from far away:
"Spanish ships of war at sea! We have sighted fifty-three!"
Then sware Lord Thomas Howard: "'Fore God, I am no coward;
But I cannot fight them here, for my ships are out of gear,

And the half my men are sick. I must fly, but follow quick.
We are six ships of the line; can we fight with fifty-three?

II

Then spake Sir Richard Grenville: "I know you are no coward;
You fly them for a moment to fight with them again.
But I've ninety men or more that are lying sick ashore.
I should count myself a coward if I left them, my Lord Howard,
To these Inquisition dogs and the devildoms of Spain."

By comparing these stanzas with Raleigh's history we can see how historical poetry derives its end from history, and yet departs from history in ways
that make it resemble imitative poetry. In Raleigh's history, the speaker who
announces the coming of the Armada is identified as one Captain Middle-
ton, who, "being in a very good sailer, had kept company with the Armada
three days before, of good purpose both to discover their forces the more, as
also to give advice to my Lord Thomas of their approach. He had no sooner
delivered the news but the fleet was in sight." Tennyson omits all the facts
of how intelligence of the Armada's arrival reached the English, for they are
not relevant to Sir Richard's actions, but the suddenness of the arrival *is* relevant, for it left Sir Richard and his men unprepared for an encounter with
the Spanish fleet. The suddenness of the arrival is expressed dramatically by
the single pinnace that in one sentence becomes fifty-three ships. The simile
of the fluttered bird and the excited shout that announces the presence of
the Armada are not in Raleigh but add dramatic vividness to the account.

We cannot suppose that either Lord Howard or Sir Richard spoke in
rhymed verse, but rhymed verse is a poetic "sweetener" (*hēdusma*) that makes
the language more pleasant. Lord Howard and Sir Richard were on different
ships and could not speak directly to each other, but by imagining an exchange between them Tennyson is able to present dramatically essential information that Raleigh supplies about their situation, attitudes, and actions.

Tennyson's evidence for Sir Richard's attitude is Raleigh's statement that
when he was urged by the ship's master and others to turn the ship, he "ut-
terly refused to turn from the enemy, alleging that he would rather choose to
die, than to dishonor himself, his country and her Majesty's ship." Tennyson
presents the refusal, but not these reasons for it, which are more nearly approximated in Sir Richard's farewell speech, where they can be combined
with his satisfaction in the choice he has made and provide a satisfactory
closure to his life in the manner of an imitative poem.

The reference to the Spanish and their country as "these Inquisition dogs and the devildoms of Spain" is not in Raleigh's history, which rather accuses the Spanish of filling the world with false reports to conceal the shame and dishonor of their defeats. By bringing in the Inquisition and calling the Spaniards dogs and their kingdoms devildoms, all in a single line, he provides a moral and religious context in support of Sir Richard's actions.

The changes that Tennyson makes in the history—the omissions, additions, condensations, re-orderings, and modifications of the facts, and the dramatic and pleasing presentation of them—can all be understood as consequences of the end or principle of the imitation, the praise of the heroic actions of Sir Richard and his men. Since the power of the poem derives from the actual occurrence of these actions, they must be truly presented in whatever relates to their heroism, while in other respects Tennyson creatively reconstructs the account to bring it into accord with the requirements of imitative poetry. This is an illustration of why nonimitative poetry belongs to the same method as imitative poetry. If he had simply imagined a single English ship successfully encountering the entire Spanish Armada without this having actually occurred, this might pass as a pleasant fantasy, but would altogether lack the power of a poem based on actual events.

Let this suffice for our discussion of the difference between historical poetry and history.

3. HISTORICAL POETRY AND IMITATIVE POETRY

We now turn to the difference between historical poetry and imitative poetry. We may begin by noting that this difference is not a matter of whether or not the poetry in fact imitates history, for any kind of poetry may imitate history. Aristotle writes, "And even if he [the poet] happens to produce incidents that have arisen, he is nonetheless a poet [that is, an imitative poet], for nothing prevents some incidents which have arisen from being the sort of incidents that are likely or possible, and it is in respect of this aspect of the incidents that he is a poet" (9.1451b29, trans. Telford). Whether the events have actually occurred is essential to historical poetry, but accidental to imitative poetry.

This difference can be illustrated by comparing Tennyson's account of the last fight of the *Revenge* with Shakespeare's account of the battle of Agincourt in *Henry the Fifth*. Both imitate historical events, but the power of Tennyson's poem comes from the actual occurrence of the events that it recounts. If the events had not actually occurred, there would be nothing to praise. The power of Shakespeare's play, on the other hand, does not depend on the actual occurrence of the victory at Agincourt, but on the universals present in the play itself, which make the outcome of the battle probable whether it occurred or not. Shakespeare is concerned to portray Henry V, both before and during the battle, as the kind of person who makes such a victory possible. All of Shakespeare's tragedies except Othello have their source in historical events, but none of them is historical poetry, because the source of their ends lies in the plays themselves. They are self-sufficient works, made independent of the actual events from which they originate.

Improbabilities thus have a contrasting status in imitative and historical poetry. In historical poetry the very improbability of what is imitated may be the principal factor in its interest and power. *The World's Fastest Indian* (2005), starring Anthony Hopkins, derives much of its interest and power from the improbable fact that an old guy in New Zealand tinkering with his Indian motorcycle actually ends up breaking the world speed record for its class on the Bonneville salt flats in Utah. Relying on history for the possibility of the outcome, the film is free to accentuate its improbability. In fiction, on the other hand, it is easy to make up all kinds of improbabilities, and the improbabilities that give interest and power to historical poetry may ruin imitative poetry by making it unconvincing.

To say that imitative poetry does not depend on whether the events imitated have actually occurred is not to say that whether they have occurred has no effect on how the poem is received by the audience. Poetics as a science is concerned only with internal relations within the work itself, and not with the effect it may happen to have on an audience. But Aristotle says that if the audience believes that the events have actually occurred, this is persuasive with respect to their possibility, which he gives as the reason why poets retain traditional names in their tragedies: "The cause of this is that the possible is persuasive, and while we are not yet persuaded that what has not happened is possible, what has happened is clearly possible, for it would not have happened if it were impossible" (9.1451b16–19). Even if we do not know whether Shakespeare's *Henry the Fifth* is historically accurate, the fact that we know that Henry V was a historical king who defeated the French at the battle of Agincourt contributes to our sense of the possibility of the events imitated. The actual occurrence of tragic events can persuade us of their possibility, which is essential to imitative poetry. Persuasion, however, is the concern of rhetoric rather than poetry, for persuasion depends on the audience. The imitative poet makes the universal relations in the poem, but their effect on an audience depends on the nature of the audience and is not made by the poet. Thus, although the actual existence of tragic events may contribute to the end of tragedy, it is accidental to it as imitative poetry.

Just as the historical reality of persons and events contributes to our belief in their possibility in tragedies, so the historical reality of persons and
events may contribute to the pleasure and laughter produced by comedies.
Aristophanes is notorious for making fun of actual individuals, and these
topical references doubtless contributed to the pleasure of his audience. It
is said that when Bob Hope entertained the troops in the Second World
War he sent advance agents to the bases where he was to perform to find
out the particular grievances of the troops at those bases, and those who
heard him can testify that when his jokes hit upon such topics the pleasure
and laughter were particularly pronounced. Jon Stewart in his fake news
program makes fun of what actual individuals have said or done, and anyone who watched the program during the dark years of the Bush administration will have noticed how disposed his audience was to laugh at jokes
about this administration. Once when making fun of Hillary Clinton he
apparently anticipated a lesser response, for he followed the joke with "Oh,
I'm sorry. Oh. Oh, I see, not so funny when it's your guy, huh? Interesting"
(*The Daily Show*, August 16, 2007). As it happened, this addition was inap-
ropos, for he had to interrupt laughter and applause in order to deliver it, an
indication that his concern is topical comedy rather than comic invective.
But the point is that comedians such as Aristophanes and Bob Hope and
Jon Stewart all make use not only of the forms of the laughable, which are
universals independent of history, but of topical materials that contribute
to the pleasure and laughter of the audience for rhetorical rather than poetic
reasons, just as in tragedies the use of historical names can help to persuade
the audience of the probability of the events imitated. The actual response
of an audience to a joke depends on both the universal forms of the laughable that are the proper concern of comedy and also topical considerations
that affect how the jokes are received.

The comic poet in his concern to arouse laughter will therefore welcome
actual events that illustrate the universal forms of the laughable, and especially those whose actual occurrence can be expected to contribute to the
laughter of his audience. At the beginning of a program devoted entirely to
Dick Cheney's shooting a friend in the face, Jon Stewart lifted his eyes to
heaven and piously whispered "Thank you, Jesus," incidentally adding to the
original comic wrongness of shooting a friend in the face (the friend was not
seriously hurt) the wrongness of giving thanks for a misfortune, and to Jesus
(Jon Stewart is Jewish), and in the indirect mode appropriate to comedy,
since it was not yet clear why he was giving thanks at all. What is relevant

here is that not only was he given an ideal instance of comic wrongness that could be developed in various ways, such as issuing a solemn warning to all parents not to let their children go hunting with Dick Cheney, "because, if you do, he will shoot them in the face," but a wrongness actually perpetrated by a person at whom his audience was disposed to laugh.

4. HISTORICAL POETRY AND RHETORIC

We have considered how historical poetry differs from history and how it differs from imitative poetry. It remains to consider how it differs from rhetoric. Rhetoric, like historical poetry, can imitate particular individuals, and the encomium, which is a form of historical poetry, is also a form of epideictic rhetoric (*Rhet.* i.9.1367b28). We therefore have the specific problem of distinguishing the poetic encomium from the rhetorical encomium.

Rhetoric is defined as "the power of seeing (*theōrein*) in each case the possible persuasive" (*Rhet.* i.2.1355b26). The possible persuasive depends on the person or persons being persuaded, that is, on the audience. Rhetoric must therefore take the audience into account, whereas the universals of poetic science are independent of the audience, as we have just seen in distinguishing what belongs to poetry from what belongs to rhetoric in historical tragedy and topical comedy.

I have heard members of the Chicago school express the difference between poetry and rhetoric as the difference between presupposing a universal audience and a particular audience. This is a rhetorical form of the Aristotelian distinction and neglects Aristotle's conception of science as the self-determination of a subject genus, which requires that poetry be determined by poetic principles and not by external factors such as an audience. The universals of human nature that the rhetorical theory brings in through the audience are already contained in Aristotle's poetic theory, as, for example, the difference between virtue and vice is incorporated in the account of character. The theory that poetry presupposes a universal audience fails to distinguish between poetry and rhetoric when rhetoric is addressed to a universal audience, as it sometimes is. Consider, for example, Neil Armstrong's statement when he stepped from the lunar module onto the moon, "That's one small step for (a) man, a giant leap for mankind." This is a good example of epideictic rhetoric addressed to a universal audience. It is addressed not only to those hearing him as he spoke, and not only to his fellow countrymen, but to all mankind, but this does not make it poetry. It combines metaphor and antithesis (the latter unintentionally improved in form when it was spoken without the bracketed "a") in an exemplification of a high point of rhetorical style, sayings that are elegant (*asteios*) and memorable (*eudokimos*) (*Rhet.* iii.10.1410b7).

A poetic encomium, then, praises a historical subject, but poetically, without regard to an audience, while a rhetorical encomium also praises a historical subject, which is why both are encomia, but rhetorically, with a view to an audience. This difference can be illustrated by the beginning of Tennyson's "The Revenge: A Ballad of the Fleet," a poetic encomium, and the beginning of Lincoln's Gettysburg Address, a rhetorical encomium. Tennyson's poem begins, "At Flores in the Azores Sir Richard Grenville lay . . ." This situates the subject of the encomium in history, at Flores in the Azores in the naval struggle between England and Spain at the end of the sixteenth century, but the encomium itself, not being directed to an audience, is unsituated in history. The Gettysburg Address begins, "Fourscore and seven years ago our fathers brought forth on this continent a new nation, conceived in liberty and dedicated to the proposition that all men are created equal. Now we are engaged in a great civil war, testing whether that nation, or any nation so conceived and so dedicated, can long endure. We are met on a great battlefield of that war. We have come to dedicate a portion of that field as a final resting place for those who here have given their lives that that nation might live." Here the subject is defined by a progressive limitation beginning from the new nation and its conception and dedication, to a great civil war, to a great battlefield of that war, to a portion of that field now to be dedicated to those who gave their lives that the initial inclusive subject, the new nation, might live. Thus the encomium itself, as well as the events it praises, is situated in the life of the nation. It is delivered with a view not only to the immediate audience, but to the larger national audience, and permits the kind of analysis provided by Garry Wills in *Lincoln at Gettysburg: The Words that Remade America* (1992). A comparable analysis of the effects of Tennyson's poem would be an analysis only of accidental effects, not of effects essentially related to the poem's intent. We may note in passing that the opening sentences of Lincoln's address provide a compact illustration of Lincoln's dialectical method, bringing together whole and part; past, present, and future; and life and death. (For what I mean by a dialectical method, see Watson 1985, 84–91.)

There are further consequences of the difference between poetical and rhetorical encomia that are illustrated by Tennyson's poem and Lincoln's speech. Tennyson's encomium is in rhymed verse, Lincoln's in prose. The poetic encomium is free to use poetic diction and meter in a way that the rhetorical encomium is not, for the end lies in the poem itself, whereas the end of rhetoric is to be effective with respect to an audience. The rhetorical encomium must avoid poetic diction and meter as drawing attention to what it is and away from what it is designed to effect. Aristotle discusses these differences in speaking of rhetorical style, which concerns *how* something is said as distinguished from *what* is said (*Rhet.* iii.1.1403b15). Rhetorical style (*lexis*) thus includes not only what in the *Poetics* is called diction (*lexis*) but also meter, which is not included in diction in the *Poetics*.[3] Aristotle begins his discussion of rhetorical style by criticizing the poetical language of Gorgias as obsolete even in poetry. "The style of prose (*logos*)," he says, "is different from that of poetry" (*Rhet.* iii.1.1404a27). After giving examples of the epithets of Alcidamas, Aristotle concludes that such poetical language by its inappropriateness introduces into speeches the laughable, the frigid, and the unclear. In the translation of W. Rhys Roberts, "We thus see how the inappropriateness of such poetical language imports absurdity (*to geloion*) and tastelessness (*to psuchron*) into speeches, as well as the obscurity (*to asaphes*) that comes from all this verbosity—for when the sense is plain, you only obscure and spoil its clearness by piling up words" (iii.3.1406a32).

Not only is the language of poetry rejected in rhetoric, but also the use of meter. Meter in rhetoric is rejected as not persuasive, for it seems contrived (*peplasthai*) and draws attention to itself (iii.8.1408b22). Thus meter and poetic diction, although they do not make a work poetry, are characteristic of poetic encomia but not of rhetorical encomia. The meter and poetic diction of the opening lines of Milton's "Lycidas," "Yet once more, O ye laurels, and once more, / Ye myrtles brown, with ivy never sere," make it good poetry but poor rhetoric. The poet is free to pursue the enjoyments of language and meter in a way that would interfere with the rhetorician's end of persuasion.

The counterpart of the poetical invective (*psogos*) or lampoon (*iambos*) is the rhetorical accusation (*katēgoria*). The concern of rhetoric is to transform the actual historical situation, whereas the concern of satire is to ridicule it. Of course, any kind of poetry may actually effect a transformation of the historical situation, but this is accidental to it as poetry, for the poetic concern, as we have said more than once, is with the connection of principles and consequences within the poem, and not with its effect on an audience, whereas the rhetorical concern is with the power to affect an audience, particular or universal. The difference between satire and accusation can be illustrated by the difference between Voltaire's *Candide* and Émile Zola's *J'Accuse*. In the former, Dr. Pangloss adheres steadfastly to Leibniz's doctrine that this is the best of all possible worlds, and, as a poetic work, it is concerned to ridicule this doctrine, although it may incidentally have rhetorical effects. Zola's account of the Dreyfuss affair, on the other hand, is concerned to correct an injustice, as it helped to do.

Summing up the differences between historical poetry on the one hand, and history, imitative poetry, and rhetoric, on the other, we can say that historical poetry differs from history as all poetry does, in being ordered to an end coming from the poet, that it differs from imitative poetry in deriving its end from actual historical facts, and that it differs from rhetoric, as all poetry does, in achieving its end within itself rather than looking to an effect external to the poem.

Chapter 11
EDUCATIONAL POETRY

Educational poetry is either guiding or theoretical.
The epitome tells us only the generic name of educational poetry and that it has two species, guiding and theoretical, neither of which is subdivided. In the preliminary examination of the epitome we concluded that it derives its end from philosophy and raised the question of why it is called educational rather than philosophic. To fully answer this question, we need to examine the meaning of both "philosophy" and "education."

1. POETRY AND PHILOSOPHY

In the proper sequence of Aristotle's works, philosophy is first discussed in the philosophical preface to the theoretical sciences, as we have seen. "Rightly also is philosophy called science of the truth (*epitstēmēn tēs alētheias*). For of theoretical science the end is truth (*alētheia*), of practical science a work (*ergon*), and if practical men are concerned with how things are, they do not consider the cause in virtue of itself, but as relative and in the present" (*Metaph.* ii.1.933b19). The division of philosophy into theoretical and practical evidently corresponds to the division of educational poetry into theoretical and guiding poetry, although "practical" has been replaced by "guiding," a word that appears nowhere else in the Aristotelian corpus. It is appropriate here because it avoids excluding the productive from the practical, and thus unambiguously includes education in making as well as acting, as by a film showing how to make films. It also unambiguously includes education of character as well as intellect, as by *The Little Engine that Could* and other children's stories. The reason why theoretical poetry and guiding poetry are not further subdivided is presumably that the differences within them belong properly to the different arts and sciences that are being taught and not to poetics.

The further subdivisions of philosophy conform to the division of the sciences. "There must, then, be three theoretical philosophies, mathematics, physics, and what we may call theology, since it is obvious that if the divine is present anywhere, it is present in things of this sort" (*Metaph.* vi.1.1026a18, trans. Ross). This last philosophy is most universal in its truth, while physics, which considers only natural things, is second philosophy (*Metaph.* vii.11.1037a15). Physical truth in turn is wider in its scope than mathematical truth, for mathematics considers only quantity, which is an attribute of physical things. When Aristotle comes to practical philosophy in the *Ethics*, he calls ethics and politics taken together "the philosophy of human things" (*hē peri ta anthrōpeia philosophia, Eth.* x.10.1181b15). Thus philosophy explicitly includes both the theoretical and practical sciences.

When we come to poetics we might expect Aristotle to say, following the example of the theoretical and practical sciences, that poetics is the philosophy of poetry, meaning that it is concerned with the truth about poetry, but this is not what he says. What he says is that "poetry is more philosophic and more serious (*philosophōteron kai spoudaioteron*) than history" (9.1451b5). Instead of speaking about *poetics* as philosophy, he speaks about *poetry* as philosophic. This indicates that the primary contribution to truth, and hence to philosophy, in the domain of poetics lies not in poetics, but in poetry. Poetics is not for the sake of itself, but for the sake of poetry, poetry is imitation, and imitation can have a universality and truth that cannot be formulated in poetics or any other science.

The relatively slight contribution of poetics to scientific truth can be illustrated by the small number of books in the Aristotelian corpus that are devoted to it. If we omit as redundant the *Eudemian Ethics* and *Metaphysics* Kappa (11), we get a total of 100 authentic books, a convenient number for calculating percentages. The numbers of books and the percentages of the total are as follows: Organon, 15; Physical Sciences, 18; Biological Sciences, 31; Philosophy, 13; Practical Sciences, 18; Poetics, 2; Rhetoric, 3. Something like these percentages would be found in libraries today, but if we were to include poetry, or imaginative literature, along with poetics, the number of books assigned to it would generally exceed that of any of the sciences. Those who write about truth in the domain of poetics write not about truth in poetics, but truth in poetry. George Santayana wrote a book on three philosophical poets, not a book on three philosophical poetics. Perhaps there is more truth in a good poem than in any poetics. Some critics, as we noted earlier, even treat poetry as if it were philosophy.

Poetry is more philosophic than history, and contains more truth, but it is not philosophy or science. In fact, science as such has no place in poetry. Poetry about science, such as Sinclair Lewis's *Arrowsmith* (1925), Michael Frayn's *Copenhagen* (2000), *A Beautiful Mind*, starring Russell Crowe (2001), or Peter Parnell's *Trumpery* (2007), does not present scientific demonstrations or aim at the pleasure they provide, but rather presents the actions and passions of scientists as human dramas. Thought in the *Poetics* is a part of poetry, but for its treatment Aristotle does not refer us to the scientific treatment of thought in *On the Soul*, or to the treatment of scientific thought in the *Posterior Analytics*, or to the fullest realization of scientific thought in the *Metaphysics*, but to the *Rhetoric*, where the treatment of thought is not scientific at all.

Nevertheless, poetry is more philosophic than history, which is to say that it contains more of truth than history, and it contains more of truth because it speaks more of universals. Universality in poetry cannot be the same as universality in the sciences, however, or poetry would be philosophy, and not just more philosophic than history, and we must inquire what poetic universality is. Here we encounter an objection to Aristotle's *Poetics* that is in a way opposite to one that was mentioned in the chapter on poetry as imitation, which was that imitation means copying, and poetry is not copying. This objection in effect accuses Aristotle of assimilating poetry to history. The present objection is that, because poetry imitates universals, it imitates kinds or types rather than individuals. This objection in effect accuses Aristotle of assimilating poetry to philosophy. However implausible this view may be, either as what poets do or as what they ought to do, some have not hesitated to attribute it to Aristotle. Among them is none other than the great American Aristotelian John Dewey, whom we would expect to recover Aristotle's theory rather than condemn it. We have already noted that both Aristotle and Dewey treat art or poetry as autonomous, and that Dewey's three-stage account of the development of art as experience parallels Aristotle's three-stage account of the development of poetry as imitation.

Dewey quotes Aristotle's account of universals in poetry as follows:

"The universal is the *kind* of thing which a person of a certain character would necessarily or probably do or say. And this is what poetry aims at, though it gives proper names to the persons. The particular, for example, is what Acibiades did or underwent."

Dewey then goes on to interpret this statement:

Now the term here translated "character" is likely to give the modern reader a totally wrong impression. He would agree that the deeds and sayings attributed to a character in fiction, drama, or poetry should be such as to flow necessarily or with great probability from that individual's character. But he thinks of character as intimately individual, while "character" in the passage signifies a universal nature or essence. To Aristotle the esthetic significance of the portrayal of Macbeth, Pendennis, or Felix Holt consists in fidelity to the nature found in a class or species. To the modern reader, it signifies fidelity to the individuals whose career is exhibited; the things done, underwent, and said belong to him in his unique individuality. The difference is radical. (Dewey 1934, 348)

It should be noted first that Dewey thinks the modern reader would agree that the deeds and sayings attributed to a character in fiction, drama, or poetry should be such as to flow necessarily or with great probability from that individual's character. This is precisely why for Aristotle poetry is universal, for in poetry events are connected by probabilities and necessities rather than by the way they may happen to occur, as in history. Dewey is able to disagree with Aristotle only by adding to this conception of poetic universality the further requirement that it be the universality of a class or species rather than an individual, a requirement that for Aristotle would be appropriate only to universality in the theoretical sciences. We have already noted in chapter 1 that the universals of the theoretic sciences are true of every case, the universals of the practical sciences are outline universals that need to be filled in for the particular case, while what is universal in poetic action is left to intuitive mind.

This is confirmed by the passage that Dewey quotes when it is literally translated: "Universal (*katholou*) is any such and such things (*ta poia atta*) as such and such a man (*ho poios*) happens to say or do with probability or necessity . . . , while the particular (*to kath' hekaston*) is what Alcibiades did or what he suffered" (9.1451b8–11). Dewey's "the *kind* of thing" is literally "any such and such things" and his "a person of a certain character" is literally "such and such a man." "Such and such" is an indefinite such, a "such" with no implied identification of the particular "such" that it is. Thus Dewey's emphatic "*kind*," his "character," his "universal nature or essence," and his "nature of a class or species" are not in Aristotle, but are all Dewey's interpretations of Aristotle's "such." It is by interpreting "such" to mean "character" and character to be a theoretical universal, that Dewey is able to conclude that poetic universality is the universality of a class or species rather than an individual.

"A universal signifies a 'such,' not a 'this'" (*Metaph.* vii.13.1039a15). What the poetic individual, such as Macbeth (in the play) or Pendennis or Felix Holt, says or does with probability or necessity is a "such"; whereas what the particular individual, such as Macbeth (the historical king of Scotland) or Alcibiades, did or suffered is a "this." This is the distinction that Aristotle is drawing between the poetic universal and the historical particular. The historical particular can also be a "such" and a universal, for, as we noted earlier, "of the things that have happened, nothing prevents some from being such as might probably and possibly happen" (*Poet.* 9.1451b30), but, since not everything that happens is probable, poetry is more universal, and so more true, and so more philosophic, than history.

Shakespeare is our prime example of an author whose characters are individualized. Shakespeare was not available to Aristotle, but Homer was, and Aristotle says of him, "Homer, after making a short preface, at once brings in a man, woman, or other character, none of them characterless, but each possessing his own character" (*Poet.* 24.1460a10, trans. Telford).

Thus when Dewey says that to the modern reader, the esthetic significance of the portrayal of Macbeth, Pendennis, or Felix Holt consists in fidelity to the individuals whose career is exhibited, that the things done, underwent, and said belong to him in his unique individuality, he is recovering Aristotle's view after all, as his principles require him to do, but he does so by opposing "the modern reader" to a fictitious "Aristotle." This is not the only instance in which Dewey recovers Aristotelian ideas in opposition to "Aristotle," nor is Dewey the only thinker who has furthered Aristotelian ideas in this way. Werner Jaeger goes so far as to say of Aristotle, "His historical importance as the intellectual leader of the West is certainly not lessened by the fact that the evolution of independent philosophical achievement in European culture has taken the form of a five-hundred-years' struggle against him" (Jaeger 1948, 368). Dewey is our great anti-Aristotelian Aristotelian, whose antipathy to "Aristotle" leads him to think through his problems independently, although in an Aristotelian way, and thus to come up with Aristotle for the modern reader.

Poetic necessity and probability, like the equitable, cannot be determined by reasoning, but depend on intuitive mind. That this universality cannot be reduced to formulated universals is why the truth of poetry lies in poetry rather than poetics, and also why, as is commonly and rightly said, the meaning of art cannot be formulated as a set of propositions. A great work of art supports indefinitely many intellectual analyses, and its meaning is not exhausted by any one of them, or by all of them taken together. It is also why, as Dewey says, "art is more moral than moralities" (Dewey 1934, 348). The equitable is universal, common to all the good (*Eth.* vi.1143a31), but it cannot be formulated as a moral rule. To take one example of many that might be given, Fanny Price in Jane Austen's *Mansfield Park* has the virtue of justice (Watson 1985, 162), even if she has no other unusual qualities or external advantages that could contribute to her happiness. But justice is complete virtue in relation to another (*Eth.* v.1.1129b26), and the novel shows us how in the end justice alone can lead to happiness. Fanny Price's feelings and choices provide a better test for our own sense of justice than any formulations of what justice is, for they concern individual cases, and those who think Fanny Price should not have acted as she does would do well to look more closely at the novel or their own moral values, or both.

Imitative poetry, then, because of its universality, is more philosophic than history, but its universals are neither the formulable universals of theoretical philosophy nor the outline universals of practical philosophy. Poetry for both Aristotle and Dewey is the home of individualized universality, or universal individuality, in all its infinite variety.

2. POETRY AND EDUCATION

We must now consider education, and how poetry can be educative. "Education," like "cause," is a trans-disciplinary term with a meaning in all disciplines, but a meaning that is only analogically the same in different disciplines, and Aristotle develops its meaning, as he developed the meaning of "cause," by considering it in four different disciplines.

His account of education, like his account of philosophy, begins in the philosophical preface to the theoretical sciences, and we have already referred to it in our Introduction as identifying the difficulty that confronts the modern reader in trying to understand Aristotle. Aristotle argues that the customary (*to sunēthes*) determines how we receive the sciences, and presents education as an alternative to custom. "Therefore one must be educated as to how each discourse should be received, since it is out of place to seek at the same time both science and a mode of the science and it is not easy to attain either. The minute accuracy of mathematics is not to be demanded in all subjects, but in those that do not have matter. Therefore its mode is not physical, for presumably the whole of nature has matter" (*Metaph.* ii.3.995a12). From this we learn that education arises from the reflective effort to transmit the results of inquiry. It replaces unreflective custom or tradition with mind and rationality, and is the mode of a science possessed by a person prepared to learn that science. The person educated in physics, for example, will understand the difference between physical and mathematical geometry, and will expect physical proofs in physical geometry and mathematical proofs in mathematical geometry.

This conception of education is defined at the beginning of the *Parts of Animals.* Aristotle writes,

With respect to every theory and method, the most lowly and the most esteemed alike, there seem to be two modes of the habit, one rightly called the science of the subject, the other a kind of education. For to the mode of the educated person belongs the ability to make judgments that hit the mark as to what the speaker has set forth well or not well. For such indeed we think the universally educated person to be, and to be educated to be able to do this. Except we consider universally educated some one person who is able to be thus critical with respect to all subjects, and not merely with respect to some subject separated off, for another person may have the same ability with respect to a part. It is thus clear that also in learning by inquiry about nature there must be some canons (*horoi*) such that, relative to them, the mode of showing things is acceptable, regardless of how the truth is, whether as shown or otherwise. (*Parts of Animals* i.1.639a1–15)

Aristotle goes on to formulate a series of canons or criteria for judging what is set forth with respect to the parts of animals. From the quotation as a whole we learn that to be educated in a subject is to be able to judge well what is set forth in that subject, and that every subject has its own canons and requires its own education. There is no general knowledge that would make one educated in all subjects. The unity of education is found in the educated person rather than in his knowledge. The educated person plays a key role in Aristotle's philosophy, for he is the proper hearer of the sciences. Being able to judge what to accept and what to reject in the sciences, he himself determines the content of his own mind, and becomes in this respect self-determining or autonomous. Descartes, beginning his philosophy from the individual mind, makes such autonomy of mind fundamental to philosophy itself. This autonomy of the individual mind is the reason why education is properly conceived as universal education, for unless the education is universal, the mind is not fully autonomous.[1]

Aristotle's third discussion of education is in his preface to the practical sciences (*Eth.* i.3). Aristotle there lists three prerequisites for a person learning them. The first applies to all sciences, for it belongs to the educated person to look for accuracy in each genus just so far as the nature of the subject admits. There are two further prerequisites for instruction that are peculiar to the practical sciences. A young man is not a proper hearer of ethics and politics, for he is inexperienced in the actions that occur in life, but its arguments begin from these and are about these. Further, being inclined

to follow his passions, hearing lectures will be for him vain and unprofitable, since the end is not knowledge but action. This discussion of education is concerned with the adaptation of education to its subject matter,
corresponding to the discussion of causes in On the Generation of Animals.
The last two prerequisites for hearing lectures on ethics are well illustrated, and taught, in the novels of Jane Austen. Emma has the nature and
external advantages appropriate to the social leader of her community. Practical wisdom (phronēsis) is the virtue that enables people to see what is good
for individuals and communities, and is the virtue of a leader. Emma has all
the moral virtues required for practical wisdom, but unlike Knightly, she is
young and inexperienced in the actions that occur in life, and therefore her
efforts to assist Harriet Smith in finding a suitable husband, in disregard
of Knightly's good advice, have an effect opposite to her good intentions.
Again, Marianne in Sense and Sensibility is inclined to follow her passions
rather than reason, but, unlike her sister Elinor, and in disregard of her good
advice, she does so, and her attempt to achieve happiness in this way ends in
misery. These novels illustrate how poetry can be educative, and the specific
education necessary to be a proper hearer of lectures on ethics, but they are
imitative rather than educational poetry, and so raise a question for Aristotle to answer in his analysis of comedy, how such educational plots as we
find in Jane Austen's novels contribute to them as comedies.

Education, as we see in the division of educational poetry, is of two
kinds. On the one hand it aims at autonomy in determining theoretical beliefs, and on the other it aims at autonomy in judging what is said about how
to live one's own life and what is proposed for the good of the community
and who should be elected to public office. The educated man can thus be
a good man and a good citizen even though he is not an expert in ethics or
politics. Speaking of education in relation to the role of the citizen in the
state, Aristotle emphasizes that the judgment of an educated person is not
inferior to that of the expert. He distinguishes three kinds of healers or phy-
sicians: "A physician is the practitioner and the master physician and, third,
the person educated in the art, for there are such persons also in nearly all
the arts, and we attribute judgment no less to the educated than to the experts" (Pol. iii.11.1282a3). In his discussion of education in the Politics, he
gives a complete discussion of education in music in relation to its different
possible ends: amusement (paidia), entertainment (diagōgē) that is an end
in itself, education (paideia), and catharsis (katharsis). We shall say more
about these when we come to discuss catharsis. That music is for Aristotle
the paradigmatic liberal art and a means by which the young acquire the

character that accords with the values of the community is an extremely important point that could be developed at length.

Education for Aristotle, then, has its origin in the use of mind to transmit the achievements of mind; education in a subject is the ability to judge well what is said about the subject, and universal education is the ability to be thus critical in all or nearly all subjects; it must be adapted to its subject matter; and a full account of education in music ordered to its various ends is given in the *Politics*.

We can now answer the question raised at the beginning of this chapter, why poetry that takes its end from philosophy is called educational rather than philosophic. Philosophy is scientific knowledge of the truth, and scientific knowledge is universal, whereas poetry is imitation of universal particulars. Knowledge of universal particulars is not yet science, but it is by knowing them that the mind is prepared to understand the universals of science. Consequently the proper function of poetry with respect to science and truth is to prepare the mind to understand the universals of science by exhibiting them in particulars, and the poetry that does this is educational poetry. Poetry, as imitation, cannot present the universals of philosophy or science as such except incidentally, as by imitating someone who is presenting philosophic or scientific arguments, as in Parmenides's poem or Socratic dialogues. But because such scientific demonstration is incidental to what it is as poetry, whereas its educational function belongs to it as poetry, the poetry that takes its end from philosophy is properly called educational rather than philosophic. As such, it can teach the ability to judge scientific demonstrations and practical questions and works of art.

Instruction (*didaskalia*) is for Aristotle instruction by argument, whether dialectical or scientific. Educational poetry, because it does not present universals as such, but only in particulars, is not properly didactic (*didaktikos*), for this would imply instruction by argument (*Post. An.* i.1.71a1; *Rhet.* i.1.1355a25).

Educational poetry is a recognized kind of poetry, so there is no need for an extensive list of examples. Some have already been mentioned. Socratic dialogues were mentioned as a form of imitative prose existing in Aristotle's time. Sheldon Sacks chooses Samuel Johnson's *Rasselas* to illustrate what he calls the apologue, which for Aristotle would be educational poetry.

At the lofty level of the *Divine Comedy*, Milton's *Paradise Lost* deserves mention. Plato discusses educational poetry in Book II of the *Republic*, and distinguishes the "greater stories" (*meizous muthoi*) from the lesser (*Republic* ii.377c). The greater stories would include the fundamental religious stories that are found in every culture, such as Genesis or the Bhagavad Gita. Less inclusive are moral allegories, such as Spenser's *Faerie Queene*, or Bunyan's *Pilgrim's Progress*, and morality plays such as *Everyman*. Tolstoy wrote fables to educate children, and children's stories are a major subgroup of educational poetry. Bruno Bettelheim has analyzed the educational function of fairy tales (1976). The new media make possible new forms of educational poetry, such as the television series *Supernanny*, already mentioned as illustrating rational rule in the family. The episodes have a common dramatic structure, beginning from scenes of children misbehaving, proceeding to scenes in which Jo Frost observes the family, talks with its members, and initiates appropriate new activities of various kinds. These scenes are interspersed with scenes of Jo and the family members telling us their own thoughts. She then leaves the family for several days and returns to critique how well the parents have done on their own, and the drama ends with scenes of family harmony or at least the hope that it will be achieved. Embodied in educational poetry, Jo Frost's practical wisdom is likely to have an enduring impact on a large number of parents and family counselors.

Chapter 12

TRANSITION TO THE SPECIFIC ENDS OF IMITATIVE POETRY

Imitative poetry is either narratable or dramatic and actable; the latter is comedy or tragedy or mimes or satyr plays.
The external sources of the ends of historical and educational poetry provide starting points for saying something about these kinds of poetry, but the internal source of the end of imitative poetry simply directs us back to what this poetry is, which is imitation, and which has been discussed in *Poetics* I. Our starting point for the further discussion of the end of imitative poetry must therefore be what has been said about it in *Poetics* I. Let us review this, omitting from consideration what is said about the specific end of tragedy and all that follows from this, for our concern is with the generic end of imitative poetry.

In *Poetics* I, at the beginning of the account of the genesis of poetics, it is said that "all men delight in imitations. A sign of this is what happens in the presence of the works (*epi tōn ergōn*)" (4.1448b 8–10). The natural delight in imitation leads to imitations that are made for the sake of the delight in them, and in which delight is a cause of itself, and this imitation is imitative poetry.

If the end of imitative poetry in general is pleasure in the imitation, then the end of each species of imitative poetry will be pleasure in the imitations that belong to that species, or, as Aristotle says, "one ought to seek in tragedy, not every pleasure, but that which is appropriate" (14.1453b11, trans. Telford). Comedy also has an appropriate pleasure, which is not that of tragedy (13.1453a36). What is common to all imitative poetry as an end is pleasure in the imitation for its own sake, and the end of each species is its pleasure in the imitation that belongs to that species.

Pleasure, however, is relative to the things that are pleasant, and the things that are pleasant are indeterminate in number and nature and do not constitute a determinate genus. Therefore to say that the end of imitative poetry is pleasure in the imitation for its own sake, although true, is not an adequate statement of the end of poetry. Nevertheless, it can be used to solve certain problems with respect to the end of poetry, including the problem left over from Book I, whether tragedy or epic is more achieving to their common end, and the problem under consideration in the part of Book II corresponding to the part of the epitome that we are now considering, which appears to be, what are the species of poetry whose ends we need to examine?

If Aristotle were simply to discuss the ends of all existing species, we would have no reason to think the discussion formally complete, and this procedure would also entail much repetition, since the ends of different species resemble each other or may even be the same, as in the case of tragedy and epic. Aristotle therefore begins with the general distinction between narratable and actable poetry, and asks which more fully realizes the common end of imitative poetry, which is pleasure in the imitation for its own sake. This serves to answer also the question raised at the end of *Poetics* I with respect to tragedy and epic, which is more achieving of their end.

On what ground can actable poetry be said to be more pleasant than narratable poetry? In our time this problem takes the form of the relative merits of novels and films. No argument can show that every drama is more enjoyable than every narration, for this is not the case. All that can be shown is that one manner of imitation offers a greater potentiality for enjoyment than the other. Although we know from the epitome what Aristotle's conclusion is, we do not know what argument he used to reach it. An argument based on the parts of poetry, to the effect that spectacle, with its psychagogy or power to influence the soul (6.1450b16), is a source of pleasure possessed by actable but not by narratable poetry, and therefore dramatic poetry is superior to narrative poetry in its ability to produce pleasure, is found in his dialogue *On Poets* (Janko 2010, 359). It is not conclusive, however, for, as Aristotle argues in chapter 24, there are also advantages that narration has over stage presentation, as in being able to present many things occurring at once and in presenting the wonderful (*thaumastos*).

Perhaps Aristotle based his argument on the power to set things before our eyes (*pro ommatōn*). In the construction of elegant and memorable sayings, Aristotle says we should aim at metaphor, antithesis, and actuality (*energeia*), and actuality is achieved by words that set things before our eyes (*Rhet.* iii.10.1410b33–6). Explaining what he means by "before the eyes," Aristotle says, "I mean that things are set before the eyes by words that signify actuality" (ibid., 11.1411b25, trans. Freese). If actuality is attained in speech by words that set things before our eyes, still more will it be attained when events themselves are actually set before our eyes, as in dramatic poetry. Since pleasures are relative to what is pleasing, and are greater when what is pleasing is more fully actualized, if we take pleasure in events that are nar-

rated, our pleasure will in general be greater if the events are acted. Therefore the fullest realization of the pleasures of poetry will be possible in actable rather than narratable poetry.

The next problem is which of the four kinds of dramatic poetry, comedy,
tragedy, mimes, and satyr plays, most fully achieve the end of imitative poetry. Aristotle mentions the mimes of Sophron (*Poet.* 1.1447a28), of which
many fragments survive (Hordern 2004). These mimes are in prose and,
like comedies, imitate the actions of characters worse than ourselves, but
are without choral songs or dances. We have complete mimes by Herodas
from a later period (c. 300–250 BCE) which are similar to those of Sophron and are like abbreviated comedies. Since everything that is in mimes,
and more besides, is in comedies, we can conclude that comedies are more
achieving of the end than mimes. There is no counterpart to the mime in
the case of tragedy, that is, a single-episode tragedy, because the arousal and
removal of pity and fear require a number of episodes, whereas laughter can
be aroused and removed in a single episode.

In the satyr play, the noble hero of tragedy finds himself among satyrs.
The only satyr play that survives entire, the *Cyclops* of Euripides, is based on
the Cyclops episode of the *Odyssey*. It presents Odysseus as a thoroughly
admirable character who rescues the feckless satyrs from the dominion of
the brutal Cyclops. Satyrs tend to dwell on the lawless frontiers of civilization, and the poetic possibilities of the satyr play therefore resemble those
of a classic Western such as *High Noon*. The characters are sharply divided
into the good, the bad, and the intimidated, and the noble hero rescues the
intimidated from the oppression of the formidable villains. Such plays are
happy-ending tragedies, in which the full emotional possibilities of tragedy are not realized, for the hero himself does not suffer a tragic fate. The
pleasures of tragedy are therefore more fully realized in tragedies than in
satyr plays.

If the satyr play is to remain distinct from comedy, the dignity of the hero
must be preserved. The advice of Horace to writers of satyr plays suggests
there was some tendency for satyr plays to become comedies. He writes:

The poet who in tragic song first competed for a paltry goat soon
also brought on unclad the woodland Satyrs, and with no loss of
dignity (*gravitas*) roughly essayed jesting (*jocus*), for only the lure and
charm of novelty could hold the spectator, who, after observation of the
rites, was well drunken and in lawless mood. But it will be fitting so to
seek favour for your laughing, bantering Satyrs, so to pass from grave

to gay (*vertere seria ludo*), that no god, no hero, who shall be brought upon the stage, and whom we have just beheld in royal gold and purple, shall shift with vulgar speech into dingy hovels, or, while shunning the ground, catch at emptiness. (*Ars poetica* 220–30, trans. H. Rushton Fairclough)

If the tragic hero retains his dignity, and the action arouses pleasure and laughter, the pleasure will fall short of that of comedy, because the hero cannot himself be made a figure of fun. If the hero does not retain his dignity, the play becomes a comedy, and will not achieve a greater pleasure than comedy. Whether the satyr play is a happy-ending tragedy, or a comedy with a noble hero, or becomes a comedy, it does not achieve a fuller realization of pleasure than tragedy or comedy. There is no converse of the satyr play in the sense of a species of poetry in which a comic hero suffers a tragic fate, for this would hardly be pleasant at all. Neither mimes nor satyr plays, then, are more achieving of the end of imitative poetry than tragedy and comedy. Tragedy and comedy themselves clearly attain ends different in kind. Therefore, since the fullest realization of the ends of imitative poetry is in tragedy and comedy, and tragedy, except for its end, has already been discussed in Book I, Book II proceeds to complete the discussion of tragedy by discussing its end or power.

PART IV. *The End Of Tragedy*

Chapter 13
THE END OF TRAGEDY AS CATHARSIS

The end (*telos*) of tragedy can be considered either as its function (*ergon*), what it does, or as its power (*dunamis*), what it is able to do, as the first sentence of the *Poetics* says that it will speak about what the power of each species is. But since powers are defined by their function, a statement of the end of tragedy will be a statement of its function.

We have two statements of the function of tragedy; one is a part of the definition of tragedy in Book I; the other is in the epitome: our concern is to interpret the epitome's statement, but in order to do this, we must first account for the differences between the two formulations of tragedy's function.

Tragedy is an imitation . . . achieving through pity and fear a catharsis of such emotions (*Poet.* 6 1449b24–8).

Tragedy removes the fearful emotions of the soul by compassion and dread; it aims to have a symmetry of the fearful; it has as its mother pain (Epitome 3).

The first statement is part of a definition, and definition for Aristotle involves differentiating a genus: "He who defines a subject must put the subject into its genus and then add the differentiae" (*Topics* vi.1.139a28, trans. Forster). The genus of tragedy is imitation, and it is differentiated by its object, means, manner, and function. Three of the differentiae, the object, means, and manner of the imitation are essential to what it as imitation, while the fourth, its function, is not essential to imitation but to the union of imitation with a poetic end to make it poetry. The function of tragedy is said to be a catharsis through pity and fear of such emotions. If the function of other poetic species is also a catharsis, the catharsis of tragedy will be differentiated from other kinds of poetic catharsis by the emotions that are involved, pity and fear.

This statement of tragedy's function in the definition of tragedy is indeterminate in two respects. First, the function is said to be a catharsis, but catharsis is left undefined. Many have endeavored to recover Aristotle's meaning of catharsis, without reaching any generally accepted result, which gives particular interest to Aristotle's own account. Secondly, the definition of tragedy distinguishes two groups of emotions involved in catharsis, the removing emotions and the removed emotions, but the removed emotions are stated only indefinitely as emotions such as pity and fear.

The account of the function of tragedy in the epitome appears to be a definition of that function having the same form as the definition of tragedy. The genus of tragic catharsis is a removal of something from the soul rather than from a body. Catharsis of the soul as a function of tragedy is differentiated by what is removed from the soul, by what, to what end, and from what mother. These differentiae are again of two kinds. The removal of something from something and by something are essential to catharsis and apply to any catharsis, just as the three differentiae of imitation are essential to imitation and apply to any imitation. The end and mother of the catharsis, on the other hand, are not essential to what it is as catharsis, but to the union of emotional catharsis with an aim and a mother to make it the function of a poetic species.

Katharsis is an ordinary Greek word whose ordinary meaning is that of the English "cleansing." The definition of tragedy's function begins from its genus, which restricts the ordinary meaning to a catharsis of the soul. The phrase "of the soul" would be superfluous in a nondefinitional context because it would be taken for granted that emotions are emotions of the soul. Nearly all of the uses of *katharsis* in Aristotle's writings in fact refer to the catharsis of bodies.[1] Aristotle also uses the term to refer to the religious purification in Euripides's *Iphigenia in Tauris* (*Poet.* 17.1455b15), which includes both the purification of the soul from wrongdoing and guilt and the purification of sacred objects from the touch of polluted persons. The pollution requiring catharsis is imagined as permeating the body from the soul and transmitted to other bodies by touch. The metaphorical extension of catharsis from bodies to the soul is familiar from many examples. Lady Macbeth by washing her hands attempts to cleanse guilt from her soul, as baptism and other religious rituals represent a cleansing of sin from the soul. Macbeth seeks from the Doctor a psychotropic drug that would "cleanse the stuffed bosom of that perilous stuff / Which weighs upon the heart" (5.3.45–46). The two genera of catharsis are analogous as removals, but they are only analogous, not species of a genus.

"Tragedy removes the fearful emotions of the soul." The indefinite "emotions such as pity and fear" are here made definite as "the fearful emotions." The fearful emotions in a tragedy are removed when the feared events actually occur, for once they occur there is no longer occasion to fear that they are about to occur. The fearful emotions are replaced by different emotions, compassion and dread, which are the pity and fear aroused by the actual occurrence of what is feared. The pity and fear that precede the actual oc-currence of the tragic events are anticipatory, and, since anticipated pity is properly fear, pity disappears as a separate emotion when the removed emotions are specified, and we are left with only the fearful emotions as the emotions that are removed.

Similarly, the removing emotions are not stated generically as pity and fear, but specifically as compassion and dread. The definition of tragedy states the generic emotions of tragedy that characterize the work as a whole without distinguishing the emotions of its different parts. The account of pity and fear in Book I thus makes no distinction between the pity and fear that precede the tragic event and the pity and fear that follow it: "Pity relates to the misfortune of one who does not deserve it, fear to the misfortune of one like ourselves" (13.1453a4). Nothing is said or implied about whether the misfortune has actually occurred. The definition of tragic catharsis, on the other hand, requires that the emotions that are removed be distin-guished from the emotions that remove them, for otherwise there would be no removal and no catharsis. What are needed are terms to designate the species of pity and fear that are aroused by the actual occurrence of the tragic events, and for this compassion and dread, or however we choose to translate *oiktos* and *deos*, will do. Compassion, as distinguished from pity, does well enough in this respect, for the generic pity might be said to be-come compassion if the pitiable events actually occur. The English "dread" is only half right, however, as was said in the note to the translation, for it includes the awe and reverence that belong to *deos*, but not the alarm or affright that results from the actual occurrence of the feared event. The En-glish phrase "shock and awe" brings together the two components of *deos*.

This is not the first time the terms "compassion" and "dread" have ap-peared in the *Poetics*, as Janko has noted (1984, 137). Their first appearance is in adjectival form: "We must ask, therefore, among the things that befall us, what sort are those that appear dreadful (*deinos*) and lamentable (*oiktros*)" (14.1453b14). This is a context, like that of defining tragic catharsis, in which whether or not the suffering actually occurs must be taken into account, and in fact the occurrence or non-occurrence of the incident of suffering is a variable that is in this context explicitly introduced. There are also two other uses of *deinos* in Book I (13.1453a22, 19.1456b3), both of which are speaking of a response to an actually occurring event. The usage of "compassion" and "dread" in the epitome is thus consistent with the use of the corresponding adjectives in Book I, and Aristotle's terminology, although it may appear to be loose, is, once its dependence on context is taken into account, precise.

The change from the anticipatory to the actualized emotions begins with the change in the hero's fortunes. "In every tragedy there is both complication (*desis*) and resolution (*lusis*). . . . By complication I mean everything from the beginning of the tragedy to the last part before the change in fortune, by resolution the part from the beginning of the change to the end" (18.1455b24–29). The fearful emotions that are removed are therefore the emotions of the complication, and the compassion and dread that replace them are the emotions of the resolution. The meaning of catharsis that is embedded in the definition of the function of tragedy thus turns out be something that is found in every tragedy and is familiar to everyone. It is just the removal of fearful emotions by the actual occurrence of the feared events. This is catharsis, but not yet the function of tragedy. Catharsis simply as catharsis requires two further differentiae if it is to be catharsis as the function of tragedy.

We know from Aristotle's general requirements for a science that the end or function of poetry must belong to the same genus as its other causes, and the genus is in this way self-determining. When tragedy is considered simply as an imitative whole, as it is in Book I, the parts of tragedy other than the plot are for the sake of the plot, and "the incidents and the plot are the end of tragedy" (*Poet.* 6.1450a21–4, trans. Telford). When the tragedy is considered as an emotional whole, as it is in Book II, the incidents and the plot are for the sake of the emotions they arouse or remove, and the emotions of the complication are aroused for the sake of their removal in the resolution, and this is catharsis and the end of tragedy. There are thus in the tragedy two parallel sequences, the sequence of incidents and the sequence of emotions. Both may be expected to conform to Aristotle's general philosophic method in which parts and wholes are mutually interdependent. We can therefore expect from the imitative end some analogical guidance as to the nature of the emotional end.

The plot is a whole with beginning, middle, and completion (*teleutē*). A completion is that which itself naturally exists or comes to be after something else but after which there is nothing (7.1450.b27–31, trans. Telford). If the sequence of emotions in poetry corresponds to the sequence of incidents, its end will naturally exist or come to be after other emotions and be an emotion of completion that leaves nothing further to be felt, that is, the emotional end will be a resolution in the sense of a fulfillment, satisfaction, sufficiency, closure. If a tragedy simply removed the fearful emotions by actualizing the feared event, this would be a catharsis, but not the end of tragedy, because it would leave the painful emotions associated with the tragic events unresolved.

"Tragedy aims to have a symmetry of the fearful." Since symmetry is said to be the aim of the tragedy, it is a differentia that needs to be added to catharsis to make it the end or function of tragedy. The emotions that are symmetrical with the fearful emotions must be aroused along with the fearful emotions in the complication, for not only is the resolution generally too brief to permit the introduction of a new set of emotions symmetrical with the fearful emotions of the complication, but any new emotions introduced after the tragic events would tend to be consolatory emotions weakening the power of the tragedy by minimizing rather than maximizing the loss.

With the occurrence of the tragic events, the fearful emotions are removed, while the emotions symmetrical to them are carried over into the resolution. There thus enter into the resolution both the emotions aroused by the occurrence of the tragic events and the nonfearful emotions carried over from the complication. The emotional resolution of the tragedy unites these two sets of emotions in a completion which is self-sufficient and leaves nothing further to be felt. The pain of the tragic loss, when experienced as inevitably connected with symmetrical emotions deriving from what we value most, becomes incorporated in a resolution which, taken as a whole, is pleasant and self-sufficient.

The mother of tragedy is pain. This is the second differentia that needs to be added to make catharsis the function of tragedy. The mother of tragedy precedes the birth of tragedy. and the pain that is the mother of tragedy is the real pain of human existence. The painful events of real life and their imitation in poetry belong to different genera, however, and cannot be connected by a scientific statement about poetry itself, but they are here connected by a metaphor in which the pain of real life is said to be the mother of tragedy. The pain of tragedy is not identical with the pain of real life, but the pain of tragedy comes to be from the pain of real life and resembles it. The two emotional components of the resolution, the pain that results from the occurrence of tragic events and the nonfearful emotions that are necessarily connected with them and make the resolution possible, are thus analogous to the emotions that we feel when we really experience tragic events and try to reconcile ourselves to them. The way in which tragedy reconciles us to pain is thus an imitation of the way in which we become reconciled to pain in real life. This is not to say that the purpose of tragedy is to teach us how to deal with pain, which would transform tragedy into educational poetry. The purpose of tragedy is enjoyment for its own sake, and one of the things that is enjoyable for its own sake is experiencing in the tragedy painful events in a way that reconciles us to their pain. Any educational effect is incidental to the poetic end.

We can test whether these four components of the function of tragedy provide a complete account of its function by seeing whether they can be referred to the four causes, just as the four differentiae of imitation in the definition of tragedy provide a complete definition of tragedy.

The independent clause with which the epitome's statement begins, "Tragedy removes the fearful emotions of the soul," states what tragedy does, which would make it the formal cause of tragedy's function. As the formal cause of tragedy's function, it justifies calling the function as a whole a catharsis.

The dependent clause which follows states by what the fearful emotions are removed, which would make it an efficient cause. We would tend to think of the efficient cause of the removal as the change in the hero's fortunes, but this is neither homogeneous with the removal of emotions nor the proximate efficient cause of that removal. The homogeneous and proximate cause of the removal is the emotions by which the removal is effected.

The second principal part of the epitome's statement says the aim of tragedy's function is a symmetry of fearful, which is a "for the sake of what" and a final cause.

The third principal part of the epitome's statement says that tragedy has as its mother pain, which is a metaphorical statement that identifies that from which tragedy's function comes to be and is present in it, which would be its material cause. The interpretation of the mother of tragedy as a material cause is supported by *The Generation of Animals*, which says that the male provides both the form and the beginning of motion, the female the body and the matter (i.20.729a9). It is also supported by the other instance in which Aristotle uses "mother" metaphorically, in the first book of the *Physics*. In this instance, the metaphor derives from Plato, who, in the *Timaeus* (50c–d) distinguishes three principles of becoming: that which comes to be, that in which it comes to be, and that of which it is a likeness. Plato identifies that in which it comes to be as the receptacle (*chōra*) or mother, that of which it is a likeness as the pattern (*paradigma*) or father, and that which comes to be (*to gignomenon*) as the offspring. Aristotle likens these three principles to his own principles of matter, form, and composite: "What persists is the joint cause, with the form, of what comes to be, like a mother" (*Phys.* i.9.192a14).

The epitome, then, gives us a complete set of the causes of the function of tragedy. Let this suffice as an initial account of the function of tragedy.

Of the many who have endeavored to recover Aristolte's meaning of tragic catharsis, the two that I know of who have most closely approximated to it are Jonathan Lear and Goethe. Lear examines "all the important tra-ditional interpretations" of catharsis under three heads: (1) a purgation of emotions, understood as similar to a medical purgation, (2) a purification of emotions, and (3) an education of emotions. The different ways in which these interpretations fall short enable Lear to formulate seven constraints which any acceptable interpretation of tragic catharsis must satisfy. Offering an interpretation that fits within these constraints, he concludes:

> In the *Rhetoric* Aristotle says that those who have already experi-enced great disasters no longer feel fear, for they have already experi-enced every kind of horror (ii.5.1383a3–5). In tragedy, we are able to put ourselves imaginatively in a position in which there is nothing further to fear. There is consolation in realizing that one has experienced the worst, there is nothing further to fear, and yet the world remains a rational place in which a person can conduct himself with dignity. Even in tragedy, perhaps especially in tragedy, the fundamental goodness of man and the world are reaffirmed. (1992, 335)

Here we clearly see the Aristotelian conception of tragic catharsis as the removal of fears through their actualization. That the world remains a ratio-nal place in which a person can conduct himself with dignity presupposes the feelings carried over from the complication which are required for a resolution that reaffirms the fundamental goodness of man and the world. Putting ourselves imaginatively into the resolution implies the possibility of an analogous resolution in real life.

Reconciling culmination is a topic that is common to the different accounts of tragic catharsis, but the accounts differ according their *archai*, and can be initially distinguished by their method. Goethe shares Aristotle's resolu-tive method, and his interpretation of Aristotle's tragic catharsis brings out the essential role of a resolution or reconciling culmination. Goethe writes (1967, 12:342, trans. Wenning), "Every one who has concerned himself to some extent about the theory of poetic art in general, but of tragedy in par-ticular, will recall a passage from Aristotle which has given much trouble to commentators, without their having been able to agree entirely about its complete meaning. . . . My ideas and conviction about the passage in ques-tion I believe can best be expressed by a translation of it." He translates the catharsis clause as "after a period of pity and fear, the play ends with an adjustment (*Ausgleichung*) of these passions." Aristotle's *summetria* is what makes possible Goethe's *Ausgleichung* ("equalling out"). Goethe goes on to say, "He [Aristotle] understands by catharsis this reconciling culmination (*aussöhnende Abrundung*) which is really demanded of all drama, and in fact of all poetic works" (1967, 12:343, trans. Wenning). Although Goethe shares Aristotle's resolutive method and essential realities and is thus in remarkable agreement with Aristotle on the need for a reconciling culmination in all poetry, his creative principles and personal perspectives prevent him from giving further content to the resolution, which depends on the creativity of the individual poet. There is no mention of a removal of fears through their realization, and the catharsis is simply the reconciling culmination itself. It is left to the poet to "produce in a definite way something attractive, worth seeing and worth hearing." The poet fulfills his duty by "raising important issues and worthily solving them" (ibid., 12:345).

Hegel's dialectical method also leads to a reconciling resolution, but the reconciliation is achieved, not through the symmetry of the opposed emotions, but through a higher emotion afforded by a glimpse of eternal justice. Commenting on Aristotle's definition of tragic catharsis, Hegel writes, "Above mere fear and tragic sympathy therefore stands that sense of reconciliation [*Gefühl der Versöhnung*] which the tragedy affords by the glimpse of eternal justice. In its absolute sway this justice overrides the relative justification of one-sided aims and passions because it cannot suffer the conflict and contradiction of naturally harmonious [*ihrem Begriffe nach einigen*] ethical powers to be victorious and permanent in truth and actuality" (Hegel 1975, 2:1198). This glimpse of eternal justice which reconciles the conflicting ethical powers of the tragedy is comparable to the glimpse of the form of the good in Plato which reconciles seemingly opposed goods.

Another possibility is represented by Milton. In "Of that sort of Dramatic Poem which is calle'd Tragedie" which precedes his *Samson Agonistes*, Milton, himself a Christian agonist (Watson 1985, 75), interprets Aristotle's catharsis to be the outcome of the action of antagonistic passions on each other: "Tragedy, as it was antiently compos'd hath been ever held the gravest, moralest, and most profitable of all other Poems: therefore said by *Aristotle* to be of power by raising pity and fear, or terror, to purge and reduce them to just measure with a kind of delight, stirr'd up by reading or seeing those passions well imitated" (Milton 1982, 133). Here the pity and fear raised by the tragedy are purged and reduced to just measure by the delight stirred up by the imitation itself. In all of these interpretations we can see how Aristotle is interpreted to accord with the method of the interpreter.

David Hume, following the method of Newton described in the first chapter, which explains the whole by the laws governing the parts, writes,

"It seems an unaccountable pleasure, which the spectators of a well-written tragedy receive from sorrow, terror, anxiety, and other passions, that are themselves disagreeable and uneasy" (1987, 216). "The pleasure, which poets, orators, and musicians give us, by exciting grief, sorrow, indignation, compassion, is not so extraordinary or paradoxical, as it may at first sight appear. The force of imagination, the energy of expression, the power of numbers, the charms of imitation; all these are naturally, of themselves, delightful to the mind: And when the object presented lays also hold of some affection, the pleasure still rises upon us, by the conversion of this subordinate movement into that which is predominant. The passion, though, perhaps, naturally, and when excited by the simple appearance of a real object, it may be painful; yet is so smoothed, and softened, and mollified, when raised by the finer arts, that it affords the highest entertainment" (ibid., 222–23). The pleasure of tragedy is first the sum of the component pleasures which for Milton purge and reduce to just measure the pity and fear raised by the tragedy, but which, for Hume, by its predominance, converts a subordinate painful passion to its own movement, implying a common substrate that can be converted from pain to pleasure, although Hume's phenominalism does no permit him to go beyond the phenomena, as is the case also in his analysis of causality. Hume's explanation of the pleasure of tragedy is not presented as an interpretation of catharsis, but if it is viewed as an interpretation of catharsis, the removal of the painful emotions in the resolution of tragedy would be the result of a necessary law of the passions in accordance with which subordinate motions are converted to predominant ones.

The reconciliation of tragedy can thus be conceived as a reconciling union of symmetrical feelings, as in Aristotle, Goethe, and Lear; or as a reconciliation of opposed feelings through a higher feeling which unites them, as in Hegel; or as a purging and reducing of emotions by emotions of an opposite kind, as in Milton; or as a predominant emotion converting a subordinate emotion to its own movement, as in Hume. They are all talking about the same thing, but formulate its essence in accordance with their respective *archai*.

Let us now proceed to a fuller account of each of the components of the function of tragedy.

Chapter 14
THE FEARFUL EMOTIONS

The symbolon argument noted several points at which *Poetics* I is incomplete because all discussion of the ends of poetry is deferred to *Poetics* II: the analysis of comedy, the explanation of catharsis, and whether tragedy or epic is more achieving of their common end. We recognized another incompleteness, the absence of generic accounts of melody and spectacle, when we found it supplied by the epitome. Knowing that the end of tragedy is the removal of the fearful emotions of the soul, we can now add yet another incompleteness in Book I and discover from the epitome how it is to be supplied. The incompleteness is in the rationale for the distinction among the species of tragedy as given in Book I, which we would expect to depend, like the difference among the kinds of poetry, upon differences in their ends. But Book I says only that the species correspond to the parts of the plot that had been mentioned: (1) recognition and reversal, (2) suffering, (3) character, and (4) spectacle. No explanation is given as to why these parts distinguish the species of tragedy. We can now see that these parts distinguish the species of tragedy because they are the sources of the fearful emotions that are aroused and removed in the tragedy.

(1) In the complex tragedy the whole is reversal and recognition, and the fearful emotions are aroused by the prospect of these changes. These changes are the means by which tragedy produces the greatest effect upon the soul (6.1450a33), and therefore, just as tragedy is the paradigmatic species of serious poetry, so the complex tragedy is the paradigmatic species of tragedy.

(2) In the tragedy of suffering, the whole is suffering, and the fearful emotions are aroused by this suffering. Suffering as a part of the plot is defined as destructive or painful action such as the appearance of death, severe pain, woundings, and the like (11.1452b12). But in tragedies in which the whole is suffering, we find that the suffering is psychological rather than physical. Sophocles's *Ajax* is cited as an example of the tragedy of suffering, and in this play the proud Ajax is successively more dishonored as a result of his attempts to regain his honor. The case is incidentally interesting because it shows how Ajax can suffer even after death by being refused burial, an example of suffering befalling the dead (*Eth.* 1.11.1101a32). The proud care about being honored after death. In Aristotle's other example of the tragedy

of suffering, the Ixion tragedies, Ixion presumably suffers disgrace when he embraces a cloud thinking it to be Hera, much as Ajax suffers dishonor when he kills sheep and cattle thinking them to be those who have dishonored him.

(3) In ethical tragedies, or tragedies of character, the action begins from the choice or task of a character, and the fearful emotions are aroused by this choice or task. One of Aristotle's examples is *Peleus*, which we do not have, but Peleus in the myth, like Joseph in Genesis, is confronted with the advances of the wife of a person in authority who has helped and befriended him, and we may suppose the choice that leads to his suffering is his refusal of her advances. Most of Shakespeare's tragedies are tragedies of character—Juliet chooses Romeo against the wishes of her family; Richard the Third is determined to prove a villain in a piping time of peace; Brutus joins the conspiracy against Caesar; Hamlet is charged with avenging his father's murder; Macbeth goes along with his wife's plan for fulfilling the witches' prophesy that he will become King of Scotland; Antony prefers Cleopatra to Roman politics, Coriolanus treats the plebeians with contempt.

(4) In tragedies of spectacle, the fearful emotions are aroused by the spectacle. Aristotle's first example is *The Daughters of Phorcys*. Phorcys is remarkable for his monstrous daughters—the three Graiae, who had but one eye among them, the three Gorgons, of whom Medusa was one, and Scylla. The *Prometheus* is cited as a second example of the tragedy of spectacle. At the beginning of Aeschylus's *Prometheus Bound*, we see Prometheus chained to a lonely peak in the Caucasus, a wedge driven through his breast into the rock, and there he remains, suffering physically but psychologically defiant, throughout the entire play. Tragedies taking place in Hades are also cited. In our time the cinema has greatly expanded the possibilities for tragedies of spectacle. The early horror films such as *Frankenstein, Dracula,* and *The Strange Case of Dr. Jekyll and Mr. Hyde* belong to this species, as well as later ones such as Alfred Hitchcock's *Psycho*. More recently, the technology of special effects has led to a plethora of fearful spectacles—perfect storms, tornadoes, volcanoes erupting, towering infernos, man-eating sharks, dinosaurs resurrected, asteroids headed toward the earth, war, nuclear devastation, global climate change, and invasions of aliens from outer space.

Chapter 15
THE REMOVAL OF EMOTIONS BY EMOTIONS

We have found a reflexive self-determination of tragedy in both the plot and the catharsis of emotions. In both cases the reflexive self-determination of the whole depends on the reflexive self-determination within the ruling part. In the case of tragedy considered simply as imitation, the self-determination of the whole depends on the self-determination of the plot. In the case of tragedy considered as an emotional whole, the self-determination is found in the removal of emotions by emotions in catharsis.

This reflexivity in the whole because of a reflexivity in the ruling part is illustrated by the other Aristotelian disciplines. The self-determination of formal logic depends on the self-determination of the syllogism by its premises. The self-determination of nature depends on the internal principles of motion or natural bodies. The self-determination of living bodies depends on the self-determination of the soul. The self-determination of the universe depends on an immanent God whose thinking is a thinking on thinking (*noēsis noēseōs noēsis*) (*Metaph.* xii.9.1074b34). The self-determination of a rational agent depends on his own rationality, and the self determination of the community depends on the rationality of its rulers. The self-determination of rhetorical persuasion depends on the mind of the audience inventing itself (Watson 2001, 391).

All imitative poetry is self-determined by its end, and the definition of tragic catharsis makes clear that this self-determination is the removal of emotions by emotions. Catharsis is thus the self-activity of imitative poetry, and the ends of its different species will be catharses distinguished by the emotions that are removed. Differences in the emotions removed by catharsis are differences in the end of imitation that are the counterpart of the differences in the means, object, and manner of imitation that are formulated in *Poetics* I. All our emotions are accompanied by either pleasure or pain (*Eth.* ii.5.1105b23; *Rhet.* ii.1.1378a21), and the primary difference among emotions is therefore between those that are accompanied by pleasure and those that are accompanied by pain. The emotions removed in tragic and comic catharsis differ in this respect, and this makes their catharsis paradigmatic with respecto to the possibilities for emotional catharsis.

The treatment of tragedy in Book I is about tragedy as imitation. Emotions enter into the argument from time to time, but only in order to determine what the imitation should be. The treatment of tragedy in Book II, on the other hand, is all about tragedy as emotional. Catharsis is concerned throughout with emotions: it is the removal of emotions, it removes them by emotions, the end of tragedy is a symmetry of emotions, and the mother of tragedy is an emotion.

Emotions have important roles in other disciplines besides poetics. In psychology the emotions are treated theoretically as attributes of living things. In ethics the dispositions to feel emotions are matter formed by the virtues and vices. In politics, the legislator is concerned with the formation of virtue in the citizens, with the removal of excessive emotions, and with the emotions as a cause of revolution. Rhetoric arouses emotions not in order to remove them, which would in rhetoric be pointless, but so that they will influence our judgment. These differences depend on the different disciplinary perspectives, and what distinguishes the poetic treatment of emotions is that the emotions are aroused and removed for their own sake. An anthology of poetry is a collection of emotions to be valued for their own sake, and a library of imaginative literature is like a grand museum of feeling. In poetry we find a variety and richness and depth of emotion that go beyond what we could otherwise experience. It is the most intense emotional experiences of tragedy and comedy that provide the paradigms for the treatment of emotions as ends in themselves.

Emotions are self-determining only in a very limited way. Emotions are themselves undergoings, but they are capable of producing effects. In biology, we see them producing biological effects on heart rate, perspiration, facial color, pupillary size, and much else. In ethics we see them determining our choices, and even, in the case of incontinence (*akrasia*), overruling the choices of the whole self-system with its good habits and rationality. In politics, they produce revolutions. In rhetoric, they influence our judgment.

But in poetry, where we are concerned with the effects of emotions on emotions rather than on anything else, we find that all they do is remove each other. The activity of emotions is simply catharsis. They are generated by the incidents of the plot, but have the power to remove preceding emotions, including themselves as preceding emotions. Considered as an imitation of action, the form of tragedy is a plot in which beginning, middle, and completion are united by necessity or probability. Considered as emotional, its form is a catharsis in which emotions aroused in the complication are removed in the resolution.

The removal of the fearful emotions in tragic catharsis is through the emotions aroused by the actualization of the fears, but the fearful emotions can also be removed by emotions of an opposite kind. Aristotle in the *Rhetoric* cites Gorgias on this point: "Gorgias said that you should kill your opponents' earnestness with jesting and their jesting with earnestness, in which he was right" (iii.18.1419b4, trans. Roberts). These two possibilities for the removal of emotions give rise to two kinds of catharsis of the fearful emotions. In the best kind of tragedy, fears are removed by their own actualization, and in the second-best kind, they are removed without their actualization. The *Odyssey* is an epic rather than a tragedy, but it illustrates the second-best kind of tragic plot. Odysseus survives one fearful situation after another, principally through his own ingenuity, but with help from Athena, and our fears for what may happen to him are finally removed when he slaughters the suitors. Here the removal is the result of the hero's own action in removing the cause of the fears. In *Iphigenia in Tauris*, the fear that Iphigenia will unknowingly sacrifice her brother is removed by her discovery of who he is.

We have already noted how Goethe's resolutive method leads him to recognize Aristotle's tragic catharsis as resolutive. It also leads him to recognize the second possibility for the resolution, as well as its limitations. Aristotle, he says, "understands by catharsis this reconciling culmination which is really demanded of all drama, and in fact of all poetic works. In tragedy this takes place by a kind of human sacrifice; now it may really be achieved or, by intervention of a favoring deity, be fulfilled by a substitute, as in the case of Abraham and Agamemnon; enough, a reconciliation, a solution at the close is indispensable, if the tragedy is a complete poetical work. This solution, however, when accomplished by means of a favorable and desirable outcome, approaches a mediocre kind of art, as in the return of Alcestis" (Goethe 1967, 343, trans. Wenning).

The contexts in which each type of catharsis is best are discussed by Aristotle in chapters 13 and 14 of the *Poetics*. The different problems of the two chapters are stated in inverse order at the end of chapter 14: "Concerning the construction of the incidents and of what sort the plot ought to be, then, what has been expressed is adequate" (1454a13–15, trans. Telford). In chapter 13, which concerns the problem of what sort the plot ought to be, it is argued that the most beautiful tragic plot is completed in misfortune, and that the plot which is completed in contrary fortunes for the better and the worse, like the plot of the *Odyssey*, ranks second. The pleasure in the second-beat kind of tragic catharsis, Aristotle says, is not that of tragedy, but rather that which is appropriate to comedy (13.1419b4). In chapter 14, on the other hand, which concerns the problem of the construction of incidents of suffering, it is argued that the most beautiful treatment of actions that cause suffering is for the agent to be about to perform the action, but, recognizing the victim in time, not perform it, as in *Iphigenia in Tauris*. The action which is done in ignorance and followed by the recognition ranks second. This difference between the suffering that is best as a part of a tragic plot and the suffering that is best as an incident of suffering may be a problem for Platonists, who suppose that all goods derive from one good and must be compatible, but not for Aristotle, for whom different goods are only analogous and relative to that of which they are goods. A tragic outcome is best for a tragic plot, in which the whole complication can be used both to make the outcome inevitable and to arouse nonfearful emotions that persist after the tragic outcome and make the final resolution possible. If such a complication does not end in a tragic outcome, we feel cheated. The full poetic potentialities of the catharsis of fearful emotions are not realized. But if we consider simply the incident of suffering itself, the best way of treating it is not through its actual occurrence, which in itself is simply painful, but rather the way it is treated in the second-best plot, in which the suffering is a potentiality that is not actualized. This kind of catharsis has poetic possibilities of a different kind from those of tragic catharsis in the strict sense. These are illustrated by the plot of the *Odyssey*, in which such incidents are repeated a number of times before the final incident, in which all occasion for further fear is removed.

This kind of catharsis resembles in its form the catharsis of comedy, which we also need to consider here. The statement of the function of comedy in the definition of comedy corresponds exactly to the statement of the function of tragedy in the definition of tragedy: comedy achieves "through pleasure and laughter the catharsis of such emotions." Elder Olson, following Bernays and Bywater, views this as an aping that reveals the author's failure to understand the definition of tragedy. Speaking of the Tractatus Coislinianus, which, with Janko's emendations, we are calling the epitome, and using Bywater's improbable dating, Olson writes,

The *Tractate* is an anonymous piece, written somewhere before the first century B.C. by someone who knew Aristotle's definition [of tragedy], but—in my opinion, at least—did not quite understand it or its function, for in aping it he assigns to comedy the power of catharsizing, through pleasure and laughter, pleasure and laughter themselves. Why anyone should want to get rid of pleasure or be pleased by getting rid of pleasure, or how he could get rid of pleasure and still have it, he fails to say. (Olson 1968, 45)

Olson's objections seem somewhat obtuse, since he has just said that pleasure and laughter are removed *through* pleasure and laughter. We want to be pleased and to laugh, and insofar as pleasure and laugher are removed *through* pleasure and laughter, there is no way we can have them without removing them. What we experience, however, is the pleasure and laughter, not their removal.

This in fact is what Aristotle's choice of the defining word of catharsis indicates. The Greek *huphairei* has connotations that "removes" does not have. There is no English word that captures the connotations of the Greek word, which corresponds etymologically to the Latin *surriptei* (takes away secretly), the verb from which we have the English "surreptitious." *LSJ* offers the following English equivalents of the Greek verb: "*draw or take away from under. 2. take away underhand, filch away; diminish gradually; purloin, steal; remove; gradually take away.*" The removal of emotions in catharsis may therefore be gradual and unnoticed. We do not experience the removal of pleasure and laughter in comedy as a removal of these emotions, but simply the pleasure and laughter themselves, and it is only afterward, when we are laughed out, so to speak, that we may become aware of it as a removal, which in this respect is like a theft. It is only in the second best kind of tragedy that we are likely to experience catharsis as a removal; in the best kind of tragedy and in comedy we simply experience the emotions themselves.

The catharsis of laughter produced by a joke may involve an expectation of a punch line, but the catharsis of laughter in comedy is not said to be the catharsis of an expectation of laughter, but of laughter itself. What, then, removes the laughter? It is not the laughter of the next joke, for the laughter ordinarily ceases before the next joke is told. In this case the laughter removes itself through its own actualization—it is removed by laughing, by the expression of the laughter. The catharsis of emotions in both tragedy and comedy is through the actualization of their defining emotions, although the actualization of anticipatory emotions takes place through the actualization of what is anticipated, while the actualization of non-anticipatory emotions takes place directly through their expression.

There is a difference also in the form of the catharsis as a whole. Every joke is a mini-catharsis, and the comedy as a whole achieves a catharsis of laughter as the cumulative effect of many small catharses. In this respect it resembles the catharsis of fearful emotions in the second best kind of tragedy, for this, too, can depend on the cumulative effect of a number of small catharses. The difference between the one big catharsis of the best kind of tragedy and the many small catharses of comedy explains why the form of tragedy in Book I, the plot, becomes in Book II one part of its matter, whereas the form of comedy as treated in Book II is not a single big form of the laughable, but many different forms of the laughable, each of which can be the form of a joke.

The fearful emotions are anticipatory, and are realized by the actual occurrence of the feared events, whereas laughter is not an anticipatory emotion, and is removed simply by its expression. Pleasure, the other generic emotion of comedy, can, however, be anticipatory, and while comedies need not have plots of complication and resolution, most in fact do. The incidents of the plot lead us to hope for and expect a happy resolution, and when this occurs, there is a catharsis of these anticipatory emotions by emotions that are not the same as the anticipatory emotions, but are also pleasant. The counterpart in comedy of the second-best tragic plot would be a comic plot in which pleasant anticipations were removed by emotions of an opposite kind, as by the discovery that the anticipated happiness is forever impossible. But no one writes comedies with tragic endings, except perhaps to show that there are no constraints on the freedom of the poet.

Chapter 16
THE AIM OF TRAGEDY: SYMMETRY

Tragedy . . . aims to have a symmetry of the fearful.
Symmetry is the right proportion of two or more things to each other, as health is said to be the symmetry of the hot and the cold (*Phys.* vii.3.246b5). It is the poetic analogue of the ethical mean, for just as the ethical mean discriminates better and worse in the functioning of man, symmetry discriminates better and worse in the functioning of tragedy. Everyone acts, but only the actions of a good person are in accordance with the mean, and similarly all tragedies achieve a catharsis, but only a good tragedy achieves a catharsis though symmetry. A tragedy that aroused only fearful emotions and then removed them by the realization of the fear would have a catharsis, but it would be a bad tragedy. Symmetry thus has an important role in the analysis of the function of tragedy, for it is the principle that distinguishes better and worse in the functioning of tragedies.

Both symmetry and the mean are general formulas for ends that depend on particular circumstances and are apprehended by mind rather than demonstration. The ethical mean is not right because it is between two extremes (this is the rhetorical mean — see *Rhet.* i.6.1363a2), but a mean because it is right, that is, because it accords with both ourselves and the situation as they actually are, not as we might mistakenly think them to be. Similarly, tragic symmetry is not the result of applying a general rule, but of making the play in accordance with a true perception of the emotional import of the fearful and nonfearful components in their relation to each other.

The ethical mean and poetic symmetry differ from one another, however, insofar as the ethical mean is a single term occupying the right place between the extremes of excess and deficiency, whereas symmetry is the right proportion of two terms to each other, and each of them may be made as great or as small as possible provided the other is kept in the right proportion to it. Tragic symmetry does not moderate or limit the intensity of the tragic emotions, but is rather the principle in accordance with which they can be made as intense as possible. In ethics one may be disposed to be too fearful, but in tragedy an extreme of fear is desirable provided the fear is subject to catharsis, that is, to removal.

Symmetry is Aristotle's answer to the problem of how excellence in the imitative arts can be formulated. We can expect it to be universal in its application to all imitative art, and it applies to emotions as embodied in the individual work. It can apply to any emotion, and, because it is a ratio rather than a mean, to emotions of any intensity.

The symmetry of fear implies other emotions that are symmetrical with fear. What these may be is left indefinite, which implies that they *are* indefinite, not species of a genus. Fear is a painful emotion, and all our emotions are accompanied by either pleasure or pain (*Eth*. ii.5.1105b23; *Rhet.* ii.1.1378a21). What balances fear is therefore presumably feelings accompanied by pleasure. Since pleasure is indefinite in its causes, so are the feelings accompanied by pleasure.

Milton and Hume view the pleasures of tragedy as pleasures deriving from the imitation itself. But tragedy cannot imitate the reconciliation possible in real life if the pleasures that are symmetrical with the pains are the pleasures of the imitation itself, for these can hardly be balanced by the delights of imitation,. They must rather be balanced by emotions of an opposite kind which also arise from what is imitated. Poetry can then feelingly realize the symmetry of pains and joys in the human condition and so reconcile us to it. The two basic requirements for a good tragedy are the plot with the inevitability of a painful outcome, which belongs to the tragedy as imitation and is treated in Book I, and the symmetry of the nonfearful to the fearful, which is required for tragic catharsis and is treated in Book II.

We have said that the emotions that are symmetrical to the fearful emotions must originate in the complication. If the nonfearful emotions are to be symmetrical with the fearful emotions of the complication and balance them, they must be comparable to them in magnitude. Since the whole of the complication is concerned to arouse fearful emotions, the arousal of the nonfearful emotions must be a substantial part of the tragedy. Scenes of comic relief are not what is intended. Further, the cause of the nonfearful emotions must be consistent with the requirements of the tragic plot set forth in Book I. If we think of introducing the nonfearful into a plot imitating one action with incidents bound together by necessity or probability, it is evident that the nonfearful cannot be something extraneous to the tragic plot, but must be inseparably bound up with the tragic plot itself. The fearful and the nonfearful must be like the two sides of a symmetrical figure. Further, opposed emotions tend to drive each other out, as is implied by Aristotle's approving citation of Gorgias in the *Rhetoric* already quoted. But if the nonfearful drives out the fearful, the catharsis is ruined rather than perfected. What is needed, therefore, is a symmetry between the fearful and the nonfearful in which the nonfearful is not only enjoyable for its own sake but also increases the fear. It is difficult to see how the conditions which the nonfearful must meet can in fact be met.

Since we are here discussing the principle that perfects the emotional power of tragedy, we may expect it to be exemplified in all good tragedies. We need not try to solve the problem of symmetry ourselves, since we can observe how it has already been solved by the tragic poets. It will suffice here to look for the principal symmetry in an ancient and a modern example of each species of tragedy.

(1) Beginning with tragedies of reversal and recognition, and with *Oedipus the King*, it appears that what balances the fearful in this tragedy is our pleasure in Oedipus's uncompromising determination to solve the riddle of the Theban plague and the process of inquiry and discovery to which this determination leads. Aristotle says at the beginning of the *Poetics* that learning is most pleasant, not only to philosophers, but to others as well, however little they share in it (4.1448b13). The ideal plot from the standpoint of symmetry is thus one in which the activity of inquiry, which should lead to the greatest happiness, leads instead to the greatest misery. This particular symmetry helps to make *Oedipus* the paradigmatic tragedy of the paradigmatic species of a paradigmatic art. The magnitude of our enjoyment of inquiry and discovery is comparable to that of the fearful because the whole of the complication is inquiry and discovery. It is part of the necessary and probable sequence that leads to the feared outcome because it is precisely through inquiry and discovery that the feared outcome comes to pass. This pleasure in inquiry and discovery does not drive out the fear, however, but rather intensifies it because with each new inquiry and discovery the fearful outcome appears more inevitable and our fears are increased. As we might expect, we have in *Oedipus the King* a paradigmatic example of the symmetry of the fearful and the nonfearful, the nonfearful being in this case the pleasure of inquiry and discovery.

Othello is also a tragedy of recognition and reversal, but the tragic outcome is not the result of a sustained inquiry, but of a sustained deception. It is essential to the plot that Othello make no discovery at all until the final recognition and reversal. The source of the fearful emotions is the likelihood that the love of Othello and Desdemona will be destroyed by the machinations of Iago. The machinations of Iago are fearful because of his demonic skill and uncertain motivation. His skill is a cleverness (*deinotēs*) without moral virtue (*Eth.* i.12.1144a25), and is a principal source of interest in the play. Because it is distinct from moral virtue, it can be appreciated as a skill even when it is being used for an abhorrent purpose. This appreciation does not imply ambivalence in the moral judgment of Iago nor any mitigation of the final injunction, "the torture—O enforce it!" But the skill obviously increases rather than diminishes our fears, because the greater it is, the more likely a tragic outcome. Two other sources of nonfearful emotions are the nobility of Othello and the perfection of feminine virtue in Desdemona. David Grene once remarked that Shakespeare's heroines are frequently overacted, but the possibilities of Desdemona are seldom realized. These sources of emotion also do not diminish our fears, but rather increase them, and not simply because they make the loss of Othello and Desdemona a greater loss, but because they make it more probable. This last point depends on Iago's motivation, which we do not know, nor does Iago, for the reasons that he gives to himself and others for his actions are patently spurious. Motivation of which the agent is unaware is unconscious motivation, and we know what it is only from what it attempts to do. What Iago's actions attempt to do is destroy Othello's love for Desdemona and ultimately even Desdemona herself, but Othello's death is entirely his own action. This suggests that his unconscious wish is to replace Desdemona in Othello's affections, but even if his motivation were thought to be simply the Satanic hatred by the evil of the good, the result would still be that the greater the nobility of Othello and the virtues of Desdemona, the greater the likelihood of the tragic outcome. We have, then, in *Othello* another fine example of the symmetry of the fearful and the nonfearful. The contrast between the pleasure in inquiry and discovery and the interest in skillful deception that escapes discovery makes clear why the nonfearful side of tragic symmetry is not a determinate genus.

(2) *Hamlet* is a tragedy of character, in which the fearful arises from the choice or task of a character. Hamlet's task is to avenge his father's foul and most unnatural murder, a task for which he rightly perceives himself particularly unsuited: "The time is out of joint; O cursed spite, / That ever I was born to set it right!" (1.1.189–90). What balances the fearful in *Hamlet* is our pleasure in Hamlet and all that he says and does. He is a true friend, a perceptive and accurate judge of others, richly introspective, witty, humorous, a master of the verbal arts, a discerning critic of drama, a man who acts with speed and skill in a crisis, an expert swordsman, a soldier, scholar, courtier, the glass of fashion and the mold of form, the observed of all observers, loved by the populace, and likely, had he been put on, to have proved most royal. He can do everything well, it seems, except avenge his father's murder, or solve the mystery of why he cannot. "I do not know / Why yet I live to say, 'This thing's to do'" (4.4.43–4). Hamlet, like Iago, does not know why he acts as he does—Shakespeare did not have to wait until Freud before accurately portraying the workings of the unconscious. As in the previous cases,

the arousal of pleasure and the arousal of fear are two symmetrical sides of the same thing. Both sides of the symmetry here lie in Hamlet himself, our pleasure in what he is, and our fear that, being what he is, tragedy will ensue.

We have noted that most of Shakespeare's tragedies are tragedies of character, and we may add that their most memorable component is often that which balances the fearful. Just as symmetry distinguishes a good from a poor tragic catharsis, so it is particularly in their achievement of symmetry that the great poets are distinguished from the lesser. The love of Romeo and Juliet balances the enmity of their families. Their love for each other increases rather than diminishes our fears not only by making the realization of the fear more probable but also by making it a greater evil. The love whose function is to bring new life here brings only death. This is the respect in which the Prince of Verona can appropriately say at the end, "For never was a story of more woe / Than this of Juliet and her Romeo." The endless fascination of Cleopatra balances the claims on Antony of the struggle for supremacy in Rome. The witches in *Macbeth* balance the fearful actions to which their prophecies lead. The success of *Coriolanus* when performed depends on our enjoying his pride.

(3) Turning to tragedies of suffering, and the *Ajax* of Sophocles, what balances the great suffering of Ajax is his great pride, particularly as exhibited in his responses to any slights to his honor. He prefers to fight alone rather than accept aid from Athena. He feels dishonored by the award of the panoply of Achilles to Odysseus, and when he attempts to vindicate his honor, he is, by the intervention of Athena, dishonored yet further, and sees no way to recover his honor except by death. His death makes it possible for Menelaus and Agamemnon to attempt to dishonor him yet further by denying him burial. In this way his pride is the cause of his dishonor, and the greater his pride, the more acutely he suffers from dishonor.

King Lear is also a tragedy of suffering—"I am a man / More sinn'd against than sinning" (3.2.59). There is in *King Lear* suffering of both body and soul, but the physical suffering is a foil for the psychological. The physical suffering of Gloucester is a foil for the psychological suffering of Lear, and the physical suffering of Lear himself is a foil for his psychological suffering— "But where the greater malady is fixed, / The lesser is scarce felt" (3.4.12). What balances the suffering in Lear is similar to the prideful responses of Ajax. It is the prodigious vigor of his responses to it, which contrasts with the passivity of Gloucester's responses to his suffering. What balances the fearful is not our pleasure in its cause, as in the previous cases, but in its effect. Lear himself provides the symmetry to the fearfulness of his suffering.

Each new indignity that Lear suffers calls forth fresh indignation, and the intensity of his responses, though in itself not fearful, serves to intensify rather than mitigate the perceived fearfulness of his sufferings. In the madness scene (4.6) Shakespeare takes advantage of nature's way of dealing with excessive grief, and Lear's comic appearance and antic behavior balance the grief that we know to be their cause. The final scene, with the death of Cordelia, provides a fine instance of emotional continuity, for the suffering reaches an intensity that can be balanced only by death itself, which appears not as fearful, but as desirable: "He hates him that would, upon the rack of this rough world / Stretch him out longer" (5.3.378–9).

(4) Finally we come to tragedies of spectacle and to Aeschylus's *Prometheus*. The tragedies of Aeschylus use a dialectical method, which unites opposites in a new synthesis, a method that is Plato's rather than Aristotle's. Nevertheless, we can see that the Aristotelian symmetry becomes in the *Prometheus* the symmetry of the dialectical opposites. It is the foreknowledge of Prometheus that balances the power of Zeus to inflict suffering. It enables Prometheus to endure his sufferings, to dismiss without regret the offer of Oceanus to intercede with Zeus on his behalf, to give to Io such comfort as comes from knowing the pain that is still in store for her, and, in the end, to show himself more powerful than Zeus insofar as Zeus for all his power cannot force from Prometheus the knowledge that would prevent Zeus's overthrow. Zeus's response to Prometheus's defiance is a further display of power, which only makes more evident the balancing power of Prometheus. The resolution of the opposition of knowledge and force requires the other two plays of the trilogy.

Shakespeare wrote no tragedies of spectacle, for which, Aristotle says, he cannot justly be censured (*Poet.* 18.1456a3–10), but modern tragedies of spectacle are plentiful, as we said. In Steven Spielberg's *Jurassic Park* (1993) our fears for what the dinosaurs may do are balanced by the pleasure of seeing these fearful creatures alive and in action, and our pleasure in their power is symmetrical to the fear of the harm this power may do.

We have been considering principally first-rate tragedies because we expect them to have symmetry, but inferior tragedies may also have symmetry and therefore powerful catharses. The film *Bonnie and Clyde* (1967) is not a great tragedy, if only because its characters are not superior people. Yet there is a fine symmetry between the zest with which Bonnie and Clyde pursue together their life of crime and the increasing inevitability of a fatal outcome. Our enjoyment of them and our fears for them increase until the final sustained fusillade realizes our fears, and, by realizing them, ends them.

Chapter 17

THE MOTHER OF TRAGEDY: PAIN

Tragedy . . . has as its mother pain.
This cause is stated by an analogical metaphor: as a mother is to her off-spring, so is pain to tragedy. Scientific predication must be within the same genus, as we have said, and analogical predication is therefore not scientific. Although a metaphorical expression is always obscure (*Topics* vi.2.139b34), it does make its meaning known to some extent because of the likeness in-volved (ibid., 140a9), and Aristotle does make use of metaphors in his sci-ences. To see why they are used, let us consider his use of them.

Aristotle in the preface to the theoretical sciences uses two metaphors with respect to truth. Truth is like the proverbial door that no one can fail to hit, and in this respect the investigation of truth is easy (*Metaph.* ii.1.993b5). But that it is also difficult is shown by the fact that it is possible to have a whole without the part (ibid., ii.1.993b6), that is, to see that it is a door but not what its parts are.[1] The cause of this difficulty lies in us rather than in things, for as the eyes of bats are to the blaze of day, so is the mind in our souls to the things that are by nature most evident of all (ibid., ii.1.993b9). A related metaphor with respect to truth appears at the beginning of the science of being: if the truth were to lie in what is apparent to us, to seek the truth would be to pursue flying game (ibid., iv.8.1009b38). An extended metaphor is used at the end of the *Metaphysics* (xii.10.1075a16, trans. Ross): "And all things are ordered together somehow, but not all alike,—both fishes and fowls and plants; and the world is not such that one thing has nothing to do with another, but they are connected, For all are ordered to-gether to one end, but it is as in a house, where the freemen are least at lib-erty to act at random, but all things or most things are already ordained for them, while the slaves and the animals do little for the common good, and for the most part live at random; for this is the sort of principle that consti-tutes the nature of each." This analogy is continued in the final sentence of the *Metaphysics* which, as was said in the first chapter, provides a transition to politics.

In the *Ethics*, Aristotle uses two metaphors with respect to happiness. At the beginning it is said that it is necessary to add to the definition of happi-ness as activity of soul in accordance with virtue, "in a complete life," "for one swallow does not make a summer, nor one day, and so too one day or a short time does not make a man blessed and happy" (*Eth.* i.7.1098a18, trans. Ross). At the end of the *Ethics* it is said that pleasure completes the activity that is happiness "as an end that supervenes as the bloom of youth does on those in the flower of their age" (ibid., x.4.1174b31, trans. Ross).

In the *Poetics*, Aristotle says at the beginning of the discussion of tragedy that the plot is the principle and, as it were, the soul, of tragedy (6.1450a38) and at the end that the mother of tragedy is pain.

Three things are common to these uses of metaphor. First, the metaphors are used in explaining the principles of the sciences, and, in particular their ends. Truth is the end of the theoretical sciences, and the highest truth concerns the good in the universe as a whole. Happiness is the end of the practical sciences. The plot is the form of tragedy and the end of tragedy as imitation (6.1450a22), and its functioning is the end of tragedy. As the soul is the form of the animal, and the end of its parts, and the activity or functioning of the soul is the end of the animal, so the plot is the form of tragedy, and the end of its parts, and its activity or functioning, catharsis, is the end of tragedy. The reason why first principles are explained by analogies is because, as first principles, they do not admit of demonstration or explanation within the genus.

The second thing that appears from the examples is that metaphors with respect to principles are of two kinds, initial and final, or in the case of the remarkable metaphorical transition from the end of the *Metaphysics* to the beginning of the *Ethics*, both at once. In between are the demonstrations of science, which are not metaphorical. At the beginning of a science, the principle is for the student a hypothesis, and metaphors are used to make its meaning clear. At the end of a science, the principle can be seen as ordering the whole, and thus understood as a principle, and metaphors are then used to make clear how the principle orders the whole.

Thus, at the beginning of the theoretical sciences metaphors are used to make clear the easiness of saying something true about nature, and the difficulty of discovering principles that are true of the whole, and at the end a metaphor is used to make clear the way in which the supreme good in the whole of nature orders the whole. In the *Ethics*, analogies and a metaphor are used at the beginning to make clear the principle, the definition of happiness, and its scope, and at the end a metaphor completes the account of happiness by making clear how pleasure is included in this ordering principle.

The third thing that appears from Aristotle's use of metaphors is their appropriateness to the sciences in which they are used. In the theoretical sciences they relate the abstruse to the familiar—the truth is like a barn door, the sophists are pursuing flying game, the universe is like a household. In the practical sciences, they make vivid what is obscure—happiness is like a summer with many days, pleasure is like the bloom of youth. In the poetic sciences, the initial metaphor of the plot as the soul of tragedy projects an ideal for the poet to imitate, the poem as a living thing. The final metaphor of pain as the mother of tragedy takes us back to the beginning of the *Poetics* when the antecedents of tragedy were discussed and thus relates the whole analysis of tragedy to its antecedents in human life. If pain, and particularly death (*Eth.* iii.6.1115a26), and particularly our own death and the death of those we care most about (*Poet.* 14.1453b19), were not an inescapable part of human life, we would have no tragedies. When it is said that pain is the mother of tragedy, it projects an ideal for the poet with respect to the end of tragedy, which is to make something wonderful and enjoyable out of pain.

Pain alone is not tragic. If pain is to become tragic, a father as well as a mother is required, and this is the art of tragedy through which pain becomes a source of pleasure. The so-called paradox of tragedy is that it derives pleasure from pain. Aristotle's metaphorical formulation of pain as the mother of tragedy implies both the paradox and its solution, for, while pain is indeed the mother of tragedy, it takes the whole art of tragedy to make the pleasure symmetrical with the pain. The derivation of pleasure from pain can be taken as the task of the tragic poet with respect to its end. This is not a matter of some formula or device, but requires all the skills of the tragic poet used to make a full-length tragedy with a symmetry of the fearful and nonfearful and an inevitable tragic end. This is why the metaphor of pain as the mother of tragedy concludes the entire discussion of tragedy, for only in relation to all that has preceded it in the *Poetics* do we understand how tragedy derives pleasure from pain.

Nietzsche in *The Birth of Tragedy from the Spirit of Music* (1872) uses the metaphor of the mother of tragedy, which he probably took from the epitome in Bernays's edition (1853). Nietzsche, like Bernays, had been a student in the Schule Ritschls and certainly knew Bernays's work.[2] Whether or not Nietzsche got the idea of a mother of tragedy from the epitome, his conception of the mother of tragedy is the same as Aristotle's so far as this is possible within their differing *archai*. Both Aristotle and Nietzsche use the metaphor to explain the role of tragedy in redeeming human existence from suffering. The identification of what the mother is reflects the archic differences between Aristotle and Nietzsche. Aristotle and Nietzsche are completely heteroarchic, that is, they have none of their *archai* in common. Aristotle's account of tragedy is in a poetic science that can be shared by all, whereas Nietzsche's account is an individual view, although he says in *An Attempt at Self-Criticism* (Nietzsche 1967, 24), "How I regret now that in those days I still lacked the courage (or immodesty?) to permit myself in every way an individual language of my own for such individual views and hazards." Tragedy for Aristotle is an imitation of an action, whereas for Nietzsche the tragic artist "imitates" the art impulses or drives (*Tribes*) of nature (ibid., 38). For Aristotle the functioning of tragedy is self-determined, whereas for Nietzsche it is the functioning of these art impulses of nature. The method of tragedy for Aristotle unites matter and form in a whole, whereas for Nietzsche the art impulses of nature are in perpetual strife with only periodically intervening reconciliations. Tragedy is such a reconciliation, and it is this anomalous reconciliation of the fundamental strife that makes it possible for both Aristotle and Nietzsche to use the same metaphor of tragedy as the offspring of two parents. The mother of tragedy is for Nietzsche the Dionysian art impulse toward intoxication and unity with the truly existent primal unity, ever suffering and contradictory, the analogue of Aristotle's pain. The father of tragedy is for Nietzsche the Apollonian art impulse toward dreams and symbolic images, the analogue of the artistic form that for Aristotle the poet gives to pain.

Chapter 18
POETRY AND THE PRACTICAL SCIENCES

1. POETIC AND THERAPEUTIC CATHARSIS

Aristotle speaks of catharsis not only in the *Poetics* but also in the *Politics*, where it is one of three benefits (*ōpheliai*) of music: education (*paideia*), catharsis (*katharsis*), and entertainment (*diagōgē*) for both relaxation and rest from exertion. Catharsis is described in the following often-quoted passage:

> For feelings such as pity and fear, or again, enthusiasm, exist very strongly in some souls, and have more or less influence over all. Some persons fall into a religious frenzy, whom we see as a result of the sacred melodies—when they have used the melodies that excite the soul to mystic frenzy—restored as though they had found healing (*iatreia*) and purgation (*katharsis*). Those who are influenced by pity or fear, and every emotional nature, must have a like experience, and others in so far as each is susceptible to such emotions, and all are in a manner purged (*gignesthai tina katharsin*) and their souls lightened and delighted. The purgative melodies (*ta melē ta kathartika*) likewise give an innocent pleasure to mankind. (*Pol.* viii.7.1342a5–17, trans. Jowett)

Jacob Bernays in his 1853 paper on the epitome gave the discussion of the epitome a start in a wrong direction by supposing that Aristotle's meanings are independent of context, and, in his 1857 paper on the function of tragedy he did the same, and for the same reason, with respect to the bearing of the account of catharsis in the *Politics* on the interpretation of catharsis in the *Poetics*. Having in his 1953 paper found the account of catharsis in the epitome "worthless for the right knowledge of Aristotelian doctrine" (1880, 141), in his 1857 paper he argues that the account of catharsis in the *Politics* provides a touchstone for the correct interpretation of catharsis in the *Poetics*:

> "*Katharsis* is a term transferred from the physical to the emotional sphere, and used of the sort of treatment of an oppressed person which seeks not to alter or to subjugate the oppressive element but to arouse it and draw it out and thus to achieve some sort of relief of the oppressed. . . . Anyone who, after such unequivocal statements could still think it possible that the definition [of tragedy] in the *Poetics* should

relate catharsis to quite a different object must indeed nurture strange ideas of Aristotle's use of terms. . . . Rather, an interpretation that is proved on the touchstone of the *Politics*, however surprising it may seem to a modern aesthetician, may confidently be accepted as the correct one" (1979, 160, 162).

This is a fine restatement of what Aristotle says in the *Politics*, but it can be applied to tragic catharsis only insofar as the two kinds of catharsis are the same. What it overlooks is the possibility that when catharsis is combined with other elements to form therapeutic or tragic catharses, the results may not be the same. The distinction of the causes of tragic catharsis in the epitome enables us to distinguish the respects in which the two catharses are the same or different.

Both catharses are a removal of emotions, and the emotions removed may even be the same. Pity and fear are mentioned twice in the above quotation, although enthusiasm is the emotion of the example, and presumably any kind of emotion might be removed by this kind of catharsis. The emotions removed in poetic catharsis depend on the species of poetry, the fearful emotions in the case of tragedy and emotions such as pleasure and laughter in the case of comedy.

Both catharses also remove emotions by emotions, although the removal in the catharsis of the *Politics* uses music rather than poetry. Both arouse and remove emotions through imitation, but music in general arouses and removes the feelings directly by imitating the feelings, whereas poetry and painting in general do so indirectly by imitating external actions, objects, and events. The removal of emotions by the catharsis of the *Politics is* thus by direct expression of the emotion, which is like the removal of laughter in comedy. In the example, enthusiasm is removed through a frenzied dance to the music. The removal of fear through this kind of catharsis would not be by removing its cause or by the occurrence of what is feared, but only by the expression of the fear.

The other two causes are not the same in the two kinds of catharsis. The benefit of the catharsis of the *Politics*, as indicated by the medical analogy, is a healing, and it is for this reason that the catharsis can be called therapeutic. It is thus a means to the end of psychic health rather than an end in itself, like poetic catharsis.

The mother of therapeutic catharsis, which need not be expressed metaphorically because the emotion removed is an emotion of real life, is indicated by the opening words of the quotation, which say that the emotions to be removed "exist very strongly in some souls," is any excessive emotion. The mother of poetic catharsis is again relative to the species of poetry, pain in the case of tragedy and laughter in the case of comedy. The particular pain or laughter that is removed does not preexist as an excessive emotion, but is aroused by the poem.

Thus the two kinds of catharsis are the same as emotional catharses, that is, as the removal of emotions by emotions, but differ in the use that is made of this catharsis. In poetic catharsis, it is made into the end of poetry, while in therapeutic catharsis it is used to remove unwanted emotions.

The analogy of catharsis to medical purgation is instructive with respect to therapeutic catharsis because both are therapeutic processes that restore the body or soul to health by removing what is in excess. The analogy is not appropriate to poetic catharsis because, (1) what the poet makes is not the actual catharsis in the souls of the audience, but only the potentiality for this (this will be discussed in the next section). The analogue of the poet's work would thus be the work of the pharmacist who prepares the purgative drug, but even this analogy fails because (2) poetic catharsis is an end in itself rather than a means to psychic health, and (3) poetic catharsis does not presuppose an excess of emotion that needs to be removed, but itself arouses the emotions that catharsis removes. Inference from therapeutic to poetic catharsis or vice versa is possible through the definition of emotional catharsis that they both share, but not through the distinctive features of each.

If we wish to include the psychotherapeutic catharsis of Breuer and Freud in our account of the different kinds of catharsis, we need only add to Aristotle's account of therapeutic catharsis the possibility represented by the second-best kind of tragic catharsis, the removal of fears by the removal of their cause. The therapeutic catharsis in this case is accompanied by the discovery that the disposition to feel the emotion has been preserved in the unconscious from an earlier situation which no longer obtains. The actualization of the emotion without the insight is incomplete and not psychotherapeutic because it does not remove its cause.

2. IS CATHARSIS IN THE POEM OR IN THE AUDIENCE?
In addition to the differences between therapeutic and poetic catharsis already noted, there is a fundamental difference in the genus of things to which they belong, for therapeutic catharsis is a subject of the practical sciences, and poetic catharsis is a subject of the productive sciences. This difference is formulated in the *Metaphysics*, which tells us that each science has its own subject genus, and that the productive sciences concern things

made, whose principle is in the maker, while the practical sciences concern things done, whose principle is choice (vi.1.1025b1–25).

The therapeutic catharsis of the *Politics* is clearly in the souls of the audience. The legislator chooses to benefit the citizens of the state by relieving them of unwanted emotions. If the catharsis did not remove emotions from the souls of the audience, there would be no benefit. The account from the *Politics* is concerned to show the benefit of catharsis to the citizens in general and not just to particular individuals, as would be the case in psychotherapeutic catharsis. The account begins from the individuals who can benefit most from catharsis and shows that the benefit extends to everyone. The universal audience appears three times in this brief passage in three guises, as all souls (*pasai psuchai*), all men (*pantes*), and mankind (*anthrōpoi*).

Since the epitome says that tragedy removes the fearful emotions of the soul, it might be thought that the emotions are removed from the souls of the audience, as they in fact are. But the art of the poet is only concerned to make the poem. He makes the poem, and he makes the self-activity of the poem, which is catharsis, but he does not make the response of the audience, which depends on factors that do not belong to his art. Goethe states the point emphatically: "Could Aristotle in his way of indicating his object, because in actuality he speaks only of the technique of tragedy (*der Konstruktion des Trauerspiels*), think of the effect, and, what is more, the remote effect, which tragedy would probably have on the spectator? By no means! He expresses it clearly and accurately: when tragedy has passed through a course of actions that arouse pity and fear, it should finally close on the stage with an adjustment and a reconciliation of these passions" (1967, 12:343, trans. Wenning).

The distinction between what belongs to the poetic art and what depends on the audience appears several times in Book I. It is the distinction between what tragedy is in itself essentially and what it is in relation to the audience (4.1449a7). The latter problem is said to belong not to poetics but to another discourse. It is the distinction between determining the right length of the plot from the nature of the thing itself rather than from the dramatic contest and its perception (7.1451a6). The latter is said not to belong to the poetic art. It is the distinction between the ending required by tragedy and what the audience may prefer because of its weakness (13.1453a34). It is thus clear that it is the poetic work and not the response of the audience that belongs to poetics. A poetic work may be excellent even if never witnessed by any audience.

There are two steps between the work of the poet and the mind of the audience. First, there is the art of producing a performance of what the poet has written, which, as was said in chapter 3, depends on a number of auxiliary arts such as the art of the scene painter, the costume maker, the choral directors, and the art of elocution. After this, there is the step from the performance to the mind of the audience, which is always mediated by the soul's own autonomy and thus rules out the possibility of the result being determined simply by the poet. All the arts which attempt to influence the soul directly take the soul to be influenced into account. Rhetoric achieves persuasion by making its conclusion a consequence of pre-existent opinions. Education by instruction depends on pre-existent knowledge. Education by habituation depends on the activity of the person being educated. The therapeutic catharsis of the *Politics* and the catharsis of laughter in comedy depend on the expression of emotion by the person involved. Psychotherapeutic catharsis depends on the person making discoveries about himself. The catharsis of fearful emotions in tragedy depends on the identification which is a consequence of the hero's being like oneself or somewhat better. There is no necessity in the relation between the work of the poet and what transpires in the mind of the audience.

There is a sense, however, in which poetic catharsis also can be said to be in the audience. The poet makes a potential catharsis, and, although he does not make it actual, he makes it for the sake of its actualization in an audience. The catharsis in the audience can be said to be made by the poet so far as it actualizes the potential catharsis that he has made. We can rightly speak of the poetic catharsis as in the audience if we mean what the poetic catharsis would be if it were actualizsed in an audience. But we cannot investigate tragic catharsis by examining the response of an audience because we will not know what in the response of the audience corresponds to the poetic work and what does not. We must examine poetic catharsis by examining the text, not the audience.

3. IS CATHARSIS EDUCATIVE?

In the *Politics*, catharsis as a benefit of music is distinct from education as a benefit of music. If therapeutic catharsis were essentially educative, the two benefits would not be distinct. From this we can conclude that therapeutic catharsis is not essentially educative. Similarly, poetic catharsis as an end of poetry is distinct from education as an end of poetry. If poetic catharsis were essentially educative, the ends of the two kinds of poetry would not be distinct. From this we can conclude that poetic catharsis is also not essentially educative.

In the absence of the epitome and its distinction between imitative and educational poetry there has been a long tradition of interpreting catharsis as educative. We have already cited Milton as saying that tragedy is moral and profitable because, by purging the passions, it tempers and reduces the passions to just measure.

Corneille sees tragedy as a kind of morality play. "Pity from the misfortunes which we see befalling one of ourselves awakens fear in us lest a similar misfortune befall us; the fear awakens the desire to avoid it and this desire an endeavor to moderate, to improve, even to exterminate the passion, by means of which the persons suffering whose misfortunes we pity, for reason tells every one that we must cast off the cause if we wish to avoid the effect" (1965, 29, trans. H. Zimmern). To this it must be said that there is nothing that prevents this kind of moral effect of tragedy, but it is not the end of tragedy. It is rather an accidental effect of that end.

Lessing makes clear what catharsis would have to do if it were essentially educative: "Since (to put the matter briefly) this purification rests in nothing else than in the transformation of passions into virtuous habits, and since, according to our philosopher each virtue has two extremes between which it rests, it follows that if tragedy is to change our pity into virtue it must also be able to purify us of the two extremes of pity, and the same is to be understood of fear. Tragic pity must not only purify the soul of him who has too much pity, but also of him who has too little; tragic fear must not simply purify the soul of him who does not fear any manner of misfortune, but also of him who is terrified by every misfortune, even the most distant and improbable" (Lessing 1769, no. 78, p. 193). For Aristotle, however, habits are transformed by actions, not passions.

Janko, I regret to say, continues the tradition of catharsis as educative. He writes,

By representing pitiable, terrifying and other painful events, tragedy arouses pity, dread and other painful emotions in the audience, for each according to his own emotional capacity, and so stimulates these emotions as to relieve them by giving them moderate and harmless exercise, thereby bringing the audience nearer to the mean in their emotional responses, and so nearer to virtue in their characters; and with this relief comes pleasure. Comedy works on the pleasant emotions in the same way. (Janko 1987, xix–xx; cf. 1984, 142)

I have already said enough about why Aristotle's science of poetry is independent of the emotions of the audience, and will speak here only to the argument that catharsis is educative because it brings the emotions of the characters nearer to the mean of virtue. Character is changed by habituation (*ethismos*), and habituation is the self-formation of character through action, and requires the active engagement by the character in the action by which it is formed. "It is by doing just acts that the just man is produced, and by doing temperate acts the temperate man; without doing these no one would have even a prospect of becoming good" (*Eth.* ii.4.1105b10). Catharsis as an effect on the audience is an undergoing (*paschein*) rather than a doing (*poiein*) and therefore does not affect the character. All catharsis can do is remove emotions, and whether or not the resulting feelings are in accord with the moral mean makes no difference—the character is unaffected insofar as the removal is not its own doing. The therapeutic removal of excessive or undesirable emotions can have a moral benefit insofar as these emotions would otherwise impede action in accordance with choice, but their removal does not affect the character directly. And if it did have such an effect, it would always be working in opposition to habituation. Music educates us by habituation insofar as we make the virtues and feelings imitated our own, whereas catharsis, if it were educative, would educate us to rid ourselves of the feelings imitated. Thus the ethical music that by habituation makes us more virtuous would by catharsis make us less virtuous, if not positively vicious. But catharsis does not in fact work against the good effects of habituation, for it does not affect the character directly. Imitative poetry is indeed educative insofar as it habituates us to enjoy the feelings and actions of characters better than ourselves, or to laugh at the faults of those worse than ourselves, but it has this effect through habituation, not catharsis. Aristotle's answer to Plato's criticism of the imitative arts is not to be found in an assimilation to Plato that unites artistic and educational ends, but in distinguishing artistic from educational ends and in distinguishing the kinds of art best suited to achieve each.

4. THE PRACTICAL ENDS OF POETRY

Aristotle in the *Politics* distinguishes four kinds of practical ends of music. He first (viii.3) distinguishes entertainment (*diagōgē*) in leisure, which is an end in itself and not a means to further ends. To this he adds (viii.5) amusement (*paidia*) for the sake of relaxation (*anesis*) and rest (*anapausis*), and education (*paideia*) in virtue (*aretē*). Finally (viii.7) he lists three benefits (*ōpheliai*) of music: education, catharsis, and entertainment for relaxation and rest. Entertainment for its own sake is not included, for it is an end in itself rather than a benefit. Entertainment for relaxation and rest would be what was previously called amusement, which indicates that the Greek *diagōgē* has the same ambiguity as the English "entertainment" and can mean either entertainment for its own sake or entertainment for the sake of relaxation and rest. Catharsis is now mentioned for the first time, with a promise to speak about it more clearly in the *Poetics*.

All four of these ends can also be ends of poetry. Poetry can be entertainment for its own sake. It can also be used for education, and the poetry that aims at this is educational poetry. It can also be used for therapeutic catharsis, although it is not so suitable for this as music. The chanting of the Shakers,

Shake, shake, out of me,
All that is evil,

used words accompanied by shaking for the sake of therapeutic catharsis.

When poetry is used for the sake of poetic catharsis, it is entertainment for its own sake, and the end of poety as catharsis and the practical end of entertainment here coincide and are the same thing considered in the different perspectives of the two disciplines. Considered as the function of the poetic work, poetic catharsis is a thing made and belongs to poetics. Considered as a desirable use of leisure, it is a thing chosen and belongs to the practical sciences. Poetic catharsis is not mentioned in the *Politics* because the practical sciences are concerned with how poetry is used, not how it is made. Similarly, entertainment is not mentioned in the *Poetics* because poetics is concerned with how the work is made, not how it is used.

Here is what Aristotle says about the entertainment provided in ancient times by the recitation of epic poetry to the accompaniment of a lyre (*Pol.* viii.3.1338a22–29). The translation is that of Jowett, but with *diagōgē* translated consistently as "entertainment."

There remains, then, the use of music for entertainment in leisure; which is in fact evidently the reason of its introduction, this being thought an entertainment appropriate to free men; as Homer says—
"But he who alone should be called to the pleasant feast,"
and afterwards he speaks of others whom he describes as inviting
"The bard (*aoidos*) who would delight them all."
And in another place Odysseus says there is no better entertainment than when men's hearts are merry and
"The banqueters in the hall, sitting in order, hear the voice of the minstrel (*aoidos*)."

The question being discussed in this quotation is the reason for introducing music into education. This is a practical question of choice and action, and the answer depends on its appropriateness to the audience. The use of music for entertainment is appropriate to free men, men who have the leisure that enables them to enjoy activities that are ends in themselves and not means to further ends. The practical context here is that of the political community, and the banquet and the entertainment that follows, with the banqueters sitting in order and sharing the banquet and the entertainment, are a sort of simulacrum of the state and its ends, for the state is a community that in its origin aims at survival, but ultimately aims at the good life for its citizens.[1] We should note also, as particularly relevant to our own time, that the music enjoyed is not what we would call patriotic music, but music that is enjoyable by all mankind.

PART V. *Comedy*

Chapter 19
THE DEFINITION OF COMEDY

Comedy is an imitation of action laughable and with no share in magnitude, complete, in speech made pleasing by accessories whose forms are different in different parts, by acting and not by narration, through pleasure and laughter achieving a catharsis of such emotions.
The science of comedy, like the science of tragedy, begins with its definition. It is a four-cause definition which parallels the four-cause definition of tragedy.

The object of imitation is generically the same in both tragedy and comedy, a complete action, but in tragedy the complete action is serious (*spoudaias*) and possesses magnitude (*megethos*), whereas in comedy the complete action is laughable (*gelotas*) and with no share in magnitude. The means of imitation are the same in both, language made pleasing by accessories that are different in different parts. The manner of imitating the action is also the same in both, imitating by acting and not by narration. The end of the imitation is generically the same, a catharsis of emotion by emotion, but the emotions are pleasure (*hēdonē*) and laughter (*gelōs*) rather than pity (*eleos*) and fear (*phobos*).

That the object of imitation in comedy is laughable rather than serious is what we would expect from the statement in Book I that comedy imitates the laughable (3.1449a34). To say that the action of comedy has no share in magnitude is puzzling, since as a whole with beginning, middle, and end it would necessarily have magnitude in the sense of length, *mēkos*. That magnitude in the definition of tragedy is also not magnitude in the sense of length is implied by what is said in Book I: "We have posited tragedy to be imitation of a complete and whole action having some magnitude, for there is also a whole having no magnitude" (7.1450b26). The requirement that the complete and whole action have some magnitude would be superfluous if magnitude in the sense of length were intended. Comedy is almost certainly the whole without magnitude that is referred to, and reassures us that the statement in the epitome is authentic, although it was perhaps one reason why Bywater thought the definition a sorry fabrication.

What, then, is meant by tragic magnitude if not length? This can be inferred from the account of its genesis: "The magnitude, from small (*mikros*) plots and laughable diction, by the change from satyric drama, at length assumed solemnity (*apesemnunthē*)" (4.1449a19). Satyric drama with its small plots had magnitude in the sense of length, but no magnitude in the sense of gravity or solemnity. The verb *aposemnunō* is here in the middle or reflexive voice, indicating that magnitude as gravity or solemnity was a self-development or epigenesis from magnitude as length. As the plots increased in length, they finally became grave or solemn. We see the same sort of evolution in English when a large magnitude is called great or grand or grave or gross, and from their designation of quantities these terms come to designate qualities. The quality which emerged in the development of tragic magnitude is indicated by the embedded word *semnos*, for which *LS* offers "*august, holy, solemn, awful*: at Athens, esp. of the furies or Erinyes, who were called *semnai theai* or *Semnai*. Of men, *grave, solemn, stately, majestic*. Of things, *stately, solemn, august, grand*." It was the relative gravity or frivolity of poets that produced the initial split that resulted in hymns and encomia on the one hand and invectives on the other, from which tragedy and comedy are descended. "The graver (*semnoteros*) poets imitated noble (*kalos*) actions and the actions of those of their sort, while the more frivolous (*eutelosteros*) imitated the actions of base (*phaulos*) men, producing invectives at first as the former produced hymns and encomia." (4.1448b25). Hymns to the divine may be solemn, but invective has no share in solemnity. The object of imitation in comedy is thus a complete action that is laughable and has no share in magnitude in the sense of *to semnon*, the grave or solemn. It is a stretch in English to interpret magnitude as gravity or solemnity, as it also seems to be in Greek to interpret *megethos*, magnitude, as *semnotēs*, gravity or solemnity, for *LSJ* gives only "importance" as the English meaning of *megethos* when predicated of actions, and *LS* nothing more. Let us try to make the stretch in English: "A satisfactory distinction between tragedy and comedy is not as easy to find as one might think. Both evoke emotions of joy and sorrow with a view to an ultimate pleasure. Both may have laughable characters who are worse than we are and serious characters who are like us or better. The action of tragedy is serious and the action of comedy laughable, but it is also the case that there may be laughable components in the action of tragedy and an overall seriousness in the action of comedy. But perhaps there is a quality that is found to some degree in all tragedies but not at all in comedies. It could be called magnitude in the sense of gravity or solemnity."[1]

This brings us to pleasure and laughter as the defining emotions of comedy. It is no surprise to see laughter here, for the object of comedy is the comic or laughable (*to geloion*), and laughter (*gelōs*) is what the laughable produces. And, quite apart from the *Poetics*, it is laughter that marks the success of a joke or a comedian. The Greek *to geloion*, which I am translating as the laughable or funny, is used also in the plural *ta geloia* (*Rhet.* i.11.1371b35), for which the best English translation is not the funnies, which has a special meaning, or the laughables, but jokes. A joke that does not produce laughter fails as a joke. A stand-up comedian who does not get laughs fails as a stand-up comedian. As Steve Martin said to Jon Stewart on *The Daily Show* (October 28, 2008), "The bottom line is, did it get a laugh?" When Hamlet tells us that Yorick was wont to set the table on a roar, this alone tells us that he performed well the function of a jester. Situation comedies may also aim at laughter. When Jerry Seinfeld was interviewed by Charlie Rose in connection with *Bee Movie* (2007), he said that in writing the Seinfeld series he aimed at laughter. He added that even with his own children he will do anything to make them laugh, and feels rewarded by the beautiful sound of their laughter.

There are many comedies, however, such as those of Henry Fielding and Jane Austen, which do not consist of jokes and aim more at pleasure than at laughter. We can see here both the need for the distinction that is made in the last section of the epitome between old, new, and middle comedy and the need for pleasure as well as laughter in the emotions through which comic catharsis is achieved.

There is a formal parallel between the two emotions of tragedy, pity and fear, and the two emotions of comedy, pleasure and laughter. In the initial differentiation of objects of imitation in Book I, Aristotle distinguishes characters as better than we are, worse than we are, or such as we are, and adds that comedy aims to imitate characters worse, and tragedy better, than those of now. But in stating the objects of imitation in the definitions of tragedy and comedy the distinction of character does not appear as such. This distinction is not suited to distinguish the objects of imitation in tragedy and comedy because characters of any moral type can be imitated in either tragedy or comedy. Yet in the case of tragedy the distinction has not disappeared, but is implied by the presence of fear in the definition, for fear is felt for the misfortunes of one like ourselves. Pity, however, does not imply this distinction of character, for pity is felt for undeserved misfortune even if the misfortune is not of one like ourselves. Thus the primary emotion of tragedy, fear, requires characters like ourselves, but the secondary emotion, pity, is also felt for characters who are not like ourselves.

Similarly, comedy imitates characters worse than ourselves, and this is not stated as such in the definition but is implied by the presence of laughter in the definition, for we laugh at characters worse than ourselves. Pleasure, however, does not imply this distinction of character, for we are pleased by the good fortune of those like ourselves as well as by the laughable in characters worse than ourselves. Thus the primary emotion of comedy, laughter, requires characters worse than ourselves, but the secondary emotion, pleasure, is felt for characters who are not worse than we are. In Jane Austen's *Pride and Prejudice*, for example, we find both characters who are laughable because of their vices, the obsequious Mr. Collins and the conceited Lady Catherine, with whom we do not identify, and characters like ourselves or somewhat better, notably Elizabeth and Darcy, who are not laughable, but whose fortunes and misfortunes engage us, and by whose good fortune we are pleased. Similarly, in Shakespeare's *Twelfth Night* we laugh at the vain Malvolio with his cross-gartered yellow stockings, but feel sympathetic concern for the fortunes of Viola and Sebastian. Thus the laughter of comedy requires characters worse than we are, just as the fear of tragedy requires characters like us or somewhat better, but the pleasure of comedy may be felt for characters like us or somewhat better just as the pity of tragedy may be felt for characters worse than we are.

Finally, we come to the power of comedy, the power of achieving through pleasure and laughter the catharsis of such emotions. As we said earlier, laughter is not an anticipatory emotion and most be removed by its own actualization in laughing, whereas pleasure may be anticipatory and removed by the actual occurrence of the anticipated events. A comic plot is said in section 11 of the epitome to have its construction around laughable actions, and laughable actions do not themselves require a composition and a resolution, although anticipatory and realized pleasure would certainly admit of such a distinction, which would then be found in the comic plot.

Chapter 20
THE MOTHER OF COMEDY: LAUGHTER

Comedy . . . has as its mother laughter.
The definition of comedy is immediately followed in section 4 of the epitome by the statement that comedy has as its mother laughter. This statement is evidently the counterpart of the earlier statement that tragedy has as it mother pain, but the statement about the mother of tragedy occurs at the end of the account of tragedy, whereas the statement about the mother of comedy occurs at the beginning of the account of comedy. In the light of what we have said about the different function of metaphors at the beginning and the end of sciences, it appears that the metaphor of pain as the mother of tragedy helps us to understand the whole tragedy as a derivation of pleasure from pain, whereas the metaphor of laughter as the mother of comedy helps us to understand laughter as the starting point for the whole analysis of comedy.

This suggests that we have hit upon the contrast between tragedy and comedy that is the reason why tragedy is discussed in Book I and comedy in Book II. The analysis of tragedy begins with its parts and the plot as the end of the other parts and the principle of the whole. The generic plot has a definiteness which, in the analysis of tragedy, is emotionalized to become a tragic plot in which the definiteness is used to achieve the end of tragedy, the catharsis of fearful emotions. The analysis of comedy, on the other hand, begins with the laughable, which produces the laughter which is the end of comedy. The laughable has a formal definiteness which is the basis for a scientific account of the laughable. Of the two generic sources of poetry, imitation and emotional end, it is imitation that supplies the form that is emotionalized in tragedy, and the emotional end of laughter that supplies the forms that are realized in the imitative material of comedy. The general difference between tragedy and comedy is the difference between an imitative form emotionalized and an emotional form imitationalized.

This enables us to solve the problem of why a complete poetics needs to analyze only three species. Science concerns what is necessary, but the existence of particular species is contingent, and, as we have said, we have no reason to suppose that all possible species of poetry already exist. Completeness with respect to poetic species is therefore a matter of exhausting formal possibilities rather than actual species. All poetry unites imitation and an end, and for a complete poetics we need, first, generic analyses of both imitation and end. For the species of poetry, we need analyses of the two species that represent highest fulfillment of the ends of imitative poetry in each of the two ways in which these components can be united, and these are found in the two dramatic species, tragedy and comedy. We also need an analysis of the species that represents the fullest realization of the poetic possibilities of non-dramatic or narrative poetry, and this is epic poetry. Therefore it suffices for a formally complete poetics to analyze poetry in general and three of its species, tragedy, comedy, and epic poetry.

Lyric poetry is not included in this list nor is there any separate treatment of it in the *Poetics*. We must consider why this is so. One possibility is that the treatment of lyric poetry belongs to another discipline. This possibility is represented by W. D. Ross, who writes, "Aristotle no doubt held the lyric to belong to the theory of music rather than to that of poetry." (Ross 1949, 290). But this cannot be right. If the music is for the sake of the words, as in tragedy and comedy melody sweetens the words, the work belongs properly to poetics, and music is a subordinate art used for poetic ends. Thus we see in section 15 of the epitome that melody is proper to music and its use in tragedy and comedy is referred to the art of music. Conversely, if the words are for the sake of the music, as in opera, songs, oratorios, and other choral music, the work belongs properly to music, and poetics is a subordinate art used for musical ends. In either case, the lyrics belong properly to poetics and the melody to music.

Another possibility is that the *Poetics* as we have it is incomplete and needs to be supplemented by a poetics of the lyric. This possibility is represented by Elder Olson, himself a lyric poet. His first paper on the lyric, "'Sailing to Byzantium': Prolegomena to a Poetics of the Lyric," "attempts to discover—through the analysis of a particular poem—some index as to how, eventually, a poetics of the lyric might be framed" (Olson 1942, 4). But if a poetics of the lyric is possible, lyric poetry would need to be a definable species of imitative poetry, and this would require that it have a determinate end, like the catharsis of pity and fear in the case of tragedy and the catharsis of pleasure and laughter in the case of comedy. We see, however, that lyric poetry is not limited to any single emotion or pair of emotions, but can seek to arouse any kind of emotion, and therefore it is not a definable species of imitative poetry with consequences that belong to it as lyric poetry.

How, then, does lyric poetry fall within the framework of analysis provided by the *Poetics*? First of all, a lyric poem is imitative poetry in the sense of having its end in itself. This means that the whole generic analysis of imitative poetry will apply to it. It will have its own object, means, manner, and end, and the parts that derive from these, both qualitative and quantitative. Further, it must derive its form either from the materials of imitation, like tragedy, or from its emotional end, like comedy. It is perhaps even more evident than in the case of comedy that lyric poetry imitationalizes emotion. In Shakespeare's sonnet 30, for example, "When to the sessions of sweet silent thought," there is no necessary or probable connection between the old woes that the speaker remembers in the complication and the dear friend who is thought on in the resolution, but there is a powerful emotional symmetry between the losses and sorrows of the complication and the restoration of all losses and ending of sorrows in the resolution. The analysis of lyric poetry must therefore follow the example of comedy and begin by identifying its mother, the emotions that are realized in the poem, and proceed to show how the principle of the poem gives rise, through the character of the speaker, to these emotions by organizing the materials of imitation. The principle of the poem is the principle of self-determination of the lyric, analogous to the tragic plot as the principle and soul of tragedy and to the laughable as the corresponding principle of comedy.

As an example of this procedure we may cite Olson's analysis of Yeats's "Sailing to Byzantium" in the paper already referred to. "The procedure reduces to an attempt to discover some principle in the work which is the principle of its unity and order" (Olson 1942, 5). Olson discovers this principle in the poem's argument. But since lyric poetry is not a species, the principle or argument of "Sailing to Byzantium" can determines its unity and order only as an individual poem and not as a member of a supposed species of lyric poetry. Olson's analysis of "Sailing to Byzantium" therefore cannot and does not provide an index of how a poetics of the lyric might be framed, but only an index of how a lyric poem can be analyzed. The analysis of a lyric poem moves directly from the generic account of imitative poetry to the individual poem without the mediation of a rational structure belonging to it as a lyric poem. It depends directly on the perceptions of intuitive mind without the help that might be provided by a poetics of the species.

In order to assure ourselves that lyric poetry is not a definable species, let us follow through to its conclusion Olson's effort to frame a poetics of the lyric. His next work on lyric poetry is section IV of "An Outline of Poetic Theory" (Olson 1949). He writes, "We may illustrate the nature of a special poetics a little further by outlining briefly that of the species to which Yeats's "Sailing to Byzantium belongs" (Crane 1952, 563; Olson 1976, 286). He proceeds to state the object, means, manner, and end of the poem, and to specify the argument of the poem as a deliberation. He thus outlines what might be a subspecies of the lyric if the lyric were a species, but without supplying a definition of the lyric. Since a species is derived from its genus by differentiation, we do not have here a subspecies of lyric poetry, but only a topic or place in which to put other poems resembling "Sailing to Byzantium" in aiming to arouse "a kind of noble joy or exaltation."

Finally, twenty-seven years after the publication of the "Prolegomena," Olson published a paper entitled simply "The Lyric," not "A Poetics of the Lyric." He writes, "I do not propose in this paper to attempt definitions or the statement of principles or the construction of a poetics. I propose something far more simple, far more modest: to see whether we can establish, so to speak, a geography of the lyric; to delineate its boundaries, so that we may at least know where it begins and where it leaves off" (Olson 1969, 213). This more modest attempt employs the topical method that Olson has in fact been using all along. Olson concludes, "We have found, I think, the boundaries of lyric territory, but we are far from knowing everything these boundaries contain. It should be clear even from this much consideration that there are different forms ruled by different principles, so that we can no longer speak, with any confidence at least, of the lyric in the sense of a single form. . . . A further thing is clear—that it is futile to attempt a definition of lyric" (219). We end up with a territory or place for the lyric, but without a definition of it. Without a definition of the lyric there can be no poetics of the lyric, in Aristotle's sense. Olson's efforts with respect to framing a poetics of the lyric thus provide a kind of empirical confirmation of the theoretical argument that lyric poetry is not a definable species because it has no determinate end. This does not mean that it is not possible to use the Poetics to analyze the lyric, for this is what Olson did so well in his first paper, but only that there are no scientific arguments specific to lyric poetry that can be used in doing this, and this is why Aristotle has offered none.

Returning to the account of laughter as the mother of comedy, we have said that its appearance at this point indicates not only the inversion of method in the analyses of tragedy and comedy, but also provides the starting point for the analysis of comedy. At the beginning of an investigation, Aristotle characteristically states both the subject to be investigated and the starting point of the investigation. Thus the opening sentence of the Poet-

ics states both the subject to be investigated and where it will begin, and we have noted that Book II begins with an expanded subject and a new starting point. Section 4 of the epitome, with its definition of comedy and its identification of the mother of comedy as laughter, does the same with respect to comedy.

Chapter 21

THE LAUGHABLE

Laughter arises from the diction and from the incidents.
Laughter can be investigated in disciplines other than poetics—in physiology and psychology and sociology, for example. The laughter that concerns the poet is the laughter that he produces, and this results from the diction and incidents of the comedy rather than from, for example, a tickling of the feet. Just as the poet produces a potential rather than an actual catharsis, so he produces potential rather than actual laughter, that is, he produces the laughable. The relation of the laughable to laughter is evidently highly contingent. Sometimes a person will find nothing funny, and sometimes everything will seem funny. A joking mood, in which one is inclined to disregard customary restraints and inhibitions and to tolerate any sort of wrongness that is not painful or destructive, contributes greatly to our laughter at jokes, which is why comedians warm up the audience before a broadcast of their performance. A person who is not in a joking mood can read a whole joke book without laughing. A person who, being introduced to a comedian, says, "A comedian, eh? Well, then, make me laugh!" makes a joke, because it is within his power to laugh or not to laugh. The scientific analysis of laughter (*gelōs*) in the *Poetics*, then, is limited to the laughable, *to geloion*. The word has no English cognate, and has been translated using Latin roots as the ridiculous (Twining 1789; Bywater 1924; Golden 1968), or the ludicrous (Butcher 1895; Cooper 1913; Grube 1958; Telford 1961), and, using the English root, as the laughable (Fyfe 1927; Else 1957; Halliwell 1995; Janko 1987), while in informal English it is the funny. I shall translate the adjective *geloios* as "laughable" or "funny" interchangeably. There is, however, a major problem in translating *to geloion* by any single English substantive, which is that in English we use the word "jokes" for a particular kind of the laughable, whereas in Greek there is no separate word for jokes. Therefore it should be kept in mind that the laughable includes jokes, and often, particularly in the plural, the meaning is better conveyed by "joke" than by "laughable." I shall therefore sometimes refer to the forms of the laughable as joke-forms and to the laughable in the singular as a joke and in the plural as jokes, but this should not be understood to imply that Aristotle makes a distinction between the laughable and jokes.

1. THE DEFINITION OF THE LAUGHABLE

The definition of the laughable is not given in Book II, but in the account of the genesis of comedy: in Book I:

> Comedy, as we have said, is an imitation of the more base (*to phauloteron*), not, however, with respect to every kind of vice (*kakia*), but with respect to that part of the disgraceful (*to aiskhron*) which is the laughable (*to geloion*). For the laughable is a wrongness (*hamartēma*) or disgrace (*aiskhos*) that is painless (*anōdunos*) and not destructive (*ou phthartikos*), as the comic (*geloios*) mask is ugly (*aiskhros*) and distorted (*diestrammenos*) without pain (*aneu odunē*). (5.1449a33–6)

This statement is puzzling because there seem to be three different genera to which the laughable is being assigned: vice, the disgraceful, and wrongness. Its context, however, is that of the evolution of poetry, and just as the evolution of poetry enabled us to understand the apparent contradiction between the ordinary meaning of imitation used in Book I and the technical meaning used in Book II, so the evolution of comic imitation may help us to understand the apparent contradiction here. The three different generic terms used in the statement to characterize the object of comic imitation can be understood as relating primarily to different stages in the development of comic imitation. First we have the more base, referring back explicitly to the object of comic imitation as first stated in chapter 2. This baseness is the baseness of character, or vice. Vice is then replaced by the disgraceful, which is vice from the standpoint of the perceiver. This shift from vice to the disgraceful corresponds to the shift from vice or badness as an object of imitation with no ulterior purpose to vice as disgraceful and thus an object of imitation in invectives. Finally, the definition of the laughable introduces wrongness. Disgrace implies a fault in the agent, whereas wrongness need not be disgraceful. The shift from the disgraceful to wrongness corresponds to the shift from invectives and lampoons to comedy, which aims at laughter for its own sake and is not limited to the disgraceful, but can make fun of any kind of wrongness. A similar distinction appears in the well-known statement (*Poet.* 13.1453a9; cf. *Metaph.* ix.9.1051a20) that the change to misfortune in tragedies should be brought about not by vice (*kakia*) or wickedness (*mokhthēria*), but by some error (*hamartia*). In both comedy and tragedy error or wrongness marks the emergence of the properly poetic from the moral, but the laughable retains the disgraceful among the objects of imitation, for the disgraceful can be laughable if it is not painful or destructive.

All three terms, *kakia* (vice), *aiskhros* (disgraceful), and *hamartēma* (wrongness), have narrower and broader meanings. *Kakia* can refer to vice and also to badness in general. *To aiskhron* can refer to the disgraceful and also to whatever is the opposite of *to kalon*, meaning the fair, beautiful, good, noble. As the opposite of the beautiful, it is the ugly. *Hamartēma* and *hamartia* are in general interchangeable, and in the *Rhetoric* Aristotle calls comic faults *hamartiai* (ii.6.1384b10), while in the *Poetics* he uses *hamartēma* for comic wrongness and *hamartia* for tragic error. Perhaps this is because *hamartēma* is better suited to the indefinite wrongness of comedy and *hamartia* to the wrong choice of tragedy. Both terms can, however, refer not only to errors or mistakes relative to human intentions, but also to faults in things (*Phys.* ii.8.199a33, b4), and their most general sense is simply *wrongness*, the opposite of rightness, *orthotēs* (*Topics* ii.4.111a16; *N. Eth.* vi.10.1142b10). Any wrongness, provided it is not painful or destructive, can be laughable, and therefore I have translated *hamartēma* in the definition of the laughable by the most general term, "wrongness." That this is the right English word for the genus of the laughable can be confirmed inductively even by reviewing in an ordinary social conversation the different instance of the laughable to see what word best designates what they have in common. The only problem with translating *"hamartēma"* by "wrongness "is that the Greek word has a plural, *hamartēmata*, and to translate this one must either use "wrongnesses," which from the standpoint of usage is itself slightly wrong, or a circumlocution such as "forms of wrongness." The wrongness that is the source of the tragic misfortune is not any wrongness, but wrongness relative to the intention of the agent, and therefore the *hamartia* of tragedy can be suitably translated by "error" or "mistake."

In the evolution of the object of imitation in comedy its genus expands from vice to include all forms of wrongness, and at the same time is limited by its differentiae to wrongness that is not painful or destructive. We may note that the differentiae limiting the comic laughable to what is painless and not destructive result in a distinction between comic laughter and what we may call malicious laughter, which is laughter at painful or destructive wrongness.

This account of the meaning of wrongness in the definition of the laughable is confirmed by the example of the comic mask insofar as it shows that both the disgraceful and wrongness are to be taken in their broader senses. The comic mask is ugly (*aischros*), but not disgraceful in a moral sense, and its distortion is the wrongness of a thing rather than an action, and thus wrongness in the broad rather than a narrower sense. It should also be noted, however, that the comic mask retains the generic connection with us as objects of imitation in poetry, for it is an imitation of us as laughable. The laughable, then, is any sort of wrongness that is not painful or destructive. It seems that we have developed two ways of dealing with wrongness. Wrongness that is not painful or destructive becomes a source of pleasure in laughter and comedy, while wrongness that is painful or destructive requires the more elaborate method of tragedy to make it a source of pleasure.

2. ACCOUNTS OF THE LAUGHABLE

Immediately after stating the definition and mother of comedy in section 4, the epitome begins in section 5 to enumerate the sources of laughter in diction and incidents. Before considering them, we must recall that for this part of Book II we have other sources besides the epitome. One is John Tzetzes's *Iambi de Commoedia*, composed in the twelfth century. Tzetzes appears to have had knowledge of Book II through intermediaries now lost (Janko 1984, 11–12). From this source Janko has added two sources of laughter from diction that are not in the Tractatus Coislinianus but clearly needed, parody and transference.

Another source is the anonymous Prolegomenon to Comedy, of uncertain date but going back at least to late antiquity, parts of which are preserved in a number of manuscripts, primarily among introductory matter to manuscripts of Aristophanes. Janko gives a full account of these manuscripts and their relation to the *Tractatus* (1984, 8–18). The Prolegomenon provides additional material on the sources of laughter in diction and the first two sources of laughter in the incidents, as well as on the quantitative parts of comedy.

With respect to the sources of laughter in general, the epitome gives us only a schematic epitomization: "Laughter arises from the diction" and "from the incidents." The Prolegomenon gives us more: "He says that the laughter of comedy has its structure (*echei tēn systasin*) both from diction (*ek lexeōn*) and from incidents (*ek pragmatōn*)" (Janko 1984, 24). The "He says" of the Prolegomenon indicates that the author is taking the statement from another author, who can hardly be other than Aristotle. That the Prolegomenon has words of Aristotle that are not in the epitome is evidence that its author had independent access to the second book of the *Poetics*. The wording of the statement is similar to the wording of what Aristotle says about the plot in Book I, that it is "the structure (*systasis*) of the incidents" (6.1450a15) and what is said about the comic plot in the epitome, "The comic plot is one having its structure (*echon tēn sustasin*) around laughable actions." But the sentence "The laughter of comedy has its structure both from diction and from things" presents us with a difficulty that might lead us to doubt whether the Prolegomenon is really giving us the words of Aristotle. What is meant by the structure of the laughter of comedy, as is evident from what follows in the *Prolegomenon*, is the structure of laughable things such as jokes. But laughable things and the laughter of comedy are evidently different, for laughable things are in the comedy but laughter is in the audience. We have here the counterpart in comedy of the problem discussed earlier in relation to tragedy as to whether catharsis is in the play or the audience. The present problem can be resolved in the same way as the earlier one, for the laughable that the poet makes is the potentiality for the laughter of the audience, and since they are the potentiality and actuality of the same thing, the structure of the laughter will be the same as the structure of the laughable. The attribution of the common structure to the laughter clarifies the point made earlier, that tragedy derives its form as a structure of incidents from what poetry is as imitation, whereas comedy derives its form as a structure of laughter from what poetry is as realizing an end, imitation and its end being the two heterogeneric components of all poetry. It also clarifies the difference between tragic and comic catharsis, the one being a consequence of an essential structure of incidents, the other being a consequence of a structure of incidents many of which have the essential structure of comedy.

3. THE CAUSES OF THE LAUGHABLE

The essential structure of comedy is the structure of the laughable, while the essential structure of tragedy is the structure of incidents, or the plot. This suggests that we may expect in Book II an analysis of the laughable comparable to the analysis of plot in chapters 7–16 of Book I. The enumeration of the forms of the laughable in sections 5 and 6 of the epitome would then be only the first part of the analysis of the laughable. The forms of the laughable are the stable and determinate forms that provide the basis for a science of the laughable, but such a science would not be complete unless it included a matter for the forms, a cause that unites them, and an end for their union in comedy. Looking at all the sections of the epitome that are concerned with the laughable, we see that sections 5 and 6 concern the forms of the laughable (analogous to chapters 7–11 on the structure of the plot), section 7 concerns the manner of the laughable (analogous to chapters 17–18 on how the poet should construct his plots), section 8 concerns the material out of which the laughable is constructed (analogous to chapter 12 on the quantitative parts of tragedy), and section 9 concerns the aim or end of the laughable (analogous to chapters 13–16 on the functioning of the plot). The Prolegomenon thus helps us in interpreting the epitome by supporting the idea that the analysis of the laughable, although very different from the analysis of plot, is nevertheless an analysis of a structured whole in terms of its causes. Before discussing the forms of the laughable, therefore, let us first look at the other causes so that we shall be able to discuss the examples of the forms of the laughable in the context of the whole theory of the laughable.

Comedy differs from abuse, since abuse recounts without concealment the bad attributes, whereas comedy has need of indirection.
Comedy and abuse both present human faults, but they differ essentially in whether they are presented without concealment or only indirectly, which is a difference in the manner of presentation. In ordinary social conversation, a *sotto voce* delivery may take the place of indirection; the hard of hearing often have to ask a neighbor to repeat a punch line.

The mocker aims to reproach wrongnesses of the soul or of the body.
The relation of this to the preceding sentence is clarified by the statement in the *Ethics* (iv.8.1128a 30) that the mock or gibe (*skōmma*) is a kind of abuse (*loidorēma*), so the mocker (*skōptēs*) will be to the comedian as a gibe is to a joke. The aim of reproaching others is not the aim of the comedian, who aims at laughter for its own sake. Both the mocker and the comedian make use of some material, wrongness of the soul or of the body, and what these are is most evident in the abuse of the mocker, since he presents them without concealment. Therefore the identification of the matter of the laughable is made by presenting it as what the mocker aims to reproach.

This is the only occurrence in the epitome of the generic term for the laughable, wrongness. Taken with the sources of laughter in words and incidents, it completes the three kinds of laughable things listed in the *Rhetoric*: men (*anthrōpoi*), words (*logoi*), and deeds (*erga*) (i.11.1371b35). Wrongness in us as objects of laughter, however, which I shall call material wrongness, plays a different role in the laughable from the wrongness of words or incidents that supplies the forms of the laughable and which I shall call formal wrongness. The forms of the laughable taken by themselves provide opportunities for what we call wit, which may be clever or witty without being particularly funny. The material of the laughable, in contrast, taps into the emotional sources of laughter that produce laughter that is in general more explosive and less voluntary than the polite laughter occasioned by wit. Section 8, with its unique occurrence of the key generic term *hamartēmata*, wrongnesses, makes a most important point in Aristotle's theory of the laughable, that in addition to the formal wrongness of diction or incident, there is a material wrongness in that at which we laugh. We can expect the laughable in its full realization to unite wrongness of form with wrongness of matter, while the indirect manner of the laughable is a sort of screen behind which the material wrongness is partially concealed, and which makes possible its union with formal wrongness in a joke and also provides an additional source of pleasure in discovering what is concealed, that is, in getting the joke.

There aims to be a symmetry of fear in tragedies and of the laughable in comedies.
A laughable incident aims to produce a laugh, but a comedy aims to produce a catharsis of laughter by means of many laughable incidents. The catharsis of laughter in comedies is perfected by symmetry, just as the catharsis of the fearful emotions in tragedies is perfected by symmetry. The beginnings of both comedy and tragedy go back to the split at the very beginning of poetry into invectives on the one hand and hymns and encomia on the other. We are such that we cannot be fully engaged in the fearful emotions of tragedy unless these are balanced by nonfearful emotions, nor can we be fully engaged in the laughter of comedy unless the laughter is balanced by serious emotions. The painful and the laughable taken by themselves call upon only a part of our emotional nature, and the fullest engagement of the emotions occurs when emotions of one kind are dominant and controlling but symmetrical with emotions of an opposite kind.

It is through symmetry that the laughable is integrated into the more inclusive theory of comedy. A joke may be laughable without symmetry, but if we are thinking of the catharsis of laughter in comedy, comedy aims at a symmetry between the laughable and the serious. In the case of tragedy, it was not at once evident what symmetry could mean, and we examined ancient and modern tragedies in trying to determine how it is possible for the nonfearful to be symmetrical with the fearful. In the case of comedy, however, the meaning of symmetry is more evident, and it will suffice to list a series of comic writings and authors in which the serious component is easily recognized. We have first of all the example of Aristophanes, whose plays, most evidently those concerned with the war, have a serious component. We can also answer the question raised earlier as to how Jane Austen's concern with the moral virtues is compatible with comedy. To Aristophanes and Jane Austen we can add, among others, Molière, Mozart's *Cosi Fan Tutte*, Henry Fielding, Mark Twain's *Huckleberry Finn*, Will Rogers,

Charlie Chaplin, Tom Lehrer, Mort Sahl, Russell Baker, and Jon Stewart. In Shakespeare's *As You Like It*, peace and love in the Forest of Arden are symmetrical with the strife in the world beyond the forest. The greater the strife in the world beyond the forest, the more we enjoy the benign world of the forest. For *Twelfth Night* I cannot do better than quote Charles Isherwood's review of the 2009 production in Central Park directed by Daniel Sullivan: "Despite all the present mirth Mr. Sullivan weaves throughout the production an equally present melancholy. For much of the play's running time it is clear that the pursuit of love is a pastime as vexing, troubled and potentially humiliating as any human endeavor, a kind of emotional shipwreck that, like real ones, can end either in disaster or salvation. The dark strains in the music, the complicated colors of all the major performances, even the dependable uncertainty of the weather in Central Park, where for much of June it seemed as if 'the rain it raineth every day'—all contribute to the moving sense that the richest joys are hard won, the triumph of love just a hair's breadth away from the heartbreak of loss" (*New York Times*, June 26, 2009).

The four aspects of the laughable can be referred to its causes in the following way. The sources of laughter in words and incidents are the forms of the laughable, as they are called in the *Rhetoric*; the indirect manner in which the laughable is expressed can be referred to its efficient cause, wrongnesses of soul and body to its material cause, and the aim of symmetry to its final cause.

To see in a preliminary way how the different causes unite to produce the laughable, let us first consider a classical joke. It was well known as a joke about Augustus Caesar (Macrobius 1969, 172) and appears again in Freud (1963, 68) and Holt (2008, 71). I quote Holt's version: "A royal personage was making a tour through his provinces and noticed a man in the crowd who bore a striking resemblance to his own exalted person. He beckoned to him and asked: 'Was your mother at one time in service in the Palace?'— 'No, your Highness,' was the reply, 'but my father was.'" The form of the joke is a reversal of expectation with some similarity to the plot of *Oedipus the King*. The royal personage expects to find that he is the father of a hitherto unknown son, and instead discovers that he is himself the son of a hitherto unknown father. The comic indirection lies in these momentous facts being revealed, not in an investigation that occupies an entire play, nor in an abusive statement that the royal personage is the bastard offspring of the adultery of his mother, but indirectly in ordinary polite conversation as to whether a member of a provincial family had ever served in the royal palace. The matter of the joke concealed behind the polite conversation is adultery, in this case of the Queen Mother and the consequent illegitimacy of the royal personage. The joke stands alone and is not told as part of a comedy having symmetry with the serious, but it has aspects that admit of serious treatment—the artificiality of distinctions of rank, the sexual prerogatives of alpha males, the uncertainty of paternity, the imperfect monogamy of the human species. The first three causes are needed to explain the laughability of the joke, and the last corresponds to ways in which it could be integrated into a serious comedy. The persistence of the joke since ancient times with only a change of characters is a sign that it has a stable form that makes it a possible object of a science.

Let us consider also a typical topical joke. The actress Farrah Fawcett died in the morning of June 25, 2009, and the singer Michael Jackson died in the afternoon of the same day. In the circulation of topical jokes this one reached me about two weeks later: "Farrah Fawcet died and went to heaven. There she was asked her greatest wish, to which she replied, 'I would like to see the world a better place.' Michael Jackson died." This is followed by silence. We expect a continuation in which Michael Jackson enters the afterlife and is asked his greatest wish, and are momentarily puzzled because there is no continuation. The silence in which the joke ends, and the laughter which follows, contrast with the saturated media coverage which in fact followed Michael Jackson's death. The formal wrongness lies in the broken symmetry and the unexpected silence at the end. This is united with the material wrongness, not stated but expressed indirectly, of viewing his death as something to be wished for. Jokes at funerals and wakes have the important double function of, on the one hand, relieving us from the strain of suppressing any inappropriate negative feelings we may have about the dead or any inappropriate lack of sympathy we may feel for those who are grieving, and, on the other hand, of reassuring the survivors that it is still possible for them to enjoy life and laughter together. The Michael Jackson joke, like the previous example, was an isolated joke, although it could be related to serous considerations, such as the role of pop singers and of the media in national life or the merits of Michael Jackson, but, as a topical joke, it relies on events of the time and will soon be forgotten, contrasting with the long life of the preceding joke. Nevertheless, broken symmetry and the strains of dealing with death supply an enduring form and matter for jokes.

4. LAUGHTER FROM THE DICTION

With this much by way of an overview of the synergy of causes in Aristotle's treatment of the laughable, let us now take up the forms of the laughable.

These are the part of the epitome that has been most discussed by previous authors. It will suffice here to provide one or two illustrations of each of the forms, which will at least provide additional evidence of their universality.

We should first note the difficulty in treating them scientifically. In the definition of the laughable as wrongness that is not painful or destructive, both the generic term and the differentiating terms are negations. In fact, all of the terms used for the object of comedy in the course of its evolution imply a standard or norm of which they are privations. *Phaulos*, "base," is a privation of *spoudaios*, "worthy," "serious," "good." *Kakia*, "vice," is a privation of *aretē*, "virtue." *Aiskhros*, "disgraceful," "ugly," is a privation of *kalos*, "fair," "beautiful," "good," "noble." *Hamartēma*, "mistake," "error," "fault," "failure," "wrongness," is a privation of *orthotēs*, "rightness." *Diestrammenos*, "distorted," is a privation of "the undistorted" or "the natural." Laughter is our natural response to all the kinds of harmless wrongness that we encounter in the world.

Negations cannot define an essence, as was said earlier in relation to nonimitative poetry, for essences are in their nature positive, not privative. Thus there is no science of the laughable in the sense of a determinate genus from whose definition joke-forms and their properties could be derived. It is nevertheless possible to treat them systematically, for privations as relative terms are known through their positives. Joke-forms can therefore be distinguished in relation to the forms of which they are privations. Just as the forms or species of the tragic plot can be distinguished by the sources of the fearful emotions, so the forms of the laughable are distinguished by the sources of laughter. The account of joke-forms in the epitome begins by stating two general sources of laughter in comedies, the diction and the incidents. This is not a division of wrongness or the laughable as such, but a division of what can be found in comedy into two great ordered and determinate regions within each of which wrongness and the laughable can occur, wrongness with respect to diction and wrongness with respect to the incidents.

Laughter arises from the diction.
Language is the means of imitation in comedy and diction is expression through language. Wrongness in diction includes all wrongness in expression through language, and presumably also wrongness in the sweeteners that accompany language, such as the wrongness in a musical joke, or wrongness in meter, as in:

There was a young man of Japan,
Whose limericks never would scan.

When asked, "Why so?"
He replied, "I don't know—
I simply try to get as many syllables into the last line as I possibly can!"

The epitome does not include definitions or examples of the sources of the laughter in diction, but we know from the *Rhetoric* (iii.2.1404b37– 1405a6) that the first two, homonyms and synonyms, were defined, and we may suppose that the rest were also defined. The Prolegomenon to Comedy provides a definition of paronymy by addition as well as examples of most of the sources of the laughter that it mentions, and we shall include these in our account. The examples are of particular interest because presumably they come from Book II itself.

1. *From homonymy.* Homonyms, synonyms, and paronyms are all de- fined in the first chapter of the *Categories.* All these definitions, however, are definitions of things rather than words, whereas the sources of laughter in diction are words rather than things. Hence the definitions of the *Categories* need to be turned around so as to make them definitions of words. For hom- onyms, the *Categories* has, "Homonyms are said to be those things of which the name only is common, while the formula of the essence (*logos tēs ousias*) corresponding to the name is different, as a man and the picture of a man are both said to be animal, for the name only is common, while the formula of the essence corresponding to the name is different." (*Cat.* 1.1a1). Turn- ing this around, homonymous names are those names that signify more than one thing. This accords with the account of homonymy as a source of sophistical arguments (*Soph. Ref.* 4.165b30–166a21), which are arguments from homonymous words rather than homonymous things.

The Prolegomenon offers two examples of homonymy. The first is *di- aphoroumenois*, whose primary meaning is "dispersed," used of dream im- ages in Aristotle's *On Prophesying by Dreams* (464b13). Janko proposes as an English counterpart "paying," which means both paying out (disbursing), and paying in (profitable). The second example is *metron* (measure), which can be found in the *Clouds* of Aristophanes (637–47). Instructing Strep- siades in measures, Socrates asks him which is the most beautiful measure, trimeter or tetrameter. Strepsiades replies that he thinks nothing better than the *hemiekteon*, which is a measure equal to four *choinikes*, and is in this sense a tetrameter or four-measure, and, since a *choinix* measures a daily ration of grain, it measures four daily rations of grain.

Puns that are merely puns need not be funny, and are sometimes greeted with groans rather than laughter. They can be joined with the matter of the laughable when an expected sense of the words is first established, and the word is then taken in the wrong sense, which reveals a material wrongness such as Strepsiades's ignorance of prosody.

Here is a more recent example. W. C. Fields, when asked, "Do you believe in clubs for small children?" replied, "Only when kindness fails" (Holt 2008, 83). The expected meaning of "clubs" is established by the phrase "clubs for small children," and the formal elegance of the pun results from the fact that Fields can take it in a wrong sense that also relates to small children. The manner of his reply, "Only when kindness fails," reveals indirectly not only the formal wrongness of taking "clubs" in an unintended sense, but also the material wrongness of a kindly man who, though believing in treating small children with kindness, is nevertheless not averse to clubbing them if kindness fails.

Here is another example, a favorite of my brother-in-law, the mathematician Bert Eisenstadt: "His face was flushed, but his broad shoulders saved him." The normal meaning of "flushed" is established by its use in the familiar phrase, "His face was flushed," but the second clause implies by indirection not only the formal wrongness of taking the word in an unintended sense, but also the material wrongness of flushing people down toilets. This material wrongness is accompanied by a second formal wrongness, a formal wrongness with respect to things, that broad shoulders are needed to save a potential victim from being flushed down a toilet, for shoulders of quite ordinary width would suffice. This joke may be supposed to have its material roots in the childhood experience of seeing that whatever is flushed down the toilet in a scary rush of water is never seen or heard from again, and in the thought that this is a good way to get rid of unwanted things or people. But this leads to the further thought that one might oneself be flushed down the toilet, either on purpose or by accident. This, however, is countered by the reassuring thought that probably one is too big to go down the toilet. All of these thoughts may contribute to our enjoyment of the pun, for the different forms of wrongness in question are, from the superior vantage point of the adult, not painful or injurious but comic.

If we include homophony under homonymy, which seems the best place for it, we get a different kind of pun, well represented by Bishop Whatley's "Noah's ark was made of gopher wood, but Joan of Arc was maid of Orleans." This double pun does not conceal a hidden material wrongness, but what is funny is the formal wrongness of equating different words having the same sound as if they meant the same thing. The result is an absurd double pun with the material wrongness of having no significance.

Any joke format once established provides the possibility of a new kind of wrongness and a new kind of joke that uses it. "A priest, a rabbi, and a minister walk into a bar. The bartender says, 'What is this, a joke?'" In the context of homonymy, we have "Two men walk into a bar. The third one ducks."

Or the bar may simply provide a context for more homonymy: "So a C, an E flat, and a G walk into a bar and the bartender says, 'You know I don't serve minors.' So the E flat walks out and the C and G split a fifth." Such jokes are witty but not as funny as those that tap, not into the technical knowledge of musical scales, but into the great sources of material wrongness in sex, aggression, ethnic differences, and the excretory functions.

Homonymy can be extended from words to phrases, and in order not to omit possible sources of laughter in diction, it will be well to treat homonymy, and also synonymy and repetition, as applying to phrases as well as words. Here is an example from the _Philogelōs, or Laughter-lover,_ a joke book from late antiquity. A barber asks his client, "How shall I cut your hair," and the client replies, "In silence!" (Holt 2008, 11). It is the forms of the laughable that are universal, not the particular jokes that fall under them, but, if circumstances remain the same, jokes can be viable for centuries.

Homonymy and the other forms of the laughable appear also in tragedies, where they function to intensify the pity and fear rather than as sources of laughter. This makes clear that the forms of the laughable can be used for other than comic purposes. Thus Mercutio's "Ask for me tomorrow and you shall find me a grave man" (_Romeo and Juliet_ 2.2.101) reminds us of the high-spirited, witty person we are losing. Again, in the well-known punning sequence in _Hamlet_ that precedes the play within the play, Hamlet's manic exaltation, contrasting with his preceding suicidal depression, expresses itself in a somewhat inappropriate sexual aggressiveness toward Ophelia that turns into a repeated disparagement of femininity that presumably reflects, at least in part, his anger at Gertrude for her role in the usurpation. Hamlet furthers and concludes his attack by comically protesting his innocence. Even an occasion for pleasure and laughter is not free from corruption by the task imposed on Hamlet.

Ham. Lady, shall I lie in your lap?
Oph. No, my lord.
Ham. I mean, my head upon your lap?
Oph. Ay, my lord.
Ham. Do you think I meant country matters?

Oph. I think nothing, my lord.
Ham. That's a fair thought to lie between a maid's legs.
Oph. What is, my lord?
Ham. Nothing.
Oph. You are merry, my lord.
Ham. Who, I? (3.2.119–30)

2. Synonymy. The *Categories* has, "Synonyms are said to be those things of which the name is common and the formula of the essence corresponding to the name is the same, as man and ox are both animal, for each of them is called by the common name 'animal', and the formula of the essence corresponding to the name is the same" (1.1a6). If we transform this into a definition of synonymous words, they will be different words signifying the same thing, as "man" and "ox" both signify animal. It happens that we have a confirmation that synonyms were so defined in the *Poetics*, coming from Simplicius (sixth century) saying in his commentary on Aristotle's *Categories* that Porphyry (third century) in his *Greater Commentary on the Categories*, now lost, says, "Aristotle in the *Poetics* said that synonyms are when there are several words with the same meaning" (Janko 1984, 29, 63, 88, 172–73).

As an example of synonymy, the Prolegomenon offers "*hēkō kai katerchomai*" ("I'm here and I'm back!"), to be found in Aristophanes, *Frogs* 1153. The example is in one sense defective, since to be here and to be back do not have the same meaning, and this might seem to make its provenance from Aristotle suspect, but, as Janko points out (1984, 171–72), both have the same generic meaning in the sense of Aristotle's example from the *Categories*, in which man and ox are said to be synonymous because both signify animal; so here, both "I'm here" and "I'm back" signify that the speaker is now present.

Synonymy applies to phrases as well as individual words, as in Yogi Berra's "It's like déjà vu all over again." Another example is George W. Bush's, "You teach a child to read, and he or her will be able to pass a literacy test" (Wikipedia, s.v. "Bushisms"). In addition to the synonymy between ability to read and literacy, there is here the material wrongness of making passing a literacy test the reason for learning to read, and the further formal wrongness of the "her" that should be a "she." These formal wrongnesses are accompanied by the material wrongness of occurring in a statement advocating literacy. Wrongnesses piled one upon another in this way can all contribute to laughter.

Comic synonymy may appear in tragedies, as in Shakespeare's parody,

of Marlowe: "The rugged Pyrrhus, he whose sable arms, / Black as his purpose, did the night resemble" (*Hamlet* 2.2.474; the whole speech is quoted
as parody in Macdonald 1960, 16). The synonymy does not become an occasion for laughter, however, but contributes to our sense of the artificiality
of the play from which the Player is quoting, which becomes an occasion
for Hamlet to contrast the Player's expression of passion in an artificial situation with his own idleness in the face of a real provocation.

3. *Repetition (adoleschia).* *Adoleschia* means talking to no purpose,
which might include the examples of synonymy of words or phrases just
considered. If *adoleschia* is to mean something different from synonymy, it
would here mean saying the same things in the same words, or repetition.
This is the meaning that it has in *On Sophistical Refutations*, where it means
making one's opponent say the same thing again and again (3.165b16). The
formal relation among the first three sources of laughter would then be as
follows. If we start from two words that can be either the same or different
signifying two things that can also be either the same or different, we have
four possibilities: the same word may signify different things (homonymy),
the same thing may be signified by different words (synonymy), the same
words may signify the same things (repetition), or different words may signify different things, the normal case and not a form of wrongness.

Yogi Berra supplies an example of a comic single repetition in "It ain't
over till it's over" (Wikipedia, s.v. "Yogi Berra"). My understanding of its
initial use is that it was also a parodic put-down and last word with respect
to the many expressions of the form "It's not over until . . ." An example of
comic multiple repetition is found in Shakespeare's *All's Well that Ends Well*
(2.2), in which "O Lord, sir!" is tried out as an answer that fits all questions.[1]

Sometimes an expression will become associated with a particular char-
acter and we come to expect the repetition, which adds to the enjoyment.
Weekly radio shows in the days before television sometimes had a person
who would repeat the same line each week, getting a laugh each time, as
Molly saying to Fibber McGee, "Tain't funny, McGee," or Jack Pearl as Baron
Munchausen saying, "Vass you dere, Charlie?"[2] or, on the Fred Allen show,
Titus Moody's melancholy "I'm not long for this world," or Senator Claghorn's boisterous "That's a joke, son!" A more recent example is Bugs Bun-
ny's repetition of "Anh—What's up, Doc?"

4. *Paronymy.* Paronyms are words derived from another word. We have
in the case of paronymy three relevant definitions, which together clarify
how paronymy applies to logic, poetry, tragedy, and comedy. (1) The definition of paronyms from the *Categories*: "Paronyms are said to be those things

that derive their name from another name by some difference in inflection (*ptōsis*), as from grammar the grammarian and from courage the courageous" (*Cat.* 1.1a12). (2) The definition of extended words in *Poetics* I: "A word is extended when a longer vocal element is used than what is appropriate to it, or when a syllable is inserted, e.g., *poleōs* for *poléos* and *Pēléadeō* for *Pēleidou*" (22.1457b35–1458a4, trans. Telford). (3) The definition of paronyms by addition in the *Prolegomenon*: "Fourth, from paronyms by addition, when something extraneous (*exōthen*) is attached to the standard (*kurios*) term" (Janko 1984, 31). Paronyms in the *Categories* derive from inflections, which belong to grammar. Paronymy by addition in the *Poetics* is defined in Book I as an inappropriate addition, that is, an addition not grammatically appropriate to the word, and in Book II as an exothenic addition, that is, an addition whose source is external to grammar. From this we see that "paronymy" is an analogical term meaning different things in different disciplines—in the *Categories*, paronymy results from grammatical derivations, in the *Poetics* from non-grammatical derivations. The two definitions in the *Poetics* are synonymous in the sense of saying the same thing in different words, but the definition and examples in Book I emphasize the lengthening of the sound, and Book II emphasizes the exothenic character of the addition. All three definitions are appropriate to their respective contexts. The *Categories* is concerned with words that have a determinate relation to things and thus can be used to state what is true, whereas the *Poetics* is concerned with words that have an emotional effect, either contributing to the solemnity of tragedy through lengthened or additional vowel sounds, or contributing to the laughter of comedy because they are exothenic and in this sense wrong.

Paronymy by addition. Here we have a place for the Aristotelian word preserved by the Anti-Atticist. The word begins like the comparative *kunteros*, (more shameless or doglike), but continues like the superlative *kuntatos* (most shameless), resulting in a paronym by the addition of a "to": *kuntotatos*. The effect is that of a super-superlative appropriate to a comic insult. A comparable doubling of the comparative ending is used in "No one is betterer than Roger Federer," which appeared on a banner held up by his fans at a time when he was the world's best tennis player. The additional "er" at the end of "better," a standard word, makes an extended or nonstandard word, but one that, even though it is not grammatical, is appropriate to Roger Federer because it says that he is better than better, and this accords phonetically with his name. Playfulness with respect to words is characteristic of young children and abandoned in proper adult speech, and the return to childlike speech seems to require justification by producing a true result. Examples of derogatory paronymy by addition are Gershon Legman's "cacademics" for "academics," and "Phudniks" for PhDs (Holt 2008, 33). Condensations such as De Quincey's "anecdotage" (Freud 1963, 22) are also paronyms by addition. Freud takes such paronyms, and in particular the German *familionär*, a condensation of *familiär* (familiarly) and *millionär* (millionaire), as the starting point for his analysis of jokes (Freud 1963, 16–22). The English counterpart of *familionär* would be "famillionairely," which is not as condensed nor as elegant as the German because it requires more than the addition of a "fa" or an "on." Economy of means often adds to the laughability of a joke.

Paronymy by subtraction. This is illustrated in the Prolegomenon by "I'm called Midas the Bomax," where "Midas" is a common slave's name (Janko 1984, 178) and *bōmax* is listed in *LSJ* as equivalent to *bōmolochos*, from which it is derived by subtraction. *Bōmolochos* is derived from *bōmos* (altar) and *lochaō* (to lie in wait) and properly means "one that waited about altars to beg or steal some of the meat offered thereon" (*LSJ*), but it is Aristotle's word in the *Ethics* for someone who goes to excess in the giving of amusement—that is, a buffoon (*Eth.* ii.7.1108a25). In this sense Midas would in English be saying, "I'm called Midas the Buffoon," but the paronymy is lost.

Paronymy by a diminutive. This gives a word a diminutive ending. The diminutive endings of the examples are *-ion* or *-idion*, which are the most common diminutive endings, but there are others. A full list is in Starkie 1909 (lv–lvi). The Prolegomenon offers *Sōcratidion* (*Clouds* 223) and *Euripidion* (*Acharnians* 404). Janko translates these as "Socratiddles" and "Euripidipides." Aristotle in the *Rhetoric* (iii.2.1405b30) gives four diminutives from the *Babylonians* of Aristophanes: *chrusidarion* (goldlet), *himatidarion* (cloaklet), *loidorēmation* (abuselet), and *nosēmation* (plaguelet). Diminutives are not necessarily funny, but may become so when their use involves some wrongness, as when applied to objects that are not small. They tend to be funny, however, because, like the pun on "flushed," they take us back to the world of childhood, a point to which we shall return later.

Paronymy by alteration. In general, addition and subtraction are changes of quantity, whereas alteration is a change of quality. Just as paronymy by addition results from any exothenic attachment to a standard word, so we would expect paronymy by alteration to result from any exothenic alteration of a standard word. The Prolegomenon's example is *Ō Bdeu despota* (O Mighty Fart) instead of *Ō Zeu despota* (O Mighty Zeus).[3] *Bdeu* alters the initial sound of *Zeu*, but the paronymy is lost in translation, for "fart" is not an alteration of "Zeus"—they are just different words, and we have in English what could be parody but is not paronymy. Janko proposes as an English counterpart to the Prolegomenon example, "O Clod Almighty." "Clod" is a paronym of "God" by alteration of the initial sound, but "O Clod Almighty" is not as funny as "O Mighty Fart" because it falls short in material wrongness. The comic potentialities of mighty farts have been exploited by the moderns as well as the ancients. Mark Twain in *1601: Conversation as It Was by the Social Fireside in the Time of the Tudors* (Twain, n.d.), taking off from the historical fart of Sir Walter Raleigh when making a low obeisance to Queen Elizabeth (Holt 2008, 52), reconstructs a fireside conversation in the time of the Tudors, in which Queen Elizabeth questions her companions as to who among them is responsible for a mighty fart. Sir Walter finally acknowledges that it is his, but modestly deprecates its might: "Most gracious maisty, 'twas I that did it, but indeed it was so poor and frail a note, compared with such as I am wont to furnish, yt in sooth I was ashamed to call the weakling mine in so august a presence" (Twain n.d., 35). Sir Walter proceeds to make amends for his weakling by producing for the delectation of her gracious majesty and the elegant company a truly mighty fart.

Cicero, in his account of the laughable in *De oratore* says, "Another kind of joke uses a slight change in a word, which, when it is the change of a letter, the Greeks call *paronomasia*, as Cato called a man surnamed 'Nobiliorem' (the Noble) 'Mobiliorem' (the Fickle)" (*De Orat.* ii.63.256). This example has the same form as the example in the Prolegomenon, and thus supports Janko's conclusion, reached on other grounds, that Cicero was using a source in some way related to the *Prolegomenon* (Janko1984, 73), an important point to which we shall later return.

Paronymy by alteration may be doubled by an exchange of letters, as in Spoonerisms: "How often do we feel a half-warmed fish rise within us." Or there may be an exchange of syllables rather than letters: "How do you titillate an ocelot? You oscillate its tits a lot" (Holt 2008, 78). The interchange of the stressed syllables of the two dactyls of the question yields its answer. Elegant! It has in addition the material wrongness of oscillating tits a lot, not always a proper subject of conversation, but, once the question is asked, unavoidable.

5. *Parody.* A paronym is etymologically a "beside-word," a word derivative from another word, whereas a parody is etymologically a "beside-song," a song derived from another song. Aristotle's only use of "parody" in the surviving works says that Hegemon of Thasos was the first to produce parodies (2.1448a12–14). (One might have thought that parodies began with

the *Margitēs* or earlier, but Aristotle is evidently presupposing the distinction between invective parody (*Margitēs*) and comic parody (Hegemon). The example of Hegemon suggests that parodies are derivations that do not depend upon changes in the parts of words (paronymy), but on changes of whole words and the way they are put together. They are often of some length, like Chaucer's "Tale of Sir Thopas," but a one-word parody is possible, as when Ronald Reagan replied to the question, "How was your meeting with Bishop Tutu?" with, "So-so." "So-so" is not a paronym of "Tutu," but another word that resembles it in being composed of a repeated syllable. Such words are characteristic of baby-talk and again take us back to a time when words were perceived as indicating properties of the things that they name, and so we are delighted in this case to find it confirmed by a president of the United States that a meeting with a bishop named Tutu should be so-so.

An example of parodying a sentence by subtracting a word is provided by my high school chemistry teacher. He asked a student whether, if one performed a certain experiment, one would get a certain result, and the student replied, rather tentatively, "I don't think so," to which he responded, "You can leave off the 'so.'" This was an attempt at a joke, and it might have succeeded, but the victim happened to excel in art if not in chemistry, and was popular because she was good-looking, modest, and considerate of others. Hence the wrongness attributed by the teacher to her answer was inconsiderate and not free from pain, and was an example of mockery rather than the laughable. As mockery of a student by a teacher, it is an example of wrongness in teaching, which is why I remember it, and which would make it funny as a teaching technique only if it were not painful.

Will Rogers took a parodic jab at a political wrongness by changing the last word in a familiar saying, "A fool and his money are soon elected." Or, varying the parodic form of the same material wrongness, "America has the best politicians money can buy" (Rogers 179, 63).

These jokes have become dated not because the problem has gone away, but because the current ways in which money influences politics are not reflected in the language used. Adlai Stevenson united parody with homonymy when he parried the charge of being an egghead by saying, parodying the slogan derived from the conclusion of Marx's *Communist Manifesto,* "Eggheads of the world, unite! You have nothing to lose but your yokes!"

An example of parody involving word order rather than word substitution is provided by a sentence from Wolcott Gibbs's celebrated parody of the style of *Time* magazine, which he calls Timestyle: "Backward ran sentences until reeled the mind" (Macdonald 1960, 342). The inversion of the normal order of subject and predicate in Timestyle is parodied twice in one sentence, resulting in a reeling of the mind that mirrors the turning-around of the subject-predicate order that has produced it.

The parody of the story of Cinderella and the Prince, "Prinderella and the Cince,"[4] is a parody by repeated spoonerisms. It is remarkable for the way in which the parodied original can barely be discerned through the incessant wrongness. Parody is of course a well-recognized literary form, and Dwight Macdonald has compiled a 550-page anthology of parodies, beginning with the "Tale of Sir Thopas" (Macdonald 1960).

6. Transference by sound. Transference of names has the general meaning of transferring the name of one thing to another (*Poet.* 21.1457b7). A transference of names by sound has been called a malapropism, named after Mrs. Malaprop in R. B. Sheridan's *Rivals* (1775), whose name is a paronym by subtraction of "malapropos." Her best-known malapropism is, "As headstrong as an allegory on the banks of the Nile." Shakespeare's Constable Dogberry in *Much Ado about Nothing* supplies many examples, as "Our watch, sir, have indeed comprehended two auspicious persons" (3.5.49).

Transference by sound is also illustrated by mishearings. My wife's father was an accountant, and as a child she thought he went off to work to do "taxi-turns." Such mishearings were baptized "mondegreens" by Sylvia Wright in "The Death of Lady Mondegreen" (*Harper's Magazine*, November 1954). She writes, "When I was a child, my mother used to read aloud to me from Percy's *Reliques*, and one of my favorite poems began, as I remember:

Ye Highlands and ye Lowlands,
Oh, where hae ye been?
They hae slain the Earl Amurray,
And Lady Mondegreen."
(Wikipedia, s.v. "Mondegreen")

The ending should have been, "They hae slain the Earl O'Murray, / And laid him on the green." Another example is mishearing "surely goodness and mercy" in the comforting line of Psalm 23 as "surely good Mrs. Murphy shall follow me all the days of my life." The matter as well as the form of the wrongness is important, for it brings with it the image of good Mrs. Murphy carrying her handbag and dutifully following along behind the psalmist wherever he goes. Wikipedia provides extensive lists of malapropisms, mondegreens, words in one language that sound like words in another language, and other varieties of transference by sound.

Transference by homogeneous attributes, or metaphor. Mark Twain provides an example in *1601*: the narrator, the Queen's cup-bearer, exasperated at having to endure the farts of Sir Walter without complaint, refers to him as "ye damned windmill" (Twain, n.d., 36). As a metaphor, it is imperfect, because a windmill is turned by the wind, but does not produce it, but its comic value is enhanced by the magnitude of the wind involved. Another instance is in the first act of Puccini's *La Bohème* in which the landlord Benoit comes to the loft of the Bohemians to demand the rent. The occupants ply him with wine and encourage him to reveal his amorous exploits. In feigned admiration for his prowess, Marcello exclaims, "Una quercia! Un cannone!" (An oak! A cannon!), expressing by metaphor a gross exaggeration of what Benoit has actually said. When Prince Hal calls Falstaff a "huge hill of flesh," Falstaff retaliates with a torrent of metaphors: "'SBlood, you starveling, you elf-skin, you dried neat's tongue, you bull's pizzle, you stockfish! O for breath to utter what is like thee! You tailor's yard, you sheath, you bow-case, you vile standing-tuck,—" (*Henry IV, Pt. 1* 2.4.269–74).

7. *Form of diction*. The form of diction shifts from what is said to how it is said (cf. *Rhet.* iii.1.1403b15). Wrongness of diction is not subdivided and we see Aristotle's list tailing off into indefiniteness. Different forms of diction are mentioned by Aristotle in different disciplines, and wrongness in any of them can be a source of laughter. The forms of diction mentioned in *Poetics* I are the differences between a command, a prayer, a description, a threat, a question, an answer, or anything else of this sort (9.1456b9–19). They are assigned to the architectonic art of elocution (*hupokritikē*), because what is right or wrong with respect to them depends primarily on how they are spoken. This art is architectonic because it governs all speech as spoken. Wrongness in form of diction in this sense is wrongness in the speaking of the words. Here we meet, among others, our old friend, the lady who puts the wrong emphásis upon her syllábles.

Forms of diction are also mentioned in sophistic and rhetoric. In *On Sophistical Refutations* the last of the six topics of refutation that depend upon diction is the form of the diction (*Soph. Ref.* 4.166b10–19). Fallacies can result from the form of the diction when grammatical gender differs from natural gender or when the ending of a term puts it in the wrong grammatical category. These sources of fallacy can also be sources of laughter, as when Socrates in the *Clouds* instructs Strepsiades on the agreement of grammatical gender with natural gender with respect to "trough" and "Cleon" (658–93). Another example in which grammatical wrongness produces laughter rather than fallacious arguments is provided by another Bushism:

"Rarely is the question asked: How is our children learning?" (Wikipedia). As we have noted, when the wrongness in a joke turns out to be in some way right, this enhances the joke by confirming the wrongness rather than negating it, as in this case the grammatical wrongness does indeed make the question one rarely asked.

Forms of diction are discussed twice in the *Rhetoric*, as a source of apparent enthymemes and in relation to style. The form of the diction is used persuasively when what is said, although not an enthymeme, appears to be an enthymeme because of the way it is said (*Rhet.* ii.24.1401a1–7). It can be a source of the laughable, as illustrated by the speech of the grave-digger in *Hamlet*, which has the diction of a legal argument without being one: "For here lies the point: if I drown myself wittingly, it argues an act, and an act hath three branches; it is to act, to do, and to perform; argal, she drowned herself wittingly," followed, after an attempted protest, by, "Give me leave. Here lies the water; good. Here stands the man; good. If the man goes to this water and drown himself, it is, will he nill he, he goes,—mark you that? But if the water comes to him and drown him, he drowns not himself; argal, he that is not guilty of his own death shortens not his own life" (5.1. 10–22). This comic scene begins the series of confrontations with death with which the tragedy ends. In the discussion of style in Book III of the *Rhetoric* it is said that the form of diction should be neither metrical nor without rhythm, for if it is metrical it is unpersuasive and if it is without rhythm it is not pleasant (*Rhet.* iii.8.1408b21–33). Here we have a place for the wrongness with respect to meter that we supposed at the outset to be included in the sources of laughter in diction. An example of the laughable originating from rhythm is to be found in Aristophanes's *Knights* (216): *molōmen* (let us go) spoken slowly at first but with increasing rapidity and then followed by *auto* becomes *automolōmen* (let us desert), an action that dares not speak its name, while at the same time the rhythm of the words suggests masturbation, and the comic potentialities of the similarity of desertion to masturbation are then developed.

The generality of a list such as this depends on the principles by which it is generated. It progresses from what is most definite and determinate toward what is more indefinite and indeterminate. It begins with the possibilities for wrongness that inhere in standard speech.

Such wrongness may result from a one-many relation of terms to their meaning (homonymy), or a many-one relation (synonymy), or a one-to-one relation (repetition). Next is wrongness in what is said that has its origin in deviations from the standard form of derivations from standard speech, which may involve paronymy either by a change of quantity (addition or subtraction), or by a change of quality (alteration), and the latter may have standard forms, as in diminutives, or it may not. Deviational derivation may originate from changes of the parts of words (paronymy) or in the parts of compositions (parody). We proceed from deviational derivations from standard speech to deviational substitutions for it (transference), and the transference may originate from similarities in sound (malapropism) or from similarities in meaning (metaphor). All of these concern what is said, and wrongness in how it is said (form of diction) opens up a whole new and more indeterminate domain that is not subdivided.

5. LAUGHTER FROM THE INCIDENTS

The laughter from the incidents. We now turn from the diction of comedy to the incidents of comedy as sources of laughter. Since the tragic plot is the construction of the incidents, any kind of incident is in general susceptible of either a comic or a tragic form, reminding us again that the laughable is more than its forms.

1. *From deception.* The Prolegomenon gives as an example Strepsiades believing the story about the flea was true. Near the beginning of the *Clouds*, Strepsiades concludes that if he is to free himself of his debts he must go to the school of Socrates himself and learn unjust logic. His knocking is answered by a student who consents to reveal to him some of the mysteries of the school, including how Socrates measured the length of a flea's foot:

> Student.   'Twas Socrates was asking Chaerephon,
> How many feet of its own a flea could jump,
> For one first bit the brow of Chaerephon,
> Then bounded off to Socrates's head.
> Strep. How did he measure this?
> Stu.   Most cleverly.
> He warmed some wax, and then he caught the flea,
> And dipped its feet into the wax he'd melted:
> Then let it cool, and then there were Persian slippers!
> These he took off, and so he found the distance.
> Strep. O Zeus and king, what subtle intellects!
> (144–52, trans. B. B. Rogers)

Deception plays a major role in comedies of wits and gulls, such as Ben Jonson's *The Alchemist*, as does deception with respect to identity in Shakespeare's *Comedy of Errors*, with its two sets of identical twins, and again in *Twelfth Night,* in which the twins Viola and her brother Sebastian are mistaken for each other. Deception has a tragic form in Iago's deception of *Othello.*

2. *From assimilation used towards the better or towards the worse.* The Prolegomenon gives an example of each: toward the better when Xanthias, the slave of Dionysius, is made to resemble Heracles, and toward the worse, when Dionysus is made to resemble Xanthias (Aristophanes, *Frogs* 495ff). These joke-forms are frequent in ordinary joking conversation, as when blunders are called brilliant and unusual skill is referred to as incompetence.

What are called sick jokes have the form of an assimilation of the extremely bad to the ordinary or everyday. "Aside from that, Mrs. Lincoln, how did you like the play?" Or the Little Willy jokes, such as

> Willy and some other brats
> Licked up all the Rough-on-Rats.
> Father said, when Mother cried,
> "Never mind, they'll die outside."

Or "Mom, why do I keep going around in circles?" "Shut up or I'll nail your other foot to the floor!"

The use in tragedy of assimilation toward the better is given in Book I: "As Tragedy is an imitation of personages better than ordinary men, we in our way should follow the example of good portrait-painters, who reproduce the distinctive features of a man, and, at the same time, without losing the likeness, make him handsomer than he is" (15.1454b8, trans. Bywater). The assimilation toward the better in portraits has recently been a subject of public discussion with respect to the Cobbe portrait of Shakespeare. Assimilation toward the worse is illustrated by caricature, of which examples are plentiful.

The contributions of the Prolegomenon to the sources of laughter end at this point, and we are left with only the epitome's list of sources unaccompanied by definitions or examples.

3. *From the impossible.* This is the counterpart of, and opposite to, necessity in the tragic plot. An example of impossibility is the classic Chas Addams cartoon in which we see that a downhill skier watched by another skier has made tracks that go on opposite sides of a stout tree. This joke depends entirely on the form, the matter serving simply as a vehicle for the form. It is what Freud calls an innocent, as distinguished from a tendentious, joke. One of the delights of Aristophanes is his freedom from the restraints of possibility, as Trygaeus feeding a dung beetle until it is large

enough to carry him off to Olympus (*Peace*), or the poetry contest between Aeschylus and Euripides in Hades (*The Frogs*). Another example of the comic impossible begins from the wisdom of Silenus expressed in the saying "Never to have been born would be the best thing for mortal men." The German comic weekly *Fliegende Blätter* (*Flying Leaves*) comments: "Yes, but this happens to scarcely one person in a hundred thousand" (quoted from Freud 1963, 57). The joke depends on taking the statement of Silenus in an unintended sense as meaning the best thing that can happen to mortal men once they have been born, and brings out its absurdity in this sense by trying to estimate how many of those who have been born have not been born. Materially, the joke counters the intended meaning, well formulated elsewhere by Freud (1962, 22), "Life as we find it is too hard for us; it brings us too many pains, disappointments and impossible tasks. In order to bear it we cannot dispense with palliative measures." The joke counters this meaning by making the statement itself a source of enjoyment, although, since it depends on deviating from its true meaning, we are left with the view of life of expressed by Silenus and Freud, but made more endurable by humor as a palliative measure.

4. *From the possible and inconsequential.* This is the counterpart of, and opposite to, probability in the tragic plot. It is possible rather than impossible, but is, so to speak, an attenuation of the impossible because it does not usually follow and is therefore improbable, just as the probable is an attenuation of the necessary. The comic hero, for example, may always escape unharmed from his predicaments. This is a staple of cartoon shorts, as Bugs Bunny escapes from the efforts of antagonists such as Elmer J. Fudd, Yosemite Sam, and Wile E. Coyote to destroy, eat, or otherwise get the better of him. Or the incompetent detective may always succeed, for example Inspector Clouseau (Peter Sellers) in the *Pink Panther* films, or Agent 86 Maxwell Smart (Don Adams) in the *Get Smart* television series. I recall also a scene from an early comic movie that I have otherwise forgotten in which paroxysms of laughter erupted when in the film a butcher attempts to slice up a bologna, but it keeps slipping away from him and for one reason or another always eludes his knife. The unconscious source of the material wrongness in this case was evident from the phallic appearance of bologna.

5. *From things contrary to expectation.* This can play an important role in both tragedy and comedy, for it can be a cause of pleasure and laughter in comedy and pity and fear in tragedy. "Incidents come to be most piteous and fearsome, or more so, when they arise because of one another and yet are contrary to what would seem to follow" (9.1452a3, trans. Telford). Ar-

istotle offers a comic example of contrariety to expectation in the *Rhetoric*: "'Onward he came, and his feet were shod with his—chilblains,' where one imagined the word would be 'sandals'" (iii.11.1412a20, trans. Roberts). This is an example of something contrary to expectation, but, taken in isolation, it is not a good example of a source of laughter because striding onward on chilblains would be painful. It is presumably part of a parody that did not purport to represent anything real. It is like Oscar Wilde's comment on the death of Little Nell in Dickens's *The Old Curiosity Shop*: "One must have a heart of stone to read the death of Little Nell without laughing,"[5] which reduces Dickens's account to unjustified sentimentality at which we are free to laugh. Another example of this form is Will Rogers's "I am not a member of any organized political party—I am a Democrat" (Rogers 1979, 55).

6. *From accoutering the personages toward the wretched.* Here we have all the ways in which the persons of the drama can be made laughable by their appurtenances. Circus clowns are a conspicuous example. Their voices cannot be heard, so they must rely on spectacle to produce laughter, and their costumes and equipment are made to be funny. An example of accoutering a character toward the wretched in tragedy is Edgar disguised as Poor Tom in *King Lear*. The function of the disguise is not to make us laugh, but to provide a visual counterpart to Lear's effort to do away with pretense and convention and find "unaccommodated man."

7. *From using vulgar dancing.* Vulgar dancing is to be contrasted with the stately dancing of tragedy. Comic dances could indeed be vulgar, particularly the dance called the Cordax. Starkie comments, "From the *Nubes* [*Clouds*] 540 it appears that the Cordax was so unseemly that Aristophanes prided himself, in respect of his rivals Eupolis and Hermippus, on avoiding it in his plays" (1909, lxx). In this and the remaining sources of laughter from the incidents Aristotle uses an extreme form to represent the entire class, but any form of wrongness of bodily movement is included. A classic example of comic dancing that is not vulgar is Charlie Chaplin's comic movements and dances, a few of which can now be seen on the Internet. The first comic films were silent and relied heavily on comic physical actions and facial expressions, and this carried over into early comic films generally, as in the films of Chaplin, Buster Keaton, Harold Lloyd, the Three Stooges, Laurel and Hardy, Abbott and Costello, and the Marx Brothers. A later example is provided by the Monty Python Ministry of Silly Walks. I once knew an expert ice-skater and performer who had mastered the art of appearing unable to skate, and his performance was very funny indeed. Some of the funniest comic dancing I have ever seen was by Matthew Broderick in

The Foreigner, which, so far as I know, was never recorded, and in this respect is like the great majority of comic dancing.

8. **When someone having the power to do things lets go the greatest and takes the most worthless.** This is an extreme form of wrongness of choice. As an error of choice, it belongs to the same genus as the tragic *hamartia*. A comic example in the moral sphere is provided by Jane Austen at the beginning of *Sense and Sensibility*. John Dashwood plans to give his three sisters a thousand pounds each as their share of their late father's estate, and this would be the morally right amount. We witness the declination of his choice from the morally right mean to the morally wrong extreme as his illiberal wife persuades him in a series of specious arguments to successively reduce his sisters' share until they finally get nothing at all. He has the power to do the best, but does the worst. Macbeth offers a parallel example from tragedy. He has the power to treat Duncan with appropriate hospitality, but is persuaded by the specious arguments of his ambitious wife to murder him.

9. **When the speech is disconnected and lacking any consecution.** This is an extreme form of wrongness of thought. Speech that is disconnected is scatterbrained and jumps from one thing to another. Lacking consecution is illustrated by the numerous jokes based on faulty logic, such as the well-known reply of the man accused by his neighbor of returning a borrowed pot with a hole in it: "First, I never borrowed your pot; secondly, I returned it in good condition; and thirdly, it had a hole in it when I borrowed it!" Another familiar example is the man encountered by the Arkansas traveler whose rooftree leaked like a waterfall. Asked why he doesn't mend it, the man replies, "I can't mend it now; it's a rainy day." Advised to mend it on a day that is fair and bright, "Get along," says he, "for you give me a pain. My roof never leaks when it doesn't rain!"

What structure can we discern in this list of the kinds of wrongness in the incidents? The first two, deception and assimilation, are evidently wrongness in appearance rather than reality. The appearance may correspond to nothing real, as in the case of measuring the flea's foot, or it may be an assimilation of the real to something it is not, which may be either better or worse than what it is. After wrongness in appearance comes wrongness in reality. The first is a wrongness that inheres in the thing taken by itself, its impossibility; next is wrongness in relation to something else, either other things or us. Wrongness in relation to other things occurs when something is inconsequential, and in relation to us when something is contrary to our expectation. These are forms of wrongness that may be found in any kind of thing, and after them come forms of wrongness limited to a specific kind of thing. Since the kinds of things are indefinite in number, Aristotle takes a person as the representative case because a person has the fullest range of possibilities. We see this also in the definition of "quality" in the *Categories*: "By 'quality' I mean that in virtue of which people are said to be such and such" (*Cat.* 8.8b25). People exhibit the fullest range of qualitative possibilities, and "by means of a very common sort of personification, animals become comic too, and inanimate objects" (Freud 1963, 189). To a person may belong wrongness of his accouterments, body, character, or intellect. The distinction among the four parallels the common distinction cited in the *Ethics*: external goods, goods of the body, and goods of the soul (1.8.1098b12), goods of the soul being subsequently divided into moral and intellectual (13.1103.a3–10). Thus the wrongness that belongs to a person may be wrongness in what he has or what he is. Wrongness in what he is is wrongness of body or soul, and wrongness of soul is moral or intellectual.

6. CICERO'S ACCOUNT OF LAUGHTER

We have interpreted the laughable in comedy as resulting from a synergy of causes, a formal wrongness of diction or incident united with a material wrongness of body or soul expressed indirectly, and the whole aiming at a symmetry of the laughable and the serious. Before considering how this relates to a possible science of the laughable, I want to compare it to Cicero's account of laughter in *De oratore* because Aristotle's theory is a possible source of Cicero's account.

Jokes are an important element in rhetoric as well as comedy. Aristotle in his *Rhetoric* twice refers to his account of the forms of the laughable in the *Poetics*. Cicero knew Aristotle's *Rhetoric* well, and so would have known that the *Poetics* contained an account of jokes. Would the *Poetics* have been available to him? Gerald Else writes, "I can see little firm evidence of a knowledge of *our Poetics* at any time between Theophrastus and the fourth century A.D." (Else 1957, 337n125). Cairns Lord writes, "Certainly, the idea that all of Aristotle's school treatises were unknown in the Hellenistic period can no longer be sustained. Yet it seems quite possible, considering the surprisingly slight influence exercised by Aristotle in certain of the major areas of his activity throughout this period, that some of these writings did indeed remain completely unknown. The *Politics* and the *Poetics* in particular may be mentioned as candidates for this category" (Lord 1986, 140–41). The view that the *Poetics* was not generally available in the Hellenistic period is supported by Cicero himself. In Cicero's dialogue *De oratore* the speaker who gives the account of laughter, Julius Caesar Vobiscus, says, "On seeing sundry Greek books entitled *Concerning the Laughable*, I entertained the hope of being able to learn something from them, and did indeed find much in Greek writing that was laughable and pungent, the inhabitants of Sicily, Rhodes, Byzantium, and particularly Athens having distinguished themselves in this kind of thing; all however who tried to teach anything like a theory or art of this matter proved themselves so conspicuously silly that their very silliness is the only laughable thing about them" (*De Orat.* ii.54.217, trans. Sutton and Rackham). This probably reflects the experience of Cicero himself in searching for Greek accounts of the laughable. But the dramatic date of *De oratore* is 91 BCE and the Aristotelian corpus did not reach Rome until 83. Thus Caesar's statement is not inconsistent with *Poetics* being in the corpus. Cicero does not mention the Androncus edition of the corpus, which is supposed to have been published between 40 and 20 (Düring 1957, 421). Cicero completed *De oratore* in 55, and he died in 43, so it is unlikely that he used the *Poetics* in the Andronicus edition when working on *De oratore*. But this does not mean that he did not see it when it was in the Sulla library (Sulla himself died in 78, his son in 46).

Cicero was in the habit of borrowing from the libraries of others books that were not in his own library. He writes, "I was down at my place at Tusculum, and wanted to consult certain books from the library of the young Luculllus, so I went to his villa, to fetch them, as I was in the habit of doing." Asked by the interlocutor in the dialogue, Marcus Cato, who found him at Lucullus's villa, "What, then, are the books that you must come here for when you have so large a library of your own?" he replied, "Certain treatises (*commentaria*) of Aristotle, which I knew were here" (Cicero, *De finibus* iii.2–3). If Cicero had known that the *Poetics* was in the library of Sulla and had wanted to consult it, he would most probably have done so. At the time Cicero was working on *De oratore* the corpus had been in Rome about seventy years, and it is probable that word had gotten around that the works of Aristotle and Theophrastus were in the Sulla library. Word that the works were there had evidently reached Andronicus of Rhodes, if not by this time, at least not long afterward. That Cicero would have wanted to consult the *Poetics* when writing his own theory of laughter is probable for many reasons, not least his high opinion of Aristotle's work, which is evident from *De oratore* itself. *De oratore* has the form of an imagined dialogue taking place in September 91, at the Tusculan villa of Crassus. The two principal speakers are the most accomplished rhetoricians of that time,

Lucius Crassus, teacher of Cicero, who most nearly represents Cicero's own views, and Marcus Antonius, grandfather of the triumvir, whose views resemble those of Cicero's brother, Quintus. Also present are two of their distinguished disciples, Publius Sulpicius Rufus, a disciple of Crassus, and Caius Aurelius Cotta, a disciple of Antonius. In Book II these four are joined by a pair of half brothers, Quintus Catulus, an Aristotelian rhetorician, and Julius Caesar Vobiscus.

Catulus speaks first of Aristotle: "But Aristotle, he whom I admire more than any of them [the philosophers], has set forth certain topics from which every line of argument may be invented, not only for the disputations of philosophy, but even for reasoning which we use in pleading causes; from whose notions your discourse, Antonius, has for some time past not varied; whether you, from a resemblance to that divine genius, hit upon his track, or whether you have read and made yourself a master of his writings — a supposition, indeed which seem to be more probable than the other, for I see that you have paid more attention to the Greek writers than we had imagined" (ii.36.152; Cicero 1970, 124).

Antonius says in his response, "Between this Aristotle (of whom I have read, as well as that book in which he explains the rhetorical systems of all who went before him, as those in which he gives us some notions of his own art), between him, I say, and professed teachers of the art, there appeared to me to be this difference, that he, with the same acuteness of intellect with which he had penetrated the qualities and nature of things throughout the universe, saw into every thing that pertained to the art of rhetoric, which he thought beneath him; but they, who thought this art alone worthy of cultivation, passed their whole lives in contemplating this one subject, not with as much ability as he, but with constant practice in their single pursuit, and greater devotion to it" (ibid., 38.160, p. 127).

Finally, Crassus, expressing Cicero's own view, so far as anyone in the dialogue does, sums up the importance of Aristotle for rhetoric and fore-shadows the coming of Cicero as the perfect orator, by saying, "If ever a person shall arise who shall have abilities to deliver opinions on both sides of a question on all subjects, after the manner of Aristotle, and from a knowledge of the precepts of that philosopher, to deliver two contradic-tory orations on every conceivable topic, or shall be able, after the manner of Arcesilas or Carneades, to dispute against every proposition that can be laid down, and shall unite with those powers rhetorical skill, and practice and exercise in speaking, he will be the true, the perfect, the only orator" (iii.21.80; Cicero 1970, 214–15). Cicero thus indicates the importance for his own work of the precepts of Aristotle, and I think it leaves little doubt that he would have consulted Aristotle on the laughable when treating the subject himself if he had known that Aristotle's work was in Rome, as he probably did. We may note incidentally that Cicero has Crassus make clear the difference between, on the one hand, an architectonic rhetorician such as himself (or McKeon, who uses Cicero's *De inventione* to formulate his own architectonic rhetoric [McKeon 1998, 2:197]), and, on the other hand, a disciplinary rhetorician such as Aristotle. The one treats all subjects by means of opposed arguments, the other contrasts the conflicting arguments of rhetoric with the definite knowledge of science.

Let us now turn to the influence of Aristotle on Cicero's account. The task of speaking about laughter is assigned by Antonius to Caesar because he "far surpasses all others in jokes (*jocus*) and witticisms (*facetiae*)" (ii.54.216). Caesar expresses surprise at this praise: "One thing certainly surprises me, and that is your attributing so much success to me in this sphere, instead of awarding the prize for this, as for all else, to Crassus." Antonius rejoins, "I should certainly have done so were I not now and then a little envious of Crassus in this connection; for merely to be as witty and shrewd as you please need not excite unmeasured envy, but that the most attractive and polished of all speakers should at the same time be obviously the most impressive and austere, as has been the lot of our friend alone,—this did seem rather more than I could bear" (ii.56.228, trans. Sutton and Rackham). We see here already the rhetorical counterpart of Aristotle's principle of symmetry, uniting the laughable with the serious. It appears as the high point of rhetorical achievement, which distinguishes the foremost speaker of the age, Crassus, from the second-best, Antonius. In the rhetorical account, symmetry is found in the power of the speaker, while in the poetic account of Aristotle it is found in the work that the poet produces.

Caesar begins his account of laughter with a list of questions to be answered. "As regards laughter (*risus*), five things are to be sought: one, what it is; another, whence it is; third, whether it belongs to the orator to wish to produce it; fourth, to what extent; fifth, what are the genera of the ridiculous (*ridiculum*)" (ii.58.235). Instead of Aristotle's four causes as subjects of inquiry, we have five topics, a change appropriate to rhetoric. Only the fifth, the genera of the ridiculous, is recognizable as corresponding to one of Aristotle's causes, the forms of the laughable.

The first topic, the nature of laughter, Caesar leaves to Democritus, as not pertinent to the conversation in which the group is engaged. This is the rhetorical counterpart of Aristotle's disciplinary limitation of the inquiry into laughter in the *Poetics* to what the poet makes, the laughable, which is also what the rhetorician makes. The one fundamental philosophical determinant that Cicero shares with Aristotle is his disciplinary perspective; in other respects he is a Protagorean.

The next topic is whence laughter is. "The place, then, and as it were the province of the ridiculous (for it is next to be sought) is restricted to a certain unseemliness (*turpitudo*) and ugliness (*deformitas*), for the things that are laughed at, either solely or to the greatest extent, are those which note some unseemliness and point it out in no unseemly way" (ii.58.236). The ridiculous (*ridiculum*) is the Latin counterpart of Aristotle's laughable (*to geloion*). Its place or province is the rhetorical counterpart of the genus of the laughable in Aristotle, and it looks as if Caesar's account of it is taken straight from Aristotle's definition of the laughable in Book I, replacing *hamartēma* and *aischos* with *turpitudo* and *deformitas* and leaving the differentiae for his fourth topic, which we will consider in a moment. *Turpitudo* is more suited to the material wrongness of soul and body than to the formal wrongness of diction and incident. Caesar also introduces the not unseemly way in which the faults are pointed out, corresponding to Aristotle's comic indirection.

This gives us rhetorical adaptations of all four of Aristotle's causes. Symmetry becomes the union of the laughable and the serious in the ideal rhetorician, the forms of the laughable become the genera of the ridiculous, the wrongness of soul and body become turpitude and deformity, and the indirect manner of expression becomes expression in no unseemly way. These topics work together, like Aristotle's causes, and Holt can take the epigraph for his book on the history and philosophy of jokes from Cicero's combination of two of Aristotle's causes: "An indecency decently put is the thing we laugh at hardest."

Caesar's third topic justifies the inclusion of the theory of the laughable within rhetoric, a topic required for the rhetorical treatment of laughter but not for its poetic treatment.

Cicero's fourth topic is the extent to which ridiculous things are to be treated by the orator: "For neither outstanding wickedness, such as involves crime, nor, on the other hand, outstanding wretchedness is assailed by ridicule, for the public would have the villainous hurt by a weapon rather more formidable than ridicule; while they dislike mockery of the wretched, except perhaps if these bear themselves arrogantly" (ii.58.237, trans. Sutton and Rackham). This corresponds to Aristotle's limitation of the laughable to wrongness that is not painful or destructive, but instead of limiting the wrongness by differentiae appropriate to what it is in itself, the rhetorical context leads Cicero to introduce limitations from the preferences of the audience.

The first four of Caesar's topics take up only a small part of his account of laughter (four of fifty-four sections), and the rest of his account is concerned with the fifth topic, the genera of the ridiculous. This corresponds to the large part of Aristotle's account that concerns the forms of the laughable. Aristotle's account of the forms of the laughable begins with the distinction between sources of laughter in comedy in its words and in its incidents; Caesar's account of the genera of the ridiculous begins with a like distinction between the sources of humor in words and in the things they signify. "For there are two genera of the humorous (*facetiae*), one drawn from the thing, the other from what is said" (ii.59.240). Rhetoric is a narrative rather than a dramatic art such as comedy, but the rhetorician may occasionally speak like an actor, and Caesar proceeds to discuss the first two species of the humorous in things, corresponding to Aristotle's deception and assimilation, but changes them from incidents in comic drama to incidents in which the rhetorician himself acts. Deception becomes the narration of alleged incidents, which Caesar illustrates by a speech of Crassus in which he tells a wholly fabricated but apparently hilarious story of a quarrel between his opponent, Memmius, and another man, Largus, over a little lady-friend, in which Memmius ends up taking a bite of Largus's arm, an incident then commemorated by the mysterious letters "M. M. L. L. L." (Mordacious Memmius Lacerates Largus's Limb) written on walls all over the town.

The second source of laughter in things, assimilation, becomes assimilation by the speaker to someone else, or mimicry. The first illustration, mimicry of the more noble, is provided by a speech in which Crassus, mimicking the speech of his adversary, adjures him, "By your noble rank, by your ancient lineage," and, stretching out his arm, "by your statuary!" The second illustration, corresponding to mimicry of the worse, is taken from an actor rather than an orator, and is Rocius's quavering mimicry of an old man, "For you, my Antipho, I plant these trees," in which we hear the voice of old age itself.

These two species of the humorous in things, conceived as narration and imitation, are the only species of the humorous in things that Caesar takes up at this point, presumably because these are the only two in which the rhetorician speaks like a comic actor. The remaining species are taken up after the discussion of the humorous in words. The separation of these two species of the humorous in things from the others is also found in the Prolegomenon to Comedy (cf. Janko 1984, 73, 188–89). This makes it probable that the author of the Prolegomenon was using both sources, Aristotle and Cicero, in compiling his prolegomenon.

There follows a discussion of the difference between the orator and the buffoon in the use of the humorous: "A regard, therefore, to occasions, and to moderation and temperance and infrequency in jesting itself, will distinguish the orator from the buffoon (*scurra*), and also that we joke for a reason, not to be thought funny, but to gain some advantage, while they joke all day for no reason at all" (ii.60.247). Caesar here gives a rhetorical formulation of the distinction we noted in chapter 5 between poetry and rhetoric, poetry being for its own sake and rhetoric for the sake of some ulterior purpose, which is also the distinction between comedy and abuse. We see again here the disciplinary perspective shared by Aristotle and Cicero.

Caesar next repeats in slightly different words his initial distinction between the two genera of the humorous: "Now let us set forth briefly the genera themselves of what most excites laughter. Let this, then, be the first division, that what is said humorously (*facete*) sometimes has its humor (*facetias*) in the thing, sometimes in the word, though people are most delighted when laughter is excited by the union of the two" (ii.61.248). Aristotle's distinction between sources of laughter in the incidents and diction of comedy is again the rhetorical distinction between the facetious in things and in words, and the value of their synergy is here added.

Next comes a discussion of the species of the ridiculous in words. These follow the order of the epitome and the *Prolegomenon*, and to facilitate the comparison of Cicero's list to the epitome I shall use the headings of the epitome. (1) Homonymy. This becomes in Cicero ambiguity (*ambiguitas*). It is illustrated by the comment of Publius Licinius Varus to Africanus the elder when at a banquet he was trying to put a wreath on the head of Africanus and it kept breaking: "No wonder it's too small," he said, "for it must fit the head of the whole state!" (ii.61.250). (2) Synonymy and repetition. If the orator speaking in his own person were to use these for comic effect, they would make the orator himself an object of laughter, and they are omitted from Caesar's list, although not from the *Prolegomenon*. (3) Paronymy. Here Caesar refers to the Greek *paronomasia*, and illustrates it by the example already cited, in which "Nobiliorem" becomes "Mobiliorem." (4) Parody. Caesar modifies this to make it the use of quotations, whether parodied or not: "Often too a verse, or some part of one, is wittily introduced, either just as it stands or slightly varied" (ii.64.257). (5) Transference by sound becomes taking words in an unintended sense, as when, bachelors being subject to a special tax, Cato the censor used the standard legal formula to ask Nasica, "Are you truly satisfied that you have a wife?" he replied, "No, by Hercules, I am not truly satisfied" (ii.64.261). (6) Transference by homogeneous attributes becomes in Caesar's account either a borrowed metaphor, as in the use of the proverb, "As you sow, so shall you reap"; or a new metaphor, as Scipio the elder saying, when the Corinthians were promising him a statue in the place where there were statues of other commanders, "I do not care for statues in squadrons" (ii.65.262); or the substitution of different literal words, as when Crassus was arguing a case in which the opposing advocate, Lama, was deformed, and kept interrupting him, until Crassus said, "Let us hear the beautiful youth." Laughter followed, and Lama said, "I could not form my own shape; my talents I could," to which Crassus responded, "Let us hear the learned speaker," at which the laughter was far greater than before (ii.65.262). (7) Form of diction. "The opposition of verbal contraries is one of the chief embellishments of diction, and this same device is often witty as well" (ii.65.263, trans. Sutton and Rackham). In the example, Servius Galba and Libo were nominating judges for a case in which they represented opposing sides. When Galbo submitted a list of his *familiares*, Libo said, "Galba, when are you going to get out of your own dining room?" to which Galba replied, "When you get out of other people's bedrooms." The form of diction is the same, but with contrasting content.

After treating the species of humor that depends on words, Caesar takes up those that depend on things. He refers back to narration and the example of Memmius the Mordacious, and continues with a series of various forms of humor used by rhetoricians that does not follow Aristotle's list of the sources of laughter in the incidents of comedy, although some of the items are the same, such as the impossible and what is contrary to expectation. One item suggests that Cicero is incorporating in Caesar's list the forms of humor associated with two of Aristotle's characters of comedy, the understatements of the ironic and overstatements of the boasters, but without the attachment to character, a change appropriate to their rhetorical use: "Then again there are those intentional understatements or overstatements which are exaggerated to a degree of the astonishing that passes belief, such as your own assertion, Crassus, made in a speech before a public assembly, that Memmius thought himself so exalted an individual that, on his way down into the Market Place, he lowered his head in order to pass under the Arch of Fabius" (ii.66.267, trans. Sutton and Rackham). The buffoon, who is associated with no particular kind of joke, had already been distinguished from the orator, as we noted.

Cicero has thus adapted to his account of laughter in rhetoric all of the essential features of Aristotle's analysis of laughter, including his definition of the laughable and his distinction between the sources of laughter in the diction and in the incidents. His list of the sources of laughter in words and the first two sources of laughter in things matches the epitome almost item for item, with a substitution of rhetorical for poetic examples. Morreall, working from Book I of the *Poetics*, rightly saw that Cicero was following Aristotle for the genus and differentiae of the ridiculous, but, apparently unaware of the epitome, he thought that the distinction between the ridiculous in words and in things was Cicero's own idea: "In large part he follows what Aristotle had said, but he adds at least one new idea of some theoretical importance, the distinction between humor in what is being talked about, and humor arising from the language used" (Morreall 1987, 17). The epitome enables us to see that Cicero was also following Aristotle's account in this and other ways, and I think we can conclude that Cicero was relying on Aristotle not only as a source, but as the principal source for his own account of laughter in *De oratore*.[6]

The epitome is an obscure document of which few have ever heard. It is easy to find fault with it and dismiss it or ignore it altogether, but Cicero is a central figure of the Western tradition of whom everyone has heard and whose testimony cannot so easily be dismissed or ignored. When it turns out that Cicero is relying on the same source as the epitome and the *Prolegomenon*, and which includes the lost Book II of Aristotle's *Poetics*, this brings Book II into our world of accepted realities and makes it something to be investigated through the works that derive from it. Cicero's use of Aristotle should suffice to dispel any lingering doubts as to the derivation of the epitome from Book II Also, Cicero, who had the full text of Book II and not just an epitome of it, supports a key point in our interpretation of the laughable, that it involves a synergy of the causes.

7. THE SCIENCE OF THE LAUGHABLE

We can recognize among the established disciplines of our universities all of the principal subjects for which Aristotle established a scientific treatment with the exception of the laughable, or, as it would usually be called today, humor. There is no shortage of works on humor, but they do not constitute an established discipline. Is this anomaly a result of the loss of the paradigm that would have been provided by *Poetics* II? In order to answer this question, we need first to survey the current scene. For this purpose I shall use John Morreall's survey of what he calls "the three traditional theories" of laughter in his *The Philosophy of Laughter and Humor* (1987, 129–31). Morreall's three traditional theories are also discussed by Holt (2008, 81–101). The first of Morreall's three traditional theories is the Superiority Theory:

> The oldest, and probably still the most widespread theory of laughter is that laughter is an expression of personal superiority over others. This theory goes back at least as far as Plato (*Repub.* ii.388, v.452; *Laws* vii.816, xi.935–6) and Aristotle (*Rhet.* ii.12.1389b10–11; *Eth.* iv.8.1128), and was given its classic statement in Hobbes, who said that laughter "expresses a sudden glory arising from some conception of some eminency in ourselves, by comparison with the infirmity of others, or with our own formerly" (Hobbes 1840, 46; cf. Hobbes 1909, pt. 1, chap. 6, p. 45). In our own century many have adopted versions of the Superiority Theory. Albert Rapp, for example, claims that all laughter developed from one primitive behavior in early man, 'the roar of triumph in an ancient jungle duel' (Rapp 1951, 21). Konrad Lorenz and others treat laughter as a controlled form of aggression; for them the baring of the teeth in laughing is a way of asserting one's prowess." (Morreall 1987, 129)

> The second theory I want to look at is the Incongruity Theory, which had its beginnings in some scattered comments in Aristotle, but did not come into its own until Kant and Schopenhauer. The basic idea behind this theory is very simple. We live in an orderly world where we have come to expect certain patterns among things, properties, events, etc. When we experience something that doesn't fit these patterns, that violates our expectations, we laugh. As Pascal said, "nothing produces laughter more than a surprising disproportion between that which one expects and that which one sees" (quoted in Ludovici 1933, 27). Or in Kant's terminology, "Laughter is an affection arising from the sudden transformation of a strained expectation into nothing" (Kant 1951, 177). Schopenhauer explained the incongruity behind laughter as a mismatch between our concepts and the real things that are supposed to be instantiations of these concepts (Schopenhauer 1883, 1:76). (Morreall 1987, 130)

> The last theory I want to consider is the Relief Theory. Though reference to the power of laughter to relieve us of nervous tension goes back to Aristotle's comments on catharsis in comedy, the notion that laughter is a release of nervous energy was not carefully worked out until the

nineteenth century. In an essay called "On the Physiology of Laughter" (Spencer 1911) Herbert Spencer claims that our emotions are, or at least in the nervous systems take the form of, nervous energy. And nervous energy tends to beget muscular action. . . . Laughter, even if intense, does not lead to practical action such as flight or attack. Laughing, rather, is *just* a release of energy. It occurs, Spencer says, when some emotion has built up but then is suddenly seen to be inappropriate. If someone thinks she hears an intruder in the house, for example, then upon discovering that it was only the cat she might break into laughter.

Spencer's theory influenced many subsequent theorists of laughter, including Dewey (1894) and Freud (1963). Freud's theory is complex and involves much more than the notion of the release of excess nervous energy. . . . He distinguishes three kinds of laughter situations, which he calls "jokes," "the comic," and "humor." The core of the theory is that in all laughter situations we save a certain quantity of psychic energy, energy that is usually employed for some psychic purpose but which turns out not to be needed. The discharge of this superfluous energy is laughter. In joking, he says, we save energy that is normally used to suppress forbidden feelings and thoughts; in reacting to the comic we save an expenditure of energy in thought; and in humor we save an expenditure of energy in emotion. (Morreall 1987, 131)

All these theories are about laughter, but they are about different aspects of laughter which for Aristotle belong to different sciences. Laughter as the expression of personal superiority over others belongs in the practical sciences. Laughter as the result of incongruity belongs in poetics. Spencer's physiology of laughter belongs in the natural sciences. The general subject of laughter is thus in a prescientific state; it can be treated scientifically only as belonging to a determinate genus.

It is remarkable that the three theories of laughter in this prescientific state exhibit the same set of philosophic possibilities that existed before Aristotle transformed philosophy into a group of sciences. The Superiority Theory involves the superiority of one individual to another, which belongs in the Protagorean tradition of all things measured by individuals in relation to themselves. The Incongruity Theory involves reference to general forms, which belongs in the Platonic tradition of explanation by reference to forms or Ideas. The Relief Theory involves a release of nervous or psychic energy, which belongs in the Democritean tradition of explanation by what is going on in the substratum.

It is also remarkable that Morreall finds that all of the theories have beginnings in Aristotle, but does not identify Aristotle with any of them. This corresponds to something that Sir David Ross says of a book that might be written about Aristotle: "It might be shown how almost the whole of his thought is a mosaic of borrowings from his predecessors, and yet is transformed by the force of his genius into a strikingly original system" (1949, preface). What is missing from the traditional theories of laughter is precisely the force of Aristotle's genius that would transform them into a science. But now that the epitome has shown how Aristotle did bring together the components corresponding to the principles of his predecessors into a theory of the laughable, we should have in the epitome a basis for a science of the laughable.

Of the three kinds of theories, only the Incongruity Theory treats laughter in a way that puts it in the same ballpark as Aristotle's science of laughter. It can therefore be taken as a starting point for the development of the science. Incongruity can be taken as corresponding to the formal wrongness of diction and incident. It must, however, be limited to incongruity that is painless and not destructive. William Hazlitt's definition of the essence of the laughable as the incongruous omits the qualifications, although they are implied in the use he makes of it: "The essence of the laughable then is the incongruous, the disconnecting one idea from another, or the jostling of one feeling against another" (Morreall 1987, 68). Kant's formulation, "the sudden transformation of a strained expectation into nothing" has the advantage of not requiring the qualification, since what is painful or destructive is not nothing. Stephen Leacock cites Aristotle in making the qualification explicit. "Humour may be defined as the kindly contemplation of the incongruities of life, and the artistic expression thereof" (1937, 11). He adds that what Aristotle says about the laughable "contains the essential element which the word *kindly* in the definition is meant to convey." The shift from "painless and not destructive" to "kindly" corresponds to the subject matter shift from wrongness or incongruity itself to its contemplation or expression.

Mikhail Bakhtin's "carnivalesque transgression," not included among Morreall's traditional theories, approximates to Aristotle with a shift from an ontic to a social context. Transgression is wrongness in a social context, and includes not only the formal wrongness of incongruity but the material wrongness of vice, although perhaps inclining toward the latter. We do not ordinarily call puns transgressions, although in a sense they are. "Carnivalesque" limits the transgressions by making them appropriate to a certain kind of social context in which all sorts of transgressions are permissible unless they are painful or destructive.

The basic insufficiency of the incongruity theory is not that the incongruity must be limited to incongruity that is free from pain and harmless, but that it is a one-cause theory. It fits the formal wrongness of the sources of laughter in the diction and incidents, but it is a stretch to make it include the material wrongness of the faults of body and soul or Cicero's turpitude. Starkie far exceeds everyone else in the number of examples of Aristotle's forms of the laughable that he finds, taking them from both the ancient texts of Aristophanes and other ancient writers of comedy and from Shakespeare and other modern authors writing in both English and French. But he treats the forms of the laughable as if they were Aristotle's whole theory of the laughable, and thus reduces it to a one-cause theory. In order to fit all kinds of humor into the theory he blurs Aristotle's distinctions, which in his hands lose their precision.

So far as the incongruity theory has been a one-cause theory, it is easy for Morreall, and Holt after him, to refute it in the same way that they refute other one-cause theories, by showing that some source of laughter has been left out. Morreall in his "New Theory of Laughter" attempts to deal with the limitations of traditional theories by bringing them together, not in a multi-cause theory like that of Aristotle or Cicero, but in a super one-cause theory that is general enough to include them all: "Laughter results from a pleasant psychological shift" (Morreall 1987, 133). This is instructive as indicating a way in which the theories cannot be united to form a science, for this unification is through a pseudo-genus that is so general that it contributes less to our understanding of laughter than any of the one-cause theories it is designed to replace, and which cannot be derived from it by differentiation.

The key condition for a science of the laughable is a set of stable forms, forms of wrongness or incongruity or transgression. Cicero's account of laughter adapts Aristotle's forms to the requirements of rhetoric. The only other theorist who has a comparable set of forms is Freud. His techniques of jokes in fact bear a startling resemblance to Aristotle's forms of the laughable. The names of Aristotle's sources of laughter are often equivalent to the names of Freud's techniques of jokes, as Aristotle's "homonymy" and Freud's "double meanings," or Aristotle's "paronymy by alteration" and Freud's "multiple use of the same material with slight modification," or Aristotle's "transference by homogeneous attributes," or metaphor, and Freud's "metaphorical and literal meanings." Some of Aristotle's sources of laughter in the incidents correspond to Freud's techniques of conceptual jokes, although many are treated by Freud in relation to the comic in general rather than specifically to jokes. Aristotle's impossibility corresponds to Freud's conceptual absurdity, his absence of consecution corresponds to Freud's faulty reasoning, and his vulgar dancing corresponds to Freud's comic of bodily movement, which for Freud belongs to the comic but not specifically to jokes.

It is in fact probable that Freud in his *Jokes and Their Relation to the Unconscious* was, like Niezsche, influenced by Aristotle through Jacob Bernays's edition of the epitome. Whether or not he was does not affect the present argument, but is a point of some interest. Freud's wife, Minna Bernays, was a niece of Jacob Bernays, and Freud's eldest sister, Anna, married Minna's brother, Eli Bernays. Freud and Breuer adopted the term catharsis for their own therapeutic method and would almost certainly have known of Bernays's account of the therapeutic catharsis described in the *Politics*. It is probable that Freud's library included Bernays's *Zwei Abhandlungen* (Two treatises) (1880), which contains both his treatise on catharsis and his earlier treatise on the epitome. Freud wrote his book on jokes some twenty years after Bernays's death, but having the book in his library and knowing that it contained what Bernays argued was Aristotle's theory of jokes, he would most probably have consulted it when he came to write his own theory of jokes. We know that he consulted Aristotle's theory of dreams before he published his own book on dreams (1965, 36–37).

What is relevant to our present purpose is whether the similarities between the accounts of jokes in Aristotle and Freud provide evidence that we have in them the basis for a modern science of the laughable. Let us note first that Freud's archic profile, like Nietzsche's, is totally different from Aristotle's. Aristotle's perspective is that of the writer of comedies who seeks to write good comedies, whereas Freud's perspective is that of the objective scientist who seeks to understand why people laugh at jokes. The reality that Aristotle investigates within his perspective is the essential reality of the laughable as a wrongness that is not painful or destructive, whereas the reality that is essential in Freud's investigation is the substrative reality of the psychic forces that jokes, the comic, and humor bring into play. The method by which Aristotle's reality is ordered is the resolutive method that resolves the laughable into its determination by its proper causes, whereas the method by which Freud's reality is ordered is the agonistic method of opposed psychic forces. For Aristotle, the laughable aims at a symmetry with the serious required to achieve a self-sufficient emotional catharsis, whereas for Freud the laughable effects an economy in the expenditure of psychic energy that is experienced as pleasure.[7]

Confronted with this opposition of philosophic principles, a pre-pluralistic philosophy, that is, a philosophy that holds that only one set of philosophic principles can be true, would have the impossible task of determining which principles, if any, are true, and which are false. If we are pluralists, however, we can expect that the relation of the two accounts will not be that one is true and the other false, but that they are complementary formulations of the same unformulated subject matter (Watson 1991, 196–201), which in this case is the laughable or jokes. We can expect Freud to complement Aristotle's account of the laughable by disclosing the psychological reasons why the wrongness of the laughable produces pleasure.

Freud distinguishes the comic, jokes, and humor according to their psychological sources. Freud's leading example of the comic is the comic of bodily movement, corresponding to Aristotle's vulgar dancing. "But how is it that we laugh when we have recognized that some other person's movements are exaggerated and inexpedient? By making a comparison, I believe, between the movement I observe in the other person and the one I should have carried out myself in his place" (Freud 1963, 190–91). Such a comparison is made by the preconscious, which includes whatever is accessible to consciousness, and the difference between the psychic energy required for the comic movement and what would be required without the comic exaggeration provides the psychic energy available for expression as laughter.

Freud argues in chapter 6 of *Jokes and Their Relation to the Unconscious* that the joke-work, like the dream-work, particularly in its use of condensation and displacement, involves a contribution from the unconscious which distinguishes it from the comic: "All the analyses we have hitherto made have pointed to the source of the comic pleasure being a comparison of two expenditures both of which must be ascribed to the preconscious. Jokes and the comic are distinguished first and foremost by their psychical localization; *the joke, it may be said, is the contribution made to the comic from the realm of the unconscious*" (1963, 208; italics in original).

Freud's leading example of humor is an ironic joke. A rogue being led to the gallows on a Monday, says, "Well, this is a fine beginning to the week!" (1963, 229). Freud finds the source of pleasure in this joke in a shift of psychic energy from the ego to the super-ego that saves us an expenditure of psychic energy in pity: "We obtain a dynamic explanation of the humorous attitude, therefore, if we conclude that it consists in the subject's removing the accent from his own ego and transferring it on to his super-ego. To the super-ego, thus inflated, the ego can appear tiny and all its interests trivial" (1950, 218–19).

Just as jokes add to the comic a contribution from the unconscious, so humor adds a contribution from the super-ego: "I think, therefore, that the possibility I have suggested, namely, that in a given situation the subject suddenly effects a hyper-cathexis of the super-ego, which in its turn alters the reactions of the ego, is one which deserves to be retained. Moreover, we find a striking analogy to this hypothesis of mine about humour in the kindred field of jokes. I was led to assume that jokes originate in the momentary abandoning of a conscious thought to unconscious elaboration, jokes being therefore the unconscious contribution of the unconscious to the comic, In just the same way humour would be a contribution to the comic made through the agency of the super-ego" (Freud 1950, 5:220; I have replaced Joan Riviere's translation of the German *Witz* as "wit" by "jokes" to make it consistent with Strachey's 1963 translation).

From this we can see that Freud's account of the comic, jokes, and humor is essentially an application of Freud's psychological distinctions to the subject of the laughable, as contrasted with Aristotle's account of the laughable itself. He is providing a psychology of the laughable rather than a theory of the laughable. This is why Morreall can criticize Freud's distinction between joking, the comic, and humor as "highly artificial" (1987, 132). It seems artificial because it is not a division of the laughable itself, but of its psychological sources. This shifts the problem to whether Freud in the first part of his work is talking about the same thing that Aristotle is analyzing.

Let me preface the investigation of this point by remarking that it is not necessary to a science that that its practitioners all share a common philosophy. Far from it! Different philosophic approaches play a key role in the development of sciences, as we saw in the strand from the history of physics sketched in chapter 1. Aristotle's great achievement of transforming philosophy into a system of sciences has many consequences, and one of them is that massive philosophical oppositions such as those of Morreall's traditional theories of laughter are replaced by differences in approach to particular scientific subject matters. The approaches are not identical, but only analogous. This, however, when combined with their concern with the particular subject, suffices to hold them together as all belonging to the same science. Each practitioner is, in general, able to understand and evaluate what others are doing, and each contributes in his own way to the common enterprise of advancing the science. The approaches are not identical, but the analogies between them are critical to the science as a collective enterprise.

Let us therefore see whether Freud's theory of jokes contains analogues of Aristotle's causes. We have already noted the striking similarity of Aristotle's sources of the laughable to Freud's techniques of jokes. The universal forms of the laughable provide for Aristotle the stable and enduring forms that are necessary for a science. The techniques of jokes provide for Freud a tie to his work on dreams, and bring jokes within the realm of his new science of unconscious processes. Both Aristotle and Freud see jokes as resulting from the union of these forms or techniques with another factor of a different kind, material wrongness of body or soul in the case of Aristotle, and the tendency of jokes in the case of Freud—obscene, aggressive, cynical, or skeptical. Just as Aristotle's sources of laughter give laughable form to wrongnesses of soul, so the techniques of jokes give joking expression to a tendency. And just as the union of formal and material wrongness in Aristotle produces a composite wrongness that is more wrong and more laughable than the two separately, so the union of technique with tendency in Freud produces an often much greater pleasure than the technique alone. This is because the pleasure in the technique assists the tendency in removing what inhibits it, and the psychic energy required for the inhibition is released and expressed in laughter. A full account with an illustrative example is given in Freud 1963 (134–38). For Freud, the techniques of jokes produce pleasure because they are a return to the free play of words and thoughts in childhood that has become wrong in the adult. The tendencies of jokes are ordinarily suppressed or repressed as being in some way wrong, but if the inhibition is removed, the psychic energy required for the inhibition can find expression in laughter.

We thus have analogues in Freud to two of Aristotle's causes, and to their synergy. Aristotle's third cause is the indirection which permits the introduction of the material wrongness without its being reproachful or offensive. This corresponds to what Freud calls indirect representation or allusion, which for Freud has the same psychological source as the techniques of jokes, and is therefore not distinguished as a separate factor, although Freud recognizes that it functions in two different ways. Sometimes, like the other techniques, it provides an "incentive bonus" of pleasure, and sometimes it makes it possible to present the joke without offense. Indirect representation occurs in both roles in the same joke when it is introduced in the analysis of an American anecdote:

"Two not particularly scrupulous business men had succeeded, by dint of a series of highly risky enterprises, in amassing a large fortune, and they were now making efforts to push their way into good society. One method, which struck them as a likely one, was to have their portraits painted by the most celebrated and highly paid artist in the city, whose pictures had an immense reputation. The precious canvases were shown for the first time at a huge evening party, and the two hosts themselves led the most influential connoisseur and art critic up to the wall upon which the two portraits were hanging side by side, to extract his admiring judgment on them. He studied the works for a long time, and then, shaking his head, as though there was something he had missed, pointed to the gap between the pictures and asked quietly 'Where is the Saviour?'" (Freud 1963, 74.)

Indirect representation is here used twice. First, the pictures of the two unscrupulous businessmen are taken to represent indirectly the two thieves in a Crucifixion painting. This, in Aristotle's terms, provides the formal wrongness for the joke in an assimilation towards the worse. If the joke were stated without the second use of indirect representation, it would be, "I see the pictures of two thieves without the Saviour." This is something that, as Freud says, the critic could not say. The assimilation is expressed indirectly by not mentioning thieves at all, but simply by asking, "Where's the Saviour?" This keeps the critic in his proper role of judging the paintings, not his hosts.

Freud goes on to say, "In a whole number of the examples we have already examined we remarked that the technique was not a simple one, and we now perceive that 'allusion' was the complicating factor in them" (ibid., 75). Thus Freud treats them as jokes in which allusion is combined with another technique. Here is an example: "Mr. and Mrs. X live in a fairly grand style. Some people think that by earning a lot the husband has been able to lay by a little; others again think that by lying back a little the wife has been able to earn a lot" (Freud 1963, 33). For Aristotle, the form of the joke is homonymy; Freud identifies the technique of the joke as multiple use of the same material with a slight alteration (inversion of order) combined with allusion. The allusion is the indirect expression of the activity of the wife as lying back a little, rather than more directly in a way that would have been abusive rather than comic. Thus the different function of indirect representation when combined with the other techniques can still be discerned, and the fact that Freud finds it as a complicating factor in so many jokes corresponds to Aristotle's treatment of it as a different kind of cause because of its different function.

With respect to the fourth of Aristotle's causes of the laughable, symmetry, Freud recognizes it as contributing to the total pleasure of a joke, but not as a consequence of the psychological process that for him defines a joke. "We said above that a good joke makes, as it were, a *total* impression of enjoyment on us, without our being able to decide at once what share of the pleasure arises from its joking form and what share from its apt thought content" (ibid., 132; see also 92–94, 117, 137). The concept of the thought content or substance of a joke is introduced in the following example:

> "Not only did he not believe in ghosts; he wasn't even afraid of them." Here the joke lies entirely in the nonsensical form of representation, which puts what is commonly thought less of into the comparative and uses the positive for what is regarded as more important. If this joking envelope is removed, we have, "It is much easier to get rid of a fear of ghosts intellectually than to escape it when the occasion arises." This is no longer in the least a joke, though it is a correct and still too little appreciated psychological discovery—the same one which Lessing expressed in a well-known sentence:
>
> > "Not all are free who mock their chains."
>
> . . . As our last example [the fear of ghosts joke] shows, an innocent—that is, a non-tendentious—joke may also be of great substance, it may assert something of value. But the substance of a joke is independent of the joke and is the substance of the thought, which is here, by means of a special arrangement, expressed as a joke. No doubt, just as watch-makers usually provide a particularly good movement with a similarly valuable case, so it may happen with jokes that the best achievements in the way of jokes are used as an envelope for thoughts of the greatest substance.
>
> If now we draw a sharp distinction in the case of conceptual jokes between the substance of the joke and the joking envelope, we shall reach a discovery which may throw light on much of our uncertainty in judging jokes. For it turns out—and this is a surprising thing—that our enjoyment of a joke is based on a combined impression of its substance and its effectiveness as a joke, and that we let ourselves be deceived by the one factor over the amount of the other. Only after the joke has been reduced do we become aware of this false judgment. (Freud 1963, 92)

Both Aristotle and Freud here recognize the same thing, that a good joke may be united with a serious thought. This for Aristotle increases the pleasure and perfects comic catharsis, while for Freud the additional pleasure by combining with the pleasure in the joke obscures the difference in their sources. What is for Aristotle an essential unity is for Freud only a phenomenal impression that misleads us with respect to the substrative realities.

That all of Aristotle's causes of the laughable are operative in Freud's account of jokes provides evidence that he has indeed provided a basis for a science of the laughable that would include the work of both Aristotle and Freud. While it took the better part of a century before the truths of Freud's pioneering work in psychopathology were incorporated in theories of the self by Heinz Kohut and others, it is easy enough to incorporate Freud's insights into the sources of pleasure in jokes into Aristotle's theory of the laughable, as I was already doing earlier in interpreting the wrongness from which jokes are made. A foundation for one branch of the science of the laughable has already been provided by the Herculean labors of Gershon Legman (1975), whose eighteen hundred pages of dirty jokes, together with a beginning of the analysis of the jokes both psychologically and socio-analytically, supply all the data, or, in Aristotle's terms, the history, required for the science of this form of material wrongness.

Chapter 22

THE EMBODIMENT OF THE LAUGHABLE
IN COMEDY

1. THE MATTER AND PARTS OF COMEDY

The six qualitative parts of poems are intermediate between the materials and the end of poetry. Since the analysis of poetry can begin either from its materials or from its end, the qualitative parts are treated twice. In Book I they are the means by which the materials of poetry can be made to achieve a poetic end, and, in Book II, they are the means by which a poetic end can be embodied in the materials of poetry. The four quantitative parts do not, like the qualitative parts, admit of a universal treatment, but play opposite roles in the two approaches, and therefore they also are treated twice. We shall run through the epitome's sequence of the matter and parts of comedy, comparing what is said in the epitome with what is said in Book I.

The matter of comedy: plot, character, thought, diction, melody, spectacle. The characterization of the six qualitative parts as *matter* reflects, as was said in the preliminary examination of the epitome, the context in which they are treated, which is here the one in which they are being adapted to the forms of comedy. This contrasts with the context of Book I, in which the differentiae of imitation as matter take on the forms they have in tragedy. As Dewey says, "The truth of the matter is that which is form in one context is matter in another and vice-versa" (1934, 128). The six parts are the same in both contexts and their order here is the order of importance determined in Book I. It is an enumeration of the parts necessarily belonging to both tragedy and comedy as species, although there is no necessity that all the parts be used in any particular play. The account of the parts in lyric poetry or any other species of poetry should presumably begin similarly, by identifying the parts essential to the species.

We now run through the six parts, giving for each the generic account followed by its specification to tragedy and comedy if it is so specified.

A comic plot is one having its structure (sustasis) around laughable actions. The generic plot is the synthesis (*sunthesis*) or structure (*sustasis*) of the incidents (*pragmata*) (6.1459a5, 15), and is discussed in Book I. Plot is the principle (*archē*) and, as it were, the soul of tragedy. The comic plot is not the principle of comedy, however, which is rather the laughable actions around which the plot is structured. This exemplifies the essential contrast between the two possibilities for poetry. The parts of tragedy are derived from the materials of imitation, and the plot is the end of the parts. Hence if the principle comes from the materials, it is found in the plot, as in tragedy. But if the principle comes from the end, it is found in the forms of the end, in the case of comedy, the forms of the laughable. A consequence of this difference is the inversion of priority of plot and incidents, since the end of tragedy is realized only in the plot as a whole, while the end of comedy is realized in the laughable actions. This is not to say that the plot of comedy is not the structure of the incidents, for this is the universal character of the plot, but rather that this is for the sake of the laughter that the incidents make possible.

This can be illustrated by comparing the relation of plot to incidents in *Oedipus* and in Aristophanes's *Clouds*. In *Oedipus*, each new incident contributes to the final outcome in which the catharsis of fear is realized, while in the *Clouds* each new incident presents new possibilities for the laughable that make their own direct contribution to the catharsis of pleasure and laughter. The thinking up of comic situations involves a skill somewhat different from that of thinking up the jokes. Jerry Seinfeld said in the Charlie Rose interview referred to earlier that in his collaborations with Larry David it was generally Larry David who thought up the potentially comic situations, and then he, Seinfeld, thought up the jokes that they made possible.

We may note that while in tragedy there is a possibility of a best plot in which the feared event actually occurs and a second best plot in which it does not, there is no such possibility in the case of comedy because comedy requires comic events to actually occur, and tragic events to never occur. What in tragedy is second-best, the nonoccurence of a feared misfortune, produces a pleasure that is appropriate to comedy (13.1453a36).

The characters of comedy: the buffoonish, the ironical, and the boastful.
Character here plays a role different from its role in section 8, where wrongness of soul is an object of laughter. Any vice that is not painful or destructive can be an object of laughter. For example, comedians sometimes have a characteristic vice that is the subject of repeated jokes. W. C. Fields had the characteristic vice of intemperance with respect to alcohol; Jack Benny had the characteristic vice of illiberality with respect to money. In the present context, however, character does not provide the matter for jokes, but the

motivation for producing them. It belongs to humorists as authors as well as to characters in plays and stories, and therefore Aristotle's comic characters serve to distinguish different kinds of humorists.

The role of character as originating action is also its role in Book I. Character in general is that by virtue of which we say agents are of a certain kind (6.1450a5), as courageous, temperate, just, and so on. Character in Book I is treated both generically and as specific to tragedy. The character required for tragedy is a character whose misfortune gives rise to pity and fear, that is, a character neither differing from us in virtue and justice nor changing to misfortune through vice or wickedness, but through some error (13.1453a7). Character in both tragedy and comedy is such as to produce the speech and actions through which the emotional end of the work is realized, but with the difference that the comic character chooses to produce the emotional end, whereas the tragic character does not choose the tragic emotional end, but only the mistake that leads to it. Insofar as the tragic character is like us or somewhat better, he can deal with his misfortunes with a nobility that in some way transcends his misfortunes. Simon Boccanegra, for example, in Verdi's opera of that name, uses his death as an occasion to transcend personal and civic strife and initiate a regime of love and peace. Character in lyric poetry, like character in comedy, gives rise directly to the emotions of the poem, but without the limitation of comic characters to those worse than ourselves, and lyric poems may therefore share the gravity or solemnity of tragedy.

Three and only three characters are identified as the characters of comedy: the buffoonish, the ironical, and the boastful. Let us first consider why this is so. Characters are defined in the *Ethics* by their virtues and vices. Buffoonery, irony, and boastfulness all belong to the last subgroup of the virtues and vices that are there discussed. All the virtues and vices in this subgroup concern fellowship (*homilia*), living together (*suzēn*), and sharing of words and deeds (*logōn kai pragmatōn koinōnein*) (*Eth.* iv.6.1126b11). This is the sphere within which comedy is realized, and it is only the habits belonging to this subgroup that can define the characters of comedy.

There are three virtues in this sphere and for each virtue a pair of vices that respectively exceed or fall short of the mean represented by the virtue. In the order in which they are treated in the *Ethics*, the first of these virtues is considerateness, for which there is no Greek word but which is like friendship without affection and is concerned with giving pleasure in social relations in general. The corresponding vices are obsequiousness (*areskeia*) or flattery (*kolakeia*), which go too far in this, and churlishness (*duskolia*) which does not go far enough. The second virtue is truthfulness (*alētheia*), which is concerned with truth. The corresponding vices are boastfulness (*alazoneia*), which goes beyond the truth, and irony (*eirōneia*), which falls short of the truth. The third virtue is *eutrapelia*, which is concerned with the giving of pleasure in amusement (*paidia*). The concept of a moral virtue concerned with giving pleasure in amusement originated with Aristotle, and there is no word that accurately designates it in either Greek or English. Aristotle calls the virtue *eutrapelia*, although recognizing that the word is also used to designate a quality ascribed to buffoons (*Eth.* iv.8.1128a15). Thus for the meaning of *eutrapelia* LS lists not only "wit, liveliness, politeness" but also "coarse jesting, ribaldry." The corresponding vices are buffoonery (*bōmolochia*), which goes too far in giving pleasure in amusement, and boorishness (*agroikia*), which does not go far enough.

The virtues of considerateness and truthfulness are not concerned to give pleasure in amusement, and therefore do not define characters of comedy. The virtue of *eutrapelia* is concerned to give pleasure in amusement, but with moral limitations that prevent it from defining a character of comedy. If the three virtues of conviviality are ruled out, this leaves the six vices as possibilities for the characters of comedy. We can eliminate the vice opposite to buffoonery—boorishness—for boorish characters can neither make a joke themselves or put up with those who do (ibid., 7), and thus, far from being disposed to produce laughs, they inhibit laughter, acting like wet blankets. The two vices corresponding to considerateness—obsequiousness and churlishness—can also be ruled out. They provide opportunities for comedy as objects of laughter, as we see in the obsequious Mr. Collins in *Pride and Prejudice* and the churlish Mr. Palmer in *Sense and Sensibility*, but are not dispositions to produce it. The obsequious person tries to please others, but in general, not specifically by amusing them. The churlish person does not care about pleasing others in any respect, and pleases them only if he can be made an object of laughter. This leaves for the characters who produce the laughter of comedy only the three listed in the epitome: the boastful, the ironic, and the buffoonish. We shall discuss them in the order in which they are listed in the epitome. This reverses the order in which they are introduced in the *Ethics*, an indication that the priorities of comedy are not those of ethics. We begin with the buffoon.

We have already encountered the name of the buffoon (*bōmolochos*), reduced by paronymy to "bomax." He is described in the *Ethics* in a way that makes clear why buffoonery is not a moral virtue. "Those who go to excess with respect to the laughable are thought to be buffoons and vulgar, striving wholly for the laughable, and aiming to produce laughter rather than to say what is tasteful and not painful to the mocked" (ibid., 4–7). The buffoon aims to produce the laughable, which is the aim of most stand-up comedians and of comedy that aims at the laughable without concern for symmetry. The best kind of comedy, however, would presumably exhibit speech and actions like those produced by eutrapelia, not because this kind of comedy aims at morality, but because it aims at the perfection of comedy. In this way, Aristotle's conception of goods as relative to the things that are good may in the ideal case approximate to Plato's unitary good.

Shakespeare's Falstaff is perhaps the best-known literary buffoon. He illustrates not only buffoonery, but also why it is not a moral virtue. Prince Hal enjoys Falstaff without reserve as a drinking companion, but when Prince Hal becomes King Henry the Fifth, he repudiates him as a companion. Similarly, Queen Elizabeth, according to Nicholas Rowe in the life of Shakespeare that accompanied Rowe's edition of Shakespeare's works (1709), "was so well pleased with that admirable character of Falstaff in the two parts of Henry IV that she commanded him to continue it for one play more, and to show him in love," but she expressed no wish to have such a man among her courtiers.

The buffoon is disposed to use any or all forms of the laughable in his efforts to raise a laugh, but the ironic and boastful characters, to whom we now turn, raise a laugh by means of the forms that define their characters. It is also in this way that the speaker in a lyric poem determines the form of the poem. Thus the discussion of character introduces a new and enlarged approach to the subject of comedy. The ironic and boastful characters both depart from the truth, and may do so for various reasons, but it is only when this is done for the sake of amusing others that they are properly comic characters. In considering the jokes appropriate to a rhetorician Aristotle says, "Irony better befits a gentleman than buffoonery; the ironical man jokes to amuse himself, the buffoon to amuse other people" (*Rhet.* iii.18.1419b7). The comic ironist, like the buffoon, jokes to amuse other people.

Speaking of the ironic character in the *Ethics*, Aristotle writes, "Ironic people, who understate things, seem more attractive in character [than the boastful] for they are thought to speak, not for gain, but to avoid parade; and here too it is qualities which bring reputation that they disclaim, as Socrates used to do" (*Eth.* iv.2.1127b22–6, after Ross). Socrates is Aristotle's only example of an ironic character in the surviving works, and if he speaks to avoid parade, his irony is not comic irony. Presumably Aristotle is referring to the historical Socrates, who ironically understated his own knowledge.

The irony of the Platonic Socrates, we may note in passing, is a form of truthfulness rather than a departure from the truth. When Plato's Socrates says he knows only his own ignorance he is comparing what he knows with an ideal of truth that makes it impossible to know the truth of anything without knowing the principle of all things, which he does not know.

Jonathan Swift may be taken as an example of a comic ironist. In a well-known incident in *Gulliver's Travels*, Gulliver offers to provide the King of Brobdingnag with a knowledge of the manufacture and use of gunpowder that would make him the absolute master of the lives, the liberties, and the fortunes of his people (Swift 1905, 8:137–39). The King, however, refuses the offer, "a strange effect," says Gulliver, "of *narrow principles* and *short views*." The King should not be blamed for this defect, he continues, for it results from the ignorance of the Brobdingnagians, "they not having hitherto reduced *politics* into a *science*, as the more acute wits of Europe have done." "All the scenes of blood and desolation" which Gulliver paints as the common effects of gunpowder, are, as an objection to its use, a "nice unnecessary scruple." This is an ironic understatement of the evils that result from the use of gunpowder. It is Swift rather than Gulliver who is the comic ironist, for Gulliver is not trying to amuse the King, but to "ingratiate himself further in his Majesty's favor." A similar example of Swift's irony is his *Modest Proposal* for preventing the children of the poor in Ireland from being a burden to their parents or country, and for making them beneficial to the public, by selling them for food at the age of one year. "It is not improbable that some scrupulous people might be apt to censure such a practice (although indeed very unjustly), as a little bordering upon cruelty; which, I confess, hath always been with me the strongest objection against any project, however so well intended" (ibid., 7:211).

For more recent examples of comic irony we can cite Mark Twain. An example is his well-known statement, "The reports of my death are greatly exaggerated" (cable from London to the Associated Press, 1897). This understates the wrongness of the reports by making them exaggerated rather than false, while at the same time introducing the formal wrongness of making death a matter of degree. We referred earlier to Twain's *1601: Conversation as It Was by the Social Fireside in the Time of the Tudors*. This understates the restraints on the uninhibited discussion of bodily functions in polite society, a wrongness emphasized by the refined manner of their discussion. Another example is Huckleberry Finn's deliberation as to whether to turn in Jim as an escaped slave or assist in his escape (Twain 1948, chap. 31, 212–14). On the one side are his conscience and what he has been taught in Sunday school to the effect that if he does not turn Jim in but rather aids in his escape, he can look forward to everlasting fire, while on the other side are his memories of the trip down the river with Jim. At the end, he says to himself, "All right then, I'll go to hell." What is omitted in Huck's deliberation is any questioning of the rightness of slavery and the morality that supports it.

Turning now to the boastful, they may go beyond the truth simply because it is funny, and thus be motivated to produce comedy, although more usually they go beyond the truth for ulterior motives and so they are material for comedy, like the obsequious and the churlish, rather than producers of it, like the buffoon and the ironist. In the *Ethics*, this difference between lying for its own sake and for the sake of gain or reputation is again evaluated ethically: "He who claims more than he has with no ulterior object is a contemptible sort of fellow (otherwise he would not have delighted in falsehood), but seems futile rather than bad; but if he does it for an object, he who does it for the sake of reputation or honor is (for a boaster) not very much to be blamed, but he who does it for money, or the things that lead to money, is an uglier character . . . as one man is a liar because he enjoys the lie itself, and another because he desires reputation or gain. Now those who boast for the sake of reputation claim such qualities as win praise or congratulation, but those whose object is gain claim qualities that are of value to one's neighbors and one's lack of which is not easily detected, e.g., the powers of a seer, a sage, or a physician" (*Eth.* iv.7.1127b9–20, trans. Ross). Characters who go beyond the truth for an ulterior motive, such as claiming the powers of a seer, sage, or physician, are illustrated by Ben Jonson's alchemist, Subtle, and his associates, or Moliere's Tartuffe, but in these cases they are objects of laughter rather than characters disposed to produce it.

Shakespeare's Thersites, in *Troilus and Cressida*, provides an example of comic overstatement. Here are his thoughts on Agamemnon: "Agamemnon,—how if he had boils,—full, all over, general? And those boils did run?—Say so—did not the general run then? Were not that a botchy core? Then would come some matter from him; I see none now." To Ajax: "I would thou didst itch from head to foot, and I had the scratching of thee; I would make thee the loathsomest scab in Greece." To Ajax and Achilles: "Hector shall have a great catch if he knock out either of your brains: a' were as good crack a fusty nut with no kernel." On Nestor: "Old Nestor, whose wit was mouldy ere your grandsires had nails on their toes." To Patroclus: "The common curse of mankind, folly and ignorance, be thine in great revenue! Heaven bless thee from a tutor, and discipline come not near thee! Let thy blood be thy direction till thy death! then if she that lays thee out says thou art a fair corse, I'll be sworn and sworn upon't she never shrouded any but lazars. Amen." On the Trojan War: "All the argument is a cuckold and a whore; a good quarrel to draw emulous factions and bleed to death upon. Now, the dry serpigo [a spreading skin disease] on the subject! And war and lechery confound all!" (2.1–3). Thersites overstates the vileness of everyone and everything. Boastfulness ordinarily overstates desirable rather than undesirable qualities, but the latter can also be overstated. Thersites's disparagement of others resembles boastfulness in the ordinary sense insofar as his exaggeration of the faults of others may make his own deformity seem less offensive.

Examples of characters who exaggerate their own abilities are John Thorpe in Jane Austen's *Northanger Abbey*, who can be counted on to exaggerate almost anything and is one of the funniest characters in Jane Austen. Similarly, Topper is one of the funniest characters in Scott Adams's comic strip *Dilbert*. Whenever anyone recounts anything he has achieved, Topper is sure to respond, "That's nothing," and go on to recount some fantastic achievement of his own.

For an overstating author comparable to Jonathan Swift and his understatements we may cite Laurence Sterne. Tristram Shandy, after recounting the unfortunate circumstances of his conception, affirms of Fortune "that in every stage of my life, and at every turn and corner where she could get fairly at me, the ungracious duchess has pelted me with a set of as pitiful misadventures and cross accidents as ever small Hero sustained" (Sterne, n.d., 1.5.10).

A more recent example is James Thurber. His *My Life and Hard Times* (1933) is, in the form of its humor, comparable to *The Life and Opinions of Tristram Shandy*. In the first chapter, "The Night the Bed Fell," the overturning of a cot turns into a familial disaster. The first cartoon in *Men, Women, and Dogs* (1946, 1) shows a fencer completely decapitating his opponent while saying "Touché!" The "Touché!" is an ironic understatement in relation to the decapitation, but it is so only because of the exaggeration in the act itself. Most of Thurber's cartoons have the form of overstatements. Another well-known example is the cartoon of a man returning to a house which has morphed into an angry wife (ibid., 98). The title of "The War Between Men and Women" (ibid., 215) already indicates its basic overstatement, presenting the relations between men and women as a war.

Aristotle's approach to comedy through its characters resembles Freud's approach to the comic through the psychological processes involved. Just as Aristotle's approach takes him beyond the laughable and the buffoon to ironic and boastful characters, so Freud's approach takes him beyond the psychological processes involved in jokes to those involved in humor.

Freud's leading example of humor noted earlier is an ironic joke. A rogue being led to the gallows on a Monday says, "Well, this is a fine beginning to the week!" (1963, 229). This conforms to Aristotle's definition of irony because it understates the true gravity of his situation. Freud also recognizes in his way what is for Aristotle the distinguishing feature of irony: "It is also true that, in bringing about the humorous attitude, the super-ego is in fact repudiating reality and serving an illusion" (1950, 5:220). Thus we have again the same sort of complementarity between the theories of Aristotle and Freud that we had in the case of jokes. What is for Aristotle a disposition to understatement can, at least in the case of the joke cited, be understood as the result of an intra-psychic assimilation to the better. Similarly, Socratic irony involves a shift of cathexis from the individual ego to the idea of the good. Swift's moral standpoint leads him to repudiate both the truly narrow principles and short views that make the destructiveness of gunpowder desirable, and also the inhumane treatment of the Irish poor. Twain's moral standpoint repudiates the excesses of conventional morality and its acceptance of slavery.

Applying Freud's theory of the comic to the examples of overstatement, it implies that we find them laughable because we have no need to waste psychic energy on the exaggerated bad-mouthing of Thersites, the crazy exaggerations of John Thorpe and Topper, or the exaggerated misfortunes and troubles of Tristram Shandy and the characters of James Thurber.

Freud's additions to Aristotle's account of the characters of comedy enable us to fill a lacuna in Aristotle's incorporation of Morreall's three traditional theories of laughter. We have noted that the incongruity of the incongruity theories is incorporated in the formal wrongness of the laughable and that the relief of the relief theories is the result of laughter at the material wrongness of the laughable. But the superiority of the superiority theories has been relegated to malicious laughter, whereas these theories purport to account for comic laughter as well. We can now see that superiority is involved in the humor of both understatement and overstatement, for irony depends on a superior standpoint, and the humor of overstatement depends on a superior economy in the expenditure of psychic energy.

Thought has two parts, maxim and persuasion. Persuasions are five: oaths, contracts, witnesses, tortures, and laws.
Thought in general is the power of saying what is or may be suitable and is that aspect of speeches which is the function of politics and rhetoric

($6.1450b4-7$). It exists in those speeches in which the speakers demonstrate what is or is not the case or affirms something universal (ibid., 11–12). For the thought of both tragedy and comedy we are referred to the *Rhetoric*, but to different parts of the *Rhetoric*. The parts of the *Rhetoric* needed for tragic thought concern demonstrating, solving, and rendering the passions (e.g., pity, fear, anger, and the like), and also maximizing and minimizing things ($19.1456a37-b2$). Demonstrating alone includes much of the *Rhetoric*, for it involves the forms (*eidē*) from which premises are derived, to which Book I is devoted, and the inferential topics of enthymeme, which are treated in Book II, chapters 22–24. Also in Book II are the means of arousing emotions (chapters 2–11, the solving of objections (chapters 25–26), and the maximizing and minimizing of things (chapter 19). What remain in the *Rhetoric* but are not needed in tragedy are the discussion of character, which is treated independently in the *Poetics*, as we have seen, and the discussion of style and arrangement, which is treated poetically rather than rhetorically in relation to diction and plot.

On the other hand, only two chapters of the *Rhetoric* are needed for comedy, chapter 21 of Book II on maxims and chapter 15 of Book I on the nontechnical means of persuasion: laws, witnesses, contracts, tortures, and oaths. In the rhetorical list laws come first as most persuasive and oaths last as least persuasive, while in comedy laws offer the least opportunity for jokes and oaths the greatest. Arguments as to what is good or noble or just have a place in tragedy but not in comedy, and thus demonstration belongs to tragedy and not comedy. But even in tragedy it is popular rather than scientific thought that is relevant. But comedy has no place for genuine arguments, whether scientific or rhetorical, but only for obviously spurious arguments that lack any consecution, for these are laughable. Thought in comedy goes only as far as the assertion of maxims without proofs, and the use of the nontechnical means of persuasion, which are simply external factors that can be used for persuasion, without argument as to their applicability, which is the whole burden of their treatment in rhetoric. Lane Cooper has investigated the use of the nontechnical persuasions in Aristophanes, and his results are reported by Janko (1984, 219): "Oaths are plentiful, e.g., *Frogs* 305ff.; agreements not rare, e.g., *Thesm.*116off; also the appearance of witnesses, e.g., *Wasps* 936ff.; tests and ordeals are conspicuous, e.g., Aecus flogging of Dionusus and Xanthias at *Frogs* 642ff.; the citation of laws either bogusly or humorously misapplied, is less frequent, but cf. Northrup Frye, *Anatomy of Criticism*, 166, 169."

Comic diction is common and popular. The comic poet should give their native idiom to his characters, and the local idiom to himself.
Diction in general is the expression through language and is treated extensively in Book I with specification to works in different meters. The first sentence of the epitome's statement distinguishes comic from tragic diction, for, as common and popular, it should not use strange words unless they are funny, whereas tragedy uses strange words to avoid the commonplace. The second sentence treats the important contribution of dialect to jokes and the comic. Freud observes that dialect has an effect similar to the joke-technique (1963, 108), which in Aristotle's terms means that it has an effect similar to the sources of laughter in diction, that is, it is in a way a wrongness of diction and contributes to the joking mood.

Melody is proper to music, hence one will need to take from music its starting points complete in themselves.
All that is said about melody in Book I is that what is meant by melody is the power evident to all, and that it is the greatest of the sweeteners of speech. The generic account is given in Book II because what melody should be depends not on what the poem is as imitation, but on its end. And all that is said about it is that it will need to take its starting points complete in themselves from what it is as music, and for this reason there is no specification of it to either tragedy or comedy.

The spectacle supplies a great service to dramas when in harmony with them.
This is the generic account of spectacle, and it is given in Book II because, like music, what spectacle should be depends on the end of the poem. But there is this difference, that the judgment of spectacle is not referred to another art, but belongs to poetics. Thus spectacle is discussed in Book I as a source of the fearsome and piteous, and the merely monstrous is rejected as not producing a pleasure appropriate to tragedy. We said earlier that the spectacle depends on the auxiliary arts of the scene painter (1449a18), the costume maker (6.1450b20), the choral directors (14.1453b8), and the art of elocution (19.1456b10). The principle that governs the use of all of these and integrates them into the drama as a whole is the poetic principle that they must be in harmony with the drama. Modern operatic directors sometimes feel they must put their stamp on the production by producing the work in a way that has never been done before. Their innovations are often controversial, and if they are not in harmony with the drama, the directors deserve the

opening-night boos they sometimes receive. But if the innovations are in harmony with the drama, there is no reason to reject them simply because they are not traditional.

Plot, diction, and melody are observed in all comedies; thoughts, character, and spectacle in not a few.
The corresponding statement in Book I is "Those agents who have used these forms have not, we may say, been few, for every tragedy has spectacles, character, plot, diction, melody, and thought" (6.1450a12, trans. Telford). Taken out of context, these two statements may seem to imply that tragedy necessarily uses all the parts and comedy does not, but in Book I Aristotle has derived the parts from the definition of tragedy as forms necessarily belonging to the species and available for use by tragic poets, who have in fact used them, but not necessarily all of them, for he goes on to say that the tragedies of most of the new poets are characterless (ibid., 25). In the epitome, all the parts are discussed as matter for the forms of comedy, and the concluding statement presents a summary result of their use, which is that three of them are observed in every tragedy and three in not a few.

The parts of comedy are four: prologue, choral part, episode, and exode.

This introduces the four quantitative parts, which, like the qualitative parts, are intermediate between the poetic materials and the poetic end, but they function differently in the two books of the *Poetics* and therefore are treated twice. The corresponding statement in Book I is, "The quantitative parts into which a tragedy is separately divided are these: prologue, episode, exode, choral part ..." (12.1452b15, trans. Telford). The difference in order results from the choral part of tragedy being subdivided, but the four quantitative parts, like the six qualitative parts, are the same in both books. The contexts of the two statements are, however, opposite. In the analysis of tragedy, the account of the quantitative parts is given in relation to the plot as the form of tragedy, and they are related to the plot as its material embodiment. In the analysis of comedy, the account of the quantitative parts is given in relation to the other parts as the matter of comedy, and they are related to the other parts as a formal structure for them as matter. The accounts of the quantitative parts thus occur in opposite contexts and give the quantitative parts opposite functions. The qualitative parts provide the form for tragedy and the matter for comedy, while the quantitative parts provide the matter for the form of tragedy and the form for the matter of comedy. Lyric poetry in this

respect is again like comedy—the quantitative parts provide a form for the qualitative parts, as we see, for example, in the various forms of the sonnet. We take up the quantitative parts one by one.

1. *Prologue is the first part of comedy up to the entrance of the chorus.* Book I defines the prologue as the whole part of tragedy preceding the *parodos*. The *parodos* is the whole first statement (*lexis*) of the chorus. The name is derived from the side way (*parodos*) though which the chorus, like the messengers in the plays, entered the area of the stage and the orchestra, as distinguished from the three entrances onto the stage from the building behind it. The orchestra is the place where the chorus sang and danced. The statements of Book I and the epitome are two different ways of defining the first part of the drama, but in the case of tragedy it is defined formally as a whole in relation to the whole choral part that follows, while in the case of comedy it is defined materially by what divides it from the next part, the entrance of the chorus.

2. *Choral part is the melody sung by the chorus when it has sufficient magnitude.* Book I defines the choral part by its species, the *parodos* and the *stasimon*, which are common to all tragedies, and songs from the stage and the *kommos*, which are found in some only. The *parodos*, as we said, is the whole first statement of the chorus, the *stasimon* is a choral song without anapests or trochees, which seems intended to imply that without these marching meters it remains in the orchestra, and the *kommos* is a lament (*thrēnos*) common to the chorus and the actors on the stage. The distinction between *parodos*, *stasimon*, and *kommos* mirrors the distinction of the plot into its beginning, middle, and end, whereas the epitome simply divides up the drama into parts and is indifferent to all their characteristics except their magnitude.

3. *Episode.* Book I defines the episode as the whole part of a tragedy between whole choral songs. The epitome defines the episode as the part between two choral songs. The slight difference between the two definitions, the difference between the repeated "whole" and the number "two," expresses the fundamental difference between the two sets of definitions— the one concerned with the choral songs as wholes, the other only with their numerical difference.

4. *Exode.* Book I defines the *exodus* or "way out" as the whole part of tragedy after the last choral song. The epitome defines the *exodus* as the part at the end spoken by the chorus. Here we have a real difference in what is designated by the exode. Book I treats the exode as the whole part after the

last choral song, which would be the whole resolution of the tragedy, as distinguished from the preceding complication. The part is again considered in relation to the plot and is made to fit the division of the plot into complication and resolution. The epitome, on the other hand, treats the exode as the brief chanted part with which the chorus usually exits, thus making the part between this and the preceding choral part just another episode. The reason for this is clearly because the distinction between complication and resolution is not essential to comedy, as we concluded from the analysis of comic catharsis. This entails a slight qualification in the definition of an episode, that it may be not only the part between two choral songs, but also the part between a choral song and the part at the end spoken by the chorus. We may conclude by noting that these two possible ways of conceiving the divisions of a play, as corresponding to the parts of the plot and as divisions of the matter of the play, have persisted to the present day in our thinking about them.

2. OLD, NEW, AND MIDDLE COMEDY

Comedy is—
—old, which goes to excess in the laughable;
—new, which, abandoning this, inclines toward the solemn;
—middle, which is a mixture of both.
This subject completes the sequence that Aristotle has been following in his discussion of comedy. He has discussed the form of comedy, which is the laughable, and its matter and quantitative parts. These are united in the complete work, and the principle which unites them is the end of comedy, the catharsis of emotions such as pleasure and laughter. The subject of this part of the epitome is the different ways in which this end is realized.

This corresponds to the final subject of Book I, the realization of the ends of tragedy, epic poetry, and poetry in general as imitations. Aristotle treats only one species of comedy, dramatic comedy, and instead of a discussion of the attainment of the end in different species, we have the discussion of variations in the end within the species.

Although comic catharsis involves two emotions, pleasure and laughter, the distinction in the ends of comedy depends only on the role of the laughable. Laughter has a definiteness that pleasure and the emotions in general do not, and it holds together the whole account of comedy. Laughter is the mother of comedy, the forms of the laughable provide the formal element in comedy, comedy aims at a symmetry of the laughable, and the different kinds of comedy are distinguished by the extent to which they aim at laughter. Comedy aims at a symmetry of the laughable, and the different kinds of comedy can be distinguished as those that aim at this symmetry or depart from it in one or the other of two opposite ways. This is not a sharp distinction of species, but a distinction of regions on a continuum, The distinction itself is nontemporal, which implies that all the possibilities are always present and any of them may be realized at any time, but the kinds are given names appropriate to a temporal sequence, which implies an internal dynamic by which one kind leads to the next within the series. Since laughter is the mother of comedy, it is an ever-present starting point for the series. Comic laughter, as distinguished from the laughter of invective, is laughter for its own sake, and so all three kinds of comedy, so far as they aim at laughter, aim at laughter for its own sake. Invective is not included. The first comedies presumably aimed simply to raise a laugh, like the buffoon. Such comedy is unrestrained by considerations of propriety or any serious purpose. Its initial form would be that of a series of jokes, and any connection among them would be justified if it increased the laughter. Such comedy is represented today by stand-up comedy and by the episodes of situation comedy, each of which aims to raise as much laughter as it can in half an hour.

The internal motivation for a transition to middle comedy is simply to perfect the comedy as producing laughter. This leads to the introduction of emotions other than laughter and to emotional symmetry in which the end of laughter is most fully achieved. Middle comedy attains, to a greater or lesser degree, a symmetry of the laughable. Aristophanes has already been referred to as exhibiting such a symmetry. That he best represents Aristotle's ideal of comedy is suggested by the citing of Sophocles, Homer, and Aristophanes as exemplary of the three great species of poetry in Book I (3.1448a27). This conclusion is supported by his use of Aristophanes to provide examples of the forms of the laughable in Book II., and by Janko's thorough investigation of the whole question of the three kinds of comedy (Janko 242–50). Most of the comic dramas that we admire are middle comedies—those, for example, of Shakespeare, Molière, Oscar Wilde, or George Bernard Shaw.

If middle comedy perfects comedy, what motivates the transition to new comedy? I think it is an unrealized possibility with respect to comedy. Laughter is only one of the two emotions of comedy, and it requires characters worse than we are. What if we subordinate laughter and characters worse than we are to pleasure and characters like ourselves or somewhat better? This is certainly an attractive possibility and deserves development.

We do not know what comedies Aristotle had in mind as illustrating new comedy, but we do know the kind of end that such comedy requires. From a modern perspective we can see that the tendency toward new comedy in fact led to a new poetic species, the comic novel. The best examples that we have of works that attain the end of new comedy are not dramas, but novels such as those of Henry Fielding and Jane Austen. Laughter is social and is best aroused by performances before a live audience. When a performance of Oscar Wilde's *The Importance of Being Earnest* was filmed and shown in movie theaters, most of the laughter, at least in the showing I saw, came from the original audience. If there is no live audience, the comedy is usually accompanied by a laugh track. Comedy that aims at pleasure rather than laughter, however, does not need a laughing audience. If we include narrative as well as dramatic comedy under the general head of comedy, Aristotle's distinction becomes a very useful way of distinguishing the comedian, the comic drama, and the comic novel.

The principles that generate the series can give rise to new series and subseries. Richard Levin writes that the divisions of the epitome "seem to be not only a history of the genre, but also a system of classification of subgenres. English comedy went through a (roughly) similar evolution from the simple farces of Heywood to Shakespeare to the Caroline comedy of manners, and Shakespearean comedy itself evolved from early plays like *The Comedy of Errors* to the Romantic comedies (*As You Like It, Twelfth Night*) to the final romances" (pers. comm., December 8, 2007).

Aristotle's distinction among the kinds of comedies is thus useful both as providing a first cut in the analysis and evaluation of comedies and as identifying a recurrent chronological sequence in their development.

CONCLUSION

Let me conclude by summarizing the principal contributions that the epitome makes to the understanding of Aristotle's *Poetics* and to poetic theory.

1. With *Poetics* I, it provides an example of a formally complete poetics. It supplies what was missing from Book I and enables us to understand it as a component of a complete whole.
2. The evolution of imitation into poetry can now be understood as culminating in the proper subject of poetics, imitative poetry, which has its end in itself.
3. The epitome provides the basic distinction among the kinds of poetry: historical, educational, and imitative, a distinction essential to the analysis of any of the kinds.
4. It clarifies the concept of tragic catharsis in a way that makes it both an end in itself and relevant to the problems of human life.
5. It supplies a formal distinction between the two great possibilities for imitative poetry, poetry that derives its form from the materials of imitation and poetry that derives its form from the end of imitation. In so doing, it shows how the theory of lyric poetry is included in poetics.
6. It introduces the concept of symmetry as the finality of both tragic and comic catharsis. This is a principle of great power that anyone can easily use and is sure to become a commonplace of future criticism. This concept also leads to a useful distinction among comic works that provides a first step in their analysis.
7. It presents a theory of comedy to match Aristotle's theory of tragedy, including a theory of the laughable whose essential elements are found also in Cicero and Freud and which can provide the basis for a science of humor.

Insofar as these are all things that are not to be found in the existing literature on the *Poetics*, the epitome has in effect given us a new *Poetics*. We can be grateful to the unknown sixth-century epitomist who produced an epitome of Book II, and to the unknown tenth-century copyist who preserved what we have, for enabling us to recover this much of Aristotle's contribution to poetics in Book II. The floundering that, in the absence of Book II, has occurred with respect to the subjects treated in this one small part of Aristotle's scientific works suggests how great a debt we own to him for his role in establishing the full range of sciences that underlie the achievements of our modern world.

Appendix

THE ORDER AND PROVENANCE
OF THE ARISTOTELIAN CORPUS

Following the lead of Werner Jaeger (Jaeger 1948), much scholarly effort during the past century was devoted to interpreting Aristotle's thought by means of the order of composition of his works. This is one possible meaning for the order of Aristotle's works, but another is suggested by the first chapter of the *Parts of Animals*, in which Aristotle discusses the canons by which to judge the science he is presenting. He writes, "Another matter which must not be passed over without consideration is, whether the proper subject of our exposition is that with which the ancient writers concerned themselves, namely, what is the process of formation of each animal; or whether it is not rather, what are the characters of a given creature when formed. For there is no small difference between these two views" (i.1.640a10–15, trans. Ogle). The analogous distinction with respect to the order of Aristotle's works is the distinction between their order of composition and their order when composed; the latter order was followed in the first chapter. This order is the order determined by the works themselves, as was said, and can therefore be called their proper order. Since Aristotle composed the works, it is also the order in which he intended they should be placed.

The normal result of inquiries into the order of composition of the works and their proper order when completed would be two complementary accounts, the order of composition leading to the order when completed. The order of composition, however, depends on many accidental factors, Aristotle was not concerned to preserve it, and we have very little evidence for what it was. Those pursuing this order have been led to treat seeming inconsistencies as evidence of different times of composition without sufficient consideration of the possibility that the difference between seemingly inconsistent statements results from their different contexts in the order of the completed works. An example is W. D. Ross's attempt to resolve the anomaly in Aristotle's account of the material cause in the *Posterior Analytics* (note 2 to chapter 2). The result of the effort to understand Aristotle's philosophy by means of the order of composition of his works has therefore been not a better understanding of Aristotle's philosophy, but its annihilation. As Richard McKeon puts it in his Carus Lectures, "After the history of the stages of his philosophy has been worked out, he has early, late, and middle periods but he no longer has a philosophy. He begins with Plato's philosophy, ends with Theophrastus's philosophy after going through a period which is a mélange" (McKeon 1965, 26; cf. McKeon 1949, 3).

Because the proper order of the completed works depends on the works themselves, it makes use of different principles in different parts of the series. In this respect it is unlike the chronological order, which arranges all the works with respect to the time of their composition, or what may be called a logistic order, which arranges all the works from the most simple to the most compound, or a dialectical order, which may use the same contrary again and again in organizing a single whole, as Plato's *Phaedrus* repeatedly uses the contrast between rhetoric and dialectic to organize that work. The variety of principles that are used in the proper order of the works can be illustrated by briefly running through the series of arts and sciences as presented in chapter 1.

The overall order of the works is that of logical, physical, and ethical problems and propositions as these are distinguished in the *Topics* (14.105b19–31). Logic precedes physics and ethics because it is used in them, and physics precedes ethics because to the concern of physics with what is, ethics adds a concern with what ought to be.

Within logic as treated in the *Organon* the formal logic of the first three works precedes the material logic of the next three works because the first is concerned only with the formal truth by which conclusions follow from premises, whereas the second adds to this a concern with the material truth of the premises as true of things. In the first triad, the *Categories* treats the categories of single terms, *On Interpretation* treats the combination of two terms in propositions, and the *Prior Analytics* treats the combination of three terms in syllogisms. This is a simple sequence of one, two, three, or of parts to wholes, and it is also an instance of the metaphysical categories that Peirce finds everywhere — firstness, secondness, and thirdness. The sequence derives from the subject matter of formal logic and is appropriate to that subject matter, but, unless we are using the metaphysics of Peirce or a dialectic in which thought and things follow the same processes, we do not expect to find it in other subject matters. In the second triad of the *Organon*, the *Posterior Analytics* treats scientific arguments from premises that are true of things, the *Topics* treats dialectical arguments from premises that are thought to be true, and *On Sophistical Refutations* treats sophistical arguments that depend on words. This sequence is from things to thoughts to words, and it corresponds to the directness of their relation to the truth of things—the truth of things, what is thought to be the truth of things, and the formulation of what is thought to be the truth of things. The sequentiality is one of dependence with respect to existence: without things, there is nothing of which to think, and without thoughts there is nothing to express in words. McKeon has shown that this sequence characterizes the subject matters in which principles are successively sought in the historical cycles of fashions of philosophizing in the West and has used it extensively in his own work (Watson 2000, 234n29). It is because of this sequence of modes of philosophizing that Kant, in an epistemic mode, is able to give a principled formulation of the difference between logic, physics, and ethics, whereas Aristotle, in an ontic mode, is not. It is a sequence different in form from the one, two, three sequence of the first three treatises, but each sequence is appropriate to its subject matter. Thus the sequences within the *Organon* illustrate how different principles of organization are operative in different parts of the proper order.

Within physics in the broad sense as constituting the second part of the corpus, and assuming, as is argued in chapter 1, that any mathematical works would have preceded the *Physics,* the sequence is from mathematics to natural science to first philosophy or theology. Within natural science the sequence is from physics to biology. These sciences aim at truth, and the sequence is from the less true to the more true, the more true being conceived intensively as having more of truth rather than extensively as simply being true of more things. The truth of mathematics concerns quantity and is the truth about one attribute of natural things. The truth of physics is the truth common to all natural things, which is wider in its extension than the truth of living things but narrower in its intension, for the truth of living things includes the truth of nonliving things. The truth of first philosophy is the truth of all things, and if the principle of the whole has more of truth than natural living things, as we say of God that in Him is all truth, "the science of this must be prior and must be first philosophy, and universal in this way, because it is first" (*Metaph.* vi.1.1026a29, trans. Ross).

Within ethics in the broad sense as constituting the third part of the corpus, the sequence is from the practical sciences of ethics and politics to the arts, of which only two are treated, poetics and rhetoric. The theoretical sequence of physics is from the less true to the more true, while the practical sequence of ethics is opposite to this in the sense that it is from the highest good to lesser goods, where the lesser good is for the sake of the higher good. Thus the goods at which the arts aim are for the sake of the goods at which the practical sciences aim. Ethics and politics both aim at the same good, but ethics formulates what it is as an individual good and politics considers how it is to be realized in the household and state. Within the arts there is in the traditional order of the corpus an inversion of the proper order, as we shall see, for poetics, whose end is realized in the work itself, should precede rhetoric, which aims at persuasion with respect to any end, good or bad. The treatises, then, have a proper order that depends on the treatises themselves as well as on the whole of which they are parts. The books within each treatise similarly have a proper order that depends on the books themselves and the treatises of which they are parts.

The traditional order of the corpus as we have received it is in general their proper order, but there are a number of exceptions. Two are misplacements that put a book in a treatise in which it does not belong, two put the books of a treatise in the wrong order, and two put treatises themselves in the wrong order. There are also some departures from the proper order in the chapter divisions, which were made by Renaissance editors. They are in general of little consequence, and I shall not discuss them here beyond noting the most egregious of them, the absence of a chapter break in the *Rhetoric* corresponding to the major distinction between persuasion by character and emotion and persuasion by argument (ii.18.1391b23).

We begin our examination of the departures of the traditional order from the proper order by citing Porphyry's statement on the origin of the traditional order. Porphyry says, "Andronicus divided the works of Aristotle and Theophrastus into treatises, collecting related material into the same place" (*Vitae Plotini* 24, trans. in *SEP*, s.v. "Andronicus"). Porphyry had the edition of Andronicus, and had it when it still contained the second book of the *Poetics*, as Janko has shown (Janko 1984, 29, 63, 88, 172–73).

The most conspicuous instance of placing a book in a treatise in which it does not belong, noted by Ross (1949, 13) and many others, is placing the second book of the *Metaphysics*, or Little Alpha, between Books Alpha (I) and Beta (III), where it interrupts not only the Greek numbering of the books but also the explicit continuity between the end of Alpha, which proposes to enumerate aporias or difficulties, and the beginning of Beta, which begins this enumeration. Why did Andronicus place it here? Let us assume, following Porphyry, that he was dividing the works into treatises and collecting together related material into the same place, thus avoiding isolated scrolls. If this book came to him as an isolated scroll, as it apparently did, he would need to find a place for it in a larger work next to related material. The central section of Little Alpha concerns the existence of first causes, and the first book of the *Metaphysics* is concerned with first principles and causes, so, if one is collecting related material into the same place, it belongs next to the first book of the *Metaphysics*. The first book itself clearly begins the *Metaphysics*, so Andronicus placed it immediately after the first book.

What is the proper place of Little Alpha? Aristotle tells us in the *Posterior Analytics* (ii.1) that in investigating a subject such as first principles and causes, we first ask whether it exists, and having ascertained this, we then inquire into what it is. Since the central section of Little Alpha concerns the existence of first causes, and the first book of the *Metaphysics* inquires into what they are, it is clear that Little Alpha should precede the *Metaphysics*. Since Little Alpha is concerned with the existence of first causes in general, while the *Physics* is concerned with the existence of a particular first cause, the first cause of motion, and since generic causes are prior to specific causes (*Phys.* ii.3.195a29–32), Little Alpha should also precede the *Physics*. Physics is the first of the subject-matter sciences in the corpus, so the proper place of Little Alpha is immediately preceding the *Physics*. And Little Alpha itself indicates that this is where it belongs, for it concludes, "The minute accuracy of mathematics is not to be demanded in all cases, but only in the case of things that have no matter. Thus its mode (*tropos*) is not physical (*phusikos*), for presumably the whole of nature (*phusis*) has matter. Hence we must first inquire what nature is, and thus it will also be clear what things physics (*hē phusikē*) is about" (*Metaph.* ii.995a14–19). Since the inquiry into what nature is begins the scientific part of the *Physics*, it is clear that Little Alpha should immediately precede the *Physics*, where it functions as a preface to the theoretical sciences. The misplacing of Little Alpha is a clear case of a desire to avoid an isolated book that results in its placement next to the book in a larger work that has a similar subject matter, but in violation of the structure of the larger work and the internal indications in Little Alpha itself. We have discussed in chapter 1 the correspondence between the theoretical and practical prefaces and the reason why the preface to the theoretical sciences is an isolated book and the preface to the practical sciences is not.

There is another book in the *Metaphysics* that does not belong in it. What is now Book Kappa (XI) consists of shorter forms of parts of the *Metaphysics* and the *Physics*. Most scholars consider it authentic, and it is not without interest, but it is clearly not an integral part of either method. It was composed for some reason other than as a part of either the *Physics* or the *Metaphysics* as we have them. Now that we attach appendices to our treatises, if we wanted to keep it attached to the *Metaphysics* we could do so without interrupting the structure of the *Metaphysics* by making it an appendix.

Another kind of departure from the proper order puts the books of a treatise in the wrong order. With respect to this kind of departure we must show from the internal evidence why it is an error, what the proper order of the books would be, and why Andronicus, bringing related works together into the same place, departed from this order. Books Lambda (XII), Mu (XIII), and Nu (XIV) of the *Metaphysics* are all concerned with immovable and eternal substance, and Andronicus has put them all next to each other. In so doing, however, he has disregarded the internal references, for the beginning of Mu states that in considering immovable and eternal substance we should first consider what has been said by others, and this is what Books Mu and Nu do. They therefore should precede rather than follow Lambda. In their position following Lambda they are in fact anticlimactic appendages that spoil the eloquent conclusion of Lambda and its transition to the practical sciences. But book Mu begins by talking about the objects of mathematics, which may have seemed to Andronicus another subject interrupting the connection of Lambda with what precedes it, and he therefore placed Mu and Nu after Lambda.

The second instance in which Andronicus's arrangement of the books of a treatise departs from their proper order is in the *Politics*. In the traditional order of books, what is now VI preceded V (McKeon 1949, 74n6), a transposition corrected in Bekker and succeeding editions. This transposition reveals the same pattern as the first, for VI is closely related to IV in its content, and their continuity seems to be interrupted by V, but if we place IV and VI next to each other, we must disregard the references in VI to V as the preceding method, and as containing what was previously considered, and as the preceding discussion (2.1317b34; 3.1319b37; 4.1318b7). In their proper order, changes of substance, or generation and perishing, treated in V, precede changes of quality, or alteration, treated in VI.

The Bekker edition, although correcting this transposition, introduces another, which takes VII and VIII, concerned with the best state, out of their proper place following Book III and places them at the end of the work. That they should immediately follow III is clear from its conclusion: "Having determined these things about the constitution, we must now try to speak of the best, in what way it naturally comes to be and how it is constituted" (*Pol.* iii.18.1288b2–4). In this place they complete the traditional discussion of the best constitution begun in Book II and precede Aristotle's own addition of what else belongs to politics. That VII and VIII should precede V is clear from a reference to VIII in V (9.1310 a12–14). I do not know the origin of, or reason for, this transposition, but perhaps it was thought that since the discussions of finality generally come last in Aristotle's treatises, for finality is the end of the other causes, the discussion of the finality of the perfect state should also come last. Practical deliberations, however, begin from the end to be realized. Of the four methods of the *Politics*, it is not the case that the method of the best depends on the other three methods. They are rather methods to be used when the actual conditions preclude the method of the best, which does not require them for its completion, although they are required for a complete politics. It appears from the plan for the *Politics* at the end of the *Ethics* that Aristotle initially thought of placing the inquiry into the best state last, but when he came to write it reconceived the organization as depending on the scope of the initial problem. This required an initial "first discourse" (*Pol.* iii.6.1278b18) that included a genesis of the state and could incorporate much of what properly belongs in Aristotle's one-book economics (*Pol.* vii.10.1330a31–3; Diogenes Laertius v.22). The account of the preservation and destruction of states could then follow rather than precede the discussion of the best constitution, for the method of preserving or destroying states is a method for attaining what is best when the preconditions for the best do not obtain, and it is properly the last of such methods because it presupposes the least. The proper order of the books, then, in the Oxford numbering, is I, II, III, VII, VIII, IV, V, VI, which Ernest Barker tells us is the most common modern rearrangement of the books (Barker 1958, xxxix).

A third kind of departure from the proper order transposes not the books of a treatise, but treatises themselves. We have already noted that the placement of the *Rhetoric* before rather than after the *Poetics* in the traditional order of the works violates their proper order because art that aims at a good end should precede an amoral art. There are also no less than six references in the *Rhetoric* to the *Poetics*, all in the perfect tense and thus indicating that the *Rhetoric* should come after the *Poetics*. They refer to what has been distinguished (*diōristai*; i.11.1372a1) or what has been said (*eirētai*; iii.1.1404a38, 2.1404b8, 1405a5, 18.1419b5) or what has been considered (*tetheōrētai*; iii.2.1404b27) in the *Poetics*. The one reference in the *Poetics* to the *Rhetoric*, in contrast, is to what concerns thought (*ta peri tēn dianoian*) in the *Rhetoric* with no verb that would indicate the relative place of the two disciplines in their proper order. The order indicated by the tenses of a verb is normally their proper order, although it is sometimes their order of composition, as in the references to *On the Soul*, the *Prior Analytics*, and the *Topics* in *On Interpretation* (1.16a8; 10.19b11; 11.20b26). In the present case, however, there can be little doubt that the tenses are being used to indicate the proper order, for it is unlikely that the *Poetics* was composed before the *Rhetoric*, and we know from other arguments that the order they indicate is the proper order. A further argument is that all the sciences, including poetics, should be placed together, and be followed by rhetoric, which is not a science. Rhetoric may use the results of any of the sciences, including poetics, as we see from the six references to the *Poetics* in the *Rhetoric*, but the sciences as sciences seldom have need of rhetoric. Why Andronicus transposed the two treatises is even more evident than why he should not have done so, for rhetoric is used mainly in political affairs and is even thought to be identical with politics (*Eth.* x.9.1181a15; *Rhet.* i.2.1356a28). If one is collecting related works into the same place, rhetoric belongs next to politics.

A more conspicuous example of the transposition of two treatises is the transposition of the proper order of *On the Progression of Animals* and *On the Motion of Animals*. The reference to the former at the beginning of the latter makes clear that the proper order of the two treatises is that in which they were just listed. The statement at the end of *On the Motion of Animals*, "And so we have finished our account of the causes of the parts of each kind of animal, of the soul, and further of sense-perception, of sleep, of memory and of animal motion in general; it remains to speak of the generation of animals" (after Farquharson) indicates that *On the Generation of Animals* should immediately follow. This statement may be compared to the two sentences concluding *On the Progression of Animals*, "These things, then, about the parts, both the other parts and those concerned with the progression of animals and all change of place, are the way they are. These things being determined, it remains to theorize about Life and Death" (after Farquharson). Farquharson has substituted "about Life and Death" for "about the soul," but either way the second of the quoted sentences is clearly spurious, for it has no relation to what precedes it. "About Life and Death" serves only to justify some editors in placing *On the Progression of Animals* in the middle of the short natural treatises that follow *On the Soul*, where it does not belong because it is concerned with the parts of animals that are for the sake of motion and not at all with affections common to body and soul. This final sentence also interrupts what should have been a natural transition to *On the Motion of Animals*. This sentence should be athetized and the traditional order of the two treatises transposed. This also puts them into the order in which they are listed toward the end of the preceding treatise, *On the Parts of Animals*: "The cause of these serpent-like fishes being without fins is the same as that which causes serpents to be without feet. It has been stated in the treatises on progression and the motion of animals" (iv.13.696a9–1300).

This incidentally enables us to place these two treatises as composed before the *Parts of Animals*, to which Aristotle has appended them.

In the proper order of the biological treatises, then, the two on the parts required for animal motion and the common cause of animal motion follow those on the other parts, and the whole discussion of the parts of animals concludes with the identification of the part through which the motions of the whole animal are directed to its own good, the part which Aristotle thought was the heart but which we now know to be the brain or its analogues in the more primitive animals. This sequence accords with Aristotle's discussion of the first mover at the end of the *Physics*, the discussion of the first substance at the end of the *Metaphysics*, the discussion of the highest happiness at the end of the *Ethics*, and the discussion of tragic catharsis after the other causes of tragedy. The inversion of the proper order of the two treatises on the motion of animals in the traditional order of the works cannot be attributed to Andronicus, however, for there is no reason why his method of collecting related materials into the same place would lead him to makes this change. It is more probable that it resulted from an accidental transposition of the two scrolls.

The texts from which Andronicus was working apparently did not supply him with their titles, for he has had to invent titles for at least some of the works. The best-known example is his title for the *Metaphysics*, *Tōn meta ta phusika*, of the things after the physical things. This is an appropriate title for the books that he collected together under it, but it is not an appropriate title for a unified art or science. Like two other titles whose qualifying adjectives were presumably added by Andronicus, *Analutikōn proterōn* (*Prior Analytics*) and *Analutikōn husterōn* (*Posterior Analytics*), the name reflects an orientation that relates the works to each other as texts rather than as unified arts or sciences of a subject matter.

Andronicus's titles incline toward general names under which various works can be grouped rather than names that designate a unified art or science. We have *Meteōrologika* (*Meteorological Matters*) rather than *Meteōrologia* (*Meteorology*), *Ethika* (*Ethical Matters*) rather than *Ethikē* (*Ethics*), and *Politika* (*Political Matters*) rather than *Politikē* (*Politics*). His invented titles are overly general, as *Peri hermēneias* (*On Expression*), and *Organon* (*Instrument*).

Let us review the violations of Aristotelian principles in Andronicus's editorial work on the corpus. The inclusion of isolated works in larger treatises violates the integrity of a science as Aristotle conceives it. The change in the order of books in the *Metaphysics* violates the principle that dialectical inquiry precedes scientific inquiry. The change in the order of the books in the *Politics* violates the principle that inquiry into changes of substance precedes inquiry into changes of the quality of a substance. The change in the order of the treatises themselves violates the distinction between what is scientific and what is not, and the principle that scientific inquiry must precede the use of scientific results in rhetoric. Andronicus's titles violate Aristotle's conception of a science as having the unity of a self-determining genus. In general, Andronicus thinks of sciences as texts rather than as sciences of a subject matter. This last difference, however, is just the difference between the ontic mode and epoch in which Aristotle wrote and the semantic mode and epoch in which Andronicus edited what Aristotle had written (Watson 1985, 5–9).

It seems strange that a leading Peripatetic of the first century BCE should be so ignorant of essential features of Aristotle's philosophy. Evidently the Peripatetic school did not preserve Aristotle's doctrines. This accords with Ingemar Düring's statement, "The old Peripatos died with Straton" (Düring 1957, 462). Straton or Strato (for this difference of name, see note 2 to this appendix) was the third head of the Peripatetic school, after Aristotle and Theophrastus, and died in 269 BCE, more than two centuries before Andronicus edited the Aristotelian corpus. The successive heads of the Hellenistic schools were normally trained in the school and honored their predecessors and founder, but taught their own philosophies. The Platonism of the New Academy, for example, is not that of the Old. But even if the Peripatetic school, to the extent that there was one, did not preserve Aristotle's doctrines, would they not have been available in his writings? The quotation from Düring continues, "By the philosophers of the generation after Aristotle his main doctrines were already incredibly distorted; his opponents had an easy task, for except for a few dialogues and the *Protrepticus* copies of Aristotle's writings were rare and no Corpus existed until after Andronicus."

It is less surprising than it first seems, then, that Andronicus shows himself grossly ignorant of essential features of Aristotle's philosophy. It is as if he is encountering the technical works of Aristotle for the first time and is able to take into account only their most superficial features, the number of books in a treatise and their general subject matter.

The question then arises, however, as to how he knew the proper order of the works from which he chose to depart in a small number of instances. It is not credible that he worked out this order for himself and got it right except for these instances. If he had tried to work it out for himself, the first thing which he would have been likely to consider would have been the internal indications of this order, but we have seen that he repeatedly disregards such indications altogether. In addition to editing the works in the corpus, Andronicus drew up a catalogue (*pinax*) of all of Aristotle's works, including the published works and the letters.[1] In this catalogue he rightly places the *Poetics* before rather than after the *Rhetoric*, which suggests that this was indeed its original place, but he also places the practical and productive sciences and rhetoric before rather than after the theoretical sciences. This gives the wrong kind of finality to metaphysics, making it seem that the other arts and sciences lead up to it as to an end in which the principles of theory and practice would be united in Platonic fashion, rather than making it the culmination of theoretic inquiries in which the autonomy of the succeeding practical, and productive sciences was established. Andronicus's own order also eliminates many of the significant features of the proper order, such as beginning the whole sequence from the distinction between theoretical and practical philosophy, the dramatic transition from the first principle of theory to the first principle of practice, and the opening sentence of the *Rhetoric* as implying a retrospective view of all the sciences which places them between dialectic and rhetoric. Andronicus's revision of the proper order of the works in his own catalogue indicates that he did not understand the reasons for this order and is further evidence that he did not work it out for himself.

But if Andronicus himself did not put the treatises in their proper order of the works, this brings us back to the question of how they came to be in this order. If Andronicus himself did not understand it, it is unlikely that anyone else in the first century BCE did. It might have been recorded in an external document such as a catalogue, but there is no evidence that he had such a catalogue or that one even existed. The fact that he had to invent titles for some of the works is evidence that he was not working from a catalogue, for a catalogue would presumably have referred to works by their titles. If the proper order of the works was not worked out by Andronicus or made known to him by someone else or indicated in some external document, it must have been indicated by notations on the scrolls themselves or their containers. This implies that the works must have come from a single source, for if they had been assembled from multiple sources they would not have had a consistent set of notations indicating their order. And since the order indicated is their proper order, which would have been known to Aristotle and the old Peripatetics but not to those outside the school, it follows that the corpus must have come from the early Peripatetic library itself! This conclusion would have no historical probability were it not for the fact that this is exactly what the histories of the corpus in Strabo and Plutarch tell us. This kind of agreement, in which the conclusion derived from one class of facts, in this case the internal content of the corpus itself, is found to agree with the conclusion derived from another class of facts, in this case the external data on the provenance of the corpus available to the early historians, resembles what William Whewell baptized as "consilience":

> We have here spoken of the prediction of facts *of the same kind* as those from which our rule was collected. But the evidence in favour of our induction is of a much higher order and more forcible character when it enables us to explain and determine cases of a *kind different* from those which were contemplated in the formation of our hypothesis. The instances in which this has occurred, indeed, impress us with a conviction that the truth of our hypothesis is certain. No accident could give rise to such an extraordinary coincidence. No false supposition could, after being adjusted to one class of phenomena, exactly represent a different class, when the agreement was unforeseen and uncontemplated. That rules springing from remote and unconnected quarters should thus leap to the same point, can only arise from *that* being the point where truth resides.
>
> Accordingly the cases in which inductions from classes of fact altogether different have thus *jumped together*, belong only to the best established theories which the history of science contains. And as I shall have occasion to refer to this peculiar feature in their evidence, I will take the liberty of describing it by a particular phrase; and will term it the *Consilience of Inductions*. (Whewell 1847, 2: 65; 1858, 87–8).

It is also unlikely that Andronicus could have obtained all the works in the corpus from what was generally available in the first century BCE. In our discussion of the laughable in chapter 19 we cited the statements by Gerald Else and Cairns Lord that some works, the *Poetics* and the *Politics* in particular, may have been completely unknown prior to Andronicus's edition. Cicero's account in *De Oratore* of Greek discussions of the laughable available in Rome in 91 BCE, before the corpus reached Rome, is evidence that the *Poetics* was not known at this time. We also have Cicero's account of the difficulty of obtaining books such as those in the corpus. He writes to his brother Quintus in 54 BCE, "As to the replenishment of your Greek library, the exchange of books, and the collection of Latin books, I should be very glad to see all that done, especially as it tends to my own advantage as well. But I have nobody whom I could employ as my own agent in this business. For such books as are really desirable are not for sale, and cannot be got together except through an agent who is both an expert and a man who takes pains. I shall send orders to Chrysippus, however, and have a talk with Tyrannio" (*Quint.* iii.4.5, trans. Williams).

The only thing that stands in the way of accepting the histories of Strabo and Plutarch as true is that they contain manifest falsehoods. To reject them altogether on this account would be to throw out the baby of truth with the bath of falsehood. We must take the baby out of the bath, dry it off, and explain why it was ever given such a bath in the first place. We begin with the first history, that of Strabo.

Strabo was a geographer who traveled all over the ancient world at the end of the first century BCE and the beginning of the first century CE and reported his findings in the seventeen books of his *Geography*. He speaks of the history of the corpus in connection with his account of Scepsis.

From Scepsis came the Socratic philosophers Erastus and Coriscus and Neleus the son of Coriscus, this last a man who not only was a pupil of Aristotle and Theophrastus, but also inherited the library of Theophrastus, which included that of Aristotle. At any rate, Aristotle bequeathed his own library to Theophrastus, to whom he also left his school; and he is the first man, so far as I know, to have collected books and to have taught the kings in Egypt how to arrange a library. Theophrastus bequeathed it to Neleus; and Neleus took it to Scepsis and bequeathed it to his heirs, ordinary people, who kept the books locked up and not even carefully stored. But when they heard how zealously the Attalic kings to whom the city was subject were searching for books to build up the library in Pergamum, they hid their books underground in a kind of trench. But much later, when the books had been damaged by moisture and moths, their descendants sold them to Apellicon of Teos for a large sum of money, both the books of Aristotle and those of Theophrastus. But Apellicon was a bibliophile rather than a philosopher; and therefore seeking a restoration of the parts that had been eaten through, he made new copies of the text, filling up the gaps incorrectly, and published the books full of errors. The result was that the earlier school of Peripatetics who came after Theophrastus had no books at all, with the exception of only a few, mostly exoteric works, and were therefore able to philosophize about nothing in a practical way, but only to talk bombast about commonplace propositions, whereas the later school, from the time the books in question appeared, though better able to philosophize and Aristotelize, were forced to call most of their statements probabilities, because of the large number of errors. Rome also contributed much to this; for immediately after the death of Apellicon, Sulla, who had captured Athens, carried off Apellicon's library to Rome, where Tyrannion the grammarian, who was fond of Aristotle, got it in his hands by paying court to the librarian, as did also certain booksellers who used bad copyists and would not collate the texts—a thing that also takes place in the case of the other books that are copied for selling, both here and at Alexandria. (Strabo xiii.1.54, trans. Sterrett and Jones)

Let us first consider whether the history was the result of his own inquiries or was taken by him from some then current source. Although Strabo preferred the philosophy of the Stoics to that of the Peripatetics (ii.3.8 with i.2.3 and i.2.34), he is free from the anti-Peripatetic animus of the story. This can be seen in the quotation from his willingness to give Aristotle credit for being the first man, so far as he knew, to have collected books and to have taught the kings in Egypt how to arrange a library, a respect for Aristotle which is consistent with his many references throughout his works to Aristotle's scientific writings. The reference to teaching the kings of Egypt how to arrange a library refers to the work of Aristotle's pupil, Demetrius of Phaleron, who, after the Athenians had expelled him from Athens, was employed by Ptolemy I, King of Egypt, to found his library, which afterwards became known as the Alexandrian library (Aristaeus, quoted in Hadas 1954, 23). For the history of the corpus that follows this assertion, however, Strabo was apparently relying on a story that was then current; he was a geographer, not a historian, and had not made an independent investigation of the history of the corpus.

As to the falsehoods in Strabo's history, everything that is said about the corruption of the corpus before it reached Rome we know to be false because we know that it arrived in Rome in good condition. Otherwise our modern editions of Aristotle's works, all of which are based on the corpus that reached Rome, would not be as good as they are. It is not generally recognized just how good our texts of Aristotle are. The belief in the shortcomings of the texts is in part the result of uncritically referring apparent inconsistencies to the order of composition instead of resolving them by referring them to the place of the conflicting statements in the proper order of the works. The inconsistencies are then permitted to stand as inconsistencies. This and the general difficulty of understanding Aristotle have given many people the false impression that our Aristotelian texts are corrupt works, full of contradictions, and perhaps only notes for lectures, or even student notes. They have no idea of their careful composition and extraordinary consistency and coherence. Francis Fergusson's statement about the *Poetics* is typical: "The text itself is incomplete, repetitious in spots, and badly organized. It probably represents part of a set of lecture notes, with later interpolations" (Fergusson 1961, 2).

The origin of all the corruption of the texts in the Strabo story is the hiding of the books underground in a kind of trench (*diōrux tis*). From this follow the damage by moisture and moths, the need to fill the resulting gaps, and the need for copyists in Rome to collate texts. Yet the storing of papyrus scrolls underground in a kind of trench, even if done by ordinary people, is so implausible that some translators have taken the liberty of upgrading the kind of trench into a cellar. This, however, gives away the whole story, for the agents of the zealous Attalic kings would certainly have searched the cellar of a house suspected of harboring valuable books, whereas they could not search a hiding place that they did not know existed. Thus we know from external evidence that the whole story of the corruption of the texts is false, and from the internal structure of the story that all the corruption depends on an initial improbability.

As to the alleged work of Apellicon in editing and publishing the corpus, there is, as far I know, no evidence that he edited or published anything. He was a lover and collector of books, not an editor or publisher of them. As to Tyrannion paying court to the librarian, it is more likely that he was himself the librarian. Tyrannion was born in Amisus, a colony of Athens on the Black Sea. He studied in Rhodes with the grammarian Dionysius Thrax. When Amisus fell to Lucullus in 72 BCE Tyrannion became attached to the Roman army and came to Rome with Lucullus on his return in 66. In Rome he engaged in various kinds of scholarly work. His lectures were attended by the young Strabo (Strabo xii.3.16). He tutored Cicero's nephew (*Quint.* ii.4.2), organized his library (*Att.* 4a.8), and wrote a book on grammar which Cicero planned to read with Atticus (*Att.* xii.2, 6). Presumably he was employed in the Sulla library by the heirs of Sulla (Sulla died in 78 BCE). As to the corruption alleged to have taken place in Rome, we know that Andronicus did indeed make some misguided changes in the order of the books and treatises and gave them some poor titles, but these were not the result of a failure to collate texts. The charge of further corruption because of a failure to collate texts appears to be a false attribution of a common source of error to a case to which it did not apply.

That the earlier school of Peripatetics who came after Theophrastus had no books at all, with the exception of only a few, mostly exoteric works, we also know to be false. The technical works were not published by the school, but this does not mean they were not copied or that Neleus left the school with no copies of the technical works. Düring's statement that in the generation after Aristotle copies of his writings were rare is different in emphasis but not inconsistent with Leonard Tarán's statement that "copies of Aristotle's treatises must have circulated even during his own lifetime and certainly in the years following his death. So far as our evidence is concerned, during Hellenistic times there must have been copies of them or at any rate most of them not only in Athens and in Rhodes but also in Alexandria and probably other places as well" (Tarán 1981, 485–86).

There are thus many falsehoods in the Strabo story, but it does not consist entirely of falsehoods. We know that Theophrastus bequeathed his library to Neleus, for the will of Theophrastus, preserved in Diogenes Laertius, says, "The whole of my library I give to Neleus" (v.53, trans. R. D. Hicks). All that we know to be false in the history tends to discredit the Peripatetics and their texts, particularly the Andronicus edition, and this is evidently the end that requires both truth and falsehood, for scurrilous claims taken by themselves can easily be dismissed as the invention of their perpetrator, but if they can be made plausible consequences of known facts, they cannot so easily be dismissed.

At every stage of the Strabo story, the author seeks to make his defamations plausible consequences of known facts. Thus from the true facts that Neleus inherited the Peripatetic library and took a selection from it with him to Scepsis, the author falsely infers that he left behind for the school no books at all, except a few, mostly exoteric texts. That the heirs of Neleus were ordinary people is presumably true, since most people are ordinary people, and from this he falsely infers that they did not store their valuable books carefully. From the true fact that the Attalic kings sought books to build up the library in Pergamum he falsely infers that the heirs of Neleus hid the books underground in a kind of trench. From the true fact that Apellicon was a bibliophile rather than a philosopher he falsely infers that he made incorrect restorations of the (nonexistent) damage. From the true fact that the corpus came into the hands of Tyrannion he falsely infers that Tyrannion got his hands on the corpus by paying court to the librarian, and that certain booksellers did the same and used bad copyists who would not collate the texts. Thus the story at every stage uses the truth to make its defamations plausible. If we exclude the defamations, what is left has actually acquired additional probability because of the defamations, for what is left probably consists of known facts that gave the defamations plausibility.

If we exclude the false defamations of the Strabo story, we are left with the bequest of the Peripatetic library to Neleus, Neleus taking a selection of the works of Aristotle and Theophrastus (not the whole library of the school nor all the works of its two scholarchs) with him to Scepsis, the later purchase of these works from the heirs of Neleus by Apellicon, Sulla's seizure of Apellicon's library immediately after Apellicon's death, and the conveying of it to Rome, where the corpus came into the hands of Tyrannion. Such a transmission of the corpus from the Peripatetic library to Tyrannion is all that is required if Andronicus was to have known the order of the corpus from indications on the scrolls or their containers that were those of the Peripatetic library.

Plutarch, writing toward the end of the first century CE, a century after Strabo, tells us in his life of Sulla that Sulla, having taken Athens in 86 BCE, stopped there again in 84 when returning to Rome after the successful conclusion of his war with Mithridates:

> Having put to sea with all his ships from Ephesus, on the third day he came to anchor in Piraeus. He was now initiated into the mysteries, and seized for himself the library of Apellicon the Teian, in which were most of the treatises of Aristotle and Theophrastus, at that time not yet well known to the public. But it is said that after the library was carried to Rome, Tyrannio[2] the grammarian prepared (*enskeuasasthai*) most of the works in it, and that Andronicus the Rhodian was furnished by him with copies of them, and published them, and drew up the lists now current. The older Peripatetics were evidently of themselves accomplished and learned men, but they seem to have had neither a large nor an exact acquaintance with the writings of Aristotle and Theophrastus, because the estate of Neleus of Scepsis, to whom Theophrastus bequeathed his books, came into the hands of careless and illiterate people. (Plutarch, *Sulla*, 26.1–2, trans. Perrin)

Plutarch's account has three parts that appear to depend on different sources: (1) Sulla's activity in Athens, including the seizure of Apellicon's library, (2) what subsequently happened to the corpus in Rome, (3) the origin and prior history the corpus.

1. Plutarch's principal source for his life of Sulla is Sulla's own *Memoirs*, and this was presumably his source for the statement that Sulla was now initiated into the mysteries. It is less likely that Sulla would have included in

his memoirs the not altogether creditable action of seizing a distinguished Greek library for his personal use. Sulla probably used the death of Apellicon as an opportunity to seize his library. The lack of any connection between the two events except the place of their occurrence suggests that Plutarch is here incorporating in his biography something coming from another source or sources. One source available to him was the Strabo story (see paragraph 3, below), but there is no need to assume that he was relying solely on it here. That the library that Sulla had appropriated from Apellicon contained most of the works of Aristotle and Theophrastus would have become common knowledge when the works were published. That these works were not well known to the public previously would have been the consequence of the Peripatetic school not publishing them, although this would not preclude private copying, and this also was probably common knowledge. There is thus no reason to doubt anything in this part of Plutarch's history, which is not contaminated by any of the false defamations of the Strabo story.

2. Plutarch does state his source for what happened to the library after it reached Rome, namely, what is said (*legetai*). This is likely to have meant literally that it was what Plutarch had heard rather than what he had read. The Romans of the first century BCE did not have the plethora of written words that surround us today, and multiple written sources are needed before "it is said" can appropriately become a metaphor for "it is written." Also, "it is said" did not have the connotation of doubtfulness that hearsay has today, but may be, as seems to be the case here, a reliable source. Plutarch's statement resolves the inconsistency between Porphyry's statement, which mentions only Andronicus in relation to the editing of the corpus, and the Strabo story, which mentions only Tyrannion. Thus we have no reason to doubt anything in the second part of Plutarch's history.

3. For the concluding sentence in Plutarch's account he gives no source, but he appears to be relying on the Strabo story. He begins by dissociating himself from its anti-Peripatetic animus by saying that the elder Peripatetics were evidently of themselves accomplished and learned men. The Strabo story makes the distinct points that the earlier Peripatetics lacked texts and the later school lacked accurate texts, and these are condensed in Plutarch's statement that the "elder Peripatetics" did not have the writings of Aristotle and Theophrastus either largely (*pollois*) or exactly (*akribōs*). The phrase "they came into careless and illiterate hands" condenses the reason given by the Strabo story for the initial corruption of the texts. In sum, then, we can accept Plutarch's entire account except for the known falsehoods that

entered his history from the Strabo story. For that matter, we can also accept Strabo's entire account except for the falsehoods that entered his history from the Strabo story.

Let us consider how the falsehood might have originated and gained wide currency. We may suppose that the story was made up soon after the publication of the corpus and with a view to discrediting it. There would have been at the time curiosity about its provenance, and the history would probably have become more or less known. An unscrupulous opponent of Aristotle and the Peripatetics school may have seen in the history an excellent opportunity to discredit not only the new edition, but all that the school had done, by incorporating the known facts in a scurrilous history. The result is a humorous and entertaining story with unusual and sometimes graphic incidents — the hiding of the scrolls in a sort of trench to keep them from the Attalic kings, the moisture and moths eating away at the papyrus, Apellicon tying to fill up the gaps without knowing what had been lost, Sulla seizing the library and carrying it off to Rome, and Tyrannion gaining access to the corpus by paying court to the librarian. The results of these incidents are formally worthy of good comedy — the earlier Peripatetics without books having to talk bombast about commonplaces, and the later school with corrupted books able to say almost nothing with certainty. The rhetorical skill and literary merits of the story, combined perhaps with pleasure in seeing the Peripatetics discredited, led to its wide circulation. For the strength and persistence of the anti-Aristotelian tradition, see Düring 1957, 462–63. The persistence of the initial falsehoods is somewhat similar to what followed the calumniation of Aristotle in the Renaissance (McKeon 1935, 53). If one asks a physicist today for his opinion of Aristotle, the chances are that his reply will owe more to Galileo's Simplicius than to anything in the writings of Aristotle.

The histories of Strabo and Plutarch, then, once their false and defamatory content has been eliminated, can be taken as providing a true account of the provenance of the Aristotelian corpus. In spite of the interval of more than two hundred years between Neleus's selection of the works and their arrival in Rome, the papyrus scrolls seem to have been in such good condition that Tyrannion had no difficulty in making copies for Andronicus. For almost all of the interval they were stored in Scepsis, a city in a region whose average annual rainfall is now twenty-five inches, moderately dry, a little drier than the following cities are today: Oklahoma City, Oklahoma; Omaha, Nebraska; San Antonio, Texas; and Wichita, Kansas. The climate of Asia Minor in ancient times may have been somewhat different from what it is today, but it is not improbable that Scepsis was dry enough to keep the papyrus from decaying because of moisture. Neleus would certainly have informed his family of the value of the scrolls and provided good conditions for their storage. Contrary to the lies of the Strabo story, his heirs took good care of their valuable scrolls. They were probably pleased to have the opportunity to sell them at a good price to a noted Athenian book collector who would have appreciated both their special value and their good condition.

There remain, however, two elements in the history that deserve further discussion. One is why, if Theophrastus willed the library of the Peripatetic school to Neleus, it was Strato (not to be confused with the geographer Strabo) who became the third head of the school. The other is the rationale for the selection of works in the corpus. There is further information on these points in the will of Theophrastus. After the bequest of his library to Neleus, the will continues, "The gardens and the walk (*peripatos*) and the houses adjoining the garden I give and bequeath to such of my friends hereinafter named who may wish to study literature and philosophy there in common. . . . Let the community consist of Hipparchus, Neleus, Strato," and seven others who are named (Diogenes Laertius v.52–3, trans. Hicks). In the list of the seven executors of the will, Hipparchus is named first as the executor responsible for the disbursement of funds, and is again followed by Neleus and Strato in that order (ibid., 56). That the library, which was the property of the head of the school, was bequeathed to Neleus rather than to Strato, and that Neleus is given precedence over Strato both in the list of members of the community who are to possess the gardens, walk, and buildings of the school, and in the list of executors of the will, is a clear indication that Theophrastus intended Neleus to be his successor. Neleus appears to have declined the position, for there is no evidence of strife or discord within the school. There is in Theophrastus's will, however, dramatic evidence of strife and discord between the school and Athens.

The hostility of Athens to the Peripatetic school because of its association with Macedonia dates back to the Macedonian conquest and to the rule of Demetrius of Phaleron imposed by Cassander in 317 BCE. In the revolt of Athens against Demetrius Poliorcetes in 288–87, just before Theophrastus's death in 287, there had been attacks upon the school's buildings and property, particularly the bust of Aristotle. Before making the bequests already mentioned, Theophrastus provides for improving the condition of the school by repairing the damage and restoring what had been destroyed or removed: "It is my wish that out of the trust funds at the disposal of Hipparchus the following appropriations should be made. First, they should be applied to finish the rebuilding of the Museum with the statues of the goddesses, and to add any improvements which seem practicable to beautify them. Secondly, to replace in the temple the bust of Aristotle with the rest of the dedicated offerings which were formerly in the temple. Next, to rebuild the small cloister adjoining the Museum at least as handsomely as before, and to replace in the lower cloister the tablets containing maps of the countries traversed by explorers. Further, to repair the altar so that it may be perfect and elegant" (v.51–2, trans. Hicks).

Neleus's decision to leave Athens and take with him copies of the works of Aristotle and Theophrastus was most probably a response to the attacks on the school and a desire to preserve these works from damage or destruction. He may also have been reluctant to remain in such a hostile environment and still more to assume responsibility for the school in such an environment. His fear that irreplaceable writings of the school might be damaged or destroyed was probably shared by other members of the school, who would have been glad to see copies of the most valuable writings, possibly the autographs, taken to a safer place.

Neleus took from the library only the technical works of Aristotle, together with his letters. None of the published works was included, presumably because they were available elsewhere and were of lesser importance for the preservation of Aristotle's thought. The histories on which the technical works were based are also not included, with one exception, for these too would be of lesser importance and many were probably not written by Aristotle himself. The one exception is the *History of Animals*, and this was written by Aristotle himself and gives an account of the activities of animals, which do not admit of demonstration and are therefore not discussed in the scientific works.

The set of technical works is nearly complete. A one-book *Selection of Contraries* (*Metaph.* iv.2.1004b1; Diogenes Laertius v.22) is not included but much of its content was probably incorporated in the *Topics*, Book II, chapters 7–9. A one-book *Economics* (*Pol.* vii.10.1330a31–33; Diogenes Laertius v.22) is also not included, but much of it was probably incorporated in Book I of the *Politics*. Also not included is Aristotle's two-book treatise *On Plants* (*Histo. of An.* v.1.539b21; *Diogenes Laertius* v.26). But by far the most important work missing from the corpus is the eight-book *Methodics* (*Rhet.* i.2.1356b19; *Diogenes Laertius* v.23). It mediates between the general statements of the *Organon* and the methods that constitute the particular sciences. The general treatment of induction in the final chapter of the *Posterior Analytics* is brief and metaphorical, and the full account is presumably in *Methodics*. The problem corresponds to that addressed in opposition to Aristotle by Francis Bacon in his *Novum Organum* and to that addressed along more Aristotelian lines by William Whewell in his *Philosophy of Discovery* (1847), although in an epistemic mode. That is, Whewell, like Kant, is concerned with the form and matter of science (ideas and facts) rather than of things. The first part of Whewell's book deals with the suitability of different ideas to different subject matters, and it is probable that Aristotle's *Methodics* is similarly treated the suitability of different syllogistic structures to different subject matters. The *Methodics* would thus have a disciplinary particularity that is missing from the rest of the *Organon*. The second part of Whewell's work, published separately in 1858 as the *Novum Organum Renovatum*, treats the colligation of facts by ideas, corresponding to Aristotle's induction. The development of what is called the philosophy of science and its various branches, such as the philosophy of mathematics or physics or biology or psychology or life or art or sports (Paul Weiss) or football (Woody Hayes), or any subject whatever, gives contemporary interest to the problems treated in the *Methodics* and to what it means to have a philosophy *of* something. The absence of the *Methodics* is much to be regretted, but we can be grateful that it seems to be the only major technical work that is missing.

The content of the corpus as thus constituted is quite different from what might have been assembled at the time of its publication in the first century BCE, which would probably have consisted primarily of published works and would almost certainly not have included all the technical works that are in the corpus as we have it.

I think we can conclude that the histories of Strabo and Plutarch, once the false and defamatory material designed to discredit the Andronicus edition has been removed, give us a reliable account of the provenance of the Aristotelian corpus. This provenance is confirmed by the good order which Andronicus seems to have known from notations on the scrolls or their containers, an order which he, not recognizing its source, violated at a few points in his effort to improve upon it. The consistent pattern of his alterations, however, enables us to discover and correct them.

Finally, let us considered how the proper order of the works could have been indicated by notations on the scrolls. The natural way of storing papyrus scrolls in a library containing hundreds of scrolls is to stack them horizontally on shelves at right angles to the shelf, with more or less frequent vertical separators on the shelf to form compartments or scroll bins. The whole such construction was known as a *pēgma*, or bookcase. There were also scroll buckets, *capsae*, which would be useful in transporting scrolls while keeping together the scrolls of a treatise, but they would not be suitable for storing the scrolls in a large library. When stored in scroll bins, the only part of the scroll exposed to view is the outward end. We know that by the first century BCE parchment labels (*silluba* or perhaps *sittubai*) were pasted onto the ends of the scrolls so that they hung down over the end of the scroll, thus making it possible to see at a glance what was in the scroll. They are illustrated in Sider 2005. We do not know how early such labels came into use, but once a library has hundreds of scrolls, the need for something like them is obvious. They are not a difficult kind of label to invent, and Aristotle himself may have invented them. They may have been part of the system for arranging a library that Strabo says Aristotle taught the kings of Egypt. In any case, some sort of scroll label would have been needed.

As to what was on the scroll labels, three kinds of information would be necessary. First there would be need for a book number to indicate the place of the scroll in its treatise; secondly a treatise name or number to indicate the treatise to which, the scroll belonged, and thirdly an author name, or its abbreviation, to indicate the alphabetical place of the author among other authors in the library, or, more probably, among the authors working in the same field, for if the whole library were in a single alphabetical order it would be more difficult to locate particular authors and their works than if the authors were ordered according to their field of activity. And we know from the *Poetics* how Aristotle ordered the written products of the disciplines, which is what the books of a library would be. Aristotle divides them into history, poetry, and philosophy, which corresponds to the kinds of books existing at that time. The division is implied by the questions raised in the *Poetics* as to whether the work of a poetic philosopher, Empedocles, is poetry or natural philosophy (1.1447b17), and whether the work of a story-telling historian, Herodotus, supposing him to be writing in verse, is poetry or history (9.1451b2). That Andronicus had to invent titles for some of the treatises suggests that the treatises of a given author were ordered by treatise numbers rather than titles, and these could at the same time indicate an order of the treatises. Thus four notations on the scroll labels indicating respectively the place of the book in its treatise, the place of the treatise among other treatises by the same author, the place of the author among other authors working in the same field, and the place of the field among other fields, would suffice to order the scrolls of the entire library. The order could be restored no matter how thoroughly the scrolls were scrambled. If the treatises were identified by titles rather than number, a definite order of the treatises could be indicated by a number on the first scroll of each treatise. Thus it is probable that in Aristotle's well-ordered library, any order of treatises would be indicated by the scroll labels.

A continuation of this system would explain why the order of Andronicus was preserved in subsequent editions, as we know that it was. When the papyrus scrolls were copied on parchment, the original order could of course be preserved by the binding and numbering of the codices.

Were it not for the foresight of Neleus in preserving Aristotle's technical works in the dry climate of Scepsis, and their subsequent rediscovery and publication, we would probably have today no more than fragments of his writings, that is, quotations from his works in other authors, as we do of the writings of Protagoras and Democritus.

NOTES

INTRODUCTION

1. I cite passages in Aristotle in the traditional way, by an abbreviated title for the work, lower-case Roman numerals for the book, Arabic numerals for the chapter, and page numbers from the two-column Bekker edition of his works (Berlin, 1831–70), the page number being followed by an "a" or "b" to indicate the column, and this followed by the line number. Whether a number refers to a book, chapter, or page is thus immediately clear from its mode of presentation. I add the translator of the passage unless the translation is my own, in which case no translator is given.

   I generally use Telford's translation of the *Poetics* simply because it is our most literal English translation, in the tradition of William of Moerbeke's Latin translation which enabled Thomas Aquinas to understand Aristotle so well. Telford's Index of Terms enables us to know from the translation alone what Greek word is being translated.

CHAPTER 1

1. I once examined all the uses of *hermēneia* and its cognates in Hellenic texts, and found that they never refer primarily to interpretation in the sense of ascertaining the meaning of a text, but always to the opposite process, expression, which proceeds from the meaning to the text. There are a number of activities, such as translation, divination, and reciting or performing, which involve both the ascertainment and the expression of meaning, and the person who engages in these activities, and who therefore exercises the capacities both to ascertain and to express meanings, is called a *hermēneus*. But that he is so called primarily by virtue of his expressive capacity can be shown from many instances. The *Greek-English Lexicon* of Liddell, Scott, and Jones (*LSJ*) offers two instances in support of *hermēneia* as interpretation. One, from Plato's *Republic* (vii. 524a–b), requires us to think that the senses themselves *interpret* as contradictory the messages they receive, rather than, as they do, *express* to the soul messages that the soul finds contradictory. The other, from the *Theaetetus* (209a), requires us to think that a definition *interprets* a difference, rather than *expresses* it, as it does. Perhaps Liddell and Scott were seeking to connect *hermēneia* with the Latin *interpretatio*, and there is indeed a connection, which is that a *hermēneus* is also an *interpres*, since both both express and interpret, but not that *hermēneia* means interpretation. Telford has perhaps been misled by *LSJ* into translating the definition of diction in the *Poetics* (*hē dia tēs onomasias hermēneia*) as "the interpretation [of things] through language," rather than simply as "the expression through language." The *Peri hermēneias* deals with sentences that are true or false; the investigation of other kinds of sentence is more proper to rhetoric or poetics (*On Interpretation* 4.17a5).

2. In the words of John Dewey, "We live in a world which is an impressive and irresistible mixture of sufficiencies, tight completenesses, order, recurrence which makes possible prediction and control, and singularities, ambiguities, uncertain possibilities,

processes going on to consequences as yet indeterminate" (Dewey 1929, 47). Science depends on selecting out the recurrences.

3. The translation of the Greek *methodos* by the English "method" perhaps calls for an explanation. *Methodos*, "following a way," can mean either a method in the abstract, applicable to many cases, or, as here, a method in the concrete, e.g., a particular treatise or part of a treatise that employs a method. The English word "method" has also been used in both senses, as when Francis Bacon says, "Another diversity of method, whereof the consequence is great, is the delivery of knowledge in aphorisms, or in methods" (Bacon 1905, *Advancement of Learning*, II, subdivision "Method of Tradition," 125). The *Oxford English Dictionary* (*OED*) recognizes the second meaning in a series of examples ending with Bentham in 1829, but labels it obsolete. The consistent translation of *methodos* by "method" thus conforms to Greek usage and revives an earlier English usage.

4. Cf. John Stuart Mill, "The truths which are ultimately accepted as the first principles of a science are really the last results of metaphysical analysis, practiced on the elementary notions with which the science is conversant; and their relation to the science is not that of foundations to an edifice, but of roots to a tree, which may perform their office equally well though they be never dug down to and exposed to light. But, though in science the particular truths precede the general theory, the contrary might be expected to be the case with a practical art, such as morals or legislation. All action is for the sake of some end; and rules of action, it seems natural to suppose, must take their whole character and color from the end to which they are subservient. When we engage in a pursuit, a clear and precise conception of what we are pursuing would seem to be the first thing we need, instead of the last we are to look forward to. A test of right and wrong must be the means, one would think, of ascertaining what is right and wrong, and not a consequence of having already ascertained it" (Mill 1961, chap. 1, para. 2, p. 324). Mill's use of the subjunctive does not imply that our expectations or suppositions are unwarranted, but rather that, before Mill's *Utilitarianism*, they were unrealized.

5. I have translated *nous* by "mind," for, even if Aristotle's meaning does not exactly correspond to earlier meanings of *nous* or "mind," it can be understood as a development from these. By providing a starting point for understanding the new meaning, it becomes likely that the word will come to embrace this meaning. Translators of *nous* in the *Ethics* have, however, preferred to try to convey Aristotle's meaning by means of their translations, often by inventing technical phrases. (In the following list, the translators and dates are included for the information they provide, not as links to the bibliography.) Thus we have "intuitive reason" (Weldon 1892; Ross 1915), "inductive reason" (Greenwood 1909), "apperceptive intelligence" (Wheelwright 1935), "intelligence" (Rackham 1934; Rowe 2002), "understanding" (Telford 1994; Irwin 1999), and "intellect" (Crisp 2000). "Intuitive reason" is an oxymoron, for if intuitive, not discursive, and if reason, discursive. Mind is mysterious, but not self-contradictory. "Inductive reason" would as inductive eventuate in a universal and as reason be discursive, of which the first need not be true, for in practical affairs it eventuates in actions, and the second is never true, for mind is intuitive. "Apperceptive intelligence" calls attention to mind perceiving itself, which it does, but it also perceives all other principles.

"Intelligence" as we use it tends in the direction of an innate endowment, but mind in the sense relevant here is "by this time" (ēdē) and requires time and experience (*Phy.* vii. 3.248a2–3; *Eth.* vi. 9.1142a11–20). "Intellect" echoes William of Moerbeke's translation of *nous* into Latin as *intellectus*, which is right for Latin, but the English "intellect" lacks the breadth of the Latin *intellectus*. "Understanding" is in a way right, for mind understands, but since Ross uses "understanding" to translate *sunesis*, the ability to judge what someone else says about the things with which practical wisdom is concerned, we must consider which use of "understanding" is more appropriate. Aristotle says, "Where objects differ in kind the part of the soul answering to each of the two is different in kind, since it is in virtue of a certain likeness and kinship with their objects that they have the knowledge that they have" (*Eth.* vi. 2.1139a8–11). The likeness and kinship that we have with someone else and what he says about the things with which practical wisdom is concerned has its ground in the fact that we are both human beings, people of the earth, and the equitable is common to all such people. But what likeness or kinship do we have with the objects of the theoretical sciences, which are independent of us? Here the translation of *nous* by "mind" comes to our aid, for Aristotle argues that it is *nous* or mind that moves all things. Mind is the ground of our likeness and kinship with all things. For this reason, and because the attempts to translate *nous* in the *Ethics* by terms or phrases other than "mind" have produced no consensus, it seems best to follow Aristotle's example and use its English counterpart, "mind," or "intuitive mind" if this is needed to avoid confusion with rational or discursive mind.

6. Cf. a contemporary statement on the middle class: "Societies with a strong middle class tend to experience economic prosperity and social progress. Witness how the arrival of a strong middle class presaged England's golden years as a world economic and military power, or the rise of the middle class in this country after World War II. In contrast, squeezing out the middle class by allowing the tiniest top tier of the population to accumulate enormous wealth through rash tax policies, while acquiring an increasingly burdensome wartime debt, leads to stark economic and social divisions in society between the oligarchs—the 'haves and have more'—and everyone else. That will inevitably lead to economic and social decline of our country and its passing as a world power" (Charles W. Stotter, *New York Times*, November 9, 2007).

7. Aristotle was the first to formulate a science of poetry, but there are, of course, earlier writings about poetry, notably by Protagoras, Democritus, and Plato. Aristotle's neglect of the writings on poetry by his predecessors is another instance of his not doing them historical justice. Aristotle is concerned with poetics as an autonomous science, and what they wrote was not written as belonging to such a science. This is similar to the situation today, in which few works on poetry would qualify as an Aristotelian science. Plato's treatment of poetics in the *Gorgias* separates off epic poetry from other poetry and groups the rest with rhetoric as forms of flattery. While this may be a good way to approach poetry from the standpoint of its moral effect, it is not a discussion of poetry as the subject of an autonomous science. Similarly, the discussion of poetry in the *Republic* makes it part of an inquiry into justice. The subsequent history of poetic theory and the development of a pluralistic Aristotelianism have made clear that an

adequate account of poetry does not require an autonomous poetic science any more than an adequate account of the moral effect of poetry requires that poetry and morals be united in a single science.

CHAPTER 2

1. In teaching the *Ethics*, McKeon, after discussing the different discussions of pleasure, asked, "Is it clear what he is doing in each, and why there are four?" The implication was that the four accounts corresponded to the four causes, which was surprising because McKeon seldom identified the four causes as such, and had previously cautioned the class against those who claimed to find as the four causes what were not the four causes. He had previously identified in the *Ethics* as concerned with the four causes only the first four chapters of Book II. His own identification of causes in the Aristotelian texts can be found in the Introduction to McKeon 1941 and, in more detail, in McKeon 1949.

2. Thus Sir David Ross makes the following comment on the formulation of the material cause in the *Posterior Analytics*, which we have discussed:

> But even if the premises may by a metaphor be said (as in *Phys.* 195a16–19) to be an example of the material cause, it is inconceivable that if A. had here meant the material cause in general, he should not have illustrated it by some literal example of the material cause. Besides, the material cause could not be described as *to tinōn ontōn anagkē tout' einai* [the conditions from which it follows that the given thing is]. It does not necessitate that whose cause it is; it is only required to make this possible. (Ross 1965, 639; cf. Ross 1949, 51–52. I have added in square brackets Ross's English translation of the Greek, taken from Ross 1949, 51.)

If we substitute for the "material cause" in this quotation the "out of which," the argument all but disappears, for the premises as the "out of which" of the conclusion do not appear to be significantly different from the bronze as the "out of which" of the statue. The direction of the necessity seems beside the point. And since Ross recognizes that it is by a metaphor that the premises may be said to be a material cause, and since Aristotle explicitly says, in the statement quoted above in Ross's own translation, that whenever we speak of the causes in general it is only by an analogy, it follows that the direction of the necessity is in fact beside the point.

This case also supplies a good example of the difference between using the order of the completed works and the order of their composition to solve a problem. While I have pointed out that the peculiar formulation of the material cause in the *Posterior Analytics* is appropriate to that science in its place in the order of completed sciences, Ross goes on to suggest that it is appropriate to a stage in the supposed order of composition: "It may be that this chapter belongs to an early stage at which he had not yet reached the doctrine of the four causes. Or it may be that, realizing that he could not work the material cause into his thesis that the cause is the middle term, he deliberately substituted for it a type of *aition* [cause] which will suit his thesis." That is, either Aristotle's account of the four causes in the *Posterior Analytics* is not an account of the four causes, or his example of the material cause is not an example of the material cause.

Explanations using the order of composition tend to be conjectural and made at the expense of the integrity of Aristotle's works, whereas those using the order of completed sciences are not conjectural and tend to confirm the integrity of Aristotle's works.

CHAPTER 4

1. The dependence of films on many people and techniques and hence on large budgets gives a new significance to Plato's distinction between works that aim at gratifying an audience and those that do not, for large-budget films need to please large audiences.

2. Telford in translating *poiēsis* always by "making" and never by "poetry" seems to me to interpret the Moerbeke principle of word-for-word translation too narrowly. If a Greek word has two meanings that are distinct in both Greek and English, and English happens to have different words for the two meanings, then I see no reason not to take advantage of this richness of English. In the present case, translating *poiēsis* by "making" instead of "poetry" leads to a bracketed addition which still leaves the translation inaccurate: "[the process of] making."

3. The use of plural nouns with a singular meaning to designate arts appears to have originated from the Greek use of the neuter plurals of adjectives to designate the subject matters of arts or sciences and thus as names for these arts or sciences themselves. Thus Aristotle uses the neuter plural *ta phusika*, physical matters, to refer to the work he also refers to in the singular as *hē phusikē*, and whose name in translation became the plural *Physics*. Similarly, he uses the neuter plural *ta ēthika*, ethical matters, to refer to the work which is known in English by the plural name *Ethics*. There are also some arts whose names are natural plurals in English and are treated as singulars, such as mathematics; for this see the *OED*.

CHAPTER 6

1. The Greek text and numbering of sections are from Janko 1984, 22–40. Janko's photocopy of the MS shows six horizontal schemata in which a heading is connected by lines to the terms falling under it. The schemata of the kinds of poetry (sections 1–2), the sources of laughter (sections 5–6), and the three kinds of comedy (section 18) are here represented vertically in outline form, with the beginnings and endings of connecting lines represented by a dash. Each right-going dash is joined to one or more left-going dashes at the next line or indent level. The other three schemata, of the initial list of the six materials of comedy (section 10), the five persuasions (section 13), and the initial list of the four parts of comedy (section 17), are here represented simply by the heading and a colon followed by the series of items that fall under it. The English translation is my own.

2. Janko translates *amimētos* and *mimētikē* as "nonmimetic" and "mimetic." This conforms to the etymological connection of the two sets of terms and is appropriate for their technical meaning. I have translated *mimēsis* in the text as "imitation," which is accurate for its nontechnical sense, and have translated the adjectives to agree with

this. It would be possible to use the richness of English to mark Aristotle's distinction between ordinary and technical meanings by using "imitative" and "nonimitative" for the ordinary meanings and "mimetic" and "nonmimetic" for the technical meanings. Aristotle is careful to avoid ambiguity in his use of technical terms but does not attempt to avoid the ambiguity between ordinary and technical meanings. This preserves the continuity between common sense and science of which John Dewey speaks. Consistency in maintaining the distinction between ordinary and technical terms in the present case would require that we use "imitation" for the ordinary meaning of the noun and *mimēsis* or "mimesis" for its technical meaning, which would be intolerable pedantry. The confusion of the ordinary and technical meanings of these terms has indeed led to misunderstandings of the *Poetics* and to the belief that the epitome is inauthentic, but once the distinction has become clear, I think the ambiguity of the words will cease to be a problem. "Imitative" and "mimetic," and "nonimitative" and "nonmimetic," are therefore used interchangeably in the text.

3. *Mimous* and *saturous* are in the accusative case, appropriate to the grammatical object, not the nominative case, appropriate to the grammatical subject, which is used in naming the other poetic arts.

4. *Deos* is Aristotle's word for what fear in tragedy becomes when what is feared actually occurs. It has the meanings of both "fear, alarm, affright" and "awe, reverence" (LS). There is no good English equivalent. "Dread" has the component of awe but lacks the component of alarm and affright. "Shock and awe," a phrase used by the Bush administration in 2003 for the military strategy of its attack on Iraq, has the combination required. Translators of Poetics I have used "terrible," "terrifying," and "dreadful" for *deinos*, the adjectival form of *δeos* (13.1453a22, 14.1453b 14, 19.1456b3).

5. Janko translates the Greek *summetria* as "due proportion," which is a possible meaning for the term. However, in the absence of a specification of what proportion is due, the meaning of the phrase is left indefinite and seems to say only that the proportion should be what it should be. Such indeterminacy in a key term would be uncharacteristic of Aristotle, and I have therefore preferred the English cognate, "symmetry," which implies an other to the fearful emotions with which it is symmetrical.

6. Words in angled brackets are editorial additions.

7. Previous interpreters of this passage, Bernays (1880, 181), Rutherford (1905, 452), Starkie (1909, lxviii–lxx), Cooper (1922, 250–52), and Janko (1984, 197–99) all suppose that Aristotle is here developing a point made in Book I, that the characters of comedy are worse than we are (2.1448a17), by adding that the debased character of the persons of the drama is a form of the laughable. But this cannot be right, for debased character is not itself laughable, but must be made laughable by being united with a form of the laughable. Wrongness of soul is therefore a matter rather than a form of the laughable. This is confirmed both by its appearance where it does belong, in section 8, and by the fact that if it were also intended in section 6, Aristotle's own example of the laughable, the comic mask, along with all the other forms of comic accouterment, would have no place among Aristotle's sources of laughter.

8. "Indirection" translates what is literally "the so-called emphasis." The Greek "empha-

sis" here means what appears in a reflection, and thus indirectly. Janko translates the phrase as "the so-called innuendo," but the phrase must cover all sorts of comic indirection, and I have therefore preferred the more general term as closer to its meaning here.

9. Janko emends *kōmodias hulē*, "the matter of comedy," to read *kōmodias eidē*, "the forms of comedy," which brings the language into agreement with *Poetics* I. I argue in chapter 7 that the emendation is unnecessary because the different ways of referring to the universal parts of poetry are a consequence of the different starting points of the two books. For this reason I have restored the original reading.

10. Janko comments, "The MS says 'spectacle supplies harmony' (*sumphōnia*), but this makes no sense and the word must be corrupt" (1987, 171). I hesitate to question Janko on any point of philology, but I do not see why the sentence cannot be read as a straightforward double accusative. The sentence has a subject, "spectacle"; a verb, "supplies"; and two accusatives. If we read the first accusative as the primary object of the verb, we get "spectacle supplies a great service to dramas," and the second accusative, *tēn sumphōnian*, then becomes an adverbial accusative or accusative of respect, stating the respect in which spectacle supplies a great service to dramas, namely, "when in harmony with them." The same construction is found in the second sentence of the *Poetics*, in which the primary accusative tells us what the various poetic performances happen to be, namely, imitations, and the second accusative, to sunolon, states the respect in which each is an imitation, namely, as a whole.

CHAPTER 7

1. The sense in which there was or was not a Chicago school of criticism is discussed jointly by Richard McKeon and Wayne Booth in *Profession 82* (New York: Modern Language Association of America, 1982), 1–25. McKeon's contribution is reprinted in McKeon 1998 (2:11). The publications of the school include *Critics and Criticism* (Crane 1952), which contains twenty selected articles by its first generation. David R. Eastwood, of Port Washington, New York, founded, edited, and published the journal *Hypotheses: Neo-Aristotelian Analysis*, devoted to work characteristic of the school. Its first issue (Spring 1992) included a 353-item "Neo-Aristotelian Bibliography." With thirty supplements, the total at the time of the final issue, nos. 35–36 (Fall 2000–Winter 2001), was over 1,900 items. Complete files of *Hypotheses* are available at the libraries of the University of Chicago and the U.S. Merchant Marine Academy in Kings Point, New York. Members of the school may also have complete files; I plan to leave mine to the Stony Brook University Library.

CHAPTER 10

1. This of course does not imply that Shakespeare believed Othello's stories were true, or, if they were not, that Shakespeare made a poetic error, for impossibilities can be justified either because they contribute to the end of the art or because they are such as people say, or both, as is the case with Othello's stories.

2. Raleigh's account was originally printed as a pamphlet. The quotations here, and also

the quotations from Tennyson's poem, are taken from *A Book of English Literature*, edited by Franklin Bliss Snyder and Robert Grant Martin (New York: Macmillan, 1916), 103–9, 597–99.

3. *Lexis* is therefore usually and rightly translated as "style" in the *Rhetoric* and "diction" in the *Poetics*. Meter is included in rhetorical style but not in poetic diction, which is the expression (*hermēneia*) by means of language, and is the same power in verse and in prose (*Poet.* 7.1450b13). Lexis excludes meter in the *Poetics* and includes it in the *Rhetoric* because if there is, as in poetics and the other sciences, a determinate subject matter, the meanings are determined by the subject matter and can be expressed either in verse or in prose, but if, as in rhetoric, there is no determinate subject matter to determine meanings, they are left floating, so to speak, and depend both on the words and how they are said, and this includes meter and all the other things that are included in rhetorical style. The plot is the end and principal part and as it were the soul of tragedy, and language provides the material in which the soul is embodied. Rhetoric, on the other hand, has no determinate subject matter to give it life, and comes to life in the speech itself, and particularly in elegant and memorable sayings. There is for Aristotle no single art of style that applies to both poetry and rhetoric, as there is for Demetrius, Longinus, George Campbell, and others who treat poetry rhetorically. This difference affects, among other things, how contemporary departments of English conceive their mission—is there beyond the diction of poetics a universal rhetoric of style or expression, or only the styles appropriate to particular disciplines, among which rhetoric is one?

CHAPTER 11

1. We are fortunate to have an example of one way in which Aristotle's education for autonomy of mind has been achieved in higher education in the contemporary world, with its great advances in the sciences since Aristotle's time. Robert Maynard Hutchins, President and later Chancellor of the University of Chicago, recognizing the difference between education and professional instruction, made the College faculty an autonomous part of the University so that it would be free to develop the education in all subjects required for autonomy of mind. For the list of subjects Aristotle's own division of the sciences was followed, which was not difficult to do or even unusual, for, as we noted earlier, it is his divisions that have prevailed in modern universities.

The education the College faculty developed over time was, however, new in two primary ways. Instead of textbooks it used the original sources in which the achievements of the sciences were set forth. As the arguments for the new advances, or in the case of the humanities, the new advances themselves, these materials were admirably suited to develop the ability to judge what a speaker has set forth well or not well. But in order for the faculty to be able to teach these materials well, they first needed to understand them themselves, which is perhaps not as easy as it might seem. The second primary novelty of the College was the staff system developed to solve this problem. Each course was taught by a course staff, each member of which taught one or more discussion sections of the course, and contributed to lectures given to all the students in the course. Each course staff met weekly in a session led by one of its members to discuss the readings that all were teaching or about to teach. This was a device admirably suited to teach the staff itself, for when a group of teachers who have prepared themselves to teach certain materials to students meet to discuss these materials among themselves, and do so over a period of years, they eventually come to understand these materials very well, and as Joseph Schwab, probably the best-known teacher in the College, once truly said, "If I understand it, my students will understand it!"

There were other distinctive features in the College—a two-year program of common courses required for all students; voluntary class attendance; final grades determined by a single comprehensive exam prepared by a member of the course staff working in the Office of the University Examiner but approved by the course staff and graded by it anonymously; and classes conducted so far as possible in seminar rooms in which the students sat around a large oval table.

Not everyone was happy with this experiment, particularly the graduate departments in the natural sciences. "Their idea of a general education course is the first course in their own subject," McKeon once said to me. They did not like not having control of undergraduate education in their own subjects, they thought it a disgrace that students were being taught outdated science, and they found College graduates who entered their own departments insufficiently docile. The approach of the College to pre-professional education was vindicated, however, and attracted national attention, when it was found that graduates of the College, after two years of study and without a major, surpassed on the Graduate Record Examinations the graduates of four-year colleges in the very subjects in which they had respectively majored. Experts from outside the College supposed this extraordinary result must be due to extraordinary students or extraordinary teachers, but those within the College knew that what was extraordinary was neither the students nor the teachers, but the use of original sources taught by means of a staff system.

CHAPTER 13

1. Most of Aristotle's uses of *katharsis* refer to catharsis of the *katamenia*, or menstruation (e.g., *Hist. An.* vi.18.572b29), which includes the discharges following birth (*Hist. An.* vi. 20.574b4). He also uses the term to refer to the ejaculation of semen (*Gen. An.* ii. 7.747a19), and catharsis of excesses that cause bodies to be ill (*Gen. An.* ii. 4.738a27), which includes purgation of the bowels (*Phy.* ii. 3.194b36; *Metaph.* v.2.1013b1).

CHAPTER 17

1. This is explained in the opening chapter of the *Physics*, quoted in chapter 4, which immediately follows the preface to the theoretical sciences in which the metaphor is used, "What is at first manifest and clear to us is rather confused wholes; later, their elements and principles become known to us by discriminations" (*Phys.* i.1.184a21).

2. The external evidence for the influence of Bernays on Nietzsche's *Birth of Tragedy* is presented by Karlfried Gründer in the preface to the 1970 reprint of Bernays 1857.

CHAPTER 18

1. I owe this point and many others to my late friend and colleague Professor Harold Zyskind, who studied rhetoric under McKeon and the Committee on Ideas and Methods at the University of Chicago.

CHAPTER 19

1. The distinction between the serious and the solemn is essential to the theory of comedy. Russell Baker has addressed this distinction in "Why Being Serious Is Hard," *New York Times Magazine*, April 30, 1978. I am indebted to Naomi Solo for her recollection of this column. Baker begins,

> "Here is a letter of friendly advice. 'Be serious,' it says. What it means, of course, is 'Be solemn.'... Children almost always begin by being serious, which is what makes them so entertaining when compared to adults as a class. Adults, on the whole, are solemn... In politics, the rare candidate who is serious, like Adlai Stevenson, is easily overwhelmed by one who is solemn, like General Eisenhower. This is probably because it is hard for most people to recognize seriousness, which is rare, especially in politics, but comfortable to endorse solemnity, which is as commonplace as jogging. Jogging is solemn. Poker is serious.... *Playboy* is solemn. The *New Yorker* is serious. S. J. Perelman is serious. Norman Mailer is solemn.... Making lists, of course, is solemn, but this is permissible in newspaper columns, because newspaper columns are solemn. They strive, after all, to reach the mass audience, and the mass audience is solemn, which accounts for the absence of seriousness in television, paperback books found on airport bookracks, the public school systems of America, wholesale furniture outlets, shopping centers and American-made automobiles. I make no apology for being solemn. Nor should anyone else. It is the national attitude... It is hard to be serious."

Baker's fusion of humor with seriousness in his columns is exemplary, but by setting solemnity in opposition to seriousness, he risks losing the positive sense of solemnity, in which it too is serious, as in tragedy.

CHAPTER 21

1. For this example I am grateful to Harry Keyishian of the Fairleigh Dickinson Press, who was able to identify its source from my mangled recollection of the words.
2. I owe these examples to Richard Levin.
3. Janko doubts that the *Bdeu-Zeu* joke is an example of paronymy because, unlike Aristotle's example of an altered word, *dexiteron* for *dexion* (21.1458a7), it is not a change in the middle of the word, nor is it the change of a whole syllable, and he hesitantly assigns it to parody (Janko 1984, 180–81; Janko 1987, 164). But these doubts should be removed by Cicero's definition and example of *paronomasia*, quoted later in the text, and are in any case unwarranted, for where in the word the alteration occurs and whether a letter or a syllable is altered are too inconsequential to determine a major distinction such as that between paronymy and parody. Janko's argument de-

pends on taking the accidental characteristics of an example as if they were essential to paronymy by alteration in general. *Dexios*, like the English "right," is an adjective that has no comparative form. Homer, however, uses the standard form of comparative adjectives to invent a comparative for *dexios—dexiteros—*and uses it to identify the breast of Hera that was struck by Hercules's three-barbed arrow. He also uses the altered word to apply to the right hand, and Pindar uses it to apply to the right foot. It is thus not a standard word, but an altered word used by poets to mean the right one of two—see *LSJ*, s.v. "*dexiteros*." The change from *dexios* to *dexiteros* involves addition of a syllable in the middle of the word because this is a standard form for comparative adjectives, not because it is an essential requirement for the alteration of a word. If paronymy by alteration is to include all alterations that can be a source of laughter, it should not be restricted to the change of a particular kind of part at a particular location in the word.

4. I owe this example to Valerie Godfrey and her remarkable recitation of the entire parody from memory. The parody is available on the Internet.

5. I am indebted to my colleague and Wilde expert Bruce Bashford for the source and wording of this witticism. According to Richard Ellmann in his biography *Oscar Wilde* (New York: Random House, 1988), Wilde made the remark in conversation. Ellman quotes it on p. 469.

6. Janko comments, "The parallels between the Tractatus and Cicero are striking, but can be explained just as readily if Cicero's source was Theophrastus or another Peripatetic who had followed Aristotle, or in an account in another lost work of Aristotle's, presumably the published dialogue On Poets." But it is most unlikely that Aristotle would repeat the detailed analysis of the sources of laughter in the popular dialogue On Poets. The hypothesis that Cicero's source was some lost work of Aristotle or a work of Theophrastus or another Peripatetic is ad hoc and without standing unless it can be shown that such a work actually existed. So far as I know there is no evidence of such a work. The testimony of Gerald Else and Cairns Lord cited earlier is against it, and Cicero himself presents a strong argument against it when he has Caesar say that as of 91 BCE he could find no Greek work on the laughable that was not conspicuously silly. The existence of the complete *Poetics* in Rome at the time Cicero was working on *De oratore* is beyond doubt, and I think we must prefer this as Cicero's source.

7. In the technical terms of *The Architectonics of Meaning*, Freud is an agonistic Democritean working in an epistemic mode, that is, he has, like Democritus, an objective perspective, substantive reality, and elemental principles, but, unlike Democritus, has an agonistic method and is working in an epistemic rather than an ontic mode. This makes him also an objective Empedoclean, for, as Freud rightly says, "The two fundamental principles of Empedocles—*philia* and *neikos*—are, both in name and function, the same as our two primal instincts, Eros and Destructiveness, the former of which strives to combine existing phenomena into ever greater unities, while the latter seeks to dissolve these combinations and destroy the structures to which they have given rise" (Freud 1950, 5.349–50). Freud of course eschews the prophetic perspective of Empedocles for that of the objective scientist (Freud 1962, 92).

1. This catalogue can be found in Moraux 1951, 289–309; and Hein 1985, 388–439. It makes more evident the difference between the ontic epoch in which Aristotle wrote and the new semantic epoch which began in the first century BCE in which Andronicus edited what Aristotle had written. It also makes more evident the philosophic differences between Aristotle and Andronicus. Andronicus organizes Aristotle's writings by a series of trichotomies and dichotomies, a method that resembles the sophistic method exhibited in Plato's Sophist rather than Aristotle's method of analyzing self-determined wholes. The writings are distinguished as genuine (*gnēsia*), disputed (antilegomena), or spurious (*pseudemigrapha*), a primary distinction in a semantic epoch. The genuine writings are distinguished as universal (*katholou*), mixed (*metaxu*), or particular (*merika*). The language resembles the terms used by Aristotle to distinguish philosophy, poetry, and history, but for Andronicus the universal writings include poetry, the mixed writings are the writings on the constitutions of different states, which are for Aristotle histories, and the particular writings are Aristotle's letters, which are distinguishable as kinds of documents, if not by the particularity of their subject matter. The universal writings are distinguished as systematic (*suntagmatika*) and notes (*hupomnētika*), which again is a distinction of kinds of documents rather than of subject matters. The systematic writings are distinguished as exoteric (*exoterica*) or esoteric (*esoterika*) Aristotle uses "exoteric" to refer to the writings available outside the school, but never calls the technical writings "esoteric," which recalls the Pythagoreans and suggests a cult with initiation rites and secret doctrines, something very different from Aristotle's idea of the educated person as the proper audience for the technical works.

2. Tyrannion is also called "Tyrannio." This is because his Greek name, Tyranniōn, when translated into Latin falls into the class of nasal stems whose nominative form drops the final "n" of the stem and ends in "o." Thus Greek names such as Platōn, Stratōn, Strabōn, and Tyranniōn became in Latin Plato, Strato, Strabo, and Tyrannio. British scholarship, approaching Greek through Latin, brought the Greek names into English in their Latin form. French and German scholars, however, did not translate Greek names by their Latin counterparts, and this approach now seems somewhat provincial.

   Considered on its own merits, "Tyrannio" preserves the long "o" of the Greek, whereas the natural pronunciation of "Tyrannion" shortens it, but the long "o" can be preserved in one's speech if one wishes. Shortening or lengthening a vowel is in any case less destructive of the form of a word than changing or removing a consonant. The matter of a word lies in the vowels, while the consonants give it a definite form. The pronunciation of the vowels can slide around without losing the word, but the change of a consonant changes the word.

   The translations "Plato," "Strabo," and "Strato" have become well-established in English, but this is not true of "Tyrannio." In fact, current usage seems to incline toward "Tyrannion." If one searches the Internet for "Tyrannio," one accesses primarily the British scholarly tradition, somewhat buried in the list of hits, but if one searches for "Tyrannion," the man we are speaking of appears at once.

   For these reasons I have preferred "Tyrannion" to "Tyrannio."

BIBLIOGRAPHY

Apostle, Hippocrates G. 1958. "Methodological Superiority of Aristotle over Euclid."
  Philosophy of Science 25: 131–34.

Aristophanes. 1924. Trans. Benjamin Bickley Rogers. 3 vols. Loeb Classical Library.

Bacon, Francis. 1605. *The Proficience and Advancement of Learning, Divine and Human.* In
  The Philosophical Works of Francis Bacon. Reprinted from the texts and translations of
  Ellis and Spedding. Edited by John M. Robertson. London: George Routledge and
  Sons, 1905.

Barker, Ernest. 1958. *The Politics of Aristotle.* New York: Oxford University Press.

Barnes, Jonathan. 1985. "Editor's Notes." *Phronesis* 20: 103–6.

Bernays, Jacob. 1853. "Ergänzung zu Aristoteles Poetik." *Rheinischen Museum für
  Philologie* 8: 361–96.

———. 1857. *Grundzüge der verlorenen Abhandlung des Aristoteles über Wirkung der
  Tragodie.* Breslau. Repr. Hildesheim: Georg Olms Verlag, 1970.

———. 1880. *Zwei Abhandlungen übder die aristotelische Theorie des Drama.* Berlin. Repr.
  of Bernays 1857 and 1853. Repr., Darmstadt 1968.

———. 1979. "Aristotle on the Effect of Tragedy." Translation of Bernays 1857 by
  J. and J. Barnes. In Articles *on Aristotle,* vol. 4, edited by J. Barnes, M. Scofield, and
  R. Sorabji, 154–65. London: Duckworth.

Bettelheim, Bruno. 1976. *The Uses of Enchantment: The Meaning and Importance of Fairy
  Tales.* New York: Alfred A. Knopf.

Booth, Wayne C. 1995. "What Does It Take to Make a New Literary Species?" *Hypotheses*
  15:11–12.

Bywater, Ingram. 1909. *Aristotle on the Art of Poetry.* Oxford: Clarendon Press.

Cicero. 1970. *Cicero on Oratory and Orators.* Translated by J. S. Watson. Carbondale:
  Southern Illinois University Press.

———. *De finibus bonorum et malorum.* Translated by H. Rackham. Loeb Classical
  Library.

———. *De oratore.* Translation begun by E. W. Sutton, completed by H. Rackham. 2
  vols. Loeb Classical Library.

———. *Letters to Atticus.* Translated by E. O Winstedt. 3 vols. Loeb Classical Library.

———. *Letters to Quintus.* Translated by W. Glynn Williams. In *Letters to His Friends,* 3
  vols. Loeb Classical Library.

Cooper, Lane. 1922. *An Aristotelian Theory of Comedy with an Adaptation of the Poetics
  and a Translation of the "Tractatus Coislinianus."* New York: Harcourt, Brace and Co.

Confucius. 971. *Confucian Analects, The Great Learning, and The Doctrine of the Mean.*
  Translated by James Legge. New York: Dover Publications.

Corneille, Pierre. 1965. *Writings on the Theatre.* Edited by H. T. Barnwell. Oxford: Basil
  Blackwell.

Crane, Ronald S., ed. 1952. *Critics and Criticism.* Chicago: University of Chicago Press.

Darwin, Charles. 1888. *Life and Letters*. 3 vols. London.

———. 1958. *The Autobiography of Charles Darwin and Selected Letters*. Edited by Francis Darwin. New York: Dover Publications. Abridgement of preceding.

Dewey, John. 1894. "The Theory of Emotion." *Psychological Review* 1:559.

———. 1929. *Experience and Nature*. New York: W. W. Norton & Co. Repr., Dover, 1958.

———. 1934. *Art as Experience*. New York: Minton, Balch & Co.

———. 1946. *Problems of Men*. New York: Philosophical Library.

Dilworth, David. 1989. *Philosophy in World Perspective: A Comparative Hermeneutic of the Major Theories*. New Haven: Yale University Press.

Diogenes Laertius. *Lives of Eminent Philosophers*. Translated by R. D. Hicks. 2 vols. Loeb Classical Library.

DK. 1954. *Die Fragmente der Vorsokratiker*. Edited by Hermann Diels and Walther Kranz. 7th ed. Berlin: Wiedmannische Verlagsbuchandlung.

Düring, Ingemar. 1957. *Aristotle in the Ancient Biographical Tradition*. Göteborg: Elanders Boktryckeri Aktiebolag.

Eco, Umberto. 1983. *The Name of the Rose*. San Diego: Harcourt Brace Jovanovich.

Else, Gerald F. 1957. *Aristotle's Poetics: The Argument*. Leiden: E. J. Brill.

Fergusson, Francis. 1961. *Aristotle's Poetics*. New York: Hill and Wang.

Freud, Sigmund. 1950. *Collected Papers of Sigmund Freud*. 5 vols. London: Hogarth Press.

———. 1962. *Civilization and Its Discontents*. Translated by James Strachey. New York: W. W. Norton & Co.

———. 1963. *Jokes and Their Relation to the Unconscious*. Translated by James Strachey. New York: W. W. Norton & Co.

———. 1965. *The Interpretation of Dreams*. Translated by James Strachey. New York: Avon Books.

Frye, Northrup. 1957. *Anatomy of Criticism*. Princeton: Princeton University Press. Repr. Princeton Paperback Ed., 1971.

Goethe, Johann Wolfgang von. 1967. "Nachlese zu Aristoteles' Poetik." In *Goethes Werke*, 12:342–5. Hamburg: C. Wegner Verlag. Translated in part by Elizabeth L. Wenning in Smith and Parks 1939, 697–700.

Golden, Leon. 1968. *Aristotle's Poetics: A Translation and Commentary for Students of Literature*. Translation by Leon Golden. Commentary by O. B. Hardison. Englewood Cliffs, NJ: Prentice-Hall.

Guthrie, W. K. C. 1985. *A History of Greek Philosophy*. 3 vols. Cambridge: Cambridge University Press.

Hadas, Moses. 1954. *Ancilla to Classical Reading*. New York: Columbia University Press.

Halliwell, Stephen. 2008. *Greek Laughter*. Cambridge: Cambridge University Press.

Harvey, William. [1628] 1928. *Anatomical Studies on the Motion of the Heart and Blood*. Trans. Chauncey D. Leake. Springfield, IL: Charles C. Thomas.

Heath, Malcolm. 1989. "Aristotelian Comedy." *Classical Quarterly* 39: 344–54.

Hegel, Georg Wilhelm Friedrich. 1975. *Aesthetics: Lectures on Fine Art*. Translated by T. M. Knox. 2 vols. Oxford: Clarendon Press.

Hein, Christel. 1985. *Definition und Einteilung der Philosophie Von der spätantiken Einleitungsliteratur zur arabischen Enzyklopädie.* Frankfurt am Main: Peter Lang.

Hobbes, Thomas. 1840. *Human Nature.* In *The English Works of Thomas Hobbes of Malmesbury,* edited by Sir William Molesworth, vol. 3. London: J. Bohn.

———. 1909. *Leviathan.* Repr. from ed. of 1651. Oxford: Clarendon Press.

Holt, Jim. 2008. *Stop Me if You've Heard This: A History and Philosophy of Jokes.* New York: W. W. Norton & Co.

Hordern, James H. 2004. *Sophron's Mimes.* Oxford: Oxford University Press.

Hume, David. 1987. "On Tragedy." In *Essays Moral, Political, and Literary,* edited by Eugene F. Miller, rev. ed., 216–25. Indianapolis: Liberty Classics.

Hypotheses: Neo-Aristotelian Analysis. See note 1 to chapter 7.

Jaeger, Werner. 1948. *Aristotle: Fundamentals of the History of His Development.* Translated by Richard Robinson. 2nd ed. Oxford: Clarendon Press.

James, Henry. 1950. *The Art of the Novel.* New York: Charles Scribner's Sons.

Janko, Richard. 1984. *Aristotle on Comedy.* London: Duckworth. Duckworth paperback, 2002.

———. 1987. *Aristotle Poetics.* Indianapolis: Hackett Publishing Co.

———. 1992. "From Catharsis to the Aristotelian Mean." In *Essays on Aristotle's Poetics,* edited by Amélie Oksenberg Rorty, 341–58. Princeton: Princeton University Press.

———. 2001. "Aristotle on Comedy, Aristophanes and Some New Evidence from Herculaneum." In *Making Sense of Aristotle: Essays in Poetics,* edited by Ø. Anderson and J. Haarberg, 51–71. London: Duckworth

———, ed. 2010. *Philodemus, On Poems, Books 3–4, with the Fragments of Aristotle, On Poets.* Oxford: Oxford University Press.

Joyce, James. 1916. *Portrait of the Artist as a Young Man.* New York: The Viking Press.

Kaibel, G. 1899. *Comicorum Graecorum Fragmenta I.* Berlin.

Kant, Immanuel. 1951. *Critique of Judgment.* Translated by J. H. Bernard. New York: Hafner Publishing Co.

———. 1994. *Ethical Philosophy.* Translated by James W. Ellington. 2nd ed. Indianapolis: Hackett Publishing Co.

Leacock, Stephen. 1937. *Humour and Humanity: An Introduction to the Study of Humour.* London: Tomas Butterworth.

Lear, Jonathan. 1992. "Katharsis." In *Essays on Aristotle's Poetics,* edited by Amélie Oksenberg Rorty, 315–40. Princeton: Princeton University Press.

Legman, Gershon. 1975. *Rationale of the Dirty Joke: An Analysis of Sexual Humor.* First Series, New York: Basic Books and Grove Press, 1968. Second Series, New York: Breaking Point, 1975.

Lessing, G. E. [1769] 1962. *Hamburg Dramaturgy.* Translated by Helen Zimmern. New York: Dover Publications.

Levin, Richard. 2006. "Launcelot's and Huck's Moral Dilemma." *Shakespeare Newsletter* 56.3.83.

———. 2008. "Who Do the People Love?" *Shakespeare Survey* 61:289–301.

Locke, John. (1690) 1908. *An Essay Concerning Human Understanding*. In *The Philosophical Works of John Locke*, edited by J. A. St. John. London: George Bell.

LS. 1871. *A Lexicon Abridged from Liddell and Scott's Greek-English Lexicon*. Oxford: Clarendon Press.

LSJ. 1968. *A Greek-English Lexicon*. Compiled by Henry George Liddell and Robert Scott, revised by Henry Stuart Jones. 9th ed. Oxford: Clarendon Press.

Ludovici, A. M. 1933. *The Secret of Laughter*. New York: Viking Press.

Macdonald, Dwight, ed. 1960. *Parodies—An Anthology from Chaucer to Beerbohm—and After*. New York: Random House.

Macrobius. 1969. *The Saturnalia*. Translated by Percival Vaughan Davies. New York: Columbia University Press.

McCullough, David G. 2001. *John Adams*. New York: Simon & Schuster.

McKeon, Richard. 1935. "Renaissance and Method." In *Studies in the History of Ideas*, vol. 3, edited by Dept. of Philosophy, Columbia University, 34–114. New York: Columbia University Press.

———. 1941. *The Basic Works of Aristotle*. New York: Random House.

———, ed. 1943. *History of the Organization of the Sciences*. Selected Readings for the Course in Observation, Interpretation, and Integration. 1st ed. 2 vols. Chicago: University of Chicago Bookstore, 1943.

———. 1949. Original Introduction to McKeon 1941. Mimeographed from the galley proofs by his students, 1949, and referred to by McKeon as "the pirated edition." 102 pp. Online at http://www.RichardMcKeon.org.

———. 1954. *Thought Action and Passion*. Chicago: University of Chicago Press.

———. 1965. "Facts, Categories, and Experience." Lecture Notes for the Paul Carus Lectures, delivered at the American Philosophical Association, New York. 38 pp. Typescript prepared by Douglas C. Mitchell, University of Chicago Press, 1989.

———. 1990. *Freedom and History and Other Essays*. Edited by Zahava K. McKeon. Chicago: University of Chicago Press.

———. 1998. *Selected Writings of Richard McKeon*. Edited by Zahava K. McKeon and William G. Swenson. 3 vols. Chicago: University of Chicago Press.

Mill, John Stuart. 1961. *Utilitarianism*. In *The Philosophy of John Stuart Mill*, edited by Marshall Cohen. New York: Modern Library.

Milton, John. 1982. "Of that sort of Dramatic Poesie which is call'd Tragedy." In *Complete Prose Works of John Milton*, 8 vols., 8:133–38. New Haven: Yale University Press.

Moraux, Paul. 1951. *Les listes anciennes des ouvrages d'Aristote*. Louvain: Éditions Universitaires de Louvain.

Morreall, John, 1987. "A New Theory of Laughter." In *The Philosophy of Laughter and Humor*, edited by John Morreall, 128–38. Albany: State University of New York Press.

Newton, Isaac. [1687] 1934. *Mathematical Principles of Natural Philosophy*. Translated by A. Motte, revised by Florian Cajori. Berkeley: University of California Press.

Nietzsche, Friedrich. [1872] 1967. *The Birth of Tragedy* and *The Case if Wagner*. Translated by Walter Kaufmann. New York: Vintage Books.

OED. 1971. *The Oxford English Dictionary*. Oxford: Clarendon Press.

Olson, Elder. 1942. "'Sailing to Byzantium': Prolegomena to a Poetics of the Lyric." In Olson 1976, 3–14.

———. 1949. "An Outline of Poetic Theory." In Crane 1952, 546–66; and Olson 1976, 268–89.

———. 1950. "William Empson, Contemporary Criticism, and Poetic Diction." In Crane 1952, 45–82; and Olson 1976, 118–56.

———. 1968. *The Theory of Comedy*. Bloomington: Indiana University Press.

———. 1969. "The Lyric." In Olson 1976, 212–19.

———. 1976. *On Value Judgments in the Arts and Other Essays*. Chicago: University of Chicago Press.

Peirce, Charles Sanders. 1935. *Collected Papers of Charles Sanders Peirce*. Edited by Charles Hartshorne and Paul Weiss. 6 vols. Cambridge: Harvard University Press, 1931–35.

Plato. 1968. *The Republic of Plato*. Translated by Alan Bloom. New York: Basic Books.

Plutarch's Lives. Translated by Bernadotte Perrin. 11 vols. Loeb Classical Library.

Rapp, Albert. 1951. *The Origins of Wit and Humor*. New York: E. P. Dutton & Co.

Robinson, John Mansley. 1968. *An Introduction to Early Greek Philosophy*. Boston: Houghton Mifflin.

Rogers, Will. 1979. *The Best of Will Rogers*. Edited by Bryan B. Sterling New York: Crown Publishers.

Ross, W. D. 1949. *Aristotle*. London: Methuen. Reprint, University Paperbacks, 1964.

———. 1965. *Aristotle's Prior and Posterior Analytics*. Oxford: Clarendon Press.

Rutherford, William G. 1905. *A Chapter in the History of Annotation, Being Scholia Aristophanica Vol. III*. London.

Sacks, Sheldon 1964. *Fiction and the Shape of Belief*. Berkeley: University of California Press.

Schopenhauer, Arthur. 1883. *The World as Will and Idea*. Translated by R. B. Haldane and J. Kemp. London: Routledge & Kegan Paul.

Scott, Gregory. 2003. "Purging the Poetics." *Oxford Studies in Ancient Philosophy* 35:233–63.

SEP. Stanford Encyclopedia of Philosophy. http://plato.stanford.edu/.

Shields, Christopher. 2007. *Aristotle*. London: Routledge.

Sider, David. 2005. *The Library of the Villa dei Papiri at Herculaneum*. Los Angeles: The J. Paul Getty Museum.

Smith, James Harry and Edd Winfield Parks, eds. 1939. *The Great Critics*. New York: W. W. Norton & Co.

Spencer, Herbert. 1911. "The Physiology of Laughter." In *Essays on Education, Etc.* London: J. M. Dent & Sons.

Starkie, W. J. M. 1909. *Aristophanes' "Acharnians."* London.

———. 1920. "An Aristotelian Analysis of 'the Comic.'" *Hermathena* 42:26–51.

Sterne, Laurence. n.d. *The Life and Opinions of Tristram Shandy, Gentleman*. New York: Modern Library.

Strabo. *Geography*. Translated by Henry Leonard Jones. 8 vols. Loeb Classical Library.

Swift, Jonathan. 1905. *The Prose Works of Jonathan Swift, D.D.* Edited by T. Scott. 12 vols. London: George Bell and Sons.

Tarán, Leonardo. 1981. "Aristotelianism in the First Century B.C." In *Collected Papers* (2001), 479–524. Leiden: Brill.

Telford, Kenneth A. 1961. *Aristotle's Poetics: Translation and Analysis*. Chicago: Regnery Gateway Edition. Repr., Boston: University Presses of America, 1985.

Thurber, James. 1933. *My Life and Hard Times*. New York: Harper & Brothers.

———. 1946. *Men, Women and Dogs*. New York: Bantam Books.

Twain, Mark. 1948. *The Adventures of Huckleberry Finn*. New York: Rinehart & Co.

———. n.d. *1601: Conversation as it was by the Social Fireside in the Time of the Tudors*. New York: Lyle Stuart.

Vollmann, W. T. 2005. "Review of Friedrich Nietzsche by Curtis Cate." *New York Times Book Review*, 14 August.

Watson, Walter. 1985. *The Architectonics of Meaning: Foundations of the New Pluralism*. Albany: State University of New York Press. 2nd. ed. Chicago: University of Chicago Press, 1993.

———. 1990. "Types of Pluralism." *The Monist* 73:350–66.

———. 1991. "Systematic Pluralism and the Foundationalist Controversy." *Reason Papers* 16 (Fall 1991): 181–203.

———. 1994. "McKeon's Semantic Schema." *Philosophy and Rhetoric* 27:85–103.

———. 1995. "Dogma, Skepticism, and Dialogue" In *The Third Way: New Directions in Platonic Studies*, edited by Francisco J. Gonzalez, 189–210. Lanham, MD: Rowman & Littlefield.

———. 2000. "McKeon: The Unity of His Thought." In *Pluralism in Theory and Practice*, edited by Eugene Garver and Richard Buchanan, 10–28. Nashville: Vanderbilt University Press.

———. 2001. "Invention." *Encyclopedia of Rhetoric*, edited by Thomas O. Sloane, 389–404. Oxford: Oxford University Press.

———. Forthcoming. "Cultural Circumstances in Ontic Returns." In *Ontic Returns*, ed. James Ford. New York: Palgrave Macmillan.

Wellek, René, and Austin Warren. 1949. *Theory of Literature*. New York: Harcourt, Brace and Co.

Whewell, William. 1847. *The Philosophy of the Inductive Sciences*. New ed. 2 vols. London: J. W. Parker.

———. 1858. *Novum Organon Renovatum*. London: J. W. Parker. Part 2 of *The Philosophy of the Inductive Sciences*.

Wills, Garry. 1992. *Lincoln at Gettysburg: The Words That Remade America*. New York: Simon & Schuster Lincoln Library.

INDEX

The order of subheadings is suited to the subject of the main entry. The order may be from the general to the specific, the order of treatment in the text, a chronological order, an alphabetical order, or some combination of these.

Aristotelian corpus
  defined, 1, 19
  originated from Peripatetic library,
    268
  selected by Neleus, 273–74
  preservation and transmission to
    Rome, 264–71
  prepared by Tyrannion and furnished
    to Andronicus, 269
  published by Andronicus, 216
Aristotelian tradition, 35, 64, 101, 103, 106
Aristotle
  archetypal Hellenic philosopher, 30
  scientific rationality, 19–21
  philosophy consists of sciences, 22–23
  series of arts and sciences, 23–45
  archic profile, 12; disciplinary perspec-
    tives, 23, 26, 29, 99, 101, 219, 228;
    essential realities, 16, 28, 106–24,
    150–51, 228; resolutive method,
    12–13, 28, 147–48, 154, 195–96, 228,
    254; reflexive principles, 19–20, 24,
    26, 28–30, 36, 40, 42, 45, 47, 99–105,
    131, 152, 228, 284n1
  prefaces of: to the theoretical sciences,
    21–23, 125, 129–30, 257; to the practi-
    cal sciences, 32, 131; compared, 32
  proper order of works: defined, 21;
    compared to traditional order, 21,
    256–62; compared to order of com-
    position, 253–54, 255; employs many
    principles, 254–56; high point of,
    looks both ways, 32, 165; sciences lie
    between dialectic and rhetoric, 46
Armstrong, Neil, 121
Arrowsmith (Lewis), 126
assimilation. See under sources of laughter
As You Like It (Shakespeare), 195, 250
audience, universal, 121, 171
Augustine, Saint, 34, 36, 113
Austen, Jane
  Emma, 132, 214
  Mansfield Park, 129
  Northanger Abbey, 182, 242

Pride and Prejudice, 182, 238
Sense and Sensibility, 132, 214

Bacon, Francis
  condemns epitomes, 9
  Novum Organum corresponds to Aris-
    totle's Methodics, 273
  uses "method" as general and indi-
    vidual, 278n3
Baker, Russell, 195, 286n1
Bakhtin, Mikhail, 226
Barker, Ernest, 259
Barnes, Jonathan, 8–9, 86, 90
Bashford, Bruce, 287n5
Beautiful Mind, A (2001), 126
Benny, Jack, 236
Bentham, Jeremy, 278n3
Bernays, Jacob
  on catharsis, 168
  on the epitome, 2, 12, 282n7
  influence of, 6–8, 155, 166, 228, 285n2
Berra, Yogi, 201–2
Bettelheim, Bruno, 134
Bhagavad Gita, 134
Birth of Tragedy from the Spirit of Music,
  The (Nietzsche), 166, 285n2
Bishop Tutu, 206
Bonnie and Clyde (1967), 163
Booth, Wayne, 90, 108, 283n1
Broderick, Matthew, 213
Bugs Bunny, 202, 212
Bunyan, John, 134
Burns, Ken, 112–13
Bush, George W., 201, 208–9
Bush administration, 42, 120, 282n4
Bywater, Ingram, 4–8, 12, 94, 155, 179, 188, 211

Campbell, George, 284
Candide (Voltaire), 111, 123
Casanova, Jacques, 112
catharsis
  analogous to motion in nature, 100
  of bodies and of souls, 142, 285n1
  tragic, 141–46; two kinds of, 153–54

comic, 155–57, 179–82
interpreters of: Bernays, 168, 168–69; Corneille, 173; Goethe, 147; Golden, 73–74; Hegel, 147; Hume, 148–49; Janko, 173–74; Lessing, 173; Milton, 148
surreptitious, 156
therapeutic, 80, 92–93, 168–70, 175, 228
in Breuer and Freud, 170
reflexivity of, 152
in poem or audience, 170–72
educative, 172–74
causes, 51
origin in questions for inquiry, 47
nature and number, 48–49
modes of causes, 59–60
variation with subject, 50–51
completeness of kinds, 51–52
analogical nature of universal causes, 53–55
in physical sciences, 49, 49–50
in biological sciences, 50
in metaphysics, ethics, politics, rhetoric, 55–56
in poetics: generic, 59–63; specific, 63–64
Chaplin, Charlie, 195, 213
Chaucer, Geoffrey, 206
Chicago school of criticism
didactic poetry, 90, 107
particular or universal audience, 121
poetry for its own sake, 106
Cicero
opportunity and desire to consult *Poetics* on laughter, 215–18
Poetics as principal source on laughter, 218–23, 287n6
his theory multicausal, 227
supports a science of humor, 251
provides evidence for meaning of paronymy, 286n3
a source for the Prolegomenon to Comedy, 205
difficulty of obtaining desirable books, 264
relations with Tyrannion, 267

Cobbe portrait of Shakespeare, 211
comedy
definition of, 179–82
no share in magnitude, 83, 93, 179–80
genesis of, 60, 95, 189
mother of, 183–84
the laughable, 188–215
matter of, 235–46
characters of: the buffoon, 238–39; the ironic, 239–41; the boastful, 241–42
parts of, 246–48
old, middle, and new, 248–50
Comedy of Errors (Shakespeare), 210, 250
Communist Manifesto (Marx), 206
Confucius, 19
consecution, lacking. See *under* sources of laughter
consilience, 264
contrary to expectation, the. See *under* sources of laughter
Cooper, Lane, 4, 7, 11, 13, 86, 188, 244, 282n6
Copenhagen (Frayn), 126
Coriolanus (Shakespeare), 151, 162
Corneille, Pierre, 173
Cosi Fan Tutte (Mozart), 194
Cramer, J. A., 2
Crane, Ronald, 90
Crowe, Russell, 126
Cyclops of Euripides (satyr play), 137

Darwin, Charles, 28–29
Daughters of Phorcys, 151
David, Larry, 236
deception. See *under* sources of laughter
Demetrius (*On Style*), 284
Demetrius of Phaleron, 266, 272
Democritus
archetypal Hellenic philosopher, 30
only fragments survive, 276
compared with Newton, 25–26
compared with Freud, 287
represented by relief theory of laughter, 225
cited by Cicero, 218

De Quincey, Thomas, 204
Descartes, René, 131
Dewey, John
    creative Aristotelian, 101
    the distinctively esthetic, 102–3, 105
    poetic universality, 127–30
    experience a mixture of essential and
        accidental, 277–78n2
    form and matter relative terms, 235
    common sense and science, 281–
        82n1
Dickens, Charles, 213
Dilbert (comic strip), 242
Dilworth, David, 12
disconnected speech. *See under* sources of
    laughter
Dracula (1931), 151
Dreyfuss affair, 124
Düring, Ingemar, 216, 262, 268, 271

Eastwood, David R., 283
Eco, Umberto, 14
educated readers, 13–16, 60, 130–33
education
    Aristotle's account, 15, 125, 130–33
    benefit of music, 168
    depends on student, 172
    alternative to rhetoric, 45
    illustrated by University of Chicago
        College, 248n1
    education and catharsis, 45, 172–77
Einstein, Albert, 27
Elizabeth, Queen, 205, 239
Else, Gerald, 215, 264, 287n6
emotions
    in different disciplines, 153
    in tragedy and epic, 4, 81, 83, 141
    in comedy, 155–56, 179–80, 249
    parallel between emotions of tragedy
        and comedy, 181
    in lyric poetry, 184–85
    action of emotions on emotions, 146,
        152–53

emotional completion or resolution,
    144
unembodied emotion sentimentality, 76
Empedocles
    comparison with Freud, 287n7
    as poet or natural philosopher, 2–3, 67,
        70, 275
entertainment (*diagōgē*), 132, 168, 174–76
Euclides, grammarian, 5
evolution
    of life, 28–29
    of cosmos, 29
    of imitation, 73, 81, 251
    "eyes of bats . . . to the blaze of day," 16, 164

Faerie Queene, The (Spenser), 134
Falstaff (*Henry IV*), 208, 239
Fawcett, Farrah, 196
Federer, Roger, 203
Fergusson, Francis, 267
Fielding, Henry, 181, 194, 250
form of diction. *See under* sources of
    laughter
Frankenstein (1931), 151
fresh beginnings
    general account, 99
    from dialectical to scientific inquiry, 100
    from new cause, 37, 82, 87, 99
    in *Physics* II and *Poetics* II, 99–100
Freud, Sigmund
    archic profile, 228, 287
    investigation of unconscious determi-
        nants of behavior, 36–37
    uses terms of ordinary language, 28, 54
    The Interpretation of Dreams, 54
    unconscious motivation in Iago and
        Hamlet, 161
    analysis of jokes, 195, 204, 211–12, 225,
        227–34
    comic diction, 245
    comic character, 230, 242–43
    basis for a science of humor, 251
Frye, Northrup, 244

Rose, Charlie, 181, 236
Ross, Sir David, 10, 21, 184, 226, 256, 278–79n5, 280n2
Rowe, Nicholas, 239
Rutherford, W. G., 4, 7, 11, 282n7

Sahl, Mort, 195
Samson Agonistes (Milton), 148
Santayana, George, 126
Scepsis (city in Troad), 265, 268–69, 271–72, 276
Schopenhauer, Arthur, 224
Schwab, Joseph J., 285
Scott, Gregory, 42
Seinfeld, Jerry, 181, 236
Sellers, Peter, 212
Senator Claghorn, 202
Shakespeare, William
    individualized characters, 129
    tragedies of character, 151
    no tragedies of spectacle, 163
    symmetry, 168, 195
    middle comedy, 249–50
    Sonnet 30 imitationalizes emotion, 185
    political order, 43
    workings of unconscious in Iago and Hamlet, 161
    See also titles of individual plays
Shaw, George Bernard, 249
Shields, Christopher, 73–74
Simon Boccanegra (Verdi), 237
Simplicius, 1, 81, 201
1601 (Twain), 205, 208
Smart, Maxwell (Agent 86 in *Get Smart*), 212
Socrates
    Aristophanes's *Clouds*, 198, 208, 210
    Plato's *Apology*, 240
    Plato's *Gorgias*, 77, 279n7
    Plato's *Republic*, 34
    Plato's *Sophist*, 77, 288
    Aristotle's *Ethics*, 239
Socratic discourses, 67, 69, 133

Socratic irony, 243
Socratic philosophers (Erastus, Coriscus), 265
Solo, Naomi, 286n1
sonnet forms, 247
Sophocles, 249
Sophron, 67, 69, 137
sources of laughter
    homonymy, 82–83, 93, 198–99, 200, 202, 206, 209, 221, 227, 232
    synonymy, 82–83, 200, 202, 209, 221
    repetition, 83, 200, 202, 209, 221
    paronymy, 202–7, 221, 227; by addition, 83, 93, 198, 203–4; by subtraction, 83, 204, 207; by a diminutive, 83, 204; by alteration, 1, 84, 204–5, 210, 227, 232, 286–87n3
    parody, 4, 84, 191, 201–2, 205–7, 210, 213, 221, 286n3, 287n4
    transference by sound, 84, 206
    transference by homogeneous attributes, 84 (*see also* metaphor)
    form of diction, 84, 208–10, 222
    deception, 160–61, 210–11, 214, 220
    assimilation, 84, 211, 214, 220, 232, 243
    the impossible, 84, 211–12, 222
    the inconsequential, 84, 212, 214
    things contrary to expectation, 84, 212–13, 222
    accoutering toward the worse, 84, 213
    vulgar dancing, 84, 213, 228–29
    letting slip the greatest things, 84, 214
    disconnected speech, 84, 214
    lacking consecution, 84, 212, 214, 228, 244
species of tragedy, 150–51, 160
Spencer, Herbert, 225
Spoils of Poynton, The (James), 104
Spoonerisms, 205
Starkie, W. J. M., 4, 7, 11, 204, 213, 227, 282n7
Sterne, Laurence, 242
Stevenson, Adlai, 206, 286n1

Made in the USA
Middletown, DE
07 June 2023